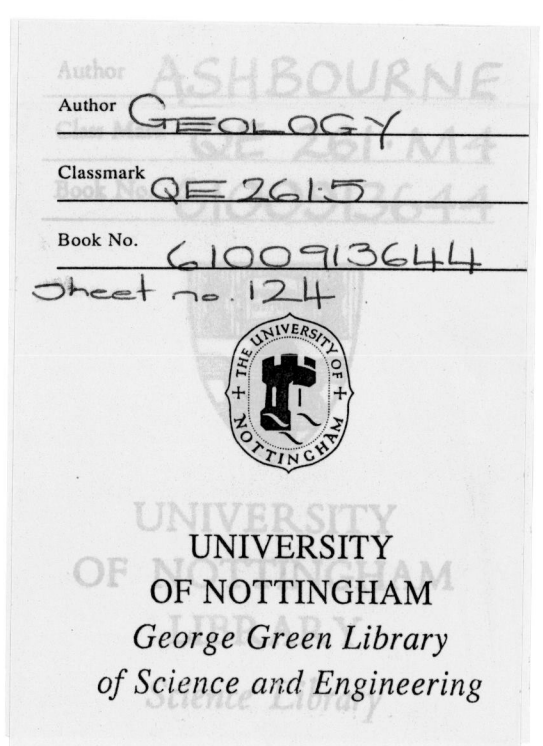
Geology of the country around Ashbourne and Cheadle

The district described in this memoir lies at the southern end of the Pennines, where the uplands of the Peak District National Park descend southwards into the Midland Plain. The National Park is famous for its scenic beauty and attracts many thousands of visitors each year.

The northern half of the district is underlain by a variety of sedimentary rocks of Carboniferous age, the most obvious of which are the limestones of Dovedale and the Manifold valley, in the centre of the Pennine upfold. The overlying sandstones form escarpments on either side, being particularly prominent in the west, around the Cheadle Coalfield. The plain to the south is underlain by red and yellow sediments of Triassic age with a veneer of Quaternary—glacial and recent—deposits. This last geological period saw the northern glaciers enter the district both from the east and from the west, to leave behind the products of their decay as a complicated patchwork of tills and outwash deposits.

The rocks contain many materials of economic value, from bulk minerals such as limestone, gravel and silica sand, to vein-minerals such as barytes, and the pressure to exploit these deposits conflicts with the need to conserve the landscape.

The memoir contains chapters on each of the main rock units in the sequence, on the geological history and structure of the district, known and inferred, and on the mineral deposits. It is primarily an explanation of the colour-printed map published at 1:50 000 scale as sheet 124 of the Geological Survey of England and Wales—and to that effect should be read in conjunction with the map. More detailed maps, at a scale of six inches to the mile, are also available.

BRITISH GEOLOGICAL SURVEY

J. I. CHISHOLM
T. J. CHARSLEY
and N. AITKENHEAD

Geology of the country around Ashbourne and Cheadle

Memoir for 1:50 000 geological sheet 124
(England and Wales)

CONTRIBUTORS

Stratigraphy
I. P. Stevenson

Palaeontology
M. Mitchell
N. J. Riley
A. R. E. Strank
G. Warrington

Petrography
N. G. Berridge

Geophysics
J. D. Cornwell

Hydrogeology
R. A. Monkhouse

LONDON: HER MAJESTY'S STATIONERY OFFICE   1988

© *Crown copyright 1988*

First published 1988

ISBN 0 11 884412 1

Bibliographical reference

CHISHOLM, J. I., CHARSLEY, T. J. and AITKENHEAD, N. 1988. Geology of the country around Ashbourne and Cheadle. *Mem. Br. Geol. Surv.*, Sheet 124.

Authors

J. I. Chisholm, MA
British Geological Survey, Edinburgh

T. J. Charsley, BSc and N. Aitkenhead, BSc, PhD
British Geological Survey, Keyworth

Contributors

N. J. Riley, BSc, PhD, N. G. Berridge, BSc, PhD, J. D. Cornwell, PhD and G. Warrington, BSc, PhD
British Geological Survey, Keyworth

I. P. Stevenson, MSc, M. Mitchell, MA, and A. R. E. Strank, BSc, PhD
formerly *British Geological Survey*

R. A. Monkhouse, MA, BSc (Oxon), BA (Oxon)
British Geological Survey, Wallingford

Other publications of the Survey dealing with this and adjoining districts

BOOKS

British Regional Geology
The Pennines and adjacent areas, 3rd Edition 1954
Central England, 3rd Edition 1969

Memoirs

Macclesfield (110) 1968
Buxton (111) 1985
Chesterfield (112) 1967
Derby (125) 1979
Burton upon Trent (140) 1955

91364

Reports

Hydrogeochemistry of groundwaters in the Derbyshire Dome with special reference to trace constituents, 71/7, 1971
A standard nomenclature for the Dinantian formations of the Peak District of Derbyshire and Staffordshire, 82/8, 1982
A standard nomenclature for the Triassic formations of the Ashbourne district, 81/14, 1982

Mineral Assessment Reports: resources of 1:25 000 sheets
Limestone and dolomite
No. 47   Wirksworth SK 25 and part of SK 35   1980
No. 129   Ashbourne SK 15 and parts of SK 04, 05 and 14   1983
No. 144 Peak District (parts of 1:50 000 sheets 99, 111, 112, 124 and 125)   1985

Conglomerate
No. 57   Cheadle SK 04   1981
No. 94   Stoke-on-Trent SJ 94   1982

MAPS

1:625 000
Great Britain South, Solid geology
Great Britain South, Quaternary geology
Sheet 2 Aeromagnetic

1:250 000
Liverpool Bay   1978
Humber-Trent   1983
East Midlands   1983
Bouguer gravity anomaly, Liverpool Bay   1977
Aeromagnetic anomaly, Liverpool Bay   1978
Bouguer gravity anomaly, Humber-Trent   1977
Aeromagnetic anomaly, Humber-Trent   1977
Bouguer gravity anomaly, East Midlands   1982
Aeromagnetic anomaly, East Midlands   1980

1:50 000 or 1:63 360
Sheet 110 (Macclesfield)   1968
Sheet 111 (Buxton)   1978
Sheet 112 (Chesterfield)   1963
Sheet 125 (Derby)   1972
Sheet 124 (Ashbourne)   1983
Sheet 139 (Stafford)   1974
Sheet 140 (Burton upon Trent)   1982
Sheet 141 (Loughborough)   1976

1:25 000
SK 06   Roaches and upper Dove valley   1976
SK 07   Buxton   1975
SK 16   Monyash   1977
SK 17   Millersdale   1976
Parts SK 25, 26, 35 and 36 Matlock   1978

Printed in the United Kingdom for HMSO

Dd 240415   C20   12/88   3933   12521

CONTENTS

1 **Chapter 1 Introduction**
Area and location 1
Outline of geological history 1

5 **Chapter 2 Pre-Carboniferous**

7 **Chapter 3 Dinantian**
Classification 7
Biostratigraphy 7
Palaeogeography and depositional history 12
Stratigraphy of shelf provinces 14
  Bee Low Limestones 14
  Kevin Limestones 14
Stratigraphy of off-shelf province 15
  Rue Hill Dolomites 15
  Milldale Limestones 16
  Ecton Limestones 26
  Hopedale Limestones 27
  Widmerpool Formation 31
  Mixon Limestone-Shales 34

36 **Chapter 4 Namurian**
Classification 36
Biostratigraphy 39
Lithology 39
Depositional history 40
Nomenclature of sandstones 40
  Minn Sandstones 40
  Hurdlow Sandstones 40
  Ipstones Edge Sandstones 41
  Cheddleton Sandstones 41
  Kniveden Sandstones 42
  Brockholes Sandstones 42
  Roaches Grit 42
  Ashover Grit 42
  Chatsworth Grit 42
  Rough Rock 42
Petrography of sandstones 43
  Protoquartzite facies 43
  Feldspathic facies 44
Stratigraphy 45
  Pendleian strata 45
  Arnsbergian strata 46
  Chokierian and Alportian strata 49
  Kinderscoutian strata 50
  Marsdenian strata 51
  Yeadonian strata 53

55 **Chapter 5 Westphalian**
Sandstone petrography 55
Stratigraphy 59
  Strata from Subcrenatum Marine Band to
    Crabtree Coal 59
  Crabtree Coal 61

Strata between Crabtree Coal and
  Woodhead Coal 62
Woodhead Coal 65
Strata between Woodhead Coal and
  Vanderbeckei Marine Band 65
Vanderbeckei Marine Band 70
Strata between Vanderbeckei Marine Band and top of
  proved sequence 70
Unproved higher strata 72

73 **Chapter 6 Dolomitisation of Dinantian
limestones**
Surface dolomites 73
Deeper dolomites 73

74 **Chapter 7 Triassic**
Pre-Triassic surface 74
Sherwood Sandstone Group 75
  Huntley Formation 76
  Hawksmoor Formation 77
  Freehay Member 80
  Lodgedale Member 80
  Hollington Formation 80
  Sherwood Sandstone Group, undivided 83
Mercia Mudstone Group 84
  Denstone Formation 84
  Mercia Mudstone Group, undivided 85

88 **Chapter 8 Pocket Deposits**
Brassington area 89
  Wall rocks 89
  Chert breccias 89
  Namurian mudstone 89
  Brassington Formation 89
  Pleistocene deposits 89
  Origin of the pockets 89
Weaver Hills 90

92 **Chapter 9 Quaternary**
Glacial deposits 92
  Area 1: Uplands with little drift 94
  Area 2: 'Older' drift with northern erratics 95
  Area 3: 'Older' drift with eastern erratics 98
  Area 4: 'Newer' drift 101
Fluvial deposits 103
  Ashbourne Gravel 103
  Higher terrace deposits 105
  Lower terrace deposits 106
  Recent alluvium 106
Periglacial deposits, processes and landforms 108
  Head 108
  Scree 109
  Silty loam 109
  Superficial structures 110

Tors   110
Dry valleys   111
Surfaces of faint relief   111
Other deposits   111
Landslips   111
Peat   112
Cave and fissure deposits   114
Denudation chronology   114

116 **Chapter 10   Structure**
Pre-Carboniferous basement   116
Intra-Carboniferous movements   116
Hercynian structures   117
Post-Hercynian structures   120
Earthquakes   121

122 **Chapter 11   Geophysical investigations**
Pre-Carboniferous basement   123
Carboniferous rocks   125
Triassic outcrop   126

127 **Chapter 12   Mineralisation**

131 **Chapter 13   Mineral products**
Limestone   131
Sandstone   131
Coal   131
Ironstone   131
Silica sand   132
Fluorspar   132
Barytes   132
Lead   132
Copper   132
Sand and gravel   132

133 **Chapter 14   Hydrogeology and water supply**

135 **References**

142 **Appendices**
1 Six-inch maps   142
2 List of boreholes and measured sections   143
3 List of petrographical samples   146
4 Geological Survey photographs   147

148 **Fossil index**

151 **General index**

FIGURES

1   Sketch map showing the general geological setting of the district   2
2   Principal physical features and drainage   3
3   Sketch map of Dinantian formations in the Peak District and adjacent areas   8
4   Dinantian formation names in the Ashbourne district compared with earlier classifications   9
5   Age relations of the Dinantian formations of the Ashbourne district   10
6   Graphic log of Caldon Low Borehole   11
7   Comparative composite sections of Milldale Limestones and parts of adjacent formations   17
8   Regional outcrop distribution of knoll-reefs in the Milldale Limestones   18
9   Section of strata in Brownend Quarry   22
10   Diagrammatic cross-section of strata from Thors Cave to Ladyside Wood   23
11   Scale section of lowest Hopedale Limestones (units A – E) resting on eroded top of Milldale Limestones at Cauldon Quarry   29
12   Sections of Dinantian strata around Tissington and Kniveton   32
13   Outcrop of Namurian rocks and location of composite stratigraphical sections shown in Figure 14   36
14   Composite sections of Namurian strata   37
15   Palaeocurrent data from the Ipstones Edge Borehole   41
16   Generalised sequence in the Cheadle Coalfield   56
17   Comparative sections in the Cheadle Coalfield: strata below the Woodhead Coal   57
18   Comparative sections in the Cheadle Coalfield: strata above the Woodhead Coal   58
19   Distribution of Froghall Ironstone and Two Foot Coal, with palaeocurrent data for Woodhead Hill Rock   59
20   Structure contours on the base of the main Triassic outcrop; contours above Ordnance Datum only   75
21   Generalised map of main Triassic outcrop, showing palaeocurrent data from Sherwood Sandstone Group and Denstone Formation   76
22   Structure, thickness and palaeocurrent data for Triassic rocks of the Leek outlier   78
23   Comparative vertical sections of boreholes in the Sherwood Sandstone and Mercia Mudstone groups   79
24   Distribution of Pocket Deposits and secondary dolomite in the Ashbourne district   88
25   Distribution of glacial deposits in the Ashbourne district; with ice-movements, ice limits and area boundaries partly defined by the distribution of erratics   93
26   Distribution of fluvial deposits, head and landslips in the Ashbourne district   94
27   Pebble counts from borehole cores in till   99
28   Main structural elements of the district and adjacent areas to the north and west   117
29   Structural features of the Ashbourne district   118
30   Diagrammatic sections showing folding in beds of the Widmerpool Formation and Tissington Volcanic Member formerly seen in cuttings of the Ashbourne to Buxton railway (now the Tissington Trail)   119
31   Bouguer gravity anomaly map of the Ashbourne district with contours at 1 mGal intervals   122
32   Aeromagnetic map of the Ashbourne district with contours at 10 nT intervals   123
33   Bouguer gravity anomaly profile AA′ (see Figure 31 for location), and a possible geological interpretation   124
34   Compilation of geophysical and relevant geological features in the Ashbourne district   125
35   Mineral deposits of the Ashbourne district   127

PLATES

1   Dovedale; River Dove flowing between
    Pickering Tor and Ilam Rock   4
2   Samples of cores from BGS boreholes at Lees Farm
    and Caldon Low   6
3   The type section of the Kevin Limestones at Kevin
    Quarry   15
4   Brownend Quarry, Waterhouses   21
5   Ravens Tor, Dovedale   25
6   Namurian turbidites, Carsington Reservoir site   48
7   Rough Rock at Wetley Rocks   53
8   Fault in Triassic sandstones and conglomerates at
    Mobberley Quarry near Cheadle   81
9   Junction of the Hollington and Hawksmoor formations
    below Alton Castle   82
10 Cemented limestone gravel in disused gravel pit,
    Weaver Hills   97
11 Section in Ashbourne Gravel, Old Grammar School,
    Ashbourne   104

TABLES

1   Namurian Stages and Zones, with a list of the main
    faunal bands found in the Central Pennine Basin   38
2   Named units in the Namurian of the Ashbourne
    district   39
3   Selected modal analyses of terrigenous clastic rocks
    from the Ashbourne district: Namurian, Westphalian
    and Triassic   44
4   Correlation of coal seams at Cheadle with those of the
    Potteries   56
5   Classification of the Triassic in the Ashbourne
    district   74
6   Drift deposits of the Ashbourne district   95
7   Relationships between deposits, faunas, floras and
    archaeology in two sections in Elder Bush Cave,
    together with comments on their environment of
    deposition   113

NOTES

Throughout the memoir the word 'district' refers to the
area covered by the 1:50 000 geological sheet 124
(Ashbourne) except where used in the name Peak District.

National Grid References are given in square brackets;
those beginning with the figure 9 lie in the 100 km square
SJ and those beginning with the figures 0, 1 or 2 lie in the
100 km square SK.

Numbers preceded by the letter E refer to the sliced rock
collection of the British Geological Survey.

The authorship of fossil species is given in the fossil index.

PREFACE

The district covered by the Ashbourne (124) Sheet of the 1:50 000 geological map of England and Wales was originally surveyed on the one-inch scale as Old Series sheets 72NW and 72NE by A. H. Green, E. Hull, J. Phillips, A. C. Ramsay and W. W. Smyth between 1852 and 1868.

A six-inch survey of parts of the western (Staffordshire) portion of the Ashbourne Sheet was carried out by G. Barrow, G. W. Lamplugh, T. I. Pocock, C. E. De Rance, and C. B. Wedd between 1886 and 1900. Small marginal areas of the Sheet were also surveyed during work on adjoining sheets between 1947 and 1963. Systematic fieldwork was started in 1973 by Dr N. Aitkenhead and Messrs T. J. Charsley, J. I. Chisholm, I. P. Stevenson and P. J. Strange, and was completed in 1980. Six-inch maps by the various surveyors are listed on p.142. The Solid with Drift edition of the map at 1:50 000 scale was published in 1983.

The writing of the memoir has been shared largely between Mr J. I. Chisholm, Mr T. J. Charsley and Dr N. Aitkenhead, who was also responsible for its compilation. Mr I. P. Stevenson contributed to several chapters and also edited the memoir. Biostratigraphical contributions to the memoir were made by Mr M. Mitchell and Drs N. J. Riley and A. R. E. Strank. Fossil identifications were provided by Mr Mitchell (Dinantian macrofaunas), Dr Riley (Dinantian, Namurian and Westphalian microfaunas and macrofaunas), Dr Strank (Dinantian foraminifera), Mr M. J. Reynolds (Dinantian conodonts), Dr W. H. C. Ramsbottom (Namurian macrofossils), Dr M. A. Calver (Westphalian macrofossils), Dr B. Owens (Carboniferous palynomorphs) and Dr G. Warrington (Triassic palynomorphs). Petrography of the sedimentary and igneous rocks is by Dr N. G. Berridge, who also contributed to the Namurian chapter; some mineralogical data were also supplied by Mr K. S. Siddiqui. The chapters on geophysics and hydrogeology are by Dr J. D. Cornwell and Mr R. A. Monkhouse respectively. The photographs, the complete collection of which is referred to in Appendix 4, were taken by Messrs K. E. Thornton, G. Moore and J. M. Pulsford.

Grateful acknowledgment is made to numerous organisations and individuals including landowners, quarrying and mining concerns, consulting engineers, research geologists and public and local authorities for assistance during the survey. In particular, Dr A. Ludford is thanked for donating his valuable collection of Dinantian macrofossils.

F. G. Larminie, OBE
Director

British Geological Survey
Keyworth
Nottingham NG12 5GG

1 August 1988

x

CHAPTER 1

Introduction

AREA AND LOCATION

This memoir describes the geology of the district covered by the 1:50 000 Ashbourne Geological Sheet (124). About two thirds of the district lies in Staffordshire and the remaining part in Derbyshire, the county boundary mostly following the course of the River Dove. The southernmost part of the Peak District National Park lies in the northern half of the district, occupying about one-seventh of the total area.

The northern half of the district is underlain by Carboniferous rocks, while the Triassic outcrop forms the southern half (Figure 1). The highest ground, reaching an altitude of over 300 m, is formed mainly by Dinantian limestones but also includes the broad Namurian sandstone escarpments of Ipstones Edge and the southern part of Morridge (Figure 2). The limestone uplands are the southernmost part of a more extensive tract in the Buxton (Aitkenhead and others, 1985) and Chapel en le Frith (Stevenson and Gaunt, 1971) districts. Typical karstic features such as dry valleys and caves are best seen in and around the deeply dissected valleys of the rivers Hamps, Manifold and Dove. Long stretches of the beds of the first two of these rivers are normally dry for many months of the year. Karstic weathering processes have given rise to spectacular scenery, particularly in the massive knoll-reef limestones that dominate Dovedale (Plate 1). To the southwest, the River Churnet, a major tributary of the Dove, has incised a beautiful wooded valley through the Upper Carboniferous and Triassic sandstones between Cheddleton and Alton. South of the Triassic sandstone belt that extends from Dilhorne in the west to Hulland in the east lie the gentle southerly-inclined dip slopes of the Mercia Mudstones, the higher parts thickly mantled by glacial till.

In summary, the district spans a major geological and scenic transition from the Carboniferous uplands at the southern end of the Pennine chain to the Mesozoic lowlands of the Midland plain.

OUTLINE OF GEOLOGICAL HISTORY

Evidence from the district allows a picture of the geological history to be drawn as far back as the end of the Devonian period. At that time, some 365 million years ago (Forster and Warrington, 1985), much of what is now Britain probably lay in the equatorial belt south of the equator and near the southern margin of the Old Red Sandstone or Laurasian continent (Johnson, 1981, p.221; Johnson and Tarling, 1985). The climate was hot and fairly arid, but there were some fast-flowing rivers in the intermontane basins between the eroding ranges of hills. This landscape was gradually submerged during a major marine transgression at the beginning of the Carboniferous Period and for the next 40 million years or so, during the Dinantian Epoch, carbonate deposition prevailed. This took place in a variety of marine environments and water depths, which probably reflected the interplay of tectonism and eustatic changes of sea level. Water depth was also affected by the abundant growth of marine organisms and the accumulation of their comminuted calcareous remains, which contributed to the deposits on shelves and surrounding ramp and slope environments. More localised buildups of organically-generated lime mud, knoll-reefs, added further variety to the sea floor relief. At times, too, volcanoes erupted on the sea floor and must have had a dramatic impact on the marine environment.

During the next 10 million years, in Namurian times, (Lippolt and Hess, 1985) deltas prograded intermittently across the south Pennine area, bringing great thicknesses of sand, silt and mud from the continental hinterland to the north and from the Wales–Brabant Island to the south. Marine deposition correspondingly decreased and by early Westphalian times, when fluvial and peat swamp conditions predominated, was confined to short-lived eustatic transgressions.

By the end of the Carboniferous, the region had drifted northwards across the equator, and the two continents of Gondwanaland and Laurasia collided to form a single supercontinent known as Pangaea (Johnson and Tarling, 1985). During the resulting Hercynian orogeny the Carboniferous rocks were folded, faulted and eroded, and by early Triassic times the semi-arid continental landscape had a scale of relief that was probably similar to that of the district today. Triassic sedimentation started with conglomeratic screes, fans and wadi fills of locally-derived rock debris. These deposits were soon buried by those of powerful rivers which brought thick sequences of gravel and sand, from the Hercynian mountain ranges to the south, forming the Sherwood Sandstone Group. These rivers gradually lost their transporting power as sea level again rose, and by middle Triassic times, when the Mercia Mudstones were deposited, the subdued landscape was probably one of broad floodplains and ephemeral lakes, at times briefly connected to the sea and at other times drying out to leave traces of salt deposition.

The lead-zinc and other minerals of the South Pennine Orefield were deposited, mainly in fissures in the Carboniferous limestone, during a long period that ranges from late Carboniferous to Jurassic, but apart from the youngest of these, there are no representatives of the long interval (about 200 million years) from the late Triassic to the end of the Oligocene in the district. There were, however, major global marine transgressions during the Jurassic and late Cretaceous (Anderton and others, 1979) which probably inundated the district and caused sediments to be deposited there. Subsequent uplift, doming of the Pennine axis and erosion during the latest Cretaceous to early Miocene interval—in part coincident with the main Alpine orogeny—removed all traces of any post-Triassic deposits that may have been present and reduced the region to a

Figure 1 Sketch map showing the general geological setting of the district

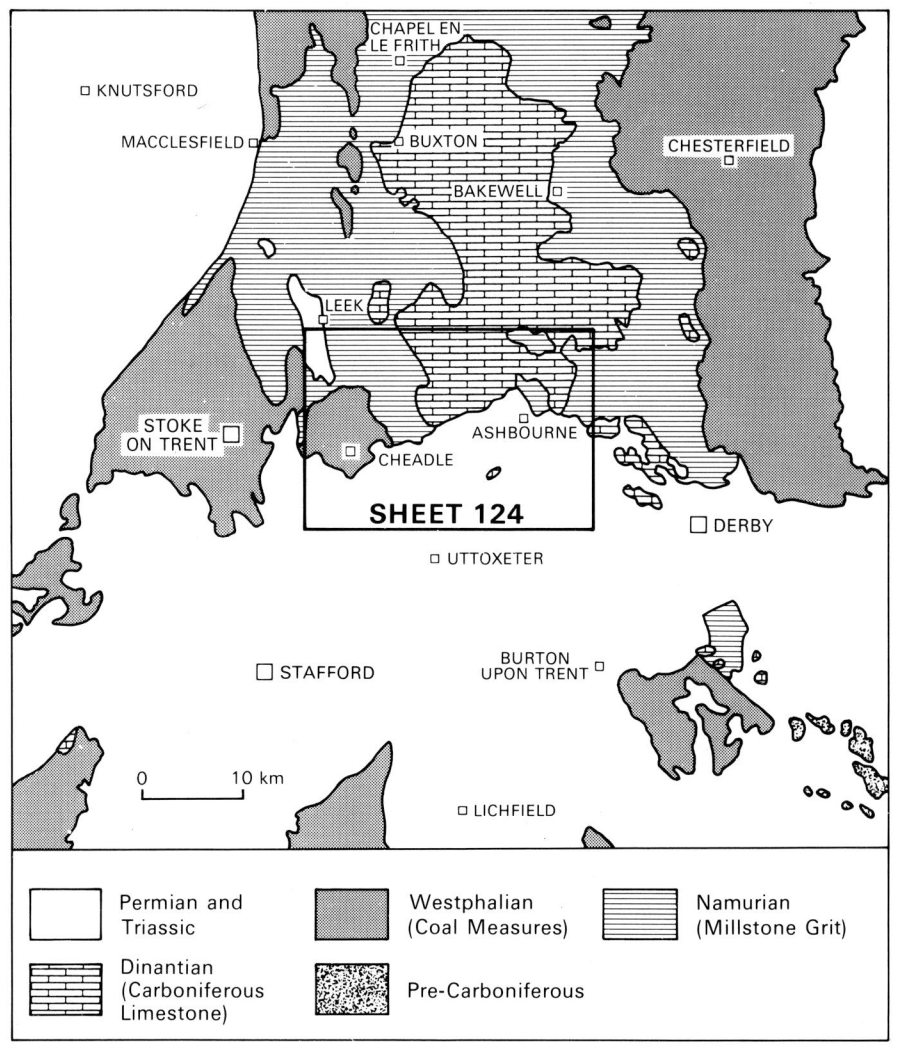

peneplain. The erosion was eventually accompanied by the deposition of sands and the overlying Pliocene clays of the Brassington Formation, which are now preserved with remnants of Namurian mudstones as Pocket Deposits in scattered dolines on the Carboniferous limestone surface.

In the current Quaternary Period, in common with most of Britain, there is another hiatus in the geological record. This is because only the last two glaciations are represented, the penultimate (?Wolstonian) and the Devensian, and these have removed any record of previous Quaternary events. Possible exceptions are some scattered patches of till on the highest ground that may be relics of an antepenultimate (?Anglian) glaciation. The different ice sheets extended into the area from different directions, the ?Wolstonian from the

east and the Devensian from the north-west, the ice-limit of the latter lying close to the western boundary of the district. To the east of this limit, the earlier glacial deposits and bedrock were deeply affected by permafrost, and accumulations of head became widespread as the climate intermittently ameliorated. The most noticeable effect of glaciation on the landscape, however, was the deep incision of the courses of the major rivers—Churnet, Hamps, Manifold and Dove—by meltwaters from the ice sheets. Cave deposits in the Manifold valley provide the main evidence in this district for the Ipswichian interglacial Stage.

Post-glacial erosional and depositional processes have continued up to the present day, either adding to or eroding the Recent deposits of head, alluvium and landslip. NA

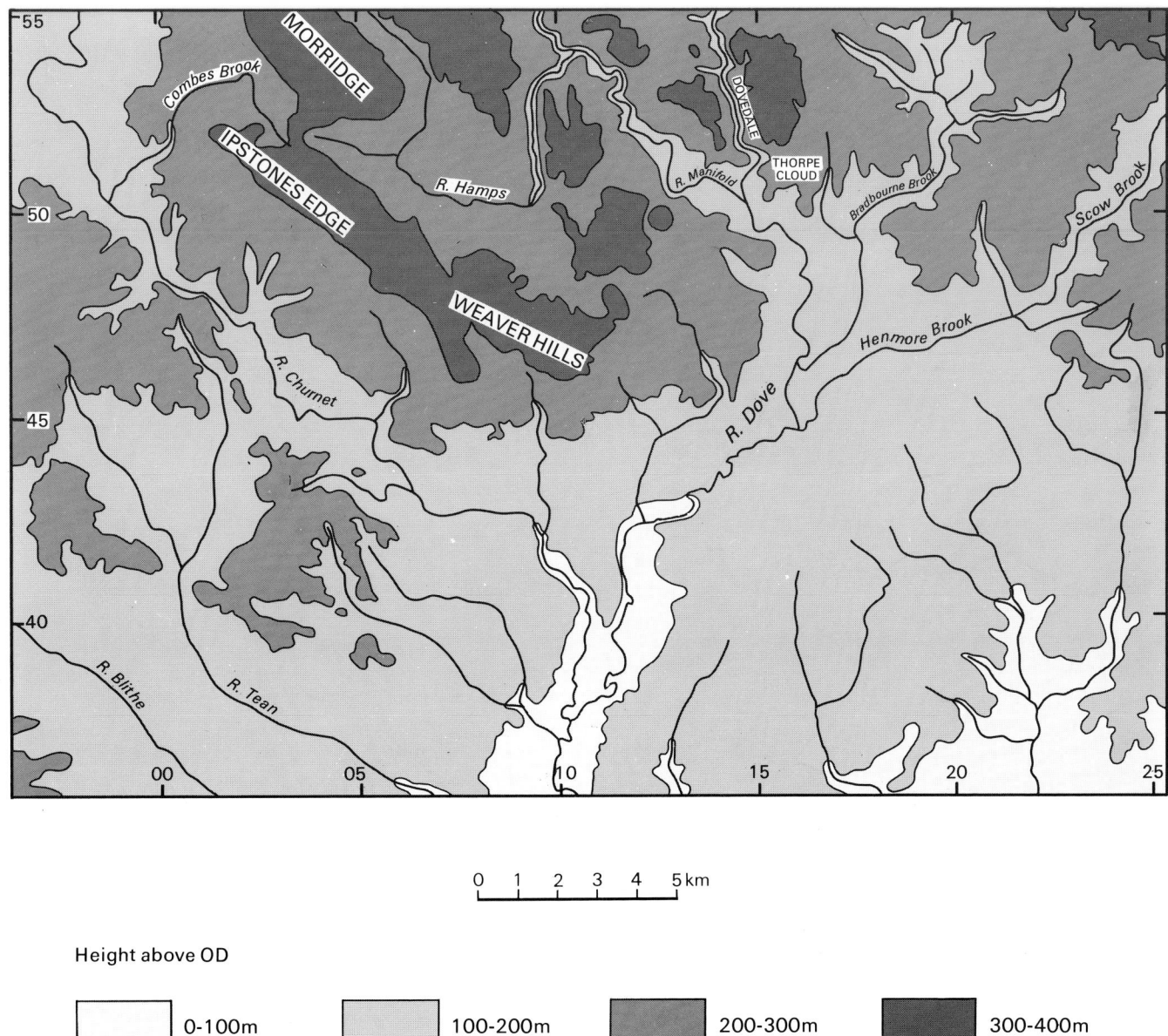

0 1 2 3 4 5 km

Height above OD

0-100m 100-200m 200-300m 300-400m

Figure 2 Principal physical features and drainage

Plate 1   Dovedale [1415 5309]; River Dove flowing between Pickering Tor (on left) and Ilam Rock (on right)

These karstic pillars of massive micritic limestone are relics of an extensive knoll-reef complex of Chadian age in the Milldale Limestones. They have been produced by solution along intersecting vertical joints and erosion by the river (L1608)

CHAPTER 2

Pre-Carboniferous

The only rocks of possible pre-Carboniferous age known in the district are the Redhouse Sandstones of Old Red Sandstone facies, proved in the basal 170.30 m of the Caldon Low Borehole (SK 04 NE/36) (Aitkenhead and Chisholm, 1982, pp.7–9). The top of the formation lies at a depth of 365.07 m, underlying the Dinantian limestones and dolomites without any discernible break. Only a few poorly preserved fossil plants and a ?palaeoniscid fish fragment have been recovered from the sediments, which are inferred to be of late Devonian or earliest Carboniferous age.

The most common rock type is pebbly sandstone. Also present are conglomerates, especially in the lowest 37 m (Plate 2.2b), non-pebbly fine- to medium-grained sandstone, and siltstone and mudstone with some concretionary carbonate. The clastic sediments are mainly red-brown in colour with minor green mottling, except between the depths of 416.52 m and 459.10 m, where they are predominantly green to pale grey and associated with sulphide mineralisation (p.129). Some crude sorting is evident in the pebbly beds, but there is little sign of well developed internal lamination and imbrication structures.

The sequence shows an overall fining-upwards trend and can also be subdivided into a number of smaller sharp-based fining-upwards cycles, each consisting of conglomerate or sandstone overlain by lesser thicknesses of siltstone and, more rarely, mudstone. Some of the sandstones may contain amalgamations of several cycles. Irregular carbonate concretions are present in the upper parts of many of the cycles. At least 25 such cycles have been recognised, with an average thickness of 6.7 m and a maximum of 14.0 m, the thickness tending to diminish upwards; in the upper 55.3 m of the sequence the average is 4.5 m. The concretions vary from white to pink in colour and range from ragged replacements with numerous irregular inclusions to nodules of relatively uniform carbonate with sharp boundaries. The concretions are similar to those generally regarded as indicative of calcareous fossil soils or caliches (see for instance Allen, 1974).

An unpublished report by N. P. Tupper of BP Petroleum Development Limited (1983), analyses eight representative samples of sandstones from the formation and indicates that both quartzose and lithic types are present. The former is cemented mainly by quartz overgrowths and fibrous illite, and the latter by various clay minerals. There is some diagenetic carbonate cement in both types. The samples show moderate to low porosity, ranging from 2.1 per cent to 8.8 per cent, and low permeability (0.02 mD to 0.12 mD).

The sequence is provisionally interpreted as representing the transition from a high-energy alluvial fan/fluvial channel environment to an alluvial plain that was eventually inundated by the sea, when the overlying carbonates of the Rue Hill Dolomites were deposited.

The nearest comparable Old Red Sandstone deposits for which there are published accounts (House and others, 1977) are in the Farlow Group of the Clee Hills 80 km to the southwest (Farlow Group: Allen, 1974). The Whittington Heath Borehole 41 km to the south (Mitchell, 1954) also proved rocks of Old Red Sandstone facies. The Caldon Low proving is thus the most northern published occurrence of the Upper Old Red Sandstone although there are other unpublished provings in the north Midlands that are commercially confidential. The nearest published occurrence of marine late Devonian is in the Merrivale No. 2 Borehole, 59 km to the south-south-east (Taylor and Rushton, 1971). A parallel may also be drawn with the Carboniferous Basement Beds of North Wales (Warren and others, 1984, p.111), although the lithologies of these are much more mixed than in the Redhouse Sandstones, the pebbly strata being interbedded with significant amounts of mudstone, limestone and dolomite.   NA

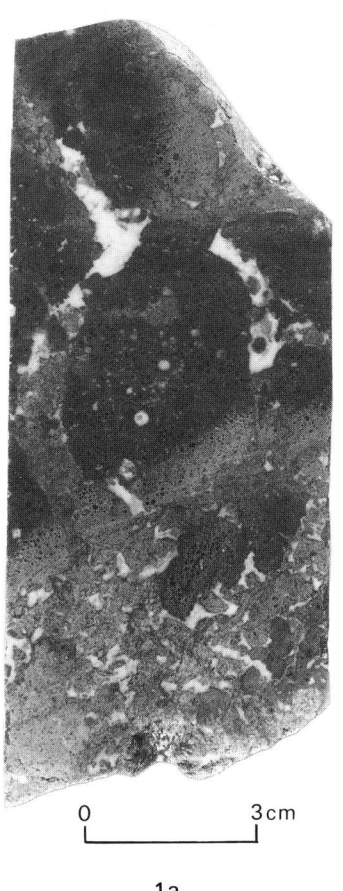

0   3cm

1a

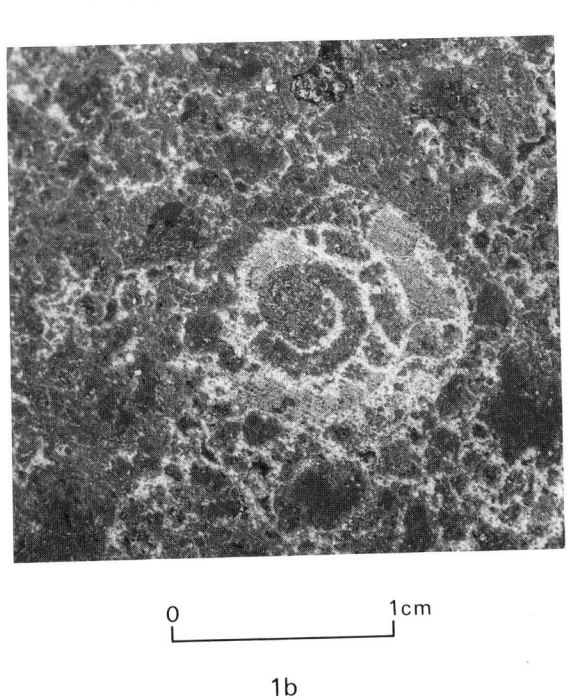

0   1cm

1b

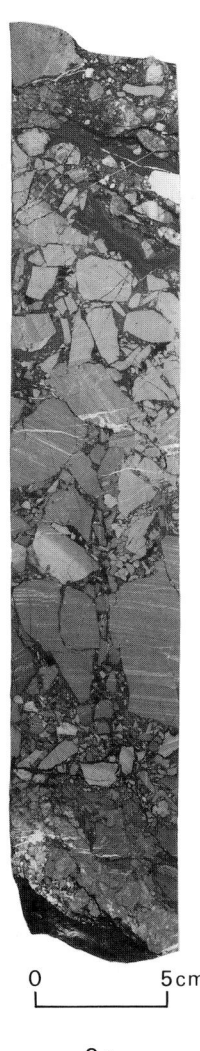

0   5cm

2a

0   5cm

2b

Plate 2   Samples of cores from BGS boreholes

1   Lees Farm Borehole (SK 15 SE/12), Tissington Volcanic Member
a   depth 173.39 m, hyaloclastite comprising clasts of dark amygdaloidal basalt
resembling pillow lava fragments with a paler chilled margin at one edge. These lie in a
matrix of small lapilli and carbonate
b   depth 162.83 m, hyaloclastite of small pumiceous lapilli (grey) and carbonate (white)
with a nautiloid that was probably trapped in a mass of hot tephra as it descended
through sea water. The darker grey patches are where clay minerals expanded and burst
out of the core surface when it was moistened with water

2   Caldon Low Borehole (SK 04 NE/36)
a   depth 328.90 m, Rue Hill Dolomites: breccia consisting of fragments of laminated
fine-grained dolomite in an argillaceous matrix, probably formed by collapse following
dissolution of evaporites
b   depth 534.30 m, Redhouse Sandstones: conglomerate comprising subrounded to
rounded clasts, dominantly of red siltstone and sandstone (greywacke type) together with
pink quartzites (conspicuous paler pebble to right of centre) and white quartz. The
largest pebble, a red siltstone, has a green reduction spot in its centre

CHAPTER 3

Dinantian

The broad outcrop of Dinantian rocks in the central part of the Peak District (Figure 3) extends into the north-eastern part of the Ashbourne district where it occupies about one fifth of the total area. Dinantian rocks are largely unproved beneath the younger Carboniferous and Triassic cover over the remainder of the district, although a small inlier of limestone is present near Snelston about 6 km south of the main outcrop. The Dinantian strata consist mainly of marine limestones and are traditionally referred to as 'Carboniferous Limestone' (Aitkenhead and Chisholm, 1982, p.1). In the highest part of the sequence, however, varying proportions of interbedded mudstone and sandstone and, locally, volcanic rocks also occur.

The maximum thickness of the Dinantian is probably about 1000 m but the base is not clearly defined since it probably lies within the Redhouse Sandstones, a poorly fossiliferous formation proved only in the basal part of the Caldon Low Borehole (SK 04 NE/36).

CLASSIFICATION

The early geological maps of Farey (1911) and those published between 1852 and 1868 by the Geological Survey showed the 'Carboniferous Limestone' undivided except for interbedded volcanic rocks or 'toadstones' (basaltic lavas). The limestone was often referred to as 'Mountain Limestone' in Geological Survey memoirs (Green and others, 1869, 1887) and contemporary publications, and the overlying argillaceous strata were known as either 'Yoredale Rocks' or 'Limestone Shale'. Many years later, Parkinson (1950, table 1) recognised areas of differing stratigraphy between Wolfscote Hill (Sheet 111) and Ilam and classified the rocks partly on a biostratigraphical basis and partly according to whether they belonged to massif, reef, or basin facies. Ludford (1951) and Prentice (1951), working in the adjacent areas to the south and west respectively, put forward their own local classifications.

During the present survey it was decided that a more uniform classification of defined formations would help clarify the stratigraphy and a new scheme was published (Aitkenhead and Chisholm, 1982) incorporating some of the earlier stratigraphical names and introducing some new ones (Figure 4). This scheme is used on the 1:50 000 and larger-scale geological maps of the district listed in Appendix 1 (p.142). Unlike previous classifications, it is wholly based on lithological changes that allow mappable units to be recognised and delineated. Previous classifications were based partly on the biostratigraphical zonal scheme of Vaughan (1905); this proved difficult to use, especially in the present district, because of the scarcity of diagnostic corals and brachiopods.

The terms shelf and off-shelf are now adopted in place of massif and basin used by Parkinson (1950) and others.

There are two shelf provinces (Aitkenhead and Chisholm, 1982, fig.8): the Derbyshire shelf that just extends into the north-eastern part of the district, and the Staffordshire shelf that includes only the extreme south-western part of the Dinantian outcrop. The latter is thought to extend at depth some tens of kilometres southwards to a penecontemporaneous landmass, the Wales–Brabant Island. The most typical formations of the shelf province are the Bee Low Limestones and the Kevin Limestones (see below). The area between the two shelves is termed the off-shelf province. These provinces are palaeogeographical features that changed with time. They were most clearly differentiated during Asbian and Brigantian times and less so during the earlier Dinantian stages. However, for convenience of description, the Milldale Limestones and Rue Hill Dolomites are described under the heading 'off-shelf' province', though they probably extend beneath the Staffordshire shelf area (Figure 5).

Knoll-reefs in the Milldale Limestones and Hopedale Limestones, and apron reefs in the Bee Low Limestones and Kevin Limestones, form both major and minor outcrops that are delineated on the geological maps. They are not given separate member status within their respective formations, however. The reefs are essentially buildups of micritic limestone and generally lack any rigid organic framework. Although the term 'buildup' (Heckel, 1974; Aitkenhead and others, 1985, p.7) is now commonly used for the various types of Dinantian reef, the terms knoll-reef and apron-reef are retained in order to be consistent with the maps and memoirs covering the rest of the region; they also better describe the morphology of the different types of reef.   NA

BIOSTRATIGRAPHY

The Dinantian biostratigraphy of the Derbyshire Dome has been discussed in a series of memoirs (Ramsbottom *in* Smith and others, 1967, pp.48–52; Mitchell *in* Frost and Smart, 1979, pp.131c and d; and Mitchell and Strank *in* Aitkenhead and others, 1985, pp.55–58). The last of these covers the Buxton district which is immediately north of the present one and is therefore particularly relevant.

The distribution of fossils has been studied to support the classification and correlation of the mapped lithostratigraphical units. The macropalaeontological work has made extensive use of the excellent collection presented to the BGS by Dr A. Ludford, and examination of thin sections for foraminifera and algae has been of considerable benefit, particularly to the study of the off-shelf province sequences which are difficult to date precisely from their contained corals and brachiopods. All specimens are stored in the Biostratigraphy Research Group collection at Keyworth. Full lists of identifications are recorded on data cards and

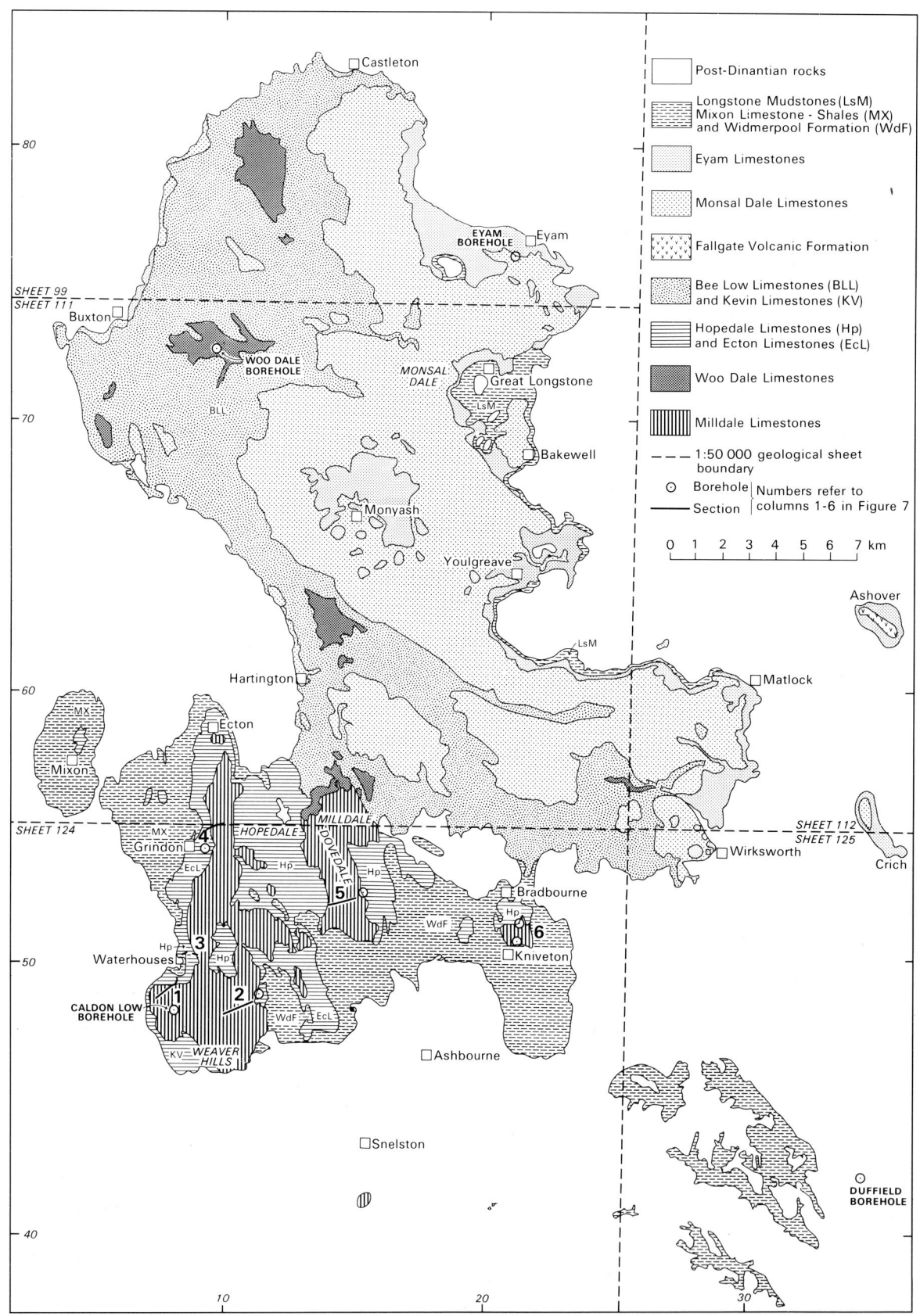

Figure 3 Sketch map of Dinantian formations in the Peak District and adjacent areas. The locations of boreholes and sections in the Milldale Limestones shown in Figure 7 are also indicated

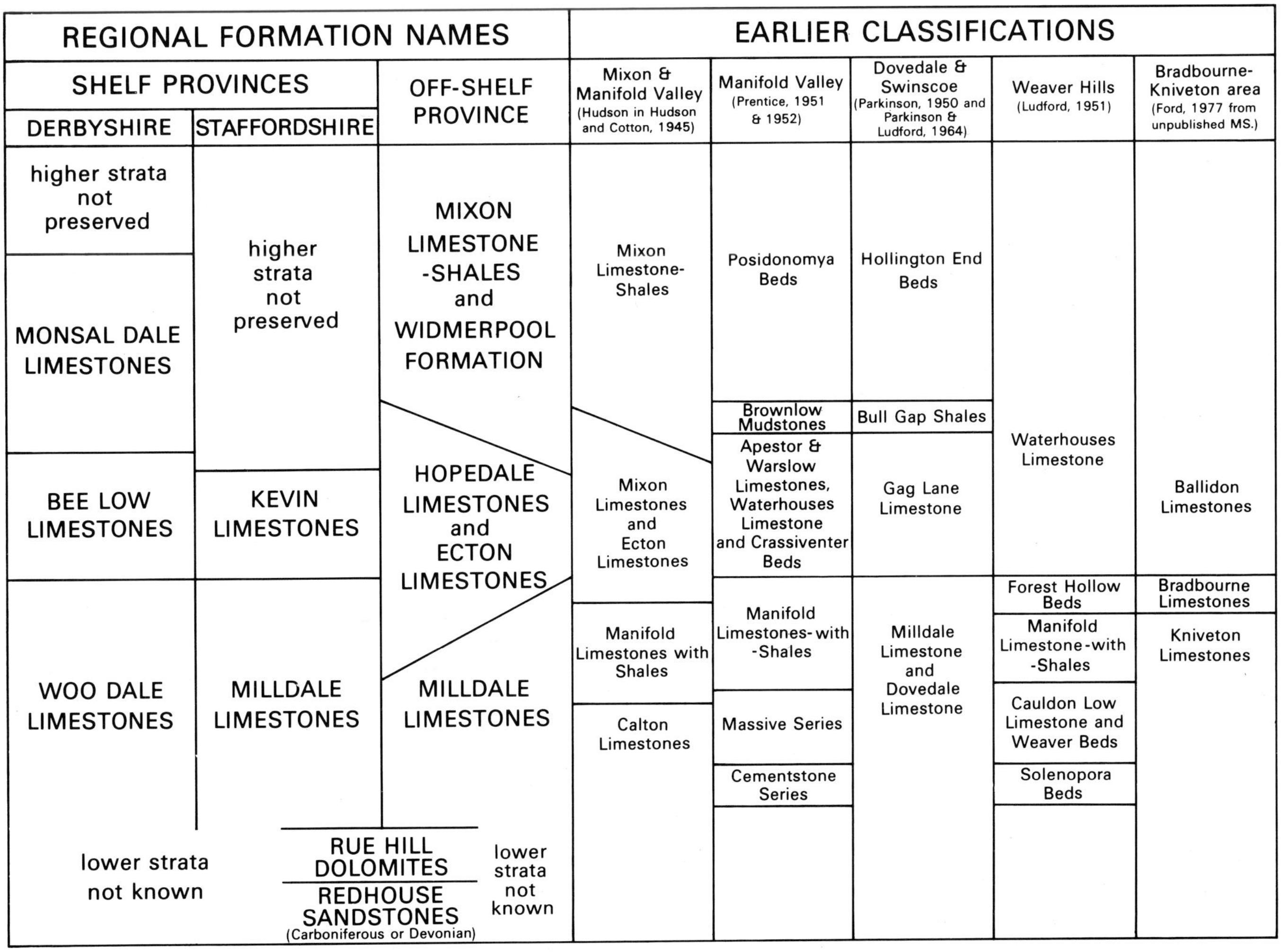

REGIONAL FORMATION NAMES			EARLIER CLASSIFICATIONS				
SHELF PROVINCES		OFF-SHELF PROVINCE	Mixon & Manifold Valley (Hudson in Hudson and Cotton, 1945)	Manifold Valley (Prentice, 1951 & 1952)	Dovedale & Swinscoe (Parkinson, 1950 and Parkinson & Ludford, 1964)	Weaver Hills (Ludford, 1951)	Bradbourne-Kniveton area (Ford, 1977 from unpublished MS.)
DERBYSHIRE	STAFFORDSHIRE						
higher strata not preserved	higher strata not preserved	MIXON LIMESTONE-SHALES and WIDMERPOOL FORMATION	Mixon Limestone-Shales	Posidonomya Beds	Hollington End Beds	Waterhouses Limestone	Ballidon Limestones
MONSAL DALE LIMESTONES							
				Brownlow Mudstones	Bull Gap Shales		
BEE LOW LIMESTONES	KEVIN LIMESTONES	HOPEDALE LIMESTONES and ECTON LIMESTONES	Mixon Limestones and Ecton Limestones	Apestor & Warslow Limestones, Waterhouses Limestone and Crassiventer Beds	Gag Lane Limestone		
						Forest Hollow Beds	Bradbourne Limestones
			Manifold Limestones with Shales	Manifold Limestones-with-Shales	Milldale Limestone and Dovedale Limestone	Manifold Limestone-with-Shales	Kniveton Limestones
WOO DALE LIMESTONES	MILLDALE LIMESTONES	MILLDALE LIMESTONES	Calton Limestones	Massive Series		Cauldon Low Limestone and Weaver Beds	
				Cementstone Series		Solenopora Beds	
lower strata not known	RUE HILL DOLOMITES / REDHOUSE SANDSTONES (Carboniferous or Devonian)	lower strata not known					

Figure 4 Dinantian formation names in the Ashbourne district compared with earlier classifications

fossil-matrix tables which can be consulted by arrangement with the Group Manager.

The more stratigraphically significant fossils are noted with the formation details (pp.14–35). In the following account of the biostratigraphy, a list of the characteristic fossils with comments on their age is given for each formation.

The classification of Dinantian formations given on the 1:50 000 sheet includes reference to the Belgian stages Hastarian and Ivorian as divisions of the Tournaisian Series. The recognition of these two stages (Ramsbottom and Mitchell, 1980) is dependent on the identification of the *Polygnathus communis carina* Conodont Biozone of Belgium, and their use in Britain has not been unanimously accepted (Clayton and Sevastopulo, 1980). Varker and Sevastopulo (1985) have reviewed the conodont evidence and suggested that the Courceyan Stage name should be retained for these beds as in the present account. The informal terms early and late Courceyan are used herein and approximate to the Hastarian and Ivorian stages respectively.

SHELF PROVINCES

Bee Low Limestones of both shelf and apron-reef facies are present between Parwich and Brassington (p.14). They yield fossils typical of the more extensive outcrops to the north (see Mitchell and Strank *in* Aitkenhead and others, 1985, p.57, table 1).

Shelf limestones (the Staffordshire shelf) also occur in the Weaver Hills to the south-west of the Dovedale off-shelf province and the Kevin Limestones of this area contain characteristic late Asbian faunas including *Axophyllum vaughani, Dibunophyllum bourtonense, Lithostrotian aranea, L. martini, L. pauciradiale, L. portlocki, Palaeosmilia murchisoni* and *Davidsonina septosa*. The scattered reef outcrops yield reef brachiopod assemblages with *Alitaria panderi, Cinctifera medusa, Eomarginifera derbiensis* [large form], *Overtonia fimbriata, Plicatifera plicatilis* and *Sinuatella sinuata*.

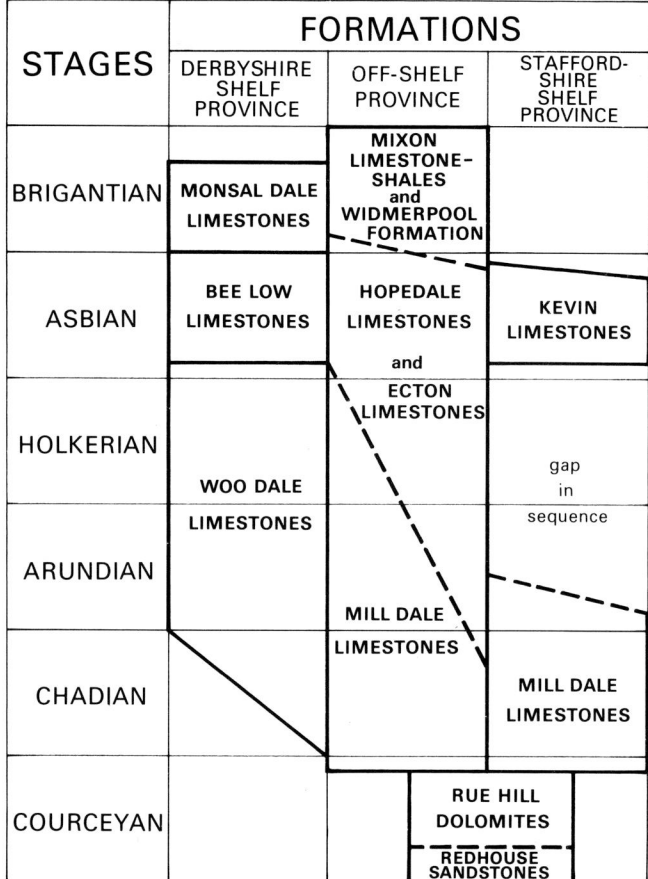

STAGES	FORMATIONS		
	DERBYSHIRE SHELF PROVINCE	OFF-SHELF PROVINCE	STAFFORD-SHIRE SHELF PROVINCE
BRIGANTIAN	MONSAL DALE LIMESTONES	MIXON LIMESTONE-SHALES and WIDMERPOOL FORMATION	
ASBIAN	BEE LOW LIMESTONES	HOPEDALE LIMESTONES and ECTON LIMESTONES	KEVIN LIMESTONES
HOLKERIAN	WOO DALE LIMESTONES		gap in sequence
ARUNDIAN		MILL DALE LIMESTONES	
CHADIAN			MILL DALE LIMESTONES
COURCEYAN		RUE HILL DOLOMITES	
		REDHOUSE SANDSTONES	

Figure 5 Age relations of the Dinantian formations of the Ashbourne district. Broken lines indicate the provisional nature of the faunal evidence

OFF-SHELF PROVINCE

Many of the varied rock types in the off-shelf province are poor in macrofossils and the biostratigraphy of these beds depends heavily on the study of foraminifera, algae and conodonts.

Redhouse Sandstones and Rue Hill Dolomites

These two formations were proved only in the Caldon Low Borehole (p.15; Figure 6). The Redhouse Sandstones probably straddle the Devonian–Carboniferous boundary, although the junction cannot be located in the arenaceous facies. Welsh and Owens (1983) recognised miospore assemblages from the lower part of the Rue Hill Dolomites (363.82 to 350.04 m) which were assigned to the V1 Subzone and to the PC Zone, indicating a Courceyan (Tn2 to early Tn3) age for these strata. The presence of the conodont *Polygnathus inornatus* at 361.40 to 360.04 m supports this age. The record of the foraminifera cf. *Brunsia spirillinoides*, *Mediocris sp.* and *Spinoendothyra mitchelli* in the upper part of the formation (318.08 m) suggests a late Courceyan or Chadian age.

Milldale Limestones

The oldest Milldale Limestones occur in the Caldon Low Borehole, where a late Courceyan or early Chadian foraminiferal assemblage including *Eblanaia sp.* is present at 268.16 m. Primitive single-walled *Koninckopora sp.* and *Endothyra laxa*, considered diagnostic of the Chadian, occur at 223.00 m, and the top 180 m of the borehole contains a diverse Chadian assemblage including the above taxa and *Eblanaia michoti*, *Eotextularia diversa*, *Latiendothyranopsis menneri*, *Palaeospiraplectammina mellina* and *Spinoendothyra sp.* The diagnostic Chadian brachiopod *Levitusia humerosa* occurs at 13.53 m.

The lowest exposed beds of the Milldale Limestones are seen in Brownend Quarry, Waterhouses (Figure 9) where Morris (1970) recorded a conodont fauna including *Scaliognathus anchoralis* and *Hindeodella segaformis*. This record was confirmed during the present survey from 31 to 44 m above the base of the section. On current understanding this would imply a late Courceyan age for this part of the Brownend section. However, the basal beds at Brownend contain *Eoparastaffella* cf. *simplex* and primitive single-walled *Konincko pora sp.*, indicating a Chadian age. This apparently anomalous distribution is possibly the result of reworking of the conodont fauna; however, diagnostic post-Courceyan conodonts do not occur below the top 13.5 m of the section, where *Gnathodus homopunctatus* first appears.

The Milldale Limestones locally contain scattered examples of typical Chadian macrofaunas including *Siphonophyllia cylindrica*, *Dorlodotia pseudovermiculare*, *Levitusia humerosa*, *Megachonetes magna*, *Faspicericyclus fasciculatus*, *Bollandia persephone*, *Phillipsia gemmulifera* and *Weania feltrimensis*. Foraminifera include *Dainella sp.*, *Endospiroplectammina conili* and *Palaeospiroplectammina mellina*.

The higher parts of the formation yield corals including *Clisiophyllum multiseptatum*, *Haplolasma subibicina*, *Palaeosmilia murchisoni* and *Siphonophyllia garwoodi* which indicate an Arundian age, although no diagnostic Arundian foraminifera have been recorded.

Knoll-reef limestones (Waulsortian buildups; see p.18) within the Milldale Limestones include rich brachiopod faunas including *Acanthoplecta mesoloba*, *Eomarginifera derbiensis* [small form], *Levitusia humerosa*, *Pugnax spp.* and *Spirifer coplowensis*, the trilobite *Phillipsia gemmulifera* and a few records of the Chadian goniatite *Faspicericyclus fasciculatus*. The youngest knoll-reef limestones so far detected occur at the summit of Thorpe Cloud and contain *Spirifer bollandensis*, *Pericyclus minimus* (type locality) and *Phillibolina worsawensis* (J. Tilsley, personal communication); these younger Chadian faunas overlie beds containing *Levitusia humerosa* and *Phillipsia gemmulifera* exposed on the northern face of the hill (J. W. Jackson Collection, Buxton Museum).

The strata recognised as 'Forest Hollow Beds' by Ludford (1951, p.221) and considered to be of S_2 (Holkerian) age are here included in the top part of the Milldale Limestones. At outcrop their fauna includes *Bollandoceras* cf. *hodderense*, *Hettonia fallax*, *Davidsonina carbonaria* and *Merocanites* cf. *applanatus*, implying an horizon close to the Holkerian/Asbian boundary. Further evidence for the age of these beds can be deduced from the assemblages present in a borehole near Caltonmoor House (SK 14 NW/5) where *Davidsonia car-*

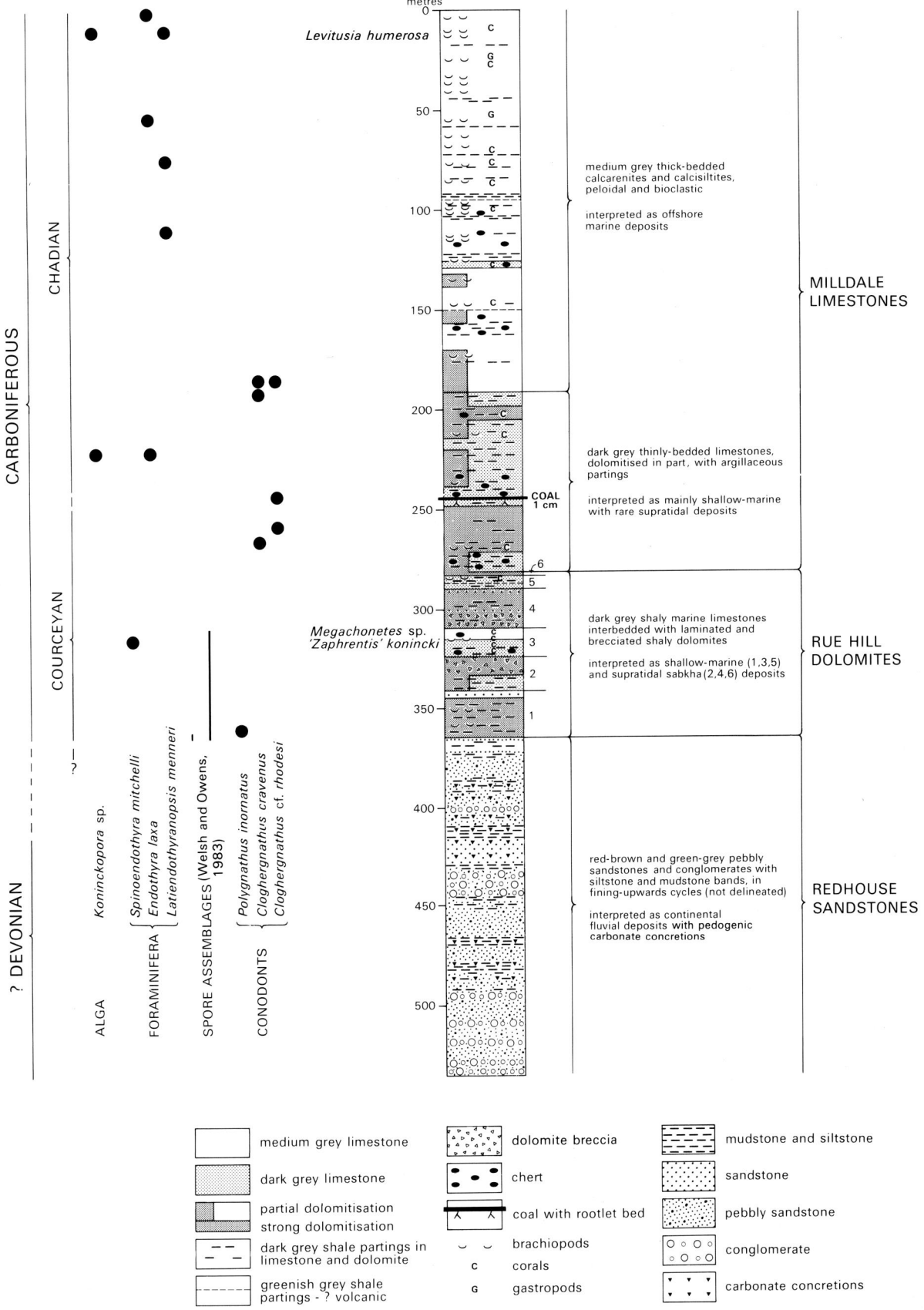

Figure 6   Graphic log of Caldon Low Borehole

bonaria (at 24.00 m) is underlain (24 to 46 m) by poorly developed *angulatus* stage archaediscids and *Draffania biloba*, again implying an horizon close to the Holkerian/Asbian boundary. An interesting feature in this borehole is the presence of a conglomerate (p.21) at the base of the 'Forest Hollow Beds' (48.93 m) which contains poorly preserved archaediscids of Arundian or Holkerian aspect, together with intraclasts containing primitive single-walled *Koninckopora sp.* indicating reworking of earlier Chadian strata.

Ecton Limestones

Corals are rare in the Ecton Limestones, but occasional records of *Clisiophyllum rigidum* and *Palaeosmilia murchisoni* suggest an Asbian age for part of the formation. However, the foraminifera indicate that other parts of the Ecton Limestones are significantly older than this. Locally, for instance at Ladyside Wood (see p.24), late Chadian faunas persist upwards from the underlying Milldale Limestones. Here, basal beds in the Ecton Limestones contain primitive single-walled *Koninckopora sp.* and *Spinoendothyra mitchelli*, in addition to the late Chadian trilobite *Winterbergia hahnorum*.

Diagnostic Arundian microfossils are known only from the Ecton Limestones in a borehole (SK 05 SE/19) near Grindon (Figure 7, column 6), where the assemblage between 115.20 and 68.50 m is dominated by *Uralodiscus spp.* and also includes *Archaediscus stilus* and *Koninckopora inflata*. Overlying this sequence are strata with a microfauna including *Pojarkovella nibelis* and an agglutinated palaeotextulariid that suggests a Holkerian age. The entry of *angulatus* stage archaediscids in the top 9.25 m of this sequence suggests proximity to the Asbian/Holkerian boundary.

Hopedale Limestones

At Brownend Quarry (SK 05 SE/29) the Hopedale Limestones, which overlie the Milldale Limestones with apparent conformity, contain a Chadian or Arundian assemblage including cf. *Eotextularia diversa* and *Koninckopora inflata*; definitive post-Chadian microfossils have not been found, although the corals *Clisiophyllum* cf. *rigidum* and *Palaeosmilia murchisoni* recorded from the highest beds in this quarry suggest an Asbian age. At Caldon Low, the Caldon Low Conglomerate at the unconformable base of the Hopedale Limestones has provided conflicting faunal evidence (p.28) indicative of ages ranging from Chadian to Asbian. However, the presence of diagnostic Asbian foraminifera (*Archaediscus spp.* at the *angulatus* stage and *Gigasbia sp.*) and the cerioid coral *Lithostrotion aranea* (which cannot be older than Holkerian) indicates that much of the material must be derived and has possibly been collected from clasts in the conglomerate.

Above the conglomerate, the Hopedale Limestones contain typical Asbian coral faunas. The assemblage from Lee House Quarries east (SK 05 SE/30 *pars*), Waterhouses, includes *Dibunophyllum bourtonense*, *Lithostrotion arachnoideum*, *L. aranea*, *L. martini*, *L. pauciradiale* and *Palaeosmilia murchisoni*. A rich and characteristic late Asbian reef brachiopod assemblage was recovered by Dr Ludford from grave diggings in Cauldon churchyard and included *Acanthoplecta mesoloba*, *Alitaria panderi*, *Avonia davidsoni*, *A. youngiana*,

Echinoconchus punctatus, *Eomarginifera derbiensis*, *Overtonia fimbriata*, *Plicatifera plicatilis* and *Productus productus*.

The upper part of the formation at Waterhouses (Lee House Quarries) has a characteristic Brigantian fauna including *Dibunophyllum bipartitum*, *Diphyphyllum lateseptatum*, *Gigantoproductus crassiventer*, *Productus hispidus*, *Pugilis pugilis* and *Striatifera striata*.

Farther north near Waterfall, early Asbian microfossils including *Archaediscus reditus*, *Globoendothyra delmeri*, *Koninckopora inflata*, *Koskinotextularia sp.* and cf. *Nudarchaediscus sp.* occur in the uppermost Hopedale Limestones in a borehole (SK 05 SE/20) between 69.45 and 56.40 m, below a late Asbian (B_2) goniatite fauna (see below), indicating the diachronous nature of the boundary with the Mixon Limestone-Shales.

Widmerpool Formation and Mixon Limestone-Shales

These strata contain the youngest Dinantian faunas in the district. In the borehole (SK 05 SE/20) near Waterfall, beds low in the Mixon Limestone-Shales yield goniatites between 57.73 m and 53.00 m; these include *Beyrichoceras* cf. *vesiculiferum*, *Goniatites moorei* and *G. struppus*, indicating an horizon in the B_2 Zone close to the Asbian/Brigantian boundary. Higher in the borehole, at 36.80 to 32.60 m, *Posidonia corrugata* and *Goniatites* ex gr. *concentricus* occur, indicating an early Brigantian (P_{1a}) horizon. The youngest Brigantian faunas seen during the survey occur in the Widmerpool Formation in an exposure [2027 4939] near Brookhouse Farm, Kniveton, where late P_{2a} faunas include cf. *Goniatites granosus*, *Sudeticeras* cf. *crenistriatus*, *Posidonia corrugata*, *P. membranacea* and the trilobite *Pseudospatulina sp.* A late P_{2a} fauna with *G.* cf. *granosus* also occurs in a stream section [1791 5119] near Basset Wood.

The youngest Mixon Limestone-Shales fauna collected was from the River Hamps (SK 05 SE/22) near Ford, where mudstones with *Sudeticeras* cf. ex gr. *stolbergi* are overlain by Namurian (E_{1a}) mudstones with *Cravenoceras* cf. *leion*. A similar section (SK 05 SE/23) is exposed in a stream at Back o' th' brook. Here mudstones with *Neoglyphioceras sp.* and *Posidonia membranacea horizontalis* are overlain by Namurian (E_{1a}) mudstones with *Cravenoceras leion*, *Eumorphoceras sp.* and *Sudeticeras sp.*   MM,NJR,ARES

PALAEOGEOGRAPHY AND DEPOSITIONAL HISTORY

Crustal stretching in late Devonian times probably initiated movement of a series of tilt-blocks or half grabens that were topographically expressed as eroding highland areas separated by intermontane basins where arenaceous deposits such as the Redhouse Sandstones accumulated. Intermittent fault movements and sea level changes caused an irregular marine inundation of this landscape and the accumulation of mainly carbonate sediments during the succeeding Dinantian. Limestone deposition was encouraged by the tropical position of the region during this epoch, favouring the abundant growth of lime-secreting organisms.

In the Caldon Low Borehole the lowest limestones are of Courceyan age (Welsh and Owens, 1983) but foraminifera from the Woo Dale Borehole, 18 km to the north (Sheet

111), show that sedimentation may not have started there until Arundian times (Strank, 1985). However, apart from a 30–50 per cent proportion of quartz sand in the dolomites below the Holkerian Griffe Grange Bed in the Ryder Point Borehole (Sheet 112; Chisholm and Butcher, 1981, p.227), there is no evidence in the late Courceyan to Holkerian rocks of continuing erosion of high-relief land areas. Such carbonate-free land areas that did exist must have been of low relief, contributing only fine-grained sediment to the adjacent seas.

The only evidence of the initial Dinantian marine transgression in the district is the occurrence of the Rue Hill Dolomites in the Caldon Low Borehole. This formation shows an alternation of shallow-water marine subtidal and intertidal or supratidal conditions. Penecontemporaneous breccias suggest solution of evaporites, giving the formation an affinity with the early Dinantian evaporite sequences proved in the deep boreholes at Eyam and Hathern in nearby districts.

Intermittent supratidal conditions probably ceased around the end of Courceyan times, the last such episode being represented by a 1 cm coal and underlying rootlet bed 36.9 m above the base of the Milldale Limestones. Thereafter, fully marine conditions prevailed over much of the off-shelf province, with subsidence and depth of water probably greatest in a broad area elongated north-west to south-east from the Manifold valley to Kniveton, but extending an unknown distance beyond these places. Little evidence has been obtained to indicate the steepness of the palaeoslopes descending to this deeper area from the north-east and south-west but developing knoll-reefs, probably concentrated in a broad belt on the south-westerly dipping palaeoslope, must have made this slope very irregular in late Chadian times.

Towards the end of the Chadian, some event, either eustatic or tectonic—perhaps associated with movement of the tilt-blocks (p.116) postulated by Smith and others (1985)—produced a turbidite influx of coarse carbonate sediment into the Manifold valley–Waterhouses area, marking the base of the Ecton and Hopedale limestones. The influx continued, with a few subordinate intervals of finer-grained deposition, throughout Arundian, Holkerian and Asbian times. However, in the Staffordshire shelf at Caldon Low there is evidence for a period or periods of erosion during the Arundian–Holkerian interval. An erosion surface is present at the base of the Hopedale Limestones on the north side of Caldon Low cut into beds of probable Chadian age, and overlain in places (Figure 11) by beds of Asbian (and perhaps Holkerian) age. It was formerly visible as a plane of angular unconformity (Ludford, 1940, p.218; 1951, p.216). To the south, the disposition of outcrops relative to fold structures suggests that the unconformity continues beneath the Kevin Limestones and cuts deeply into older Milldale Limestones (Arundian to Chadian) between Wardlow [086 473] and Walk Farm [096 470]. To the north of its area of proven extent, however, as around Waterhouses [082 502], there is no evidence of angular unconformity, though there is little exposure of the equivalent part of the sequence. The presence of siliceous pebbles in the beds immediately above the unconformity suggests that the Caldon Low area formed part of the 'Midland Barrier' at this time, for pebbles are not known to the north, in the Peak District, but are present to

the south, at Lilleshall and Breedon Cloud, localities that lie on or near the 'Midland Barrier' (Hains and Horton, 1969, pp.31–32). At Breedon Cloud (Mitchell and Stubblefield, 1941, p.205) the pebbly beds lie close above an erosion surface, as at Caldon Low. The dispersed occurrence of the pebbles at Caldon Low, accompanied by only minor amounts of quartz sand, suggests that the clastic material may have been derived from pebbly sandstones exposed on the sea bed, perhaps by tectonic agencies, because a fluviatile advance unrelated to local earth movements would have produced a large mass of clastic sediment with pebbles as a minor constituent, as exemplified by the sediments of the Namurian deltaic advances into the area. The Redhouse Sandstones are a possible source for the siliceous material.

Holkerian sediments, identified specifically only in Ecton Limestones of slope or ramp facies in a borehole (SK 05 SE/19; Figure 7) contrast markedly with beds at a similar level in the Woo Dale Limestones in the Buxton district to the north-east, which were deposited in an environment varying from open shelf to restricted lagoon (Schofield and Adams, 1985) and are about five times as thick. The margins of this Holkerian shelf are not exposed or proved in boreholes. In contrast, the margins of the shelf in Asbian times are clearly delineated by the presence of the apron-reef facies. Erosion is inferred to have removed all but a few remnants of this facies from the northern margin of the Staffordshire shelf, whose limits are therefore less well defined. In the present district, the transition from shelf to off-shelf is clearly marked only by the apron-reef along the southern margin of the Derbyshire shelf between Parwich and Carsington. This belt is highly indented with embayments and promontories, and is absent over a one-kilometre stretch between Ballidon and Brassington. To the south, in the Bradbourne–Kniveton area, minor knoll-reefs are present in the Hopedale Limestones, suggesting that this may have been a shallow-water area in Asbian times. A similar but more extensive tract is present to the south and south-west of a more extensive break in the apron-reef in the district to the north, between Parwich and Beresford Dale [128 590]. This tract extends into the present district, coinciding with the outcrop of the Hopedale Limestones, which are thought to have been deposited on an irregular ramp (Ahr, 1973) of general south-westerly inclination. The lateral passage, towards the south-west, from the Hopedale Limestones to the Ecton Limestones and Widmerpool Formation marks the transition from this ramp into the deeper water basin known as the Widmerpool Gulf. In this transition zone, deposits of the Tissington Volcanic Member provide evidence of a largely submarine volcano of probable Surtseyan type that erupted in early Brigantian times and which must have produced major local modifications to the ramp and basin environment.

Finally, the dark terrigenous muds with subordinate quartz/carbonate silt and sand, that dominated basinal turbidite deposition during Brigantian times, began to spread over the adjacent ramps and shelves bringing to an end a major episode of carbonate sedimentation.   NA,JIC

STRATIGRAPHY OF SHELF PROVINCES

The Staffordshire shelf province (p.7) is represented by the Kevin Limestones in the Weaver Hills area, and the Derbyshire shelf province by the Bee Low Limestones in the Brassington area. The Woo Dale Limestones are inferred to underlie the latter formation but have been proved only in the adjacent district (Aitkenhead and others, 1985, p.13). The Monsal Dale Limestones that normally overlie the Bee Low Limestones occur in only one small area, at Carsington Pastures; they are covered by head.

Bee Low Limestones

The Bee Low Limestones (Stevenson and Gaunt, 1971) form an extensive outcrop in the ground to the north but only a small part of this extends into the present district (Figure 3). The limestones generally comprise grey to pale grey calcarenites with thin clay bands ('wayboards') of volcanic origin (Walkden, 1972) scattered throughout the sequence. At the margin of the shelf or platform, these beds pass laterally into an apron-reef facies, characterised by micritic limestones with an abundant and varied shelly fauna, that were deposited where the shelf edge was adjacent to deeper water and subject to open marine conditions (Aitkenhead and others, 1985, pp.13–17). The algal reef core that is present in places in the apron-reef around Castleton and Earl Sterndale (Wolfenden, 1958; Stevenson and Gaunt, 1971) is absent in this area and the bedded shelf limestones pass directly into fore-reef.

NA

DETAILS

Major sections are few and much of the outcrop is dolomitised. The best sections are in Ballidon Quarry [202 554] (Aitkenhead and others, 1985, p.25), just north of the district boundary, and in the valley south-west of Black Rocks by the A524 road. Here, a disused quarry [2107 5443] exposes 11.5 m of pale massive limestone and on the opposite (south-east) side of the valley [2097 5424 to 2100 5420] a 57.5-m section in apron-reef and partially dolomitised back-reef or shelf limestones has been described by Cox and Harrison (1980, pp.86–87).

The apron-reef is best seen around Parwich where it dips at up to 40° away from the shelf area. It has yielded rich faunas (p.9) at a number of small exposures [for example 1866 5471]. The assemblage from the latter locality includes the goniatite *Bollandoceras* cf. *micronotum*, indicative of the upper B₂ Zone of the Asbian. To the south-west of the village, apron-reef is present [1860 5434] in an inlier beneath dark limestones of the Widmerpool Formation (SK 15 SE/20). To the east of Parwich, small exposures of fore-reef limestone occur at a number of places near the edge of the outcrop.

IPS

Kevin Limestones

The outcrop extends from Hoften's Cross [072 480] to a point [096 459] near Kevin Quarry, where it is overstepped by Namurian and Triassic rocks. The maximum thickness, around Kevin Quarry, is estimated at between 150 and 300 m. The formation consists mainly of pale grey, fine to coarse-grained spar-cemented calcarenites in thick beds separated by pronounced bedding planes. Thin clay wayboards, brown pedogenic crusts and rhizoliths are associated with some of the bedding planes. The limestones are of shelf facies, like the coeval Bee Low Limestones of the Derbyshire shelf.

DETAILS

The type section in Kevin Quarry (SK 04 NE/37; Plate 3) shows 131.1 m of limestone with a 6.2 m shelly band near the top bearing a typical Asbian fauna of *Dibunophyllum bourtonense*, *Lithostrotion aranea*, *L. martini*, *L. pauciradiale*, *L. portlocki*, *Palaeosmilia murchisoni* and *Davidsonina septosa*. There are good sections at lower levels in the formation in a quarry [087 468] on Wredon, at [087 472] near Weaver Villas and in Wardlow Quarry [083 472]. *Lithostrotion arachnoideum*, *L. aranea* and *L.sociale* have been collected from the thickly bedded pale limestones at the last locality and these appear to overlie a conglomeratic bed with sparse quartz pebbles; this in turn lies above Milldale Limestones with *Levitusia humerosa*, but contacts are poorly exposed. The conglomerate is regarded as a lens of the Caldon Low Conglomerate, here a basal member of the Kevin Limestones.

To the south-east of the above exposures, on The Walk [094 464], there is a lateral passage by interdigitation into a mass of pale rubbly-weathering reef-limestone with pockets of brachiopods and cavities lined with laminated limestone. The fauna includes *Lithostrotion* cf. *arachnoideum* [0931 4648], *Aulina sp.*, *Axophyllum vaughani*, *L. martini*, *Cinctifera medusa*, *Pleuropugnoides pleurodon*, *Pugnoides triplex* and cf. *Sinuatella sinuata*. The position of the reef, between shelf limestones on one side and off-shelf Hopedale Limestones on the other, suggests that this is an apron-reef analogous to that which fringes much of the Derbyshire shelf (Aitkenhead and others, 1985, p.7). It is shown as such on the published maps, but there is no topographic expression of the supposed fore-reef slope at The Walk, and it is possible that the reefs here are knolls, similar to those at the margin of the Derbyshire shelf at Narrowdale Hill (Aitkenhead and others, 1951, p.49). At the north end of the Kevin Limestones outcrop, a mass of reef-limestone is well exposed [073 480] near Hoften's Cross. It contains cavities with spectacular concentrically laminated fillings and the fauna includes *Megachonetes* cf. *papilionaceus* [0728 4803], *Nomismoceras vittigerum* [0732 4810], *Lithostrotion portlocki* and the reef elements *Cinctifera medusa*, *Overtonia fimbriata*, *Plicatifera plicatilis* and *Sinuatella sinuata*. The fauna at Cauldon churchyard (p.12) may belong to a northward extension of this reef but, in the absence of good exposures, is at present included in the Hopedale Limestones. Irrespective of its precise extent, however, the Hoften's Cross reef, like that at the Walk, is considered to be an apron-reef at the northern edge of the Staffordshire shelf (Aitkenhead and Chisholm, 1982, fig.8).

The base of the Kevin Limestones is nowhere well exposed but the field relations suggest that the boundary is a non-sequence continuous with that below the Hopedale Limestones. The top of the formation is poorly exposed in dolines (sink holes), the best section [0764 4680], at Ribden, showing 2 m of medium to dark grey cherty thinly bedded limestone dipping beneath Namurian mudstone and resting on pale massive limestone. There is no obvious angular discordance in this section but only Asbian faunas have been collected from the Kevin Limestones and it is therefore assumed that the boundary is a non-sequence. There is certainly an erosion surface in places, for an outlier of Namurian mudstone rests in a small pocket on the beds with *Davidsonina septosa* at one point [0848 4607] in Kevin Quarry.

JIC

Plate 3   The type section of the Kevin Limestones at Kevin Quarry [084 461].

The quarry exposes very thick beds of pale calcarenite with a *Davidsonina septosa* band at the top of the sequence (L2289)

STRATIGRAPHY OF OFF-SHELF PROVINCE

Rue Hill Dolomites

The formation has been encountered only in the Caldon Low Borehole (Aitkenhead and Chisholm, 1982, p.9), where it is 84.47 m thick. It may be extensive at depth in both the off-shelf and Staffordshire shelf provinces (see p.7). It consists mainly of grey fine-grained dolomite with subordinate dark grey limestone and mudstone; the dolomite is at least partly a replacement of the limestone. Thin beds of quartz-sandstone are also present. Two broad facies can be distinguished. One is of variably bedded argillaceous limestone or dolomite with a fully marine fauna; it resembles parts of the overlying Milldale Limestones and was probably deposited in a shallow subtidal marine environment. The other facies consists mainly of laminated dolomite, with rare limestone remnants, and includes many penecontemporaneous breccias. The sparse fauna of ostracods, small gastropods and serpulids indicates a restricted environment and fenestral cavities suggest that the lamination has an algal origin, perhaps on intertidal or supratidal flats. The breccias may owe their origin to penecontemporaneous solution of

evaporites, though none of these now remain. Anhydrite was present in the basal beds of the Dinantian in the Eyam Borehole, some 30 km distant (Dunham, 1973).

The Rue Hill Dolomites are probably Courceyan in age (see below).

Details

In the Caldon Low Borehole (SK 04 NE/36) the formation is present between 280.60 and 365.07 m. The two facies described above alternate and each recurs three times, giving six units (Figure 6). The lowest unit, 22.85 m thick, consists of fine-grained dolomite with many argillaceous bands. Disseminated quartz silt is common at the base but decreases upwards; thin bands of quartz sandstone are present in the lowest 9 m and at the top. Crinoid and brachiopod debris is scattered throughout, the base of the formation being drawn in an otherwise gradational lithological sequence at the lowest occurrence of this fauna.

The second unit, 16.37 m thick, is of fine-grained laminated dolomite with argillaceous wisps and thin mudstone bands. Breccias are common, most consisting of angular dolomite fragments set in a matrix of mudstone and dolomite (Plate 2.2a). Patches of partly dolomitised limestone show that the original deposits were finely laminated calcilutites, calcisiltites and, more rarely, fine calcarenites. Traces of disseminated quartz silt are present in the lowest beds. The fauna consists mainly of ostracods, with small gastropods and serpulids in some bands.

The third unit, 16.18 m thick, comprises unevenly bedded fine-grained limestone with argillaceous wisps and mudstone partings; dolomitisation is minor. Sorting is generally poor, with crinoid, brachiopod and coral debris dispersed variably through a range of calcilutites and biomicrites. A few chert nodules are present.

The fourth unit, 20.90 m thick, is mainly laminated fine-grained dolomite, showing penecontemporaneous folding, faulting and brecciation in places. Rare limestone remnants are dark grey, argillaceous and thinly laminated, with sparse ostracods and algal nodules. Fenestral vughs occur in the dolomite. Thin bands of dark grey mudstone are common, and rarer bands of coarse-grained sandstone, up to 0.6 m thick, are also present; the grains in these are of quartz, pyritic mudstone, feldspar and mica.

The fifth unit, 5.82 m thick, consists mainly of unevenly bedded limestone, partly dolomitic, with a fauna of ostracods, gastropods, brachiopod debris and algal nodules. Argillaceous wisps and thin mudstone bands are common and the limestones vary in grain size from calcilutite to calcarenite, the coarser lithologies being poorly sorted biomicrites. Sand-sized pyritic and clayey intraclasts, possibly of volcanic origin, are present in the lowest beds.

The highest unit, 2.35 m thick, is a pale-coloured fine-grained dolomite; the top part is massive but the lower part is finely laminated. Subangular intraclasts of dolomite are present.

Miospores recovered from mudstone bands in the lowest 57 m of the Rue Hill Dolomites indicate a Tournaisian age (Welsh and Owens, 1983). The assemblages with the greatest stratigraphical significance were obtained from the lowest of the six units described above, a sample 1.25 m above the base indicating the top part of the NV Miospore Zone, while two more, 4.67 m and 13.78 m higher, showed the presence of the succeeding PC Zone.　　　JIC, NA

Milldale Limestones

The Milldale Limestones (Parkinson, 1950, p.273) were re-defined by Aitkenhead and Chisholm (1982, p.10) to include the Dovedale Limestone of Parkinson, the Cementstone Series, Massive Series and Manifold Limestones-with-Shales of Prentice (1951), and the Solenopora Beds, Weaver Beds, Cauldon Low Limestone, Manifold Limestone-with-Shales and Forest Hollow Beds of Ludford (1951).

The formation crops out extensively between Thors Cave and the Weaver Hills, in the west, and around Dovedale, in the centre (Figure 3). Inliers are present between Blore and Stanton, between Bradbourne and Kniveton, and near Snelston some 6 km south of the main outcrop.

The Milldale Limestones are the oldest rocks at outcrop in the district. The base is proved only in the Caldon Low Borehole (SK 04 NE/36), together with the lowest 200 m of the formation (Figure 6). A further 270 m are estimated to be present at outcrop in the Caldon Low area making a total thickness of about 470 m. Farther north in the Hamps valley around Soles Hill [097 524], the thickness probably reaches its maximum of at least 512 m. This compares with at least 218 m near Thors Cave, 320 m around Dovedale and 215 m near Kniveton, where the lowest 100 m is proved in a borehole (SK 25 SW/19, see below).

The base of the formation in the Caldon Low Borehole is taken at a 2 cm bed of black fissile mudstone at a depth of 280.60 m, overlying 2.35 m of very fine-grained off-white dolomite at the top of the Rue Hill Dolomites. The age of the lowest beds is Courceyan (p.10; Welsh and Owens, 1983).

Figure 7 Comparative composite sections of Milldale Limestones and parts of adjacent formations, at locations shown in Figure 3

The numbers to the right of each column refer to fossil information: 1. Conodonts indicate late Courceyan to early Chadian. 2. Foraminifera indicate Chadian. 3 and 4. *Levitusia humerosa*, diagnostic of Chadian. 5. Foraminifera indicate Chadian. 6. Macrofaunal and microfaunal assemblages indicate a range from Chadian to Holkerian—probably derived—plus *Archaediscus angulatus* and *Gigasbia sp.*, diagnostic of Asbian. 7. *L. humerosa*, diagnostic of Chadian. 8. *Davidsonina carbonaria* indicates Holkerian. 9. Foraminifera indicate Holkerian to early Asbian. 10. Foraminifera indicate Chadian; *Scaliognathus anchoralis* indicates Tournaisian, but probably derived. 11. Macrofauna inconclusive; microfauna consistent with Chadian. 12. Corals and foraminifera indicate Asbian. 13. Brachiopods and foraminifera indicate Brigantian. 14,15,16 and 17. Foraminifera indicate Chadian, Arundian, Holkerian, and early Asbian or Holkerian, respectively. 18. *L. humerosa*, diagnostic of Chadian. 19. Coral fauna indicates Chadian. 20. Foraminifera indicate Chadian. 21 and 22. *Fascipericyclus fasciculatus* indicates Chadian.

The Milldale Limestones are overlain by four different formations in different places; the Kevin Limestones south of Caldon Low village in the south-west; the Hopedale Limestones around Calton, Waterhouses and much of the Manifold valley, to the east and west of Dovedale and in the Bradbourne–Kniveton inlier; the Ecton Limestones around Grindon and Blore with Swinscoe; and by the Widmerpool Formation between Ilam and Thorpe, and in the Brad-bourne–Kniveton inlier (Figure 3). The boundary is normally taken where thinly bedded dark grey to grey fine-grained cherty limestones characteristic of the Milldale Limestones pass up into paler bioclastic limestones, usually of medium to coarse calcarenite or calcirudite (conglomerate) grade. The mapped boundary is, therefore, based solely on lithology. On the basis of poor macrofossil evidence, it had been supposed that the overlying beds were generally of early Asbian age. Since the map was published, however, preliminary evidence from microfossils (see p.10 and Figure 7) has shown their age to vary from Chadian to Asbian indicating that the boundary is highly diachronous, and there remains much scope for further biostratigraphical work.

Lithology and facies variations

The Milldale Limestones in the district are normally well bedded grey to dark grey, medium- to fine-grained limestones. In the Dovedale area, however, knoll-reefs predominate; elsewhere these are isolated and relatively small (Figure 8).

The base and lower part of the Milldale Limestones are known only from the Caldon Low Borehole (Figure 6; Figure 7, column 1), where the lowest 89.85 m of the formation comprises grey-brown to dark grey fine-grained partially dolomitised bioclastic limestone. A 1 cm coal and associated rootlet bed are present, 36.9 m above the base, in-

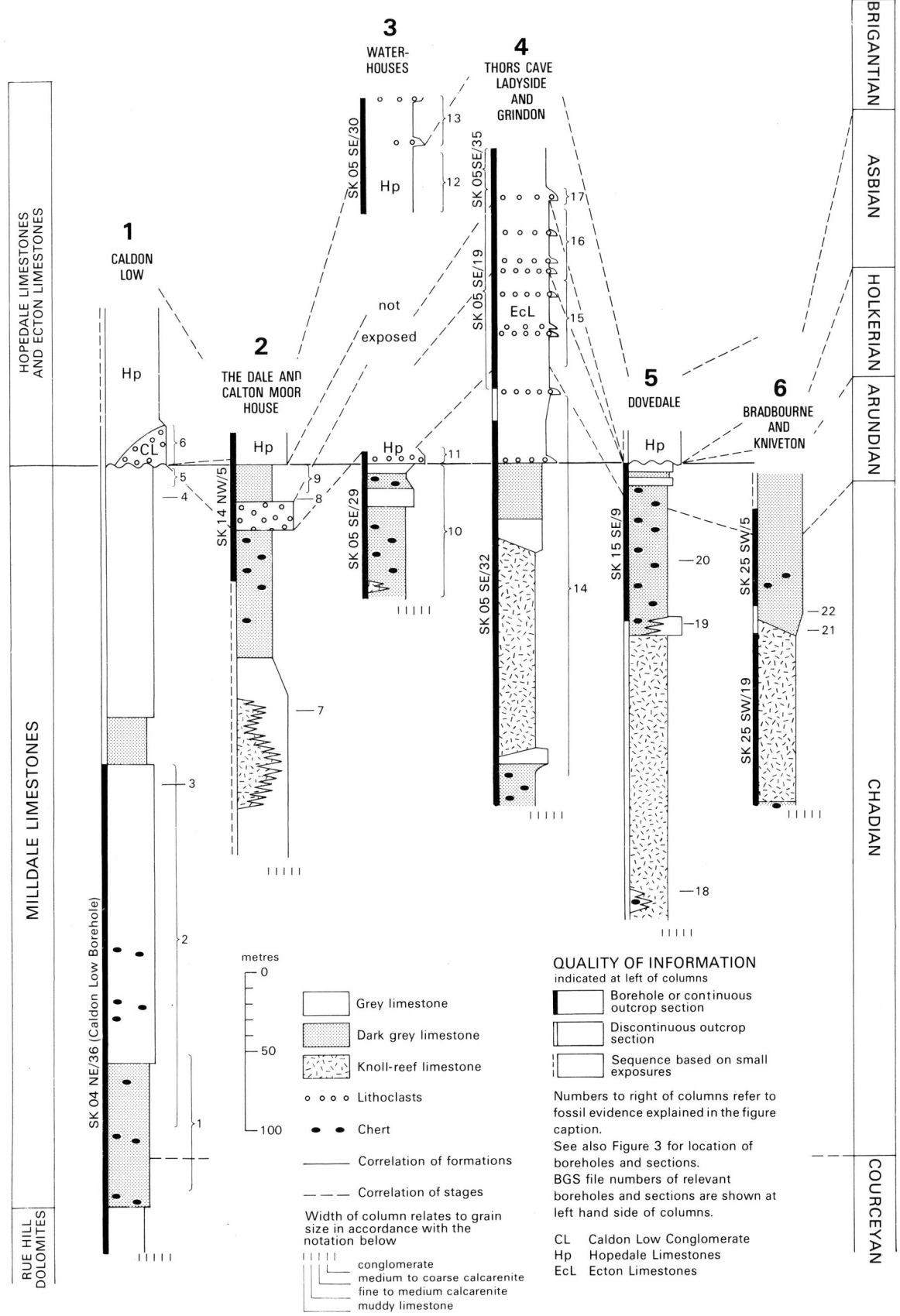

Figure 7   Comparative composite sections of Milldale Limestones and parts of adjacent formations. For details see opposite.

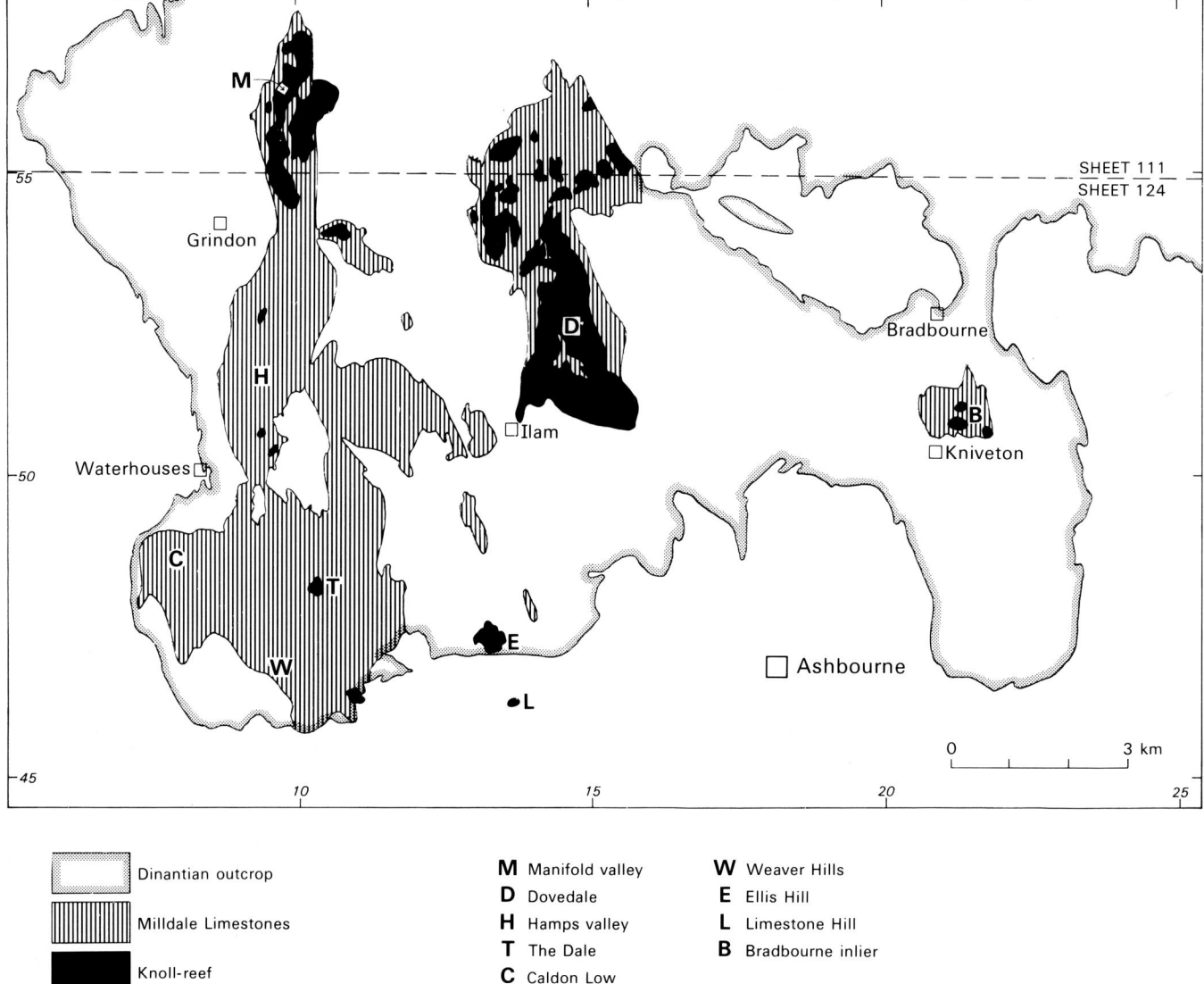

Figure 8 Regional outcrop distribution of knoll-reefs in the Milldale Limestones

dicating a temporary return of the supratidal conditions (p.15) that occurred more frequently in the underlying Rue Hill Dolomites. Above, some 380 m of predominantly grey medium-grained thickly-bedded bioclastic calcarenites with some darker finer-grained beds are known from the borehole and quarry sections at Caldon Low. Knoll-reefs are absent but the upper part includes beds with the brachiopod *Levitusia humerosa*, and probably correlates with levels in the formation elsewhere that contain knoll-reefs with this brachiopod. Around The Dale (Figure 7, column 2) grey calcarenites similar to those exposed at Caldon Low occur but in thinner beds showing a greater degree of current sorting. In the middle part of the sequence in the Manifold and Hamps valley area the beds commonly show weak graded bedding with some parallel lamination and contain scattered chert nodules. The grey beds interdigitate with and are generally overlain by darker, thinner-bedded finer-grained limestones with common chert nodules. In places, the out-

crop of this dark lithofacies is sufficiently distinctive to be shown on the geological maps.

The knoll-reef (Waulsortian buildup) facies, absent in the sequence at Caldon Low, is present elsewhere in the upper part of the formation. Since the base of the reef facies is un-proven, its stratigraphical range is uncertain although it probably spans the middle part of the Chadian. A Courceyan age assigned to part of the knoll-reef and laterally equivalent inter-reef limestones in the Manifold valley in the adjacent district (Aitkenhead and others, 1985, p.45) was based on conodont evidence and now seems doubtful.

The general lithology of the knoll-reefs is similar to that in the adjacent district in that they consist largely of obscurely bedded grey micritic limestone with calcite spar-filled cavities and scattered or clustered fossils including crinoids, ostracods, brachiopods and fenestellid bryozoa (see also Lees and Miller, 1985, table 1). Radial fibrous spar lines the walls of former cavities and fills them to varying degrees. Geopetal micritic or finely peloidal sediment is an additional cavity filling. The filled-in cavities are a typical feature of the facies and have a great range of size, shape, and form but are generally between 2 and 30 cm in width and 1–2 cm in height. They include the small flat-bottomed form sometimes known as *stromatactis* (see Lees, 1964, fig. 22). Where intact fenestellids are common, as for instance in the largest knoll-reef in the Bradbourne inlier (p.26), the facies may correspond to the Waulsortian of the type area in Belgium, the definition of which has recently been clarified by Lees and Miller (1985).

Little has been published on the petrography and palaeoecology of the knoll-reefs in the present district but petrographical details are contained in unpublished theses by Thach (1964) and Ludford (1970). Some unpublished data, mainly from the adjacent district, has also been given by Morgan (1980). Thach drew attention to the similarities in the growth forms of the knoll-reefs to the Waulsortian 'reefs' of Eire described by Lees (1964). In both regions the buildups have grown by varying degrees of vertical and lateral aggregation to produce single and composite knolls, the Dovedale knoll-reef mass being the largest composite example at outcrop in the United Kingdom.

Lees and Miller (1985), in a statistically based petrographical study of the Belgian Waulsortian buildups, have recognised the presence of four phases characterised by distinctive associations of up to 25 different components. They suggest that the distribution pattern of these phases reflects changes in the environment of deposition related to extensive sea-level movements during the early Viséan. In order to test the general application and validity of their methods, Lees and Miller analysed samples of other Waulsortian buildups, including those in the present district at Beeston Tor, Thors Cave and Ravens Tor. Preliminary results from these three localities suggest that the buildups here grew in water depths ranging from 130 to 250 m, that is from below to within the zone where there is enough light for photosynthesising organisms to live. The lower limit of this photic zone is taken at 220 m. These authors also offer an explanation of the origin of the lime mud, which is the major primary component of the buildups, preferring biogenic (microbial) in-situ generation of mud to direct physico-chemical precipitation or to the trapping of current-transported mud by skeletal organisms or algal mats. A biogenic origin is also suggested for some of the sparry calcite cavity-fills that, in total, constitute the other major component of the buildups. The origin of the cavities themselves, however, is still a matter of controversy and speculation and the subject of continuing research.

Bridges and Chapman (1988) applied the methods of Lees, Hallet and Hibo (1985) and Lees and Miller (1985) in Dovedale and Milldale and recorded assemblages of components that indicate water depths of 120–280 m. These authors also support the idea of a microbial origin for the lime mud and favour a mechanism for early cavity formation mainly by movement of marine phreatic waters beneath the mucilagenous surface of the mounds.

Chapman (1984) has examined the cathodoluminescence of cements in the Ravens Tor knoll-reef and has suggested that this buildup was subjected to an influx of fresh water, presumably during a period of subaerial exposure, that did not affect the surrounding inter-reef limestones. No time interval is suggested for this influx but one possiblity is that it was associated with a brief period of erosion in the Arundian, indicated by the presence of conglomerates and boulder beds in the Ecton Limestones in the Manifold valley (Aitkenhead and others, 1985, p.51) and possibly by the Caldon Low Conglomerate (p.28). The boulder bed exposed [1412 5347] near Dove Holes is thought to be the result of earlier penecontemporaneous submarine slumping (Parkinson, 1950, p.280).

The knoll-reefs in the Milldale Limestones (Figure 8) are concentrated in the Manifold valley, Dovedale and Bradbourne/Kniveton areas and have a widely scattered distribution elsewhere. The reefs are thus mainly concentrated in a broad, largely concealed, belt whose probable south-western limit is shown on Figure 8. The north-eastern limit is unknown but probably lies concealed not far beyond the Dovedale outcrop and certainly between the latter and Woo Dale (Sheet 111), some 18 km to the north, where a borehole (Cope, 1973, 1979) proved limestones of Arundian to Holkerian age (Strank, 1985; 1986) lying unconformably on pre-Carboniferous basement rocks. Parkinson (1950, fig.1, and p.282) envisaged a rigid block to the north-east of Dovedale, the knoll-reefs lying in a basinal area south-west of the block margin. Evidence is scarce for the presence of such a marginal feature during Chadian times when the knoll-reefs were growing. There is some suggestion of a general facies transition from shallower water in the north-east to deeper water in the south-west. Limestones in the former area include a significant proportion of grey well sorted crinoidal biosparites, whereas in the latter area, where the succession appears to reach its maximum thickness, dark argillaceous limestones and sharp-based calcarenites of probable turbidite origin are common. However, lack of precise correlation between the two areas makes direct comparison difficult. Such a transition would represent a south-westerly dipping palaeoslope or ramp and would accord with the theory that the area formed part of a tilt-block, bounded by growth faults on the north-east and south-west, that was affecting sedimentation during Chadian and Arundian times (p.116). The knoll-reefs of the Dovedale area would have a NE–SW distribution on this ramp. Lees and Miller (1985, fig.8) have suggested that similar (Waulsortian) reefs would show depth-related phases according to their position on such a ramp, an aspect recently studied by Bridges and Chapman (1988). The scarity and relatively small size of the knoll-reefs to the south-west of the main reef-belt (Figure 8) may be due to a high sedimentation rate rather than depth of water. Ther are no knoll-reefs in the south-western part of the Milldale Limestone outcrop around Caldon Low where a 'massif facies' was separately recognised by Ludford (1951) and Parkinson and Ludford (1964). This absence may also be the result of high sedimentation rates.   NA

DETAILS

Caldon Low

The Milldale Limestones are about 470 m thick around Caldon Low; they rest conformably on the Rue Hill Dolomites but their junction with the overlying Hopedale and Kevin limestones (p.27) is an erosion surface. The upper part, estimated to be about 270 m thick, is exposed in the Cauldon Anticline, a broad complex upfold centred [078 479] near School House Farm. It was called the Cauldon Low Limestone by Ludford (1951, pp.215–216). The underlying 200 m have only been seen in the Caldon Low Borehole (SK 04 NE/36; Figure 6; Institute of Geological Sciences, 1978, p.11), though it is possible that some of these beds may appear at the surface in anticlines to the east of Caldon Low.

The lowest 89.85 m of the Milldale Limestones, encountered between depths of 190.75 and 280.60 m in the Caldon Low Borehole, are of dark facies, consisting of fine-grained dark and medium grey limestone with undulating wispy argillaceous partings and rare chert nodules. Dolomitisation is widespread, about 43 per cent of the sequence being affected in this way. Most of the unaltered limestones are burrow-mottled, poorly sorted mixtures of fine-grained biomicrite and calcilutite with dispersed bioclasts. Other lithologies present are grey mudstone in rare bands 1 to 5 cm thick, some with a fragmental texture; and a 1 cm coal at 243.70 m in the borehole, underlain by limestone containing flat rootlets. The macrofauna includes algal nodules and coatings, dispersed brachiopod shells and rare corals; none is of any stratigraphical significance. Conodonts include *Cloghergnathus cravenus* and *C.* cf. *rhodesi*, indicating a probable late Courceyan–early Chadian age.

Above these dark basal beds, from 2.59 to 190.75 m in the borehole, lie 188.16 m of mainly medium grey, fine- to coarse-grained calcarenite. The lowest 100 m also include darker and paler bands and some chert nodules; patchy dolomitisation affects the lowest 57 m. A detailed log of the top 100 m of the borehole is given by Bridge and Kneebone (1983, p.27). The limestones are mainly poorly bedded bioclastic and peloidal biosparites and biomicrites, with some argillaceous wisps and bands. Burrow-mottling is common. The macrofauna consists of dispersed crinoid debris, brachiopods, including *Levitusia humerosa* at 13.53 m, rarer corals and gastropods, and common algal nodules and coatings on bioclasts and limestone intraclasts. The microfauna includes *Cloghergnathus cravenus* and *C.* cf. *rhodesi* in the lowest few metres, but no stratigraphically useful forms have been detected at higher levels. A set of fissures containing pebbles of limestone and greenish mudstone at 131.16 m in the borehole may represent a palaeokarstic surface, but no other signs of emergence have been noted.

The highest 80 m or so of the borehole sequence can also be seen at outcrop, between the borehole site and the culmination of the Cauldon Anticline. Some 190 m of limestone are estimated to lie between the borehole section and the unconformable base of the Hopedale Limestones to the north. Most of these beds are well exposed in large quarries referred to here as Caldon Low Quarry [077 486] and Cauldon Quarry [086 488] but the exact sequence is unknown, due to a prevalence of small faults. The lowest 30 m are seen in the bottom levels at the south end [077 484] of Caldon Low Quarry, where dark thinly bedded limestone alternates in units 1 to 3 m thick with medium grey thicker-bedded limestone. These are overlain, in an unquarried remnant at Hemmings Low [075 488] by about 80 m of pale to medium grey thickly bedded limestone with shelly bands. Bridge and Kneebone (1983, p.56: section SK 04 NE1S) note that the limestones in Caldon Low Quarry are fine to medium-grained calcarenites with foraminifera, compacted peloids, ostracods, crinoid debris in lenses, oncolitic nodules and dispersed brachiopods; chert is rare.

The highest beds preserved at Caldon Low are exposed in a spur [080 490] between Caldon Low and Cauldon quarries; they are mainly medium grey calcarenites, like those of Hemmings Low, and *L. humerosa* has been recorded from a locality [0805 4890] about 20 m below the unconformable base of the Hopedale Limestones.

The south end of the anticline is structurally more complex than the north and the unconformity beneath the Hopedale and Kevin Limestones appears to cut more deeply into the Milldale Limestones there, but medium and pale grey thickly bedded limestones with *L. humerosa* at the western side [083 473] of

Wardlow Quarry probably equate with some part of the sequence above the Caldon Low Borehole.

The Dale, Calton, Swinscoe and Stanton

Small disused quarries in this area reveal a variety of lithologies in an overall fining-upwards sequence at least 250 m thick. However, these exposures are too widely separated and the bedding dips too variable in both inclination and direction to allow correlation from one quarry to another.

The thickly bedded medium to pale grey limestones characteristic of Caldon Low do not persist far to the east of the quarried area (Ludford, 1951, plate 16; Bridge and Kneebone, 1983, p.14). Numerous small exposures around The Dale [099 483] and Walk Farm [096 470] show thinly bedded medium grey limestone, and a borehole at Rue Hill (SK 04 NE/10: Bridge and Kneebone, 1983, p.26) proved 61.01 m of medium and dark grey limestone. Macrofaunas collected in this area include *Siphonophyllia sp.* (*cylindrica* group) and *L. humerosa* [0920 4770], and *Megachonetes magna* [0985 4760]. These indicate a Chadian age but it is not clear whether the strata here belong to the unexposed 89.85 m of dark facies at the base of the Milldale Limestones in the Caldon Low Borehole, or whether, as Ludford (1951, p.215) supposed, they are lateral equivalents, in a thinner-bedded facies, of the exposed thickly bedded medium grey strata in the working quarries.

North-east of Caldon Low, medium and dark grey thinly bedded limestones in Huddale [090 493] underlie the Hopedale Limestones and appear to overlie the beds exposed in Cauldon Quarry. Besides these dark beds, the highest 65 m of strata beneath undoubted Hopedale Limestones include lenses of knoll-reef limestone [092 489] and a 15 m bed of coarsely crinoidal conglomeratic limestone [0929 4911]. The conglomeratic bed contains varied macrofaunas of Chadian to Arundian age: *Haplolasma* cf. *subibicina*, *Siphonophyllia sp.* (*cylindrica* group) and *Sychnoelasma konincki* [0929 4908]; *Acanthoplecta mesoloba*, *Eomarginifera derbiensis* and *Productina pectinoides* [0931 4899]; *Koninckophyllum praecursor* [0934 4908]. These beds are provisionally assigned to the Milldale Limestones on the basis of their fossil content. They may alternatively be a basal conglomeratic member of the Hopedale Limestones with faunas derived, like the limestone clasts, from the Milldale Limestones. JIC,NA

A disused quarry south-east of Huddale Farm shows a 14.8 m section (SK 14 NW/8) of thick-bedded medium to coarse bioclastic limestone with scattered corals including *Koninckophyllum praecursor*, *Michelinia megastoma* and *Palaeosmilia* cf. *murchisoni*, together with nodules of the alga *Solenopora garwoodi*. The Chadian age of these beds is supported by the presence of a poorly preserved foraminiferal assemblage that includes cf. *Baituganella sp.* and cf. *Dainella sp.* Similar bioclastic limestones with *Solenopora* in places (Ludford, 1951, pp.213–215; Parkinson and Ludford, 1964, p.171) are present to the south-west [1047 4778 and 1020 4766] in the approximate direction of the regional strike. The limestones exposed in the first of these two localities show some sharp-based graded beds and cross lamination, suggesting deposition during storms. Both exposures have yielded the Chadian brachiopod *L. humerosa*. The knoll-reefs at Stanton Dale [102 482] and Softlow Wood [109 464], south-west of Thorswood House, also appear to be at approximately the same stratigraphical level. The latter locality is poorly exposed but has yielded many brachiopods; the former stands out as a conspicuous craggy hillock in the dale where some 16 m of massive pale grey mainly micritic limestone with an abundant fauna are seen (Ludford, 1951, p.220). Other isolated knoll-reefs, which may lie at about the same stratigraphical level, occur as inliers; that at Ellis Hill [132 473, 135 476] is surrounded by overlapping Ecton Limestones and Widmerpool Formation, while the knoll at Limestone Hill [136 463] is overlapped by Triassic sandstones (Parkinson and Ludford, 1964, p.170; Charsley, 1979, p.240).

Strata inferred to be at higher stratigraphical levels than those described above are seen in scattered exposures of finer-grained grey to dark grey limestones, mainly calcilutites to finely peloidal calcarenites. Thin shaly intercalations are common in some places, with sporadic nodules and lenses of chert. Traces of bioturbation, including *Zoophycos* (cauda galli markings), are present in a 23 m section [1159 4759], north of Thorswood House. Similar beds in an old quarry [1092 4787], near Dale Abbey Farm, have yielded good specimens of *Siphonophyllia sp.* (*cylindrica* group), indicative of the Chadian stage.

The highest part of the formation and the junction with the overlying Ecton Limestones were proved between depths of 26.12 m and 100.00 m in a borehole (SK 14 NW/5) near Caltonmoor House (Bridge and Kneebone, 1983, p.36). The limestones are predominantly thickly bedded, dark grey and very fine grained with a few coarser graded bioclastic beds and streaky dark argillaceous intercalations. Several clayey bands, mainly pale brown in colour and 2–13 cm thick, are present between depths of 40.94 m and 45.35 m.

This very fine-grained succession is interrupted between the depths of 49.76 m and 68.59 m by a sequence of massive thick-bedded limestone conglomerates containing clasts of very finely bioclastic and 'reefy' micritic limestone together with very coarse crinoid debris. A few single corals, including *Rotiphyllum sp.* and *Amplexizaphrentis sp.* are also present. The conglomerate does not appear to be represented in surface exposures. It resembles the Caldon Low Conglomerate in that it contains poorly preserved microfossils

of possible Chadian to Holkerian age (p.28) but differs in having no quartzose lithoclasts.

The limestones above the conglomerate were named the Forest Hollow Beds by Ludford (1951, p.221) who assigned them to the S_2 Zone on the evidence of their coral-brachiopod fauna. A few small but typical exposures [1161 4831, 1185 4816] are present south-west of Forest Farm.

Exposures in the two inliers in the core of the Swinscoe Anticline consist mostly of grey to dark grey finely peloidal calcarenites and calcisiltites with chert nodules and lenses. Typical examples occur north of Swinscoe [1274 4951 to 1288 4957] and by the A52 road [1397 4768] south-east of the village. The disused quarry at the latter locality displays intense folding in the thinly bedded strata.

Hamps and Manifold valleys

The Milldale Limestones form broad outcrops with numerous exposures flanking the Hamps and Manifold valleys between Waterhouses and Thors Cave and between Calton and Musden Grange. The Manifold valley also cuts through inliers of the formation, for example at Beeston Tor and Ilam Hall. Fossil evidence (see below) indicates that the two best sections, at Thors Cave-Ladyside Wood [0985 5503 to 0947 5487] and Brownend Quarry, Waterhouses [0910 5019] (Plate 4; Figure 9), are both entirely of Chadian age. The quarry section (SK 05 SE/29) shows 86.85 m of the formation and its junction with the overlying Hopedale Limestones (Figure 9). The steeply dipping limestone sequence is

Plate 4   Brownend Quarry, Waterhouses [0910 5019]
Grey to dark grey mainly fine-grained limestones with small lenses of paler 'reefy' micritic limestone near the base (top right) are overlain by coarser peloidal limestone including a prominent 4.5 m bed (left of centre).
The quarry is a Site of Special Scientific Interest and Nature Reserve belonging to the Staffordshire Nature Conservation Trust (L1991)

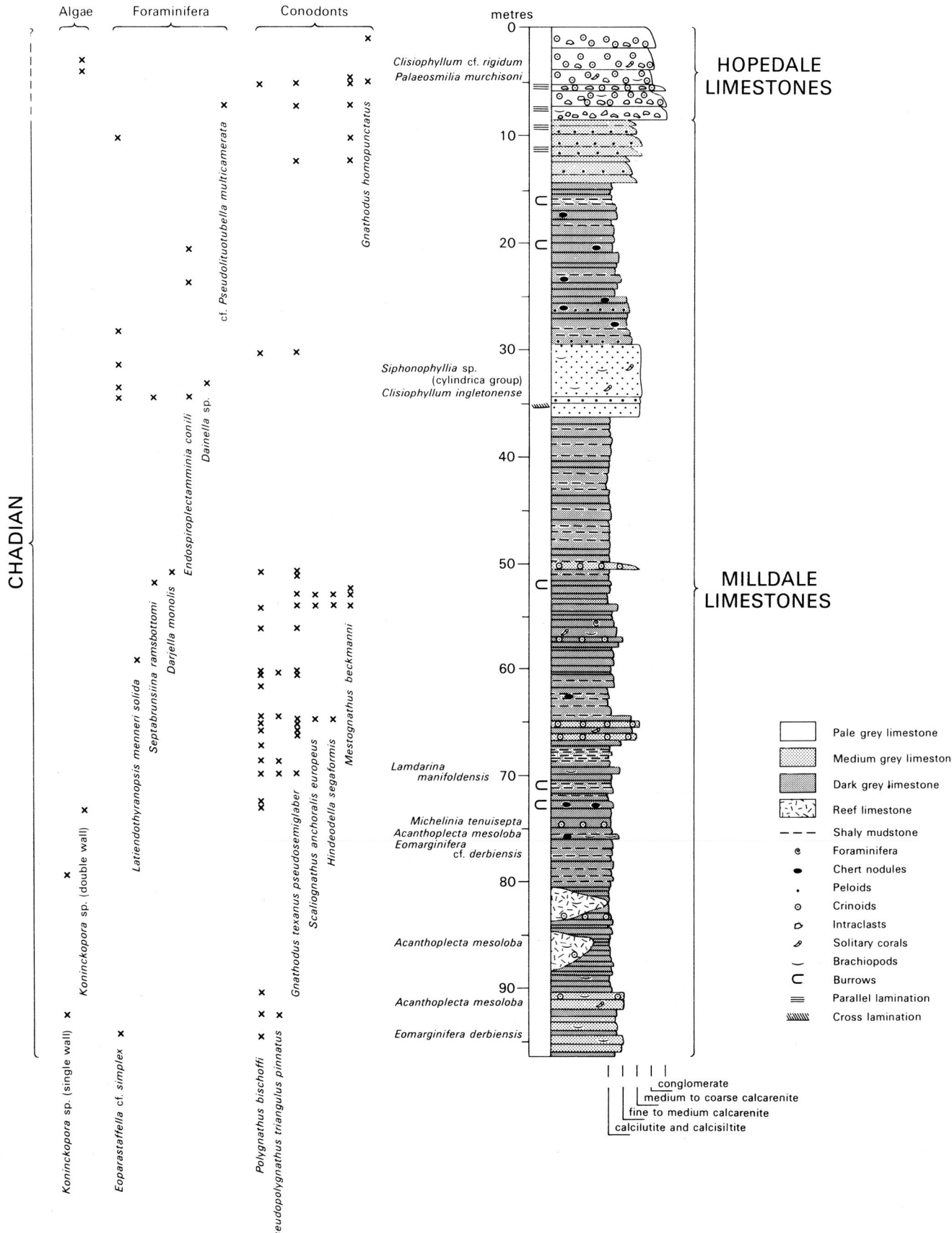

Figure 9 Section of strata in Brownend Quarry

predominantly thinly bedded, dark grey, tinged with red in places and fine-grained with scattered chert nodules and some mudstone intercalations. Two prominent lenses of micritic reef-limestone occur near the base. They appear to be diagenetically altered, with irregular siliceous bands discordant to the strike. P.Cossey and C. Edwards (written communication, January 1987) have examined a large number of geopetal cavity infills in one of these lenses which suggest that it is probably an inverted allochthonous block. Paler coarser limestones of pelsparite composition with some current-lamination are present around the middle of the sequence and include a prominent massive bed, 4.5 m thick, that has yielded a sparse coral fauna including *Clisiophyllum ingletonense*, *Cyathaxonia rushiana* and *Siphonophyllia sp.*, together with five brachiopod genera not diagnostic of age. Some sharp-based graded bioclastic beds are present in the top 6.00 m of the sequence, giving a gradational upward passage into the thickly bedded conglomeratic limestones at the base of the Hopedale Limestones (Aitkenhead and Chisholm, 1982, p.10).

The evidence for the age of the Brownend Quarry sequence is contradictory in that strata containing Courceyan conodonts overlie those with younger Chadian guide fossils (p.10). Chadian microfaunas (see p.12) also persist up into the Hopedale Limestones,

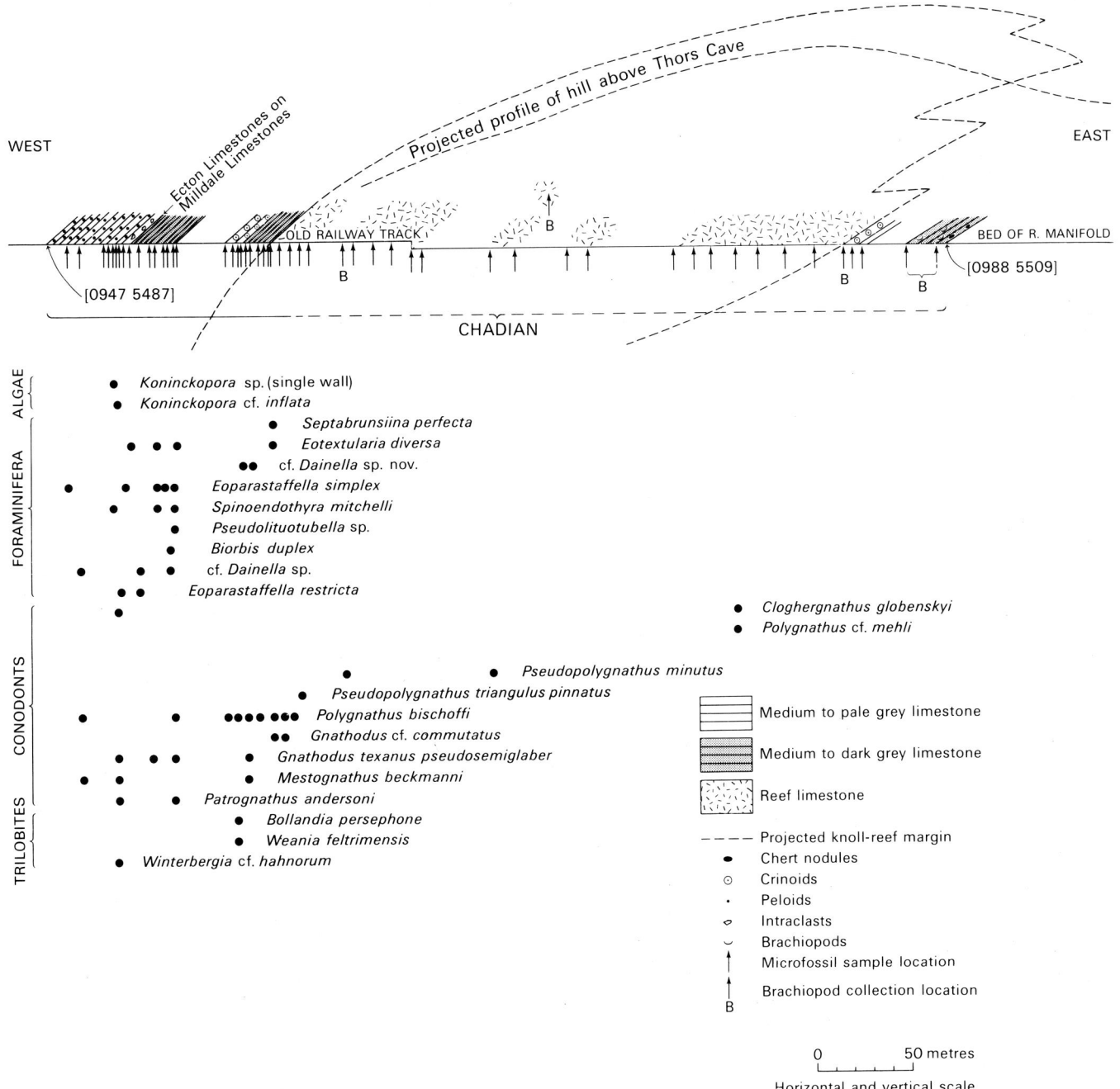

Figure 10 Diagrammatic cross-section of strata from Thors Cave to Ladyside Wood. Significant faunas are shown in direct relationship to the measured section (see also Aitkenhead and others, 1985, p.46)

which were fomerly assigned to the D_1 Zone by Parkinson and Lud- ford (1964, p.174).

The Thors Cave – Ladyside Wood section (Figure 10) spans the northern boundary of the district and lies in the bed and banks of the Manifold where the river has cut through a knoll-reef and the beds above and below it. The underlying beds (Aitkenhead and others, 1985, p.46) show an upward change from thinly bedded dark cherty bituminous limestones to thicker-bedded paler crinoidal limestones that pass up into, and interdigitate with, the basal crinoidal biomicrites of the knoll-reef. The overlying main mass of micritic reef limestones with the typical network of fibrous calcite- filled cavities forms spectacular crags at Thors Cave [0985 5495] rising 49 m above the river bed. Alignments of cavities and poorly delineated bedding structures exposed in the river bed suggest that the knoll is probably formed of a number of piled-up laterally ac- creting mounds. The upper part of the knoll-reef and 31.52 m of the overlying sequence up to the base of the Ecton Limestones are ex- posed nearby in a disused railway cutting (SK 05 SE/32; see also Figure 7 and Prentice 1951, p.180). The reef passes up into variable mainly thinly bedded grey and dark grey limestones with some crinoidal debris and dark shaly intercalations.

In the Manifold valley to the south, the bedded succession greatly expands to a total thickness of about 300 m as the Thors Cave reef mass thins. A tripartite sequence is recognised with predominantly thin dark grey fine-grained beds towards the base and top and thicker mainly grey beds in the middle. These divisions are roughly equivalent to the Cementstone Series, Manifold Limestones-with- Shales and Massive Series respectively of Prentice (1951). About 68 m of the lower dark beds are exposed in the river bed below Weags Bridge (SK 05 SE/34); they are mainly dark siliceous micritic limestones with irregular black chert. A few fossiliferous beds are present, those in the basal 25.6 m of the sequence contain- ing fenestellid bryozoa and elements of the brachiopod fauna characteristic of the nearby stratigraphically equivalent knoll-reefs. The overlying sequence of paler coarser thicker bedded bioclastic limestones is exposed partly in the river bed and partly in an old railway cutting nearby [0983 5445 to 0963 5451; Bridge and Kneebone, 1983, p.57; see also Prentice, 1951, fig.2]. This cutting also exposes about 62 m of the overlying darker thinly bedded facies.

There are numerous scattered exposures to the south-west in the Hamps valley but the stratigraphical succession here is more dif- ficult to establish owing to structural complexities. Small knoll-reefs are exposed at several localities [0934 5266, 0999 5303, 0946 5126 and 0961 5047], and a disused quarry [0980 5249] on Soles Hill shows 14.8 m of grey to dark grey bioclastic calcarenite in beds up to 1.4 m thick.

The other major knoll-reef in this area forms Beeston Tor [107 540], a crag of massive pale grey micritic limestone about 70 m high on the left bank of the Manifold. Prentice (1951, p.180) describes a penecontemporaneous breccia at the margin of the reef but this was not exposed at the time of the present survey. The reef-limestones have yielded a rich brachiopod fauna, together with the goniatite *Fascipericyclus fasciculatus* indicating a Chadian age. Field relations suggest that the base of the Hopedale Limestones could be as little as 12 m above the top of the knoll-reef but there are no exposures that demonstrate the nature of the relationship. A borehole (SK 05 SE/19), 1 km to the west, proved that some 220 m of strata separate the horizon of the top of the Thors Cave knoll-reef and the base of the Asbian (see Figure 7, column 4). Such a rapid increase in thickness over a short distance implies the presence of an interven- ing growth fault, associated with the Manifold valley plexus (p.120) that was active at intervals during late Chadian to Holkerian times.

Downstream from Beeston Tor, the probable lateral correlatives of the knoll-reef consist of well-bedded dark grey micritic limestones with dark burrows, chert lenses and thin shaly intercalations; about 57 m are exposed [1090 5376 to 1104 5361]. An exceptional 0.57 m

graded bioclastic bed about 30 m above the base has yielded cono- donts including *Mestognathus beckmanni*, together with a few brachiopods not inconsistent with an inferred Chadian age.

Between Calton and Musden Grange a borehole at Slade House (SK 15 SW/8; Bridge and Kneebone, 1983, p.50) proved 100.00 m of the formation, mainly grey to dark grey thinly bedded fine- grained limestones with chert nodules and shaly intercalations in the top 37.47 m and in the basal 27.08 m and paler coarser calcarenites in the middle part. It is not clear where this sequence fits into the overall succession, however. Variable grey to dark grey limestones form scattered exposures in Musden Wood, and about 18 m are seen by the riverside footpath at Ilam Hall [1314 5058] in a broad anticline with minor faulting. The highest part of the Milldale Limestones around Ilam Hall is characterised by grey fine- ly laminated fine-grained limestones with thin chert lenses, seen on the river bed [1280 5105 to 1282 5119] and in a 10.7 m sequence im- mediately underlying the junction with the Ecton Limestones in a disused quarry on Musden Low [1184 5034].

Dovedale

The Milldale Limestones crop out in a broadly anticlinal structure, the Dovedale Anticline, around the Dove valley and its tributaries between Milldale and Thorpe Cloud. Knoll-reefs make up much of the outcrop in this area and are described separately from the sur- rounding bedded facies.

Knoll-reef facies   Knoll-reef limestones form the greater part of the formation which has an estimated thickness of 320 m at outcrop in this area. The facies is at least 180 m thick in Dovedale but the maximum thickness is probably about 300 m since the base is not proved and the highest parts have been eroded.

The River Dove has incised a gorge 120 – 160 m deep and the knoll-reef limestones form extensive areas of steep bare rock, which have been modified by karstic solution along joints, leaving isolated towers such as Pickering Tor and Ilam Rock (Plate 1), and ridges such as Tissington Spires. The sides of the tributary valleys, such as Hall Dale and Nabs Dale, are no less precipitous.

The rock so extensively exposed consists mainly of obscurely bedded grey to pale grey fossiliferous micritic limestone with the characteristic variety of filled-in cavities (see p.19). The fabric of the rock is best seen on lichen-free surfaces exposed near the summits of hills such as Baley Hill [1451 5383], Bunster Hill [1423 5155] and Thorpe Cloud [1513 5104] where, in addition to a variety of cavity structures, a fine undulating ?algal lamination is conspicuous, in some cases disrupted by penecontemporaneous brecciation or small-scale slumping and microfaulting. This lamination is rare at lower stratigraphic levels in the knoll-reefs.

Though the knoll-reef limestones contain a sporadically abun- dant brachiopod fauna there are few age-diagnostic forms. The best Chadian indicator, *Levitusia humerosa*, has been reported by Jackson (1919, 1941) as being 'a common fossil' in the cliffs extending from the top of Nabs Dale to beyond Tissington Spires. This species was collected from Lin Dale [1565 5090] by A. Ludford (specimen LZA 5229), and from the top of the reef mass at Ilam Tops [1419 5232] during the present survey. However, the most abundant and varied reef fauna in the area is found on Thorpe Cloud. An assemblage from the lower slopes of this hill [153 511] includes *L. humerosa*, *Fascipericyclus sp.* and *Phillipsia gemmulifera*, indicating a mid-Chadian age, while the limestones at the summit [1512 5105] have yielded a slightly younger mid-Chadian assemblage including *Pericyclus minimus* and *Phillibolina worsawensis*; the last-named species was recently discovered by J. Tilsley (personal communication). Brachiopods are particularly abundant but are of limited stratigraphical value compared with the goniatites and trilobites.

Contacts between the micritic limestone of the knoll-reefs and the surrounding bedded inter-reef facies are generally gradational.

Plate 5   Ravens Tor, Dovedale [1412 5385]
A well displayed transition from massive pale micritic limestone, forming core facies of the knoll-reef or
mound, to well bedded crinoidal biosparites seen at the right-hand end of the crag (L1606)

Ravens Tor [1412 5385] (Plate 5) provides the best section showing
such a lateral passage (Thach, 1964, fig.52). The massive micritic
core of the reef passes successively into crinoidal calcilutite or
biomicrite, crinoidal biosparite of coarse calcarenite grade, and
then into finer darker calcarenite with chert nodules. In contrast,
the basal contact is sharp.

Other well exposed lateral gradational contacts are present in the
right bank of the Dove opposite Dove Holes [1424 5359], near
Reynard's Cave [1450 5254] and on the north face of Lover's Leap
[1449 5182]. Field relations indicate that the inter-reef beds at the
last two of these localities lie within the reef mass as a whole. This
implies that two originally separate knolls had grown laterally,
eventually amalgamating and causing the isolation of the inter-reef
beds. The best exposure of a sharp contact is present at the base of a
33-m rock tower known as Dovedale Church [1449 5226]. Here the
massive grey reef calcilutite, containing an abundance of
stromatactis-like cavity fills and some ?algal lamination, rests with
sharp undulating contact on 9.8 m of dark micritic limestone with
thin irregular beds, lenses and nodules of black chert. The reef-
limestone has yielded many brachiopods, especially *Schizophoria
resupinata* together with a few bivalves, corals and trilobites.
Brachiopods are also common in the underlying bedded limestones,
which have also yielded the Chadian goniatite *Fascipericyclus
fasciculatus*. A similar, more accessible, contact is present in a small
roadside quarry [1363 5476] near Milldale. Of the few good exposures of the upper contact, the best is in Nabs Dale [1476 5374]
where there is a gradational upward change from typical micritic
reef-limestone with ?algal lamination, cavity structures and a
recorded fauna of brachiopods, trilobites and nautiloids, to thickly
bedded crinoidal calcarenites. These in turn pass upwards into
darker finer-grained calcarenites with lenses of crinoid debris. The
conodont *Mestognathus beckmanni*, indicative of a Chadian or Arundian age, has been recovered from both reef and bedded facies here.

Bedded facies   A type section for the Milldale Limestones is present
in crags near the road north of Milldale village [1401 5499 to 1395
5480] (Aitkenhead and Chisholm, 1982, p.10) where about 40 m of
grey bioclastic and peloidal calcarenites, in well defined beds 0.40 to
1.50 m thick with some scattered chert nodules, are exposed.
Similar, but weathered, exposures are present south of Milldale
[1403 5438, 1401 5404] and show evidence of palaeocurrent activity
in the form of parallel and cross lamination and sorting of crinoid
debris into thin bands and lenses. At the second of these exposures,
some 9.0 m of this facies overlie 5.4 m of dark grey finer-grained
limestone with many chert nodules, typical of the inter-reef beds
that occur farther south.

Two boreholes (Bridge and Kneebone, 1983, pp.51, 54) have
penetrated parts of the formation on either flank of the Dovedale
Anticline. To the east, that near Bostern Grange (SK 15 SE/9)
started in the uppermost part of the formation and proved 100.00 m

of mainly dark grey argillaceous calcilutite in thin graded beds, some with basal calcarenite and others with chert nodules. Coarser grey to dark grey beds predominate in the top 14.2 m. Foraminifera from between depths of 65.31 m and 67.35 m indicate a Chadian age. Paler coarser limestones probably lying lateral to or slightly below the borehole sequence are exposed to the west in a disused quarry (SK 15 SE/19) where a probable Chadian macrofauna has been collected, including *Siphonophyllia sp.* (*cylindrica* group) and *Delepinea* cf. *notata*. Farther south grey thinly bedded calcarenites predominate. An exposure [1545 5167] overlying the reef at the head of the gully between Moor Barn and Thorpe Pasture shows an 11.5 m sequence with some thinly bedded dark cherty limestones, near the top, somewhat contorted by penecontemporaneous slumping. On the steep hillside flanking the gully to the north-west [1540 5168] the beds pass laterally and abruptly into a conglomerate that passes down into obscurely bedded reef-limestone (Parkinson, 1950, p.281). The bedded sequence here has yielded an Asbian microfossil assemblage that includes the conodonts *Gnathodus girtyi* and *Paragnathodus commutatus*, foraminifera including *Archaediscus sp.* and the alga *Koninckopora inflata* in abundance.

A borehole (SK 15 SW/9) to the west of Dovedale, near Stanshope, started in the Hopedale Limestones, the junction with the Milldale Limestones being taken at the base of a 1.37 m coarsely crinoidal bed at a depth of 5.43 m. The latter formation was proved to a depth of 100 m; it was mainly dark grey argillaceous limestone (biomicrosparite) with some bioturbation and a few chert nodules though 3.05 m of coarsely bioclastic crinoidal limestones with red-stained mudstone partings was present at 52.85 m. Microfossils including *Nodosarchaediscus* and *K. inflata*, indicating an Asbian age, have been identified from both this depth and from a thin bioclastic graded bed at 17.11 m. A sequence of dark cherty limestones similar to that proved in the borehole is partially exposed in Hall Dale [1309 5393], again with a bioclastic intercalation some 8.3 m thick, lying about 45 m above the top of a ?Chadian knoll-reef. An assemblage of fossils collected by A. Ludford from the bioclastic beds includes the crushed cerioid coral *Lithostrotion ischnon?*, indicating an Asbian or Holkerian age.

Bradbourne Inlier

Milldale Limestones comprising both knoll-reef and bedded facies are present in an inlier between Bradbourne and Kniveton. Contacts with the surrounding Hopedale Limestones and Widmerpool Formation are not exposed, but the latter probably has an unconformable overlapping and overstepping relationship.

There are three knoll-reefs, all with disused quarries providing good exposures. The largest quarry [2124 5084] off Standlow Lane shows a 16 m face, mainly of grey-brown dolomite, with some fossiliferous micritic limestone beneath it in places. At the western end of the face, this limestone has yielded common fenestellid bryozoa and abundant brachiopods together with bivalves, nautiloids, the Chadian goniatites *Fascipericyclus fasciculatus* and *Muensteroceras sp.*, trilobites and ostracods. A borehole (SK 25 SW/19; Cox and Harrison, 1980, pp.132–133) passed through fenestellid-rich mottled grey to dark grey micritic reef-limestone to a depth of 98.30 m, before entering bituminous dark grey micritic limestone with black mudstone partings and chert nodules. The top 20.84 m were largely dolomitised adjacent to a mineral vein (p.128). Morgan (1980) also logged this borehole and noted the similarity of the predominant mottled micrite to the blue vein facies of the type Waulsortian reefs of Belgium (Lees and others, 1977, p.293); subordinate intercalations of pale grey biomicrite and changes of dip in the core indicated the presence of several stacked mounds which together make up the knoll-reef.

A similar knoll-reef [2138 5109], near New House, has been quarried to reveal an irregular upper surface overlain by thinly bedded grey to dark grey fine-grained limestones with shaly inter-calations. These beds too are of Chadian age, as indicated by the presence of *Pericyclus sp.* in a small exposure [2143 5111] east of the quarry. Other disused quarries [2111 5084, 2101 5124] show the bedded facies to be only sparsely fossiliferous. About 60 m of these beds, faulted against Hopedale Limestones, were penetrated by a borehole (SK 25 SW/5) (Cox and Harrison, 1980, pp.128–129) north-west of New House.

Snelston Inlier

The small Dinantian inlier [154 412] near Snelston, first described by Arnold-Bemrose (1904), lies surrounded by drift-covered Triassic rocks about 6 km beyond the southern margin of the main Dinantian outcrop. The limestone is exposed in two disused quarries known as Birchwoodpark Stone Quarries. The smaller northern quarry has been largely filled leaving only 3.0 m of grey fine-grained limestone with calcite veins exposed [1547 4135] at the time of survey. The partially filled southern quarry exposes [154 412] a total of 30–40 m of massive thickly bedded limestone in its largely innaccessible faces. Samples from the lower 14 m show a grey to pale grey finely bioclastic calcarenite, dolomitised in places. A few chert nodules are present in the higher beds. The limestones have yielded a sparse fauna of brachiopods including *Delepinea sp.*, corals including *Koninckophyllum praecursor*, and foraminifera, indicating a Chadian or Arundian age. NA

Ecton Limestones

The type area for the Ecton Limestones is in the Manifold valley in the district to the north (Aitkenhead and Chisholm, 1982, p.11; Aitkenhead and others, 1985, pp.49–51). In the present district the main outcrop continues southwards from near Grindon to Waterfall, where the formation passes laterally into the Hopedale Limestones. A second outcrop is present to the south-west, around Blore with Swinscoe. The formation includes parts of the Waterhouses Limestone and Crassiventer Beds of Prentice (1951) and of the Lower Waterhouses Limestone of Ludford (1951). The total thickness is estimated to be about 258 m around Grindon and 180 m around Blore with Swinscoe. The thickness of 150 m given by Aitkenhead and Chisholm (1982) for the latter area is now regarded as an underestimate.

The Ecton Limestones in the present district have a generally more uniform lithology than the Hopedale Limestones, consisting of a thick monotonous sequence of grey, fine to coarse-grained, commonly graded-bedded calcarenites of biopelsparite composition. Many of the beds show erosive bases. Where adjacent beds are amalgamated the bedding tends to be obscure, but where fissile mudstone partings are present the bedding is much more distinct. The beds are interpreted as proximal turbidites deposited, at a somewhat deeper level than the Hopedale Limestones, on the palaeoslopes or ramps descending from the growing Derbyshire and Staffordshire shelf areas to the north-east and south-west.

Conglomeratic limestones are present, particularly in the basal part of the sequence around Blore with Swinscoe. The clasts are probably mainly derived in each case from the underlying bed. The conglomeratic nature of the deposit is therefore related to current strength rather than to the contemporaneous tectonism invoked in the case of the Caldon Low Conglomerate and some other conglomeratic beds in the Hopedale Limestones.

Fossil evidence for the age of the Ecton Limestones is sparse but certainly the upper part, and perhaps the bulk of the formation, is Asbian. The boundary with the Milldale Limestones is highly diachronous, however, ranging from late Chadian in the Manifold valley north-east of Grindon, to Asbian near Caltonmoor House and there is probably both overlap and interdigitation between the two formations.

DETAILS

Grindon to Waterfall

The Ecton Limestones reach their maximum estimated thickness of 258 m around Grindon. Of this, 124 m within the lower part of the sequence was proved in a borehole (SK 05 SE/19) (Bridge and Kneebone, 1983, p.30) and the basal 28 m is exposed in a section (SK 05 SE/32) in a railway cutting near Ladyside Wood. Only a small proportion of the upper part of the formation is revealed in small exposures. The borehole showed a rather monotonous sequence of thin to thick-bedded mostly grey fine to coarse peloidal bioclastic calcarenites with scattered coarser beds containing intraclasts and broken brachiopod and coral debris; there were no age-diagnostic macrofossils but foraminifera indicate that the sequence ranges in age from Arundian to Holkerian or early Asbian. Foraminifera, together with a trilobite assemblage, indicate that the lowest 28 m of the formation exposed near Ladyside Wood are of late Chadian age. Bedding is generally indistinct, probably due to amalgamation of successive beds. Grading is evident in some of the coarser beds with sharp bases and parallel-laminated upper divisions. Argillaceous beds are rare, being represented only by a few shaly partings. In the section at Ladyside Wood the overall upward change from the Milldale Limestones to the Ecton Limestones is gradational and the junction between the two formations is taken at the base of a massive 1.75 m graded medium to coarse bioclastic bed with a few limestone pebbles and an erosive base lying stratigraphically about 49 m above the top of the knoll-reef. This bed is overlain by calcarenites that are somewhat paler, coarser and thicker-bedded than those in the underlying formation. Chadian foraminifera and trilobites have been obtained from strata both above and below the junction. Parkinson and Ludford (1964, plate 8) recognised a 'Lower D_1' sequence faulted against 'C_2' beds in the Ladyside Wood section but no evidence for such a relationship was found during the present survey.

There are scattered exposures south of Grindon [e.g. 0933 5411, 0929 5351, 0886 5308] in the lower part of the formation but none have yielded age-diagnostic macrofossils. Conglomeratic limestones with clasts up to 0.42 m in diameter, including 'reefy' micritic lithologies, become increasingly common to the south on the eastern slopes of Waterfall Low and the little summit ridge of Pike Low; south of here the formation passes laterally into the Hopedale Limestones.

Exposures high in the formation include 3.8 m of graded-bedded bioclastic limestone by a track [0808 5233] north of Back o' th' Brook and a disused quarry at Deepdale [0825 5318] showing 3.5 m of thickly bedded grey fine to coarse bioclastic limestone. A rolled coral fauna collected from this quarry by A. Ludford includes *Lithostrotion aranea*, *L. ischnon* and *Palaeosmilia murchisoni*, indicating an Asbian age.

Blore with Swinscoe

The Ecton Limestones, Milldale Limestones and Widmerpool Formation are strongly folded in the Blore with Swinscoe area, producing a highly indented outcrop pattern. Mapped relationships indicate that both the upper and lower junctions are disconformable. This is apparent where the Ecton Limestones overlap against the Ellis Hill knoll-reef [133 473] in the Milldale Limestones and where the Widmerpool Formation overlaps and oversteps both the underlying formations.

The basal beds of the formation were proved by a borehole (SK 14 NW/5) at Caltonmoor House (Bridge and Kneebone, 1983, pp.36–37). The sequence comprised mainly grey coarse bioclastic limestones, some showing graded bedding, interbedded with subordinate dark argillaceous limestones and mudstones. The base of the formation was taken at a depth of 26.12 m, below which argillaceous limestones assigned to the Milldale Limestones predominate (p.21). Foraminifera from a temporary exposure nearby [1150 4869] include forms, such as *Nodosarchaediscus sp.*, indicative of the late Asbian. The junction with the Milldale Limestones is seen in the valley [1077 5056] south of Slade House and on the northern slope of Musden Low [1184 5034]. At both places it is taken at the base of a conglomeratic limestone bed overlying micritic or fine-grained calcarenitic limestone with chert lenses. Beds slightly above the base are well exposed in a disused quarry [1293 4964 to 1296 4969] south-east of Hazelton Clump. They consist of 24.5 m of grey medium to coarse bioclastic peloidal limestone in sharp-based graded beds up to 2.5 m thick, most of them massive below and parallel-laminated above. The thickest beds are in the lower part of the section and several contain scattered subrounded intraclasts, up to 0.35 m across, probably derived from the underlying bed. Similar conglomeratic beds are well displayed in an old quarry at Swinscoe [1365 4797] and on Musden Low [1187 4982]. West of Blore, much of the higher part of the formation is known from sections in another quarry [1305 4964] and a nearby road cutting [1317 4959] south-east of Hazelton Clump, that show similar lithologies to that proved in a borehole near Blore (SK 14 NW/6; Bridge and Kneebone, 1983, p.37). This was drilled to a depth of 100.00 m, proving a sequence of grey fine- to coarse-grained biopelsparites, commonly showing graded bedding and current lamination. Scattered nodules and bands of chert and partings of variegated clay are also present. The purity of these limestones has been considerably reduced by diagenetic dolomitisation and silicification. The highest beds in the borehole must lie very near the top of the formation; there are no sections or boreholes showing the contact with the overlying Widmerpool Formation, however.

Hopedale Limestones

The term Hopedale Limestones was introduced (Aitkenhead and Chisholm, 1982, p.10) to distinguish a formation of Asbian to early Brigantian age, intermediate in facies between the limestones of the Derbyshire and Staffordshire shelf areas and the deeper water Ecton Limestones, Widmerpool Formation and Mixon Limestone-Shales. The formation includes the Waterhouses Limestone of Ludford (1951) and the Gag Lane Limestone of Parkinson and Ludford (1964) but has not been formally subdivided here except for the separation of a basal member, the Caldon Low Conglomerate. The formation overlies the Milldale Limestones, and partly underlies and partly passes laterally into the Widmerpool Formation in the south and east; in the west it passes laterally into the Ecton Limestones.

There are extensive outcrops around the Manifold valley and to the north of Thorpe, while many less extensive areas include those around Waterhouses, Calton, Crake Low, Woodeaves and south of Bradbourne. Overall thicknesses are estimated at about 60–70 m around Calton, 120 m around Bradbourne, up to 190 m near Cauldon, 255 m near Waterhouses and over 300 m between Dovedale and Tissington.

Lithologically, the Hopedale Limestones mark an upward change from the relatively fine even-grained beds of the Milldale Limestones to coarser peloidal calcarenites interbedded with coarsely bioclastic and conglomeratic beds that are conspicuous though not predominant. The conglomerates consist mainly of discrete erosive and sharp-based beds lacking internal lamination and containing large fragments of crinoids and limestone clasts probably derived from underlying or adjacent beds. In the higher Asbian to Brigantian part of the sequence the conglomerates also contain many rolled brachiopods and some corals. The Caldon Low Conglomerate differs in being a thicker, more irregular, unit and in containing a proportion of quartz pebbles; its origin is discussed below.

Unlike the district to the north (Aitkenhead and others, 1985, p.49), knoll-reefs are only a minor part of the Hopedale Limestones in this area. The largest forms an isolated and poorly exposed outlier [106 460] south-east of the Weaver Hills; others are sparsely scattered and are associated with conglomerates and breccias, for example near Ilam Hall and Bradbourne (see below). The reefs have not been studied in detail.

The Hopedale Limestones lie in an area between the Derbyshire and Staffordshire shelves (Figures 3 and 28) though the earlier pre-Asbian parts of the formation were deposited before these shelves were clearly established as discrete entities. In places the shelf edges were marked by the presence of an apron-reef and abrupt transition to relatively deep water. However, between Parwich and Wolfscote Dale, the apron-reef is absent and the transition to deeper water was gentle, the sea floor probably having the configuration of an irregular ramp (Ahr, 1973) on which the coarser arenaceous and rudaceous beds were deposited as a consequence of occasional storms.

Coral and brachiopod faunas from the Hopedale Limestones indicate that the bulk of the succession is Asbian to early Brigantian in age (p.12). However, in the few places where the lowest beds are exposed, microfossil evidence, largely obtained since the publication of the 1:50 000 geological map, has shown that the base of the formation is highly diachronous, extending from the late Chadian or Arundian in Brownend Quarry [090 502] to Asbian at Caldon Low and near Stanshope [127 543]. The contact appears conformable at the first and last of these localities, but at Caldon Low there is an angular unconformity (see below). This implies that regionally there is interdigitation with the Milldale Limestones complicated locally by tectonism at Caldon Low.   NA

Details

Caldon Low

The thickness around the north end of the Cauldon Anticline is estimated at between 100 and 190 m. The lithology is variable, but well bedded coarsely crinoidal medium to pale grey calcarenites are common, with shells and limestone pebbles in places. There are good exposures in the dale side [088 495] by Hurst Farm and by the road [079 493] in Cauldon village. The Hopedale Limestones probably pass southwards into Kevin Limestones but the area of transition is drift-covered and a boundary has been taken at the northern side of a mass of reef-limestone at Hoften's Cross. The boundary may be more complex than shown on the map, for in Cauldon churchyard [0785 4948] there is an unexposed mass of reef-limestone which, though currently classified as part of the Hopedale Limestones, may alternatively be regarded as a northward extension of the Hoften's Cross reef.

Extensive faunal collections have been made by Alkins (1921, pp.367–369) and Ludford (1951, p.223) from material dug up in Cauldon churchyard. Re-examination of Ludford's material suggests that it is of Asbian age; the fauna comprises abundant and varied reef brachiopods (see p.12).

A basal member of the Hopedale Limestones is distinguished locally as the **Caldon Low Conglomerate**. It was first described (Jackson and Alkins, 1919) as a quartzose conglomerate consisting of small water-worn pebbles of vein quartz and quartzite, mixed with red jasper, black limestone, chert, micaceous sandstone and purple volcanic rocks, together with larger blocks of grey compact limestone, the whole cemented by a calcareous matrix. It was described as passing up into pebbly limestone and appeared to lie unconformably on the truncated edges of the 'Humerosus-beds' (now included in the Milldale Limestones). The belief that it forms part of the limestone sequence was challenged by Barke, Hind and Scott (1920) but the interpretation put forward by Jackson and Alkins (1919) has been accepted by all subsequent authors (Jackson and Charlesworth, 1920, Ludford, 1940, p.218; Ludford, 1951), whose work has also confirmed the existence of an angular unconformity at the base. The component pebbles were further described by Ludford (1951, p.217), the quartzose material ranging from sand grains to pebbles about 2 cm across, while the limestone clasts are up to 12 cm. A summary of the faunal evidence then available led Ludford to infer a C_2 age for the deposit. Later finds (Parkinson and Ludford, 1964, p.172) tended to suggest a D_1 age, however. The exposures described by the above authors lay at the north end of Caldon Low Quarry, in an area now largely obscured by tipping, but still visible in a low cliff [0770 4915] are some 6 m of medium grey well-bedded calcarenite, in the lowest 3 m of which are scattered pebbles of quartz and quartzite up to 15 mm across, rarer pebbles of green altered lava up to 5 mm, some larger limestone pebbles and many coarse grains of quartz sand. The fauna from this locality includes *Lithostrotion martini*, *Acanthoplecta mesoloba*, *Avonia youngiana*, *Linoprotonia* cf. *hemisphaerica* and *Megachonetes* cf. *papilionaceus*. It is not diagnostic of age but is more likely to be Asbian than Chadian/Arundian.

The main body of the Caldon Low Conglomerate is not now visible but is presumed to lie below the last section; the basal unconformity is also covered over. It is clear from earlier descriptions of the type section and from the exposures still remaining here, that the conglomerate is distinguished from other, unnamed, conglomerates in the Hopedale Limestones only by the presence of siliceous pebbles. The name has been applied in this account to limestone breccias with siliceous pebbles, as well as to conglomerates.

A larger exposure of the lowest Hopedale Limestones, along the northernmost face [0808 4910 to 0822 4915] of Cauldon Quarry, is shown diagramatically in Figure 11. There is a small component of tectonic dip from west to east in the diagram. The Milldale Limestones, at the left, are truncated by an uneven erosion surface on which the Hopedale Limestones rest.

Unit A consists of a mixture of massive pale calcarenite and limestone breccia containing scattered coarse grains of quartz and rare siliceous pebbles up to 1 cm. The texture of the breccia suggests that it originated as a mixture of limestone fragments and soft lime-mud; a mass of micritic reef limestone is believed to be a large clast in the breccia. The base of the breccia lies mainly below the quarry floor but at its westernmost extremity can be seen to lie on an erosion surface cut into the Milldale Limestones. The fauna of the breccia includes *Amplexus sp.*, *Caninia cornucopiae*, *Cyathaxonia rushiana*, *Koninckophyllum* cf. *praecursor*, *Zaphrentites delanouei* and *Linoprotonia* cf. *hemisphaerica*; endothyrid and tourneyellid

WEST   EAST

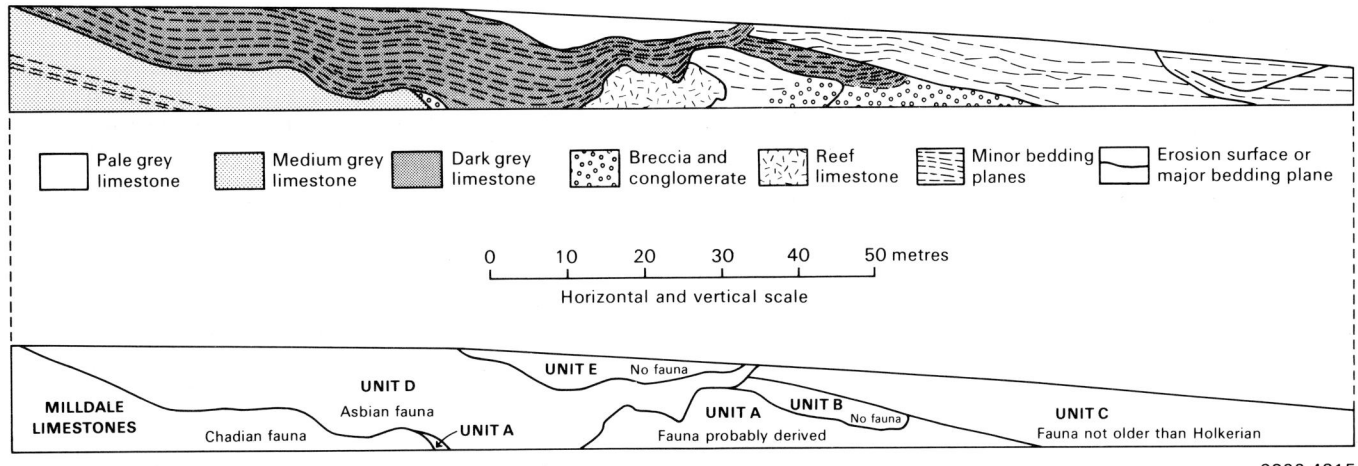

| Pale grey limestone | Medium grey limestone | Dark grey limestone | Breccia and conglomerate | Reef limestone | Minor bedding planes | Erosion surface or major bedding plane |

0   10   20   30   40   50 metres

Horizontal and vertical scale

MILLDALE
LIMESTONES
Chadian fauna

UNIT D
Asbian fauna

UNIT A

UNIT E   No fauna

UNIT A
Fauna probably derived

UNIT B
No fauna

UNIT C
Fauna not older than Holkerian

0808 4910   0822 4915

Figure 11   Scale section of lowest Hopedale Limestones (units A–E) resting on eroded top of Milldale Limestones at Cauldon Quarry

foraminifera of possible Chadian age are also present. These faunas are thought to be derived. Unit B, consisting of thinly bedded darker limestone, rests with a partly gradational contact on unit A and is thought to belong to the same mass of disturbed material. No fauna has been obtained from it.

Units A and B are overlain by erosive-based well bedded fine- to coarse-grained pale grey calcarenites (unit C) containing a variable scattering of quartz grains, up to 2 mm across, and rare quartz pebbles up to 1 cm. Several strong erosion surfaces are visible within the unit. The fauna includes *Lithostrotion aranea*, *L. martini*, *Antiquatonia* aff. *insculpta* and *Linoprotonia* cf. *hemisphaerica*, together with foraminifera indicating an Arundian to Holkerian age. The presence of *L. aranea*, however, indicates that the beds cannot be older than Holkerian.

Unit D consists of thinly bedded dark grey fine-grained limestones which contain a few grains of clastic quartz in the basal part. They rest on an uneven surface of Milldale Limestones at the west of the section, and drape over units A to C at the east. Undulating bedding is concordant with irregularities in the basal erosion surface, but some of the depositional dips are very steep and may include a component due to renewed slumping movements of units A–C during deposition of unit D, or shortly thereafter. The fauna of unit D includes *Eomarginifera derbiensis* (large form), *Pustula pyxidiformis* and the conodonts *Gnathodus texanus texanus* and *Mestognathus beckmanni*, suggesting a Chadian/Arundian age. However, the presence of the foraminifera *Gigasbia gigas* and archaediscids at the *angulatus* stage, indicates that the deposit is Asbian and implies that the older fossils are derived.

Unit E, a pale massive calcarenite, rests with a sharp erosional contact on unit D. No fauna has been obtained from it.

The basal breccia, unit A, is classified here as a lens of the Caldon Low Conglomerate on account of the presence of siliceous pebbles and sand grains. It is thought to have been emplaced by the slumping of mixed clasts of limestone and siliceous material into soft sediment, and implies the existence of steep submarine slopes nearby. Its age is not known, as the fossils are thought to be derived. The age of unit B is also unknown. Unit C is a current-laid deposit, possibly of Holkerian age. The dark limestones of unit D indicate a brief return to quieter water during Asbian times, while the overlying pale calcarenites of unit E, also presumed Asbian, are taken to lie at the base of the main body of Hopedale Limestones.

A thick conglomeratic bed containing a mixture of angular and rounded clasts of limestone and dolomite, with rare quartz pebbles, is present between the Milldale Limestones and Kevin Limestones at the south-west side [0824 4715] of Wardlow Quarry. In view of its similarity to the unit A breccia at Cauldon Quarry, it is regarded as part of the Caldon Low Conglomerate, but its top and base are poorly exposed, and its stratigraphical relationships are not clear. JIC

Waterhouses

The Hopedale Limestones are poorly exposed north of Caldon Low Quarry but in the Hamps valley around Waterhouses several disused quarries show about 83 m of the sequence. The basal 8.26 m of the formation is seen in Brownend Quarry [0910 5019 to 0897 5026] resting conformably on Milldale Limestones (SK 05 SE/29; Figure 9). The junction is taken at the base of a conglomeratic limestone in thin beds, totalling 2.96 m in thickness, with subangular to subrounded clasts of laminated calcarenite dispersed in a coarsely crinoidal matrix. The conglomerate is poorly fossiliferous but contains some foraminifera including *Pseudolituotubella multicamerata*, indicating a probable Chadian age. The overlying coarsely bioclastic beds have yielded both conodonts and foraminifera, that also suggest a Chadian age.

An area of poor exposure, representing about 150 m of strata (see below), lies to the west of Brownend Quarry and separates it from the upper part of the formation, well exposed in the adjacent Lee House Quarries, immediately north-east of Waterhouses [0868 5034 to 0851 5029]. These quarries (SK 05 SE/30) are taken as a type section for the Hopedale Limestones (Aitkenhead and Chisholm, 1982, p.10); they were previously described by Prentice (1951, p.186) and Ludford (1951, p.222). The lower part of the succession is 39.2 m thick and contains Asbian corals, brachiopods and foraminifera (p.12). The limestones are thinly to thickly bedded, grey, peloidal with some coarsely bioclastic crinoidal beds and a few partings and intercalations up to 0.18 m thick of dark grey to black mudstone. A gap of 2 m separates this sequence from the 33.8 m of overlying beds in the western quarry: grey, finely peloidal to coarsely bioclastic limestone, the coarser beds tending to a lenticular form and with erosive bases. Prominent lenticular beds up to 2.2 m thick near the base and top of the sequence contain typical Brigantian coral and brachiopod faunas (p.12). However, foraminifera including *Archaediscus sp.* (*moelleri* group) and *Howchinia sp.* from the basal 4.8 m of this sequence indicate a late Asbian to early Brigantian age. Similar beds are also exposed in disused quarries on the south side of the Hamps valley at Waterhouses.

A borehole (SK 05 SE/21) in the western quarry proved a 51.93 m sequence, corresponding to that exposed in the eastern quarry, of grey to dark grey bioclastic limestones with a few dark grey mudstone intercalations. Several beds contained oil or bituminous residue in vughs and pore spaces (Bridge and Kneebone, 1983, pp.33–34). The unexposed 150 m of the succession referred to above is partly seen in a small quarry [0864 5084] near Field House where the 6.32 m section (SK 05 SE/31) includes graded beds, up to 1 m thick, with a massive lower coarsely bioclastic division containing scattered limestone clasts and a finer-grained parallel-laminated upper division. Bases of beds are sharp and erosive and the topmost bed contains rare quartz pebbles up to 7 mm in diameter. Two of the coarsely bioclastic beds contain rich brachiopod faunas of reef affinity but not precisely diagnostic of age; the presence of *Gigantoproductus crassiventer* (Prentice, 1951, p.188; Parkinson and Ludford, 1964, p.175) has not been confirmed. Other taxa obtained include *Archaediscus sp.* and *Koninckopora sp.*, indicating a Holkerian to Asbian age. The presence of rare quartz pebbles suggests a correlation with the Caldon Low Conglomerate.

Calton

The Hopedale Limestones form a broadly synclinal outlier around Calton, the best exposures occurring to the west overlooking the Hamps valley, and at Farwall. At the former locality (SK 05 SE/33) a 12.39 m sequence of thickly bedded conglomeratic limestones contains dispersed clasts of grey calcisiltite, probably derived from the underlying Milldale Limestones, and rolled corals including *Hettonia fallax* and *Lithostrotion ischnon*, a faunal element comparable to that of the Milldale Limestones of probable Holkerian age (p.10), near Forest Farm. Disused quarries near Farwall [1013 5134, 1019 5120 and 1020 5127] expose up to 10.0 m of steeply dipping well bedded grey fine to coarse bioclastic and conglomeratic limestones yielding *Archaediscus sp.* and *Koninckopora inflata* together with a few long-ranging corals and brachiopods. A trench in the village [1014 5032] showed the highest part of the formation, which included reefy micritic lenses 4.0 m below a weathered mudstone bed marking the junction with the overlying Widmerpool Formation (p.31).

Manifold Valley

The Hopedale Limestones are well exposed in the Manifold valley from [109 543] near Beeston Tor to Ilam Hall. The limestones are mainly well bedded with some graded beds and range from grey peloidal calcarenites with some chert lenses, to coarsely bioclastic and conglomeratic limestones. Conglomeratic and coarse crinoidal beds are scattered throughout the sequence but are most common near the base, for example near Cheshire Wood [1160 5343] and near Ilam Hall [1292 5109 to 1303 5114]. At the latter locality up to 5.3 m of coarse limestone form a line of low crags and have yielded a rich brachiopod fauna of reef affinity whose Asbian age is indicated by the presence of the goniatite *Bollandoceras sp.* The relationship with the underlying unfossiliferous Milldale Limestones has not been determined.

The highest part of the sequence is best exposed in the bed of the River Manifold [1246 5163 to 1268 5176] north-east of Rushley, on both limbs of a broad anticline. One bed contains blocks, probably derived, of reefy micritic limestone up to 2.3 m across. The only in-situ knoll-reef in the Hopedale Limestones of this area occurs in the steep valley side [1139 5276] ENE of Throwley Hall, where it forms a crag of massive pale grey micritic limestone about 22.0 m high.

A 100 m borehole (SK 15 SW/7) near Throwley Hall (Bridge and Kneebone, 1983, p.48) proved the junction with the overlying Widmerpool Formation at 28.30 m and continued in Hopedale Limestones which were mainly coarsely bioclastic with some conglomeratic bands to 73.97 m, becoming finer below. The lowest 2.55 m consisted of thinly interbedded grey finely bioclastic and laminated dark grey argillaceous limestone, atypical of the Hopedale Limestones but not proved to belong to the underlying Milldale Limestones.

Hopedale and Stanshope

Hopedale [128 549] (not named on the 1:50 000 geological map), has several exposures typical of the formation named after it, but no continuous type section. Exposures include some 2.0 m of the basal conglomeratic limestones [1290 5484] consisting of crinoid and shell fragments and scattered fine-grained limestone clasts in a bioclastic matrix. In the middle part of the formation 4.2 m of massive grey micrite forms a small knoll-reef [1252 5483] and, higher in the sequence, medium to coarsely bioclastic shelly limestones yield a rich brachiopod fauna including *Productus striatosulcatus*, *Pugilis pugilis* and *Striatifera striata* indicative of the Brigantian stage [1240 5488].

To the south, in Hall Dale [1302 5406 and 1303 5399], conglomeratic coarsely bioclastic limestone beds, in scattered exposures representing about 18.0 m of strata, are assigned to the basal part of the formation. The beds contain a rich brachiopod fauna and a few corals, including *Dibunophyllum bipartitum* indicating an Asbian age. The junction with the dark cherty fine-grained facies of the Milldale Limestones is not exposed here but was proved in a borehole (SK 15 SW/9) south of Stanshope (Bridge and Kneebone, 1983, p.51).

A disused quarry [1367 5270] near Ilam Tops shows 11.6 m of thickly bedded grey to pale grey-brown peloidal and crinoidal biosparites. These limestones are atypical of the Hopedale Limestones in that the grain size is fairly uniform and in the presence of sets of cross lamination 4–16 cm thick indicating oscillatory currents, presumably of tidal or wave origin.

East of Dovedale, Tissington and Woodeaves

The irregular nature of the Hopedale Limestones outcrop east of Dovedale is due not only to folding and faulting but also to a lateral passage into the Widmerpool Formation. The interdigitation is well illustrated by the Pike House (SK 15 SE/10) and Rusheycliff Barn (SK 15 SE/8) boreholes (Bridge and Kneebone, 1983, pp.53 and 55). The former was sited in the disused Pike House Quarry which shows a 20.25 m section (SK 15 SE/16) in Hopedale Limestones comprising mainly thin-bedded dark to pale grey limestones with some chert; these beds have yielded a fauna including *Palaeosmilia murchisoni* and *Goniatites crenistria* (Parkinson, 1950, p.277) indicative of the Asbian-Brigantian junction. The borehole proved that the Hopedale Limestones here are underlain by a sequence, assigned to the Widmerpool Formation, of interbedded mainly coarsely bioclastic limestones and grey to grey-brown laminated siltstones and sandstones with dark grey mudstone intercalations. These strata passed back into Hopedale Limestones at a depth of 59.00 m, and continued in them to the bottom of the borehole at 100.01 m. The Hopedale Limestones in the Rusheycliff Barn Borehole (SK 15 SE/8; Figure 12) are highly variable and dolomitised in places, with sporadic sharp-based coarsely bioclastic beds with abundant brachiopod shells and limestone intraclasts. These beds probably correlate with similar strata proved in the Widmerpool Formation in the Lees Farm Borehole (see p.31) 3.2 km to the south. The limestone succession contains an interdigitation of the Tissington Volcanic Member (see p.31) between 21.00 and 27.40 m; this consists of bedded tuff in the upper 3.1 m and massive hyaloclastite below made up largely of vesicular lava fragments up to 5 mm in diameter. Thin pyritic tuffaceous intercalations are also present in the limestone sequence above the member, between the depths of

9.90 and 21.00 m. A disused quarry nearby [1756 5326] shows about 14.8 m of similar beds (see also Arnold-Bemrose, 1899, p.231; Bridge and Kneebone, 1983, p.69) implying that the volcanic member lies just beneath the quarry floor.

The base of the formation is not exposed in this area, but a sequence of dark limestones is present not far above the boundary in a small quarry [1506 5369] north-west of Bostern Grange. There is a non-sequence here, up to 1.0 m of beds being cut out.

Small and scattered knoll-reefs occur, particularly in the lower part of the formation [e.g. 1565 5284]. Part of such a knoll, together with a variety of associated cherty limestones displaying evidence of both erosive and constructive processes, and yielding abundant brachiopods together with corals and trilobites, is exposed in a 13.18-m section (SK 15 SE/21) north-west of Moat Low [1570 5432]. The fauna includes the Asbian corals *Axophyllum vaughani*, *Lithostrotion portlocki* and *Palaeosmilia murchisoni*, with abundant brachiopods and trilobites; Alexander (1940, p.77) reported finding *Davidsonina septosa* here.

Two cuttings [1676 5372 to 1687 5373 and 1761 5344 to 1771 5336] along the Tissington Trail provide extensive exposures of the formation and were first described by Arnold-Bemrose (1899, pp.229–230; 1903, pp.338–340). The first (SK 15 SE/18), near Newton Grange, shows a broad anticline with 31.5 m of variable limestones, grey and crinoidal in the upper part, cherty below and locally dark. The fauna includes Asbian corals in the lower part, though the upper part may extend into the Brigantian. The second cutting, east of Crake Low, shows 11.0 m of mainly rubbly shelly and coarsely crinoidal limestone with some irregular dolomitisation.

Beds near the top of the formation are exposed in a 16.3 m section (SK 15 SE/17) some 800 m SSE of the New Inn; the uppermost 0.25 m of this are dark and thin-bedded and the fauna includes the Brigantian coral *Lonsdaleia floriformis* near the top, and *Striatifera striata* near the base. The contact with the Widmerpool Formation is not exposed in this area, though it has been proved in the Pike House Borehole (SK 15 SE/10) (see above).

Bradbourne

The Hopedale Limestones crop out in an anticlinal inlier between Bradbourne and Kniveton. The junction with the Milldale Limestones is largely faulted. A borehole east of Bradbourne (SK 25 SW/18; Cox and Harrison, 1980, pp.130–131), starting near the top, proved 100 m of the formation. The limestones comprise mainly biomicrites in the upper 17 m and biosparites and pelsparites below, with many black mudstone partings. Much of the sequence below 17.32 m is dolomitised to varying degrees.

There are several good exposures on the north side of the deep valley cut by Havenhill Dale Brook. These include about 30 m of grey fine-grained thinly bedded limestone [2061 5233 to 2060 5236]; a 6.4 m section of limestone pebble conglomerate and coarsely crinoidal limestone [2076 5240]; a similar conglomerate passing laterally into a small knoll-reef [2083 5240]; and a 13.5 m bed of massive pale grey micritic limestone [2137 5238] dipping steeply to the ENE and containing conspicuous silicified *Acaciapora bradbournensis* (Thomas and Ford, 1963). These conglomeratic and minor reef developments are probably all at a level near the top of the formation and are of Asbian age. A more extensive knoll reef is seen in small exposures on Wigber Low [204 514].

Widmerpool Formation

This formation (Institute of Geological Sciences, 1968, p.88; Aitkenhead and Chisholm, 1982, p.12) includes units previously known as Bull Gap Shales (Parkinson and Ludford, 1964, p.170) and Hollington End Beds (Parkinson, 1950, p.279). It crops out continuously along the southern flank of the main Dinantian outcrop between Forest Farm [120 485] and Atlow [231 489]. In addition, small outcrops are present south-west of Thorswood, in the Manifold valley and south of Hulland. The presence of the formation beneath the Triassic cover is known only from one borehole (see below). There is one named sub-unit, the Tissington Volcanic Member (see below), which crops out in the Tissington–Kniveton area.

The formation is of similar age and facies to the Mixon Limestone-Shales, consisting mainly of silty mudstone and dark thinly interbedded limestone of turbidite facies, with chert lenses and dark fissile mudstone intercalations with a sparse goniatite/bivalve fauna. However, it differs from the Mixon Limestone-Shales in containing volcanic rocks and thin beds of quartzose siltstone or fine-grained sandstone.

As the formation is traced northwards in the area northwest of Tissington the proportion of limestone to mudstone increases and it passes laterally into the Hopedale Limestones. Farther west, field relations indicate that the formation partly overlies and partly passes laterally into the Ecton Limestones. In some areas the formation appears to lie directly on Milldale Limestones, implying an unconformable overlap, but the junction is not exposed. The maximum thickness is not known but is probably about 250 m, 219 m (corrected for dip) having been proved in the Lees Farm Borehole (SK 15 SE/12). This is less than half the thickness proved in the Duffield Borehole, 14.5 km to the ESE and near the centre of the Widmerpool Gulf (Aitkenhead, 1977).

The maximum range in age of the formation is from late Asbian (B_2) to the latest Brigantian.   NA

The **Tissington Volcanic Member** forms a continuous elongate outcrop extending over 3 km in a NW–SE direction east of Tissington. It consists largely of hyaloclastite, a rock composed of highly amygdaloidal partially carbonated basalt fragments erupted in a submarine environment. Two small outcrops of basaltic lava near Shaw's Farm [180 534] and near Brookhouse Farm [207 497] are probably associated with the same volcanic episode and are therefore included in the member (Figure 12). The volcanic rocks have been described by Arnold-Bemrose (1899, pp.224–238; 1907, pp.266–271) whose petrographical work on deposits then classified as ash or tuff, agglomerate, and lava is particularly valuable as many critical exposures no longer exist. This author recorded some 44 m of 'ash' in the former Tissington railway cutting (now part of the Tissington Trail and largely grassed over). The ash was described as 'distinctly bedded' and consisted of fragments or lapilli of a pumiceous rock 'up to an inch (25.4 mm) or so in diameter'.

The lapilli are either glassy or altered to palagonite, calcite or dolomite and their outer surfaces generally cut across the vesicles. Similar rock has been proved in boreholes near Tissington (SK 15 SE/8), Lea Hall (SK 15 SE/14) and Lees Farm (SK 15 SE/12); Figure 12 shows some comparative thicknesses. The hyaloclastite was probably produced by the ejection of magma into water in the way suggested by Tazieff (1974). More recently Kokelaar (1983), using the volcano of Surtsey as a model, has suggested that the eruptive mechanism involves intermittent to continuous jets of tephra from a vent filled with a highly mobile slurry of hyaloclastite, tephra and water, continuously replenished by vesiculating magma. Rittmann's (1962) original meaning of the term

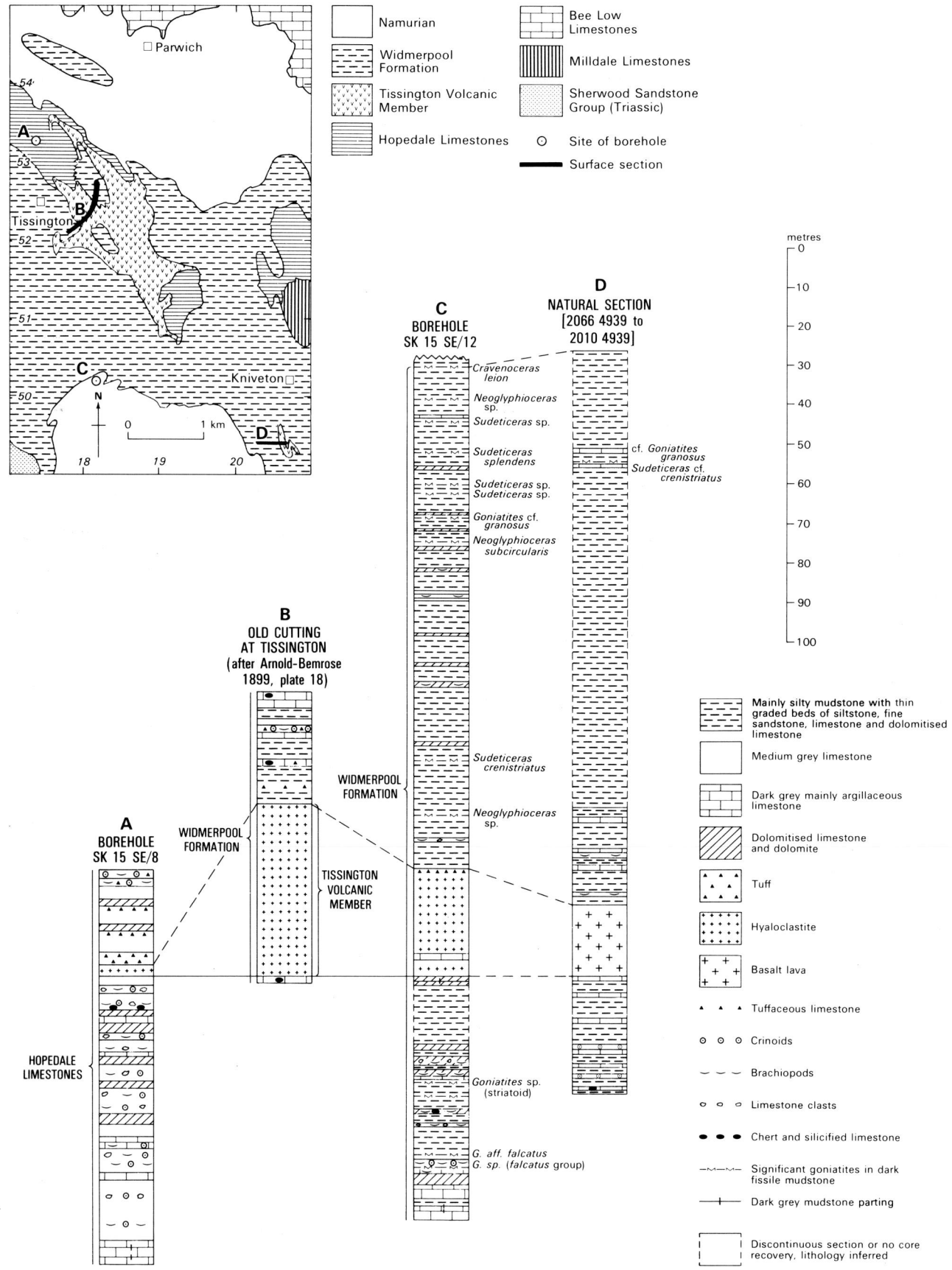

Figure 12   Sections of Dinantian strata around Tissington and Kniveton

hyaloclastite differed in that it referred to a deposit formed by the break up of the glassy shells of growing pillows. The latter process may have taken place initially as indicated by the coarser blocky deposits in the lower part of the sequence (see p.34). Arnold-Bemrose describes the lapilli in the lower part of the cutting sequence as having a spherical or discoidal shape, and notes that larger 'ejected' blocks of finely crystalline amygdaloidal lava 'up to about a foot' (0.30 m) in diameter are 'scattered irregularly through the finer ash' throughout. In the Lees Farm Borehole similar fragments, some showing chilled margins, predominate in the lower part of the sequence (Plate 2.1a).

The small outcrop of lava near Brookhouse Farm, Kniveton was first regarded as a dyke (Green and others, 1869). However, Arnold-Bemrose (1907, p.271) concluded that it was a lava on petrographic grounds and on the lack of marmorization of the limestone above and below the outcrop. The latter view is accepted here though the evidence gathered during the present survey is not conclusive. In thin-sections, the rock is a highly altered amygdaloidal porphyritic olivine basalt. Correlation with the Tissington Volcanic Member is suggested by its stratigraphic position in the marine turbiditic carbonate-mudstone succession (Figure 12). The outcrop of calcitised vesicular lava near Shaw's Farm appears from its field relations to overlie the hyaloclastites and possibly represents a late eruptive phase when access of sea water to the vent was cut off by the build up of the hyaloclastite pile to sea level.

The submarine character of the main eruptive process is also indicated by the presence amongst the lava clasts of limestone lapilli and bioclasts including coral, brachiopod and ammonoid fragments. The general turbiditic character of the parent formation also implies eruption in relatively deep water. However, the member extends north-westwards into a shallower water facies, the Hopedale Limestones, and it therefore appears to lie on a generally southward-orientated palaeoslope. The number and location of the eruptive vents is not known.   NA,IPS

Details

Swinscoe

The Widmerpool Formation outcrop west of Swinscoe has a highly indented boundary, having been folded with the underlying Ecton Limestones and Milldale Limestones. The boundary also oversteps onto both these formations but the junction is neither exposed nor proved by drilling.

There are numerous small exposures, in streams and ditches, of variably dipping thinly interbedded grey silty mudstone, dark argillaceous limestone, sandy limestone and bioclastic limestone, all with dark grey fissile mudstone intercalations and common graded bedding. The most extensive and well exposed section (SK 14 NW/7), near Coppice Barn, shows all these rock types in a 3.5 m sequence with *Sudeticeras sp.* in a mudstone intercalation 11.26 m above the base, suggesting the P_2 age of the beds. A P_{1c} age is suggested by fossils including *Dunbarella persimilis* and *Goniatites sp.* collected from dark mudstone exposed in streams [1240 4747 and 1217 4895] west of Swinscoe. Parkinson and Ludford (1964, p.170) record the presence of *Goniatites moorei* (B_2) near the latter locality.

Manifold and Dove valleys

The Dove valley north-west of Mapleton coincides with an irregular syncline containing strata of the Widmerpool Formation. In the Manifold valley, above the confluence with the Dove, the outcrop extends as far as Steeplehouse Farm, beyond which it continues as a series of outliers. Small synclinal outliers also occur at Calton [101 503] and Castern [123 525]. Limestones predominate in the lower part of the sequence east of Ilam, where they rest directly against the flanks of the Chadian knoll-reef masses of Bunster Hill and Thorpe Cloud, and pass northwards into the Hopedale Limestones. They are exposed [1397 5078] near the Isaac Walton Hotel in a 3.48-m section of dark thinly bedded limestones with graded bedding and chert lenses. Excavations for a car park [145 508] east of the hotel revealed these graded limestones with scattered septarian nodules, and weathered mudstone, in roughly equal proportions.

The outlier near Rushley contains one good exposure on the right bank of the Manifold [1246 5163] at the base of the formation. Here 0.37 m of grey bioclastic limestone rest on thinly interbedded dark grey blocky and fossiliferous fissile mudstone containing *Dunbarella* cf. *persimilis*, cf. *Goniatites crenistria* and *Nomismoceras sp.* This overlies grey bioclastic limestone assigned to the Hopedale Limestones, well exposed a few metres downstream (p.30).

A borehole (SK 15 SW/7; Bridge and Kneebone, 1983, p.48), in the outlier at Throwley Hall, proved the basal 28.30 m of the formation overlying Hopedale Limestones but no age-diagnostic macrofossils were present. The sequence consisted mainly of calcareous quartzose siltstones and fine-grained sandstones, of distal turbidite facies, with scattered graded beds, up to 0.53 m, of fine to coarse bioclastic limestone. Fissile mudstone intercalations contained *Orbiculoidea sp.* at depths of 21.50 m and 21.68 m.

Tissington – Kniveton – Atlow

The outcrop of the Widmerpool Formation is most extensive east of the River Dove especially around the Madge Hill Anticline [220 490]. The sequence includes the Tissington Volcanic Member and passes wholly or partially into the Hopedale Limestones. Between Parwich and Brassington, however, the formation is inferred to pass into the Bee Low Limestones, here mainly of apron-reef facies at the southern margin of the late Dinantian shelf, an inference supported by a borehole near Parwich (SK 15 SE/7, see below).

The best section of the formation (Figure 12) is provided by the Lees Farm Borehole (SK 15 SE/12) near Fenny Bentley (Institute of Geological Sciences, 1981, p.7), which proved some 219 m (corrected for dip) from the base of the Namurian at 12.70 m to the bottom of the hole at 251.49 m. The Tissington Volcanic Member is present between 152.28 m and 181.29 m, representing a corrected thickness of about 27.5 m. The sequence both above and below the member consists of grey to dark grey silty mudstone, mainly in thin graded beds with basal parts composed of paler laminated bioclastic limestone or quartzose siltstone. The overall proportion of mudstone diminishes with depth and the lowest 8.9 m consists largely of argillaceous limestone. Scattered thicker graded beds, up to 1.31 m, of finely bioclastic to conglomeratic limestone are also present. They are mainly dolomitised or, less commonly, silicified below the volcanic member, particularly between 205.80 m and 233.89 m. Some of these beds contain conspicuous crinoid, coral and brachiopod shell debris and clasts of dark mudstone and 'reefy' limestone. They are interpreted as turbidite deposits probably derived from shallower-water areas represented by the Hopedale Limestones and triggered by storm and earthquake events. Small quantities of oil or bitumen were noted in vughs at eight levels between 105.79 m and 246.37 m. Dark fissile mudstone intercalations with a sporadic autochthonous goniatite-bivalve fauna occur throughout the non-volcanic sequence. Diagnostic goniatites indicate a P_{1b} – P_2 age for the succession as a whole (Figure 12). The volcanic member lies somewhere in the range late P_{1c} to early P_2, probably in P_{1d} Zone.

Two other boreholes have penetrated parts of the formation. The first, (SK 15 SE/7) near Parwich (Bridge and Kneebone, 1983, p.52), showed highly variable bedded limestones alternating with brecciated apron-reef micritic limestones, representing interdigitation of the off-shelf and marginal shelf facies. The second borehole (SK 15 SE/10), at Pike House Quarry, (p.30; Bridge and Kneebone, 1983, p.55) was drilled in an area of interdigitation of the Hopedale Limestones and Widmerpool Formation, and penetrated the basal 59 m of the latter. This sequence consisted largely of dark to mid grey, fine to coarse bioclastic limestones, with subordinate thinly interbedded fine sandstones and siltstones. Graded bedding is common. Thin dark mudstone intercalations contain a few bivalves and beyrichoceratid goniatites indicating a possible late Asbian age, older than the Lees Farm Borehole succession.

There are numerous surface exposures of the formation in streams and ditches in the area. The best of these is in a stream [2066 4939 to 2027 4939] south-west of Brookhouse Farm, Kniveton (column D, Figure 12), though there are long gaps in the sequence and only sparse, poorly preserved macrofossils. These include cf. *Goniatites granosus* and *Sudeticeras* cf. *crenistriatus* in a 4.51 m exposure of calcareous mudstone with fine-grained to coarsely bioclastic graded limestone beds. Though this exposure is estimated to be high in the sequence, the goniatites suggest a P_{2a} age. A total of about 72 m of mainly limestone with interbedded mudstone strata are exposed in the lower part of the section together with a lava flow, 17.5 m thick, lying about 30 m above the base (Charsley, 1979). *Posidonia becheri* is present in intercalated calcareous mudstone both above and below the lava indicating its P_1 age and supporting its correlation with the Tissington Volcanic Member.

NA

Thin-sections (E49339 and E49340) show the lava to be a highly altered amygdaloidal porphyritic olivine basalt in which the primary minerals, probably calcic plagioclase, pyroxene and olivine are totally replaced by clay minerals, carbonate, abundant pyrite and minor leucoxene. The original porphyritic texture, however, is well preserved. The amygdales are ovoid to irregular in form, up to 3 mm across and consist mainly of carbonate, pyrite and chlorite. The chlorite is virtually colourless in thin section. NGB

The Lees Farm Borehole (SK 15 SE/12) provides the best evidence of the nature of the volcanic episode represented by the Tissington Volcanic Member. The earliest eruptive products consist of scattered angular clasts of amygdaloidal lava up to 8 cm in diameter dispersed in a slumped laminated dark grey to grey dolomitised finely granular limestone lying at a depth of 182.02 m, 0.73 m below the base of the main hyaloclastite unit. The latter consists mainly of clasts, up to 9 cm across, of greenish grey compact lava with amygdales varying in size and abundance in a matrix of poorly delineated small (<1 cm) lapilli and carbonate (Plate 2.1a). The larger clasts are rare and the small lapilli predominant in the upper half of the sequence between 152.46 m and 171.10 m; the small lapilli are highly amygdaloidal, with fractured margins cutting across the amygdales. The hyaloclastite also contains scattered fragments of limestone and bioclasts such as brachiopod shells, corals and a coiled nautiloid (at 162.83 m; Plate 2.1b).

The best natural sections of the hyaloclastite are (i) in the disused railway cutting [1812 5243] east of Tissington, now largely obscured by vegetation but showing 1.6 m of weathered igneous rock with rare clasts up to 35 mm (Figure 30; Arnold-Bemrose, 1899); and (ii) [1899 5115] near Woodeaves Farm where 4.2 m of brown-weathered igneous rock contains vesicular clasts up to 0.35 m (Arnold-Bemrose, 1894). Shallow boreholes were put down during the present survey to supplement the surface information. Tissington No. 1 Borehole (SK 15 SE/13) proved sediments of the Widmerpool Formation to 31.95 m on calcitized igneous rock and mudstone to 33.5 m. No. 2 Borehole (SK 15 SE/14) proved

sediments of the Widmerpool Formation to 26.4 m and hyaloclastite to 42.8 m. The best section here of the hyaloclastites is provided by No. 3 Borehole (SK 15 SE/15) which proved these rocks to 20.18 m; the predominant rock types were either finely comminuted lava with fragments up to 7 mm or a dark green chloritic rock, both types containing layered masses of vesicular lava (up to 0.4 m) interpreted as whole pillows, and some smaller clasts interpreted as pillow fragments. NA,IPS

Mixon Limestone-Shales

This formation crops out on the west side of the main Dinantian outcrop north of Cauldon. It reaches a thickness of about 193 m around Butterton, 1.5 km north of the district boundary, and is even thicker beneath the Namurian cover farther to the north-west (Aitkenhead and others, 1985, p.52). As the formation is traced southwards it thins and passes laterally into the Hopedale Limestones. The upward passage into the Namurian is conformable although the nature of this junction is uncertain around Waterfall, where Namurian rocks begin to overlap on to the latter formation. The mapped boundaries are highly convoluted in places, reflecting the intense folding that affects the strata. The outcrop of the Onecote Sandstones Member, which also reaches its greatest development in the adjacent district, can only be traced for about 0.5 km south of the district boundary around Bullclough [059 548].

The rocks consist mainly of silty mudstone and thinly bedded limestone, the former diminishing and the latter apparently coarsening and increasing in proportion southwards. The limestones are mostly dark and argillaceous but sandy limestones and paler beds also occur, with sand grade or coarser bioclastic or intraclastic debris in their basal divisions. Graded bedding is common, probably indicative of deposition from turbidity currents, but settling out of sediment from suspension after storms may account for this bed form in some cases. Chert lenses and intercalations of dark fissile mudstone with a sparse goniatite-bivalve fauna are commonly present. A fuller account for the ground to the north of the district is given by Aitkenhead and others (1985, pp.51–53).

DETAILS

The lowest 35.92 m (corrected for dip) of the Mixon Limestone-Shales and part of the Hopedale Limestones were penetrated by a borehole (SK 05 SE/20) near Waterfall, in the area where the two formations are inferred to interdigitate. The junction between the two is taken at the lowest substantial dark grey mudstone unit, 0.44 m thick at a depth of 55.61 m (Bridge and Kneebone, 1983, p.32). Dark fissile mudstone intercalations contain the goniatites *Beyrichoceras sp.*, *Goniatites moorei* and *G. struppus* at 53.00–53.01 m; *B.* cf. *vesiculiferum* and *G. sp.* ex gr *moorei* at 56.00–57.73 m, indicating the B_2 Zone and a late Asbian age. A thicker (5.47 m) dark mudstone unit at 33.75 m yielded *G. sp.* ex. gr. *crenistria/concentricus* at 32.80 m, indicative of the P_{1a} Zone. The limestones are mainly dark grey to grey, fine to coarse bioclastic with limestone and dark mudstone clasts in the basal parts of some beds. One such conglomeratic bed, 0.53 m thick and partially dolomitised, is present immediately beneath the mudstone unit at 33.75 m and probably correlates with the conglomeratic bed, containing the same goniatite, exposed at several places in the adjacent district (Aitkenhead and others, 1985, p.55).

The lower part of the sequence is best seen in a stream north of

Grindon [0903 5479 to 0854 5472], though exposures here are discontinuous. Parkinson and Ludford (1964, p.172) record the presence of a B_2 goniatite assemblage from a small exposure near this stream north of Grindon Church. Field evidence indicates that the exposure must lie very near the base of the formation at the core of an anticline.

The middle part of the formation is largely unexposed but higher parts are present in discontinuous exposures in streams near Ford [0634 5460 to 0625 5434], in which mudstones intercalated with thin beds of limestone have yielded *Neoglyphioceras sp.* and *Sudeticeras sp.*, indicative of the P_2 Zone (see also Morris, 1967, p.155). To the south-east, the highest parts of the sequence and conformable upward passage into Namurian strata are exposed in the banks of the River Hamps (SK 05 SE/22) and in the stream north-west of Back o' th' Brook, (e.g. SK 05 SE/23). In the former, 4.56 m of interbedded argillaceous limestones and mudstones containing *Sudeticeras* (*stolbergi* group) are separated by a gap of about 7.0 m from the overlying basal Namurian sequence, of similar lithology. A more continuous section, but with badly preserved faunas, occurs nearby [0671 5348 to 0676 5350]. In the section (SK 05 SE/23) at Back o' th' Brook 0.20 m of Namurian mudstone with *Cravenoceras leion* overlies about 1.00 m of Viséan mudstone with *Neoglyphioceras sp.* and *Posidonia membranacea horizontalis*. Here, as elsewhere, the top of the formation is taken at the Viséan/Namurian junction (Aitkenhead and Chisholm, 1982, p.12).   NA

An isolated outcrop of the formation is present around the works at Cauldon [083 496]. It consists largely of irregularly folded mudstones. Some 30 m of mudstone immediately above the Hopedale Limestones around the works [084 496] are of P_2 age, as shown by goniatites collected at various times: *Neoglyphioceras sp.* at 2.13 m above the limestone [0838 4957], *Sudeticeras splendens* about 3.65 m above the limestone [0842 4955] in temporary excavations, and *Sudeticeras sp.* at 16.6 m depth in a borehole (SK 04 NE/20). The mudstone is exposed at various places in the quarry that supplies the cement works, but cannot everywhere be distinguished from the conformably overlying Namurian mudstone on account of the prevalent folding. An exposure [0817 4959] of dark mudstone with *Posidonia corrugata*, about 8 m above the limestone, probably belongs to the Mixon Limestone-Shales and a 1.5 m band of well bedded crinoidal limestone [0809 4970] among mudstones below the *C. leion* Band is taken to mark the top of the formation. The mudstone beneath the limestone band contains some limestone bullions and graded beds of calcareous siltstone.

The lateral extent of these beds is not known, but they die out rapidly towards the south, for the mudstones resting on the limestone south of Hoften's Cross are probably of early Namurian age (p.46).   JIC

CHAPTER 4

Namurian

Namurian rocks occur in two main areas in the district. The western outcrop, where a complete sequence is present (Figure 14, columns 1–7), is a continuation of that in the Buxton district (Aitkenhead and others, 1985). The Namurian rocks occur around and beneath the Cheadle Coalfield, but to the south are concealed by the unconformable Triassic. In the north the sequence is about 1000 m thick; to the south thinning and associated facies changes indicate an approach to the basin margin. In the eastern half of the district, Namurian rocks are found in three isolated areas and as a more extensive tract continuous with the outcrop described in the Derby district (Frost and Smart, 1979). In these areas only the lower part of the succession is present, with mudstones of E_1 to R_2 age overlain by the Ashover Grit.

CLASSIFICATION

In the Pennines the term 'Millstone Grit' was originally applied to rocks of appropriate facies in a lithostratigraphic sense (Ramsbottom and others, 1978, fig. 1) but later acquired a time-stratigraphic connotation and was used, in the form 'Millstone Grit Series' for all rocks, irrespective of facies, that lie between the *Cravenoceras leion* and *Gastrioceras subcrenatum* marine bands. Strata of this age are now referred to the Namurian Series (Ramsbottom and others, 1978), and the term Millstone Grit is not currently used in any formal sense. In the absence of a formal lithostratigraphic classifi-

Figure 14   Composite sections of Namurian strata

The location of sections is shown in Figure 13. Numbered localities to the left of columns 1 and 2 refer to exposures described in the text: 1. Felthouse Wood [979 502]; 2. sections [981 519 to 984 523] near Churnet Grange, Cheddleton; 3. stream [9771 5107] near Ashcombe Park; 4. ravine [0135 5101] south of Brockholes Wood; 5. quarry [0115 5129] in Brockholes Wood; 6. Combes valley [0036 5145]; 7. The Combes [004 524]; 8. Combes valley [0066 5292 to 0063 5269]; 9. Combes Brook [0188 5333, 0192 5334], Apesford; 10. Combes Brook [0077 5292], Ballfields.

cation of these rocks, the existing names of sandstones and marine bands are retained on an informal basis within the biostratigraphic framework of zones and stages provided by the goniatite faunas. The nomenclature closely follows that established in the Buxton district (Aitkenhead and others, 1985, fig. 23). The relationship of the current names to those used by previous authors is shown in Table 2. It is worth noting that the names formerly used in this part of the North Staffordshire Basin were not always consistent with those used for the rest of the basin—for example, the Third Grit of Cheadle (Barrow, 1903) was the bed now called the Chatsworth Grit but the Third Grit of the Roaches Syncline (Hull and Green, 1866, p.52; Hind, *in* Monckton & Herries, 1910, p.580) was the next lower sandstone, the Roaches Grit (Aitkenhead and others, 1985, fig.23).

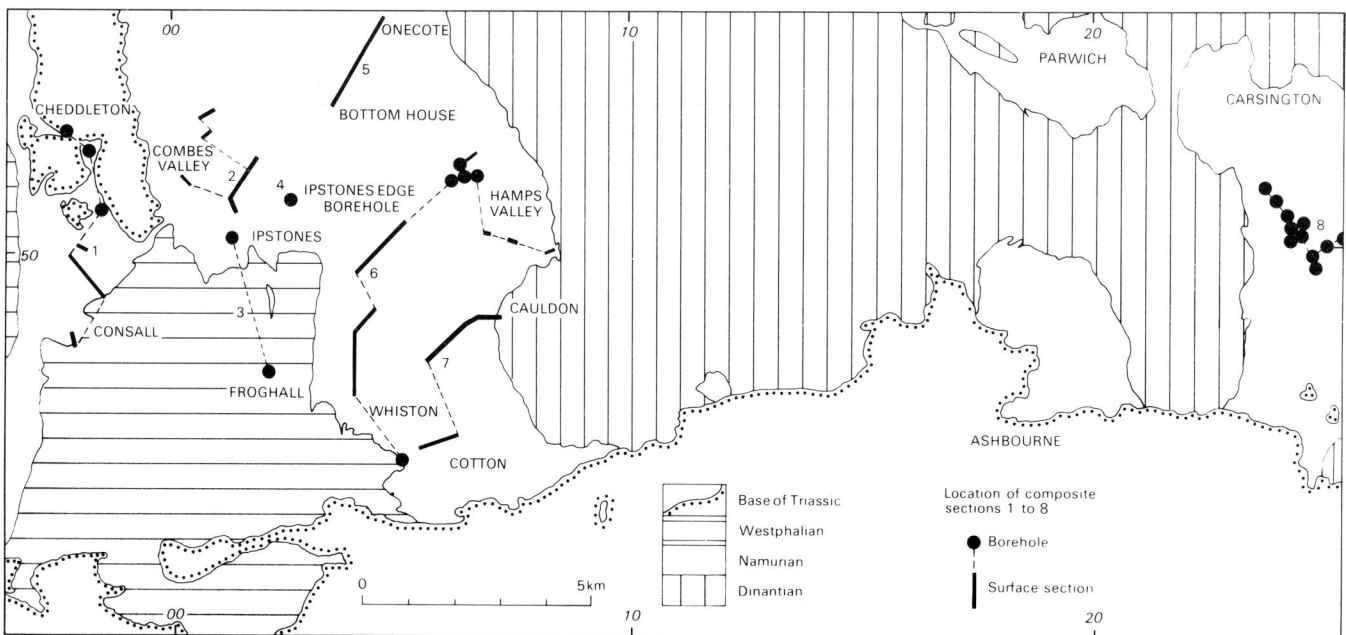

Figure 13   Outcrop of Namurian rocks and location of composite stratigraphical sections shown in Figure 14

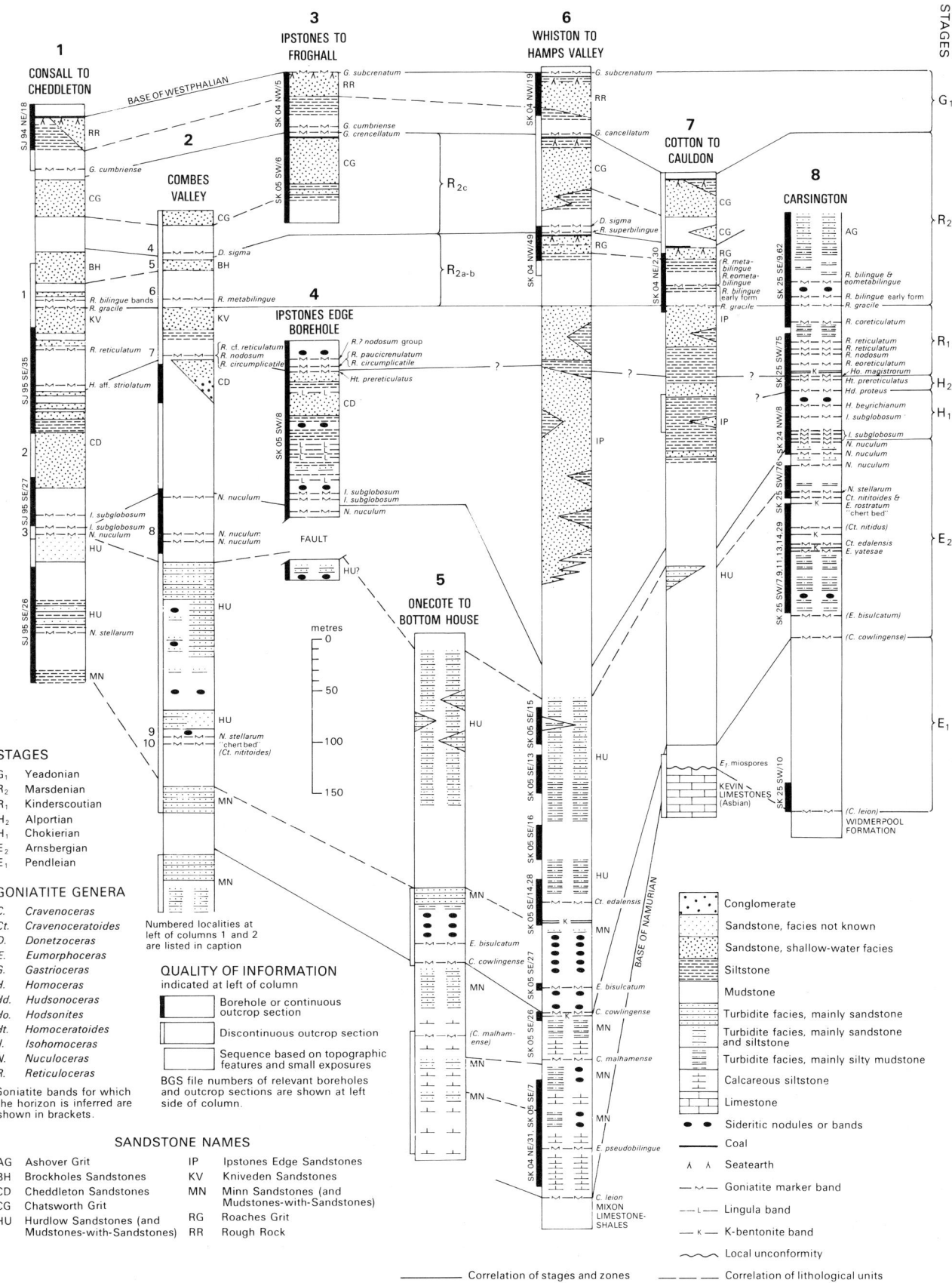

Figure 14 Composite sections of Namurian strata. For details see opposite.

Table 1 Namurian Stages and Zones, with a list of the main faunal bands found in the Central Pennine Basin (Ramsbottom, 1977, figs. 4–5). Mesothems are those of Ramsbottom

Stages	Goniatite Zones	Faunal Bands	Mesothems
Yeadonian (G$_1$)	*G. cumbriense* (G$_{1b}$)	*G. cumbriense	N11
	G. cancellatum (G$_{1a}$)	*G. cancellatum	
	R. superbilingue (R$_{2c}$)	D. sigma / *R. superbilingue	N10
Marsdenian (R$_2$)	*R. bilingue* (R$_{2b}$)	*R. metabilingue / *R. eometabilingue / *R. bilingue (late form) / *R. bilingue / *R. bilingue (early form)	N9
	R. gracile (R$_{2a}$)	*R. gracile	
Kinderscoutian (R$_1$)	R. reticulatum (R$_{1c}$)	R. coreticulatum / R. reticulatum / R. reticulatum / R. reticulatum	N8
	R. nodosum (R$_{1b}$)	R. moorei / R. stubblefieldi / R. nodosum	N7
	R. circumplicatile (R$_{1a}$)	R. dubium / R. paucicrenulatum / R. circumplicatile / Ho. magistrorus	N6
Alportian (H$_2$)	Ht. prereticulatus (H$_{2c}$)	Ht. prereticulatus / V. eostriolatus	
	H. undulatum (H$_{2b}$)	H. undulatum	N5
	Hd. proteus (H$_{2a}$)	Hd. proteus	
Chokierian (H$_1$)	H. beyrichianum (H$_{1b}$)	H. beyrichianum	
	I. subglobosum (H$_{1a}$)	I. subglobosum / I. subglobosum	N4
Arnsbergian (E$_2$)	N. nuculum (E$_{2c}$)	N. nuculum / N. nuculum / N. nuculum / N. stellarum	N3
	Ct. nitidus (E$_{2b}$)	Ct. nititoides ('chert bed') / Ct. nitidus / *C. holmesi / Ct. edalensis	N2
	E. bisulcatum (E$_{2a}$)	E. yatesae / E. bisulcatum / C. cowlingense	
Pendleian (E$_1$)	C. malhamense (E$_{1c}$)	C. malhamense	N1
	E. pseudobilingue (E$_{1b}$)	E. pseudobilingue	
	C. leion (E$_{1a}$)	C. leion	

C. = *Cravenoceras*   Ct. = *Cravenoceratoides*
D. = *Donetzoceras*   E. = *Eumorphoceras*
G. = *Gastrioceras*   H. = *Homoceras*
Hd. = *Hudsonoceras*   Ho. = *Hodsonites*
Ht. = *Homoceratoides*   I. = *Isohomoceras*
N. = *Nuculoceras*   R. = *Reticuloceras*
V. = *Vallites*

* Since the Ashbourne sheet was published, several goniatite names have been revised; the new names are in brackets: *G. cumbriense (Cancelloceras cumbriense), G. cancellatum (Cancelloceras cancellatum), R. superbilingue (Bilinguites superbilinguis), R. eometabilingue (Bilinguites eometabilinguis), R. bilingue (Bilinguites bilinguis), R. gracile (Bilinguites gracilis)* and *C. holmesi (Fayettevillea holmesi)*.

Table 2 Named units in the Namurian of the Ashbourne district

Barrow (1903)	Hester (1932)	Morris (1969)	Trewin and Holdsworth (1973)	PRESENT CLASSIFICATION			Stages
				Named sandstone units			Stages
First Grit	First Grit	Rough Rock		Rough Rock (G_{1b})			Yeadonian (G_1)
Third Grit	Roches Grits	Harston Grit		Chatsworth Grit (R_{2c})			
Sandstone in Shirley Brook		Shirley Hollow Sandstone		Roaches and Ashover grits (R_{2b})			Marsdenian (R_2)
				Brockholes Sandstones (R_{2b})			
	Churnet Shales	Ipstones Edge Sandstones		Ipstones Edge Sandstones (H_1–R_1)	Kniveden Sandstones (R_{1c})		Kinderscoutian (R_1)
		Cloughmeadow Mudstones			Cheddleton Sandstones (H_1–H_2)		Alportian (H_2)
							Chokierian (H_1)
	Morredge Grits	Morredge Sandstones	Protoquartzite unit C	Hurdlow Sandstones (E_{2c})			Arnsbergian (E_2)
				Minn Sandstones (E_{1b}–E_{2a})			
			Protoquartzite unit B Protoquartzite unit A				Pendleian (E_1)

BIOSTRATIGRAPHY

The division of the sequence into zones and stages by means of the goniatite faunas contained in the marine marker bands is now well established (Table 1). Goniatites collected during the resurvey were identified by W. H. C. Ramsbottom and N. J. Riley: all the main faunal bands have been encountered within the district. Faunal lists have not been included in the text, but are available in BGS files. Abnormal faunas are recorded in the Ipstones area, where the goniatite bands in H_1 and H_2 are represented by *Lingula* bands (Figure 14, column 4). The effect is attributed to the presence of shallow-water deltaic environments with reduced salinity close to the southern margin of the basin. Miospores, identified by B. Owens, have locally provided useful information on exposures where goniatites were not available. The floral lists can be obtained from BGS files by reference to the MPA numbers quoted.

LITHOLOGY

The sequence consists mainly of interbedded mudstones, siltstones and sandstones, with minor amounts of carbonate rocks (ironstone, dolomite, limestone) and coal. Grey to dark grey mudstones and argillaceous siltstones account for more than half the sequence, being particularly prominent in the lower half (Figure 14). Grey-brown sideritic ironstone nodules and bands occur in places among these lithologies. Subordinate dark grey to black fissile mudstones, commonly fossiliferous, are present among the grey mudstones; the thin marine marker bands with their goniatite-bivalve faunas belong mainly to this lithology, and limestone and dolomite bands and nodules ('bullions') also occur in places. There is a characteristic band of dolomitic cherty siltstone ('the chert-bed') in E_{2b} (see p.47). Pyrite is common in the dark mudstones, occurring either in scattered aggregates or replacing fossils, especially plant fragments. Thin, pale-coloured layers of potassium bentonite, (K-bentonite) probably representing wind-blown volcanic dust, are present in the mudstones of E_1 and E_2 age (Trewin, 1968; Trewin and Holdsworth, 1972). Bands of calcareous siltstone, a distinctive lithology of turbidite origin, are characteristic of the lower part of the sequence in the western part of the district (Trewin and Holdsworth, 1973, p.385) and may be present also in the east (Aitkenhead, 1977, p.6). Sandstones are of two types; a protoquartzitic variety ('crowstone'), characteristic of the lowest two thirds or more of the sequence, and a feldspathic type (including the original 'millstone grits') present in the highest part of the sequence. Rootlet horizons marking former land surfaces, with associated thin seams of coal in some areas, are also a feature of the higher strata.

As in other parts of the Central Pennine Basin, evidence of cyclic deposition is present in the alternation of faunal phases in the mudstones and in the repeated incursions of sand and silt into the basin (Ramsbottom, 1969). Both effects are attributed to eustatic rises and falls of sea level (Trewin and Holdsworth, 1973, p.397; Ramsbottom, 1977, pp.265–266). The cycles have been grouped together into mesothems, or major cycles, by Ramsbottom; the relationship of these to the goniatite zones is shown in Table 1.

DEPOSITIONAL HISTORY

The Namurian sediments were originally deposited near the southern end of the Central Pennine (or Craven) Basin, which lay between the Craven Faults and the Wales–Brabant Island (Ramsbottom and others, 1978, pp.16–23). During the earlier part of the epoch (E_1 to H_2) the existence of two subordinate basins can be recognised, each with its own characteristic sequence; the North Staffordshire Basin in the west and the Widmerpool Gulf in the east (Trewin and Holdsworth, 1973, fig. 5). However, in later times similar sequences were deposited in both areas (Ramsbottom and others, 1978, fig. 5). The earliest mudstones contain pelagic marine faunas and are considered to have been deposited in deep water (Trewin and Holdsworth, 1973, p.397). The basinal mudstone facies recurs at many higher levels, and forms a constant background to sedimentation. Where these basinal deposits overlie late Dinantian turbidite-bearing mudstones (Figure 14, columns 6, 8) the basal contact is conformable, indicating continuous sedimentation; but where they abut against, or overlie, the upstanding remnants of the Dinantian shelf provinces, the contacts are disconformable, some or all of the Brigantian rocks being absent (Figure 14, column 7). The lowest Namurian is absent or greatly condensed in these areas. The relationship is analogous to that described in detail by Aitkenhead and others (1985, fig. 25) from the reef belt at the western side of the Derbyshire Shelf.

Deposition of mudstone in the North Staffordshire Basin was interrupted at frequent intervals throughout E_1 and E_2 times by the influx of sediment carried by turbidity currents (Figure 14, columns 2, 5, 6). Calcareous siltstones from a western source appeared first, but protoquartzitic sandstones from the south or south-west came to predominate later (Minn and Hurdlow sandstones). Detailed descriptions of the lithology and sedimentology of this part of the sequence have been given by Trewin and Holdsworth (1973). In the Widmerpool Gulf the E_1–E_2 sequence is similar, with turbiditic quartz-rich sandstones derived from the south-west, but the calcareous siltstone lithology is not so well represented (Aitkenhead, 1977; Charsley, 1979).

Mudstone deposition in the Widmerpool Gulf continued with only rare pulses of coarser sediment until R_{2b} times (Figure 14, column 8), when the 'Millstone Grit' delta began to pour feldspathic sand into the region from the east (Jones, 1980, fig. 12). The earliest turbidites of this episode (Ashover Grit) are present at the eastern edge of the district. In North Staffordshire, however, the basinal mudstones of H_1, H_2 and R_1 age are interbedded with protoquartzites of shallow-water facies (Ipstones Edge, Cheddleton and Kniveden sandstones), which spread into the area from the south or south-west (Figure 14). In R_{2b} the last of the protoquartzites, the Brockholes Sandstones, are interbedded

locally with the first of the feldspathic sandstones, the Roaches Grit. The latter is equivalent to the Ashover Grit. Because this part of the basin was already almost full of sediment by this time, the Roaches Grit is thin, and entirely of shallow-water facies (Jones, 1980, fig. 3).

During R_{2c} and G_1 times, deposition of mudstone with marine bands continued but the entire south Pennine area received thick fluvio-deltaic spreads of coarse feldspathic sand from the east and north-east to form the Chatsworth Grit and Rough Rock (Figure 14); this pattern continued without major change into the succeeding Westphalian.

NOMENCLATURE OF SANDSTONES

Minn Sandstones

The name was introduced by Aitkenhead and others (1985, p.71) to include all protoquartzitic sandstones of E_{1b}, E_{1c} and E_{2a} age in the North Staffordshire Basin and was a modification of the term 'Minn Beds' used in the Macclesfield district by Evans and others (1968, p.20). The sandstones are interbedded with siltstone and mudstone and occur in groups separated by mudstones and calcareous siltstones. Trewin and Holdsworth (1973) described the petrography and sedimentology of the sandstones, showing that they are protoquartzitic turbidites derived from the Midland landmass (Wales–Brabant Island) which lay not far to the south. The last authors recognised three groups of sandstones, referred to as units A, B and C, which correspond with the three highest of four units known in the present district (Figure 14). As in the Buxton district (Aitkenhead and others, 1985, p.72) a proximal facies, in which sandstone comprises at least half the sequence, has been distinguished on the map from a distal facies in which sandstone makes up less than half the sequence. A modified name, Minn Mudstones-with-Sandstones, is used for the latter. The distribution of these facies within the present district corresponds broadly with that shown by Trewin and Holdsworth (1973, fig.5), in that distal turbidites are more common than proximal turbidites, and that all the sandstones die out eastwards (Figure 14). Unnamed sandstones at the same levels in the sequence are present farther east, in the Widmerpool Gulf, however.

Hurdlow Sandstones

The name was introduced by Aitkenhead and others (1985, pp. 74, 76) for protoquartzites deposited in the North Staffordshire Basin during E_{2c} times. They are derived, like the Minn Sandstones, from the Wales–Brabant Island to the south (Bolton, 1978; Aitkenhead and others, 1985, p.76). Within the present district they vary greatly, being thickest on Morridge (Figure 14, columns 5, 6), where lenses of proximal turbidites (Hurdlow Sandstones), some of them pebbly, are interbedded with the more prevalent distal facies (Hurdlow Mudstones-with-Sandstones). To the south-east they become thinner, passing at Winkhill into a single lens of proximal facies before dying out near Windy Harbour (Figure 14, column 7). West of Morridge the thickness and facies change rapidly in the vicinity of the Combes valley

(Figure 14, column 2). Two main leaves of turbidites are present near Apesford but south of the Sixoaks Fault these are thinner and are separated by an increased thickness of mudstone. The lower leaf, exposed in a small crag [0106 5278] near Padwick is not in a typical turbidite facies, and may be of shallow-water origin. North-west of here, in stream-side crags [9974 5402] east of Sheephouse Farm, only the lower leaf is present; it is again thin and of uncertain facies. Farther west, around Cheddleton (Figure 14, column 1) the facies is uncertain due to poor exposure, but two leaves of sandstone appear to be present. In the Ipstones Edge Borehole (Figure 14, column 4) some sandstones below a fault are thought to belong to the Hurdlow Sandstones. They occur in sharp-based beds with sole marks and ripple lamination indicating palaeocurrent flow from south to north (Figure 15).

To summarise, thin sandstones in the west, perhaps of shallow-water facies, pass eastwards into thick mainly distal turbidites; traced northwards into the adjacent district these thin gradually and become more distal (Aitkenhead and others, 1985, p.76) and to the south-east, within the present district, they thin rapidly and die out towards the upstanding mass of late Dinantian shelf-margin limestones at Caldon Low.

Ipstones Edge Sandstones

The name was introduced by Morris (1967a, fig.3; pp.25–26) for a mass of quartzose sandstones that crop out on Ipstones Edge and in the Combes valley. They were originally thought (Morris, 1969, p.148) to be entirely of R_1 age but information from the Ipstones Edge Borehole suggests (Figure 14, columns 4, 6, 7) that they probably also include sandstones of H_1 and H_2 age. The name is now used for protoquartzites of H_1, H_2 and R_1 age, but only in areas where the various component beds (Lum Edge, Stanley, Cheddleton, Blackstone Edge and Kniveden sandstones) cannot be separately recognised. Exposures and features on Ipstones Edge suggest that the sequence consists of poorly bedded, white, fine- to coarse-grained sandstone with small siliceous pebbles in places, interbedded with alternations of

fine-grained ripple laminated sandstone and purplish grey siltstone and mudstone. The sandstone facies is well exposed but the finer-grained alternations are rarely seen. All are apparently of shallow-water origin and probably represent an assemblage of fluvio-deltaic channel and mouth-bar sandstones, with overbank deposits of finer grain size. To the south-east the sandstones become thin in the Caldon Low area (Figure 14, columns 6, 7) but thicken again before disappearing beneath the Trias at Ramshorn; all are of shallow-water facies. To the north-west and north the sequence interdigitates with marine mudstone. The result, within the present district, is that the sandstones split into two named units (Cheddleton and Kniveden sandstones), both of shallow-water facies, but farther north, in the Buxton district, the sandstones become thinner, more lenticular, and turbiditic in part (Aitkenhead and others, 1985, pp.76–83). They there comprise the Lum Edge, Blackstone Edge and Kniveden sandstones, all of which die out northwards. The Ipstones Edge Sandstones, with their more distal northerly representatives, can therefore be regarded as a wedge of fluvio-deltaic sediment deposited near the south margin of the North Staffordshire Basin by rivers flowing from the Wales-Brabant Island. Palaeocurrent data from the Cheddleton Sandstones in the Ipstones Edge Borehole (Figure 15), and isolated cross-bedding measurements on Ipstones Edge, support this view. The main delta lobe was located at Ipstones Edge (Figure 14, column 6), where the sandstones are thickest and the interdigitating marine mudstones are least prominent. A similar transition, in which protoquartzites die out northwards into a marine mudstone sequence, is recorded in the Macclesfield district (Evans and others, 1968, pp.19, 34): some unnamed sandstones poorly exposed at the west margin of the present district [964 450], near Dilhorne, lie among the southernmost outcrops related to this delta lobe.

Cheddleton Sandstones

The name is introduced here to include protoquartzites of H_1 and H_2 age in the North Staffordshire Basin. It includes the Lum Edge Sandstones of the Buxton district and the Stanley

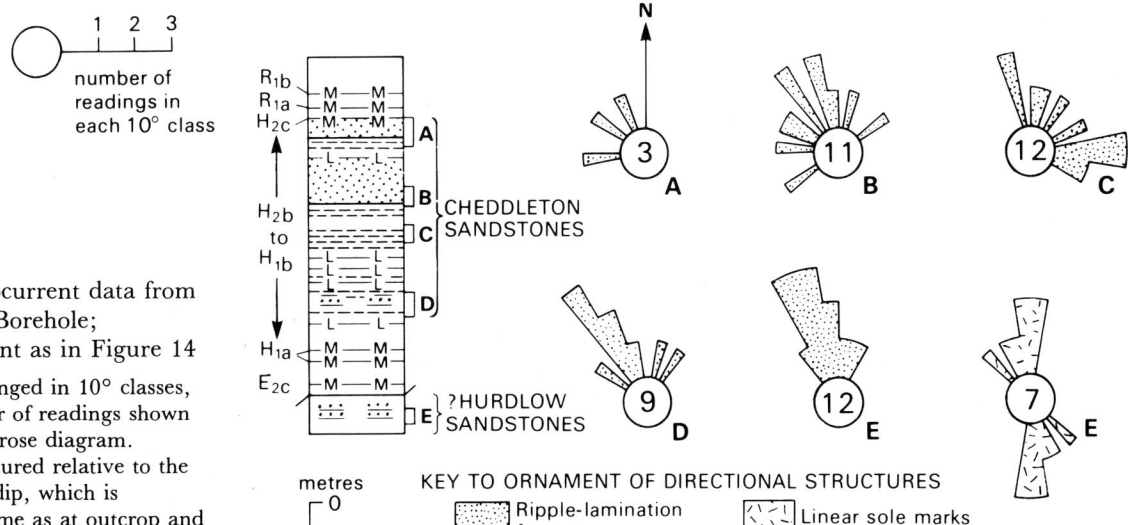

Figure 15 Palaeocurrent data from the Ipstones Edge Borehole; lithological ornament as in Figure 14

Directional data arranged in 10° classes, with the total number of readings shown at the centre of each rose diagram. Directions were measured relative to the direction of tectonic dip, which is assumed to be the same as at outcrop and consistent throughout the borehole.

Sandstone of the Stoke on Trent district. There are several exposures around the type locality (Figure 14, column 1), the best [9815 5197] showing 4 m of fine to coarse-grained well bedded white sandstone with undulating depositional dips. Other exposures show layers of purple-grey siltstone and mudstone, intraclasts of the same material, small siliceous pebbles and large plant stems. All the beds are of fluvio-deltaic facies. To the east the outcrop is discontinuous and the sandstones map out as lenticular bodies interbedded with siltstones. At Sharpcliffe Rocks [015 520] the sandstones are very pebbly (Figure 14, column 2) and have been called the Sharpcliffe Conglomerate by Morris (1967a, pp.21, 26). Cross bedding indicates palaeocurrent flow towards the south. In the Ipstones Edge Borehole the sandstones range from fine- to coarse-grained with ripple lamination which indicates palaeocurrent flow towards the north (Figure 15); the direction at Sharpcliffe Rocks is assumed to be a local effect, perhaps in a channel meander. The sandstones in the borehole were interbedded with striped siltstones and mudstones but the goniatite bands of the *H. beyrichianum*, *Hd. proteus* and *H. undulatum* zones were not present, having apparently passed laterally into a *Lingula* facies that developed in the region of the sediment source. The absence of the goniatites explains why beds named separately in more basinward areas (Lum Edge and Stanley sandstones) cannot be distinguished here. Still closer approach to the source of clastic supply is indicated farther east on Ipstones Edge, where the Cheddleton Sandstones cannot be distinguished from the overlying Kniveden Sandstones (Figure 14, columns 6, 7).

Kniveden Sandstones

The name was introduced by Aitkenhead and others (1985, p.83) for protoquartzites of R_{1c} age in the Leek area, where they are turbidites. They die out to the north. To the south, in the present district, they are of shallow-water facies, being closer to the supposed source of sediment. They can be recognised in the Cheddleton and Combes valley areas, the best sections being those in steep valley sides and landslips at The Combes [004 524]. They here consist partly of fine- to coarse-grained, poorly bedded, cross bedded and flat-bedded sandstone with scattered quartz pebbles, mudstone and ironstone intraclasts and plant stems, and partly of fine-grained ripple-laminated sandstone in thin beds with purple-grey siltstone interbeds. East of the Ipstones Edge Borehole the underlying marine bands become unrecognisable and the Kniveden Sandstones pass laterally into the upper part of the Ipstones Edge Sandstones (Figure 14, columns 4, 6, 7).

Brockholes Sandstones

The name is introduced here for protoquartzites of R_{2b} age in the North Staffordshire Basin; the sandstones are thus of the same age as the feldspathic Roaches Grit, though derived from a different source area. At the type locality [0115 5129] 5 m are exposed of fine- to coarse-grained white flat-bedded sandstone with rare quartz pebbles. The sandstones are of shallow-water facies throughout their known outcrop. They die out to the east near Ipstones and to the north near Longsdon Farm, just beyond the district boundary; at the

latter locality they are interbedded with leaves of the Roaches Grit (p.51).

Roaches Grit

In its type area, north of the present district, the Roaches Grit is the delta-top part of a thick sequence of clastic sediments that represent the infilling of the deepest remaining parts of the North Staffordshire Basin in R_{2b} times (Jones, 1980). In the present district, where it was formerly known as the Shirley Hollow Sandstones (Morris, 1969, p.167), the Roaches Grit is thin, the southern marginal part of the basin having been filled with protoquartzitic clastics from the Wales–Brabant Island by R_{2b} times. The sandstone is of feldspathic facies (Table 3; Jones, 1980, table 2) and is thus a direct correlative of the Ashover Grit. The best exposures are in Shirley Hollow (SK 04 NW/49) where the sandstone is mainly fine-grained, micaceous and ripple-laminated, with interbedded siltstone, but with a coarser-grained bed near the top (p.52); it represents a delta-top facies (Jones, 1980, p.58).

Ashover Grit

Ashover Grit is the name given to feldspathic sandstones of R_{2b} age in the Chesterfield and Derby districts (Smith and others, 1967, p.68; Frost and Smart, 1979). The name is applied to localised turbidites that lie low in the sequence as well as to the more widespread delta-top sandstones (Chisholm, 1977). The sequence is thus an eastern representative of the Roaches Grit and its associated sediments. Jones (1980, pp.62–64) demonstrated that although the palaeocurrent data from both grits indicate deposition by currents flowing across the region from south-east to north-west, broader considerations show that the source terrain must have lain to the north, in the landmass which supplied the other feldspathic grits. In the Ashbourne district the Ashover Grit is present only at the eastern margin (Figure 14, column 8) and only the lowest, turbiditic, parts are preserved. The sequence is known from boreholes (p.52).

Chatsworth Grit

Chatsworth Grit is the name given to the major feldspathic sandstones in R_{2c} (Smith and others, 1967, p.68); it has been applied to areas both east and west of the Derbyshire Dome. Sedimentological investigations in parts of this region (Mayhew, 1966; Kerey, 1978) show that the sandstones represent the channel deposits of rivers that flowed from the east or north-east. In the present district it is the thickest of the feldspathic sandstones and is generally coarse-grained, with small quartz pebbles. Cross bedding indicates palaeocurrent flow from the north-east. The best exposures are in crags and escarpments, present at intervals around the west, north and east sides of the Cheadle Coalfield (p.52).

Rough Rock

The name has been applied to the major medium and coarse-grained feldspathic sandstones of G_1 age throughout the

Central Pennine Basin. It was deposited in the channels of rivers flowing from a northern or north-eastern landmass (Shackleton, 1962). In the Ashbourne district it is generally present in characteristic facies (p.54), as at Moneystone Quarry near Whiston and at Ipstones, but it passes locally at Consall into siltstone with fine-grained sandstone bands (SJ 94 NE/18; Cope, 1946, p.4). JIC

PETROGRAPHY OF SANDSTONES

The Namurian sandstones of the district are similar to those of adjacent areas in showing a partition into 'protoquartzitic' and 'feldspathic' variants, a lack of maturity shown by rather poor rounding and sorting of grains, a commonly high degree of compaction and, in the case of the feldspathic type, the presence of abundant fresh microcline and authigenic kaolinitic clay. Modal analyses (Table 3) indicate that both lithologies are variable, but that in their proportions of two major components—lithoclasts and total feldspar—they remain mutually exclusive. The lithoclast content (excluding polycrystalline quartz varieties such as quartzite, chert, etc.) is rarely less than 4 per cent in protoquartzites but never exceeds 2 per cent in feldspathic sandstones. The total feldspar content (including authigenic kaolinitic clay, probably a feldspar decomposition product) is rarely more than 2 per cent in protoquartzites but never less than 10 per cent (commonly more than 15 per cent) in feldspathic sandstones; the contrast in microcline content is even more extreme but cannot be quantified, due to the undifferentiated nature of feldspar alteration products. The number of analysed samples is not sufficient to deduce average or general compositions for the two suites.

The nature of the lithoclasts suggests that the protoquartzites were derived from a terrain consisting of metamorphic quartzite, with some felsic volcanics and micaceous siltstones and mudstones; the composition of the feldspathic sandstones shows that they were derived from an area of coarse-grained acidic igneous rocks.

Protoquartzite facies

A sample (E51367) from a thin quartzose band among mudstones a few metres above the base of the Namurian (?Pendleian) near Caldon Low is an argillaceous carbonaceous siltstone, much finer grained than any other rock described here: the modal analysis is less accurate because the grain size is in large part much less than the thickness of the thin-section. The rock is highly compacted and the ferruginous micaceous detrital matrix is unevenly distributed. Most of the abundant organic content consists of opaque flakes concentrated in preferred bedding planes. The deficiency of feldspar in this rock is less marked than in coarser variants of the protoquartzite group, possibly because kaolinisation has been inhibited by poor primary permeability.

The **Minn and Hurdlow sandstones** are protoquartzitic throughout. E51366, from the highest of the Minn Sandstones, is a medium-grained poorly sorted rock showing very strong compaction, with sutured intergranular junctions (though with relatively little syntaxial overgrowth) and little pore space. The lithoclasts include a notably high proportion of fine-grained micaceous rocks and the matrix is also visibly micaceous. The authigenic clay content is relatively high for a protoquartzite and accessories include zircon, rutile, tourmaline and opaque oxides. E51363 and E51364 respectively represent a relatively poorly sorted coarse-grained facies and a well sorted fine-grained facies of the Hurdlow Sandstones; both show strong compaction and this, together with widespread syntaxial overgrowth, gives the finer-grained rock a granulite texture. Lithoclasts of a fine-grained micaceous lithology are especially prominent in the finer-grained E51364.

The **Ipstones Edge Sandstones** (E51347, E51348, E51354, E51357, E51358), **Cheddleton Sandstones** (E51345, E51346, E51350, E51351, E51359, E51360) and **Kniveden Sandstones** (E51344, E51352), and the overlying **Brockholes Sandstones** (E51349, E51353, E51475, E52427), are all protoquartzites. They have been sampled comprehensively, to test their variability according to regional distribution and grain size. Of those analysed modally (Table 3) E51350, E51475 and E51354 are of comparable grain size but from different parts of the outcrop, while contrasting fabrics from a single locality are represented by E51345 and E51346. E51352 is distinctive in showing a strongly bimodal fabric. The coarser rocks tend to show a higher ratio of lithoclasts to monocrystalline quartz grains, although E51352 and E51354 have very similar modal compositions despite their different grain sizes. The samples show a wide range of compaction and secondary quartz cementation textures, from the development of an almost quartzitic fabric (E51352) to relatively weakly compacted rocks (in this context) such as E51355, which was collected from a locality just beyond the western margin of the district. The variation in quartz cementation is again apparently related more to the coarseness of a lithology than to regional distribution, with the finer-grained rocks showing a higher degree of cementation. Sample E51360, a fine- to medium-grained sandstone, is noteworthy for its particularly high proportion of syntaxial quartz overgrowth, although it nevertheless retains a fairly high porosity. Partial cementation by ferric oxide is irregularly distributed, but is abundant in most samples whereas authigenic kaolinitic clay is generally rare. The ferric oxide cementation postdates syntaxial quartz overgrowth. The dominant lithoclastic content is of metamorphic quartzite with subordinate felsic volcanic lithologies and fine-grained siltstones and mudstones. Accessories include opaque oxides, zircon, rutile and tourmaline. Sample E51352 is worth separate comment because its grain size is strongly bimodal. It is a packstone consisting of angular to subrounded grains of 0.3 to 1.75 mm diameter set in a matrix of strongly welded fine-grained sandstone with a grain size of 0.06 to 0.15 mm. In addition to the usual range, lithoclasts in the thin-section include a perforate siliceous or silicified fragment of organic origin. E51359 is a poorly sorted conglomerate containing high proportions of quartzite lithoclasts and ferruginous silty micaceous clay matrix. The composition of the dominant lithoclasts in this and other protoquartzitic conglomerates (E51345 and E51346) indicates that the dominant parent rock was probably a coarsely crystalline, commonly cataclasised quartzite containing sparse and irregularly distributed schistose flakes of white mica. Minor lithoclastic lithologies include acidic to inter-

Table 3 Selected modal analyses of terrigenous clastic rocks from the Ashbourne district: Namurian, Westphalian and Triassic

	Namurian																							
Facies	Protoquartzitic facies															Feldspathic facies								
Sandstone name	? in E1	MN	HU		?HU	CD-KV-BH		CD					KV	IP	BH	RG		CG		RR				
Sample	1	2	3	4	5	6	7	8	9	10	11	12	13	14	15	16	17	18	19	20	21	22	23	24
Monocrystalline quartz	56.9	69.3	72.2	70.8	75.9	70.5	61.4	62.0	49.2	31.3	40.9	73.3	69.5	69.3	56.6	61.8	28.9	73.8	76.8	58.9	61.9	65.1	68.4	71.7
Quartz lithoclasts	3.9	11.2	19.8	13.7	13.1	10.5	18.8	20.0	33.4	49.9	37.3	12.4	17.7	17.1	19.3	7.0	35.4	1.6	1.5	10.0	23.1	10.4	18.7	10.7
Other lithoclasts	1.5	8.7	3.8	8.1	5.8	6.5	13.0	9.1	8.5	11.8	10.1	8.6	6.5	6.6	11.3	1.6	0.4	—	—	1.6	0.1	2.2	0.3	0.7
Potassic feldspar	0.5	—	—	—	—	—	—	0.1	—	—	—	—	—	—	—	3.4	23.5	10.9	8.1	10.6	6.2	10.1	5.6	8.0
Plagioclase	1.2	0.2	—	0.5	—	—	—	0.1	—	0.1	—	—	—	—	tr	1.2	0.2	1.4	1.4	1.1	—	1.4	0.4	1.0
Mica	1.6	0.4	—	1.5	0.1	0.2	—	—	—	—	—	—	1.2	0.1	0.4	1.6	0.8	0.1	0.3	1.0	0.2	0.8	—	0.3
Detrital matrix (mainly clay) / Ferric oxide (mainly cement)	29.5	8.1	3.7	4.7	5.1	11.0	6.0	8.1	8.8	6.9	11.6	5.3	4.3	4.9	11.5	10.8	2.8	3.3	4.2	8.9	1.5	4.8	1.3	2.1
Organic detritus	4.2	—	—	—	—	—	—	—	—	—	—	—	—	—	—	—	—	—	—	—	—	—	—	—
Carbonate cement	—	—	—	—	—	—	—	—	—	—	—	—	—	—	—	—	—	—	—	—	—	—	—	—
Authigenic clay (dickite and kaolinite)	—	1.5	0.2	0.3	—	0.6	0.7	0.1	tr	—	0.1	0.2	0.1	1.8	0.4	12.0	8.0	7.3	6.0	7.8	6.8	5.1	5.3	5.4
Others	—	0.6	0.2	0.4	0.1	0.7	0.1	0.2	0.1	—	—	0.2	0.7	0.2	0.5	0.6	—	1.6	1.7	0.1	—	0.1	—	0.1
Approximate maximum grain size (mm)	0.03	0.75	0.6	0.15	0.9	0.24	1.05	0.6	3	10	6	0.6	1.75	0.45	0.45	0.15	6	2	1	0.4	2	0.35	0.75	0.4

The approximate maximum grain size of each sample is appended as a guide for comparability: it is obvious, for example, that in otherwise identical situations a coarser rock will contain a higher proportion of lithoclasts than a finer-grained rock. For some Triassic samples the data are presented in alternative forms to allow direct comparability of clastic proportions without interference from large and variable amounts of carbonate cement (figures in *italic* type). All the thin sections were stained with sodium cobaltinitrite and potassiun rhodizonate, and counts of between 1000 and 2000 points, at intervals appropriate to grain size, were made to establish their modal compositions. Sample locations are given in Appendix 3.

MN	Minn Sandstones	CG	Chatsworth Grit
HU	Hurdlow Sandstones	RR	Rough Rock
CD	Cheddleton Sandstones	WH	Woodhead Hill Rock
KV	Kniveden Sandstones	CR	Sandstone below Crabtree Coal
IP	Ipstones Edge Sandstones	KY	Kingsley Sandstone
BH	Brockholes Sandstones	HUN	Huntley Formation
RG	Roaches Grit	HOL	Hollington Formation

mediate volcanic rocks and micaceous silty mudstone. Sample E51346 also shows an unusual feature in that it is partly cemented by anastomose segregations of authigenic fine-grained quartz containing minor drusy cavities partly infiltrated by ferruginous siltstone.

Feldspathic facies

The two samples of **Roaches Grit** chosen for modal analysis, E51338 and E51339, show strong contrasts in fabric and composition. The former is highly compacted, fine-grained and comparatively well sorted, and has a relatively low feldspar content compensated by a very high proportion of authigenic kaolinite, in substantiation of the theory that most of this clay is derived from feldspar decomposition. The mica content includes a proportion of altered biotite and the thin-section contains a solitary large grain of garnet. E51339 is by

contrast an arkosic conglomerate, with more than 30 per cent of potassic feldspar plus authigenic clay. The content of the latter may be even higher than recorded because the matrix is locally obscured by impregnations of ferric oxide.

Samples from the succeeding **Chatsworth Grit** are both comparatively coarse subarkosic sandstones. E51337 is the coarser of the two and is particularly immature in aspect, with poor sorting and more angular clasts than is usual. Authigenic clay occurs in forms of both relatively coarse and fine crystallinity, plagioclase is barely identifiable because of argillisation and distortion, and the rock contains a large proportion of voids; it may be inferred that much former feldspar or its decomposition products have been leached from the rock. E51623 is less coarse grained, being a medium-grained sandstone with a grittiness imparted by a small proportion of larger clasts. As in E51337 the grains are dominantly subangular and there are large proportions of

is not compensated by more authigenic clay but might be explained by leaching.

NGB

Westphalian A					Triassic				HOL	?Triassic neptunean dyke	
WH			CR	KY	HUN						
25	26	27	28	29	30		31		32	33	
53.3	55.1	61.3	77.5	46.7	17.1	20.3	17.3	23.3	53.5	25.4	54.6
10.1	15.4	14.6	18.9	6.9	13.5	16.0	18.3	24.7	20.4	14.3	30.8
1.6	1.9	1.1			47.5	56.3	29.4	39.7	8.7	2.1	4.5
8.8	9.9	11.6	—	15.5	1.0	1.2	3.0	4.0	15.3	3.3	7.1
1.6	2.3	0.5	0.1	9.4	0.5	0.6	—	—	0.8	0.1	0.2
1.8	0.7	0.6	0.1	2.4	0.1	0.1	0.1	0.1	0.1	—	—
4.4	3.0	1.9			—		—		0.8	—	—
			2.7	14.9							
tr	4.9	—			3.1	3.7	5.2	7.0	—	1.2	2.6
4.2	nd	—	—	—	—		—		—	—	—
—	—	—	—	—	15.7		25.9		—	53.5	
14.0	6.8	8.3	0.4	—	0.8	0.9	—	—	0.4	tr	tr
0.2	—	0.1	0.3	4.2	0.7	0.8	0.8	1.0	0.1	0.1	0.2
0.35	2	0.75	0.45	0.15	8		20		0.7	0.35	

Sample numbers

1 E 51367	10 E 51346	19 E 51623	28 E 51627
2 E 51366	11 E 51359	20 E 51331	29 E 51626
3 E 51363	12 E 51360	21 E 51332	30 E 51368
4 E 51364	13 E 51352	22 E 51333	31 E 51369
5 E 51361	14 E 51354	23 E 51334	32 E 51371
6 E 51356	15 E 51475	24 E 51335	33 E 51370
7 E 51355	16 E 51338	25 E 51329	
8 E 51350	17 E 51339	26 E 51624	
9 E 51345	18 E 51337	27 E 51625	

void space but very small proportions of lithoclastic grains of any sort. There is comparatively little deformation or syntaxial overgrowth and this is one of the least compacted Namurian 'grits'.

The **Rough Rock** is represented by three samples, two of which are of comparable fine grain size, from widely separated localities along the outcrop, and are moderately well sorted subarkosic grainstones. Both are compact and one, E51333, shows strong pressure solution and syntaxial quartz overgrowth textures. The other, E51335, from the south-eastern end of the outcrop, has better-rounded grains and shows less compaction than its more northern equivalent. Accessory heavy minerals include zircon, tourmaline and possible sphene and brown spinel. A coarse sample from the Rough Rock, E51334, shows an increase in quartz lithoclast proportion but also an unexpected decrease in potassic feldspar content. The reduced feldspar proportion

STRATIGRAPHY

Pendleian strata, including lower leaves of Minn Sandstones

Pendleian strata crop out mainly adjacent to the Dinantian between Ford and Waterhouses in the west, around Thorswood and Parwich, north-east of Ashbourne, and in the Carsington–Hulland area in the east. A small inlier is also present near Leekbrook [986 539] in the north-west of the district. The base is generally conformable on the Mixon Limestone-Shales or the Widmerpool Formation, though there is local unconformity where Pendleian strata rest on the Dinantian limestone sequence. The Pendleian strata consist mainly of grey to dark grey slightly calcareous blocky mudstones and siltstones of distal turbidite facies with darker fissile mudstone intercalations. The main fossiliferous horizons, including the *Cravenoceras leion* Band at the base and the *Eumorphoceras pseudobilingue* and *C. malhamense* bands above, are associated with a few thin beds of argillaceous limestone. Three leaves of protoquartzitic sandstone turbidites belonging to the Minn Mudstones-with-Sandstones are present around Morridge Side [022 544]. They pass south-eastwards into mudstones with ironstone bands and nodules. The sequence reaches its maximum thickness of about 200 m east of Morridge Side and thins southwards against the Dinantian shelf remnant south of Waterhouses. The thickness is about 125 m north-east of Ashbourne and 160 m in the Carsington–Hulland area (Figure 14).

DETAILS

The basal (E_{1a}) sequence and the upward transition from the Mixon Limestone-Shales are exposed at several localities between Bullclough, at the northern edge of the district, and Cauldon. The best sections are at Bullclough (SK 05 NE/10), Ford (SK 05 SE/22) and in a disused railway cutting [0753 4956 to 0781 4983] near Waterhouses. The last section is now largely overgrown but it was described in detail by Morris (1967b) who found eight bands, five with bullions, containing E_{1a} Zone goniatites in some 20 m of mudstone. The Bullclough section exposes 4.47 m of dark grey fossiliferous mudstone with thin beds of argillaceous limestone. The fauna consists mainly of *Posidonia corrugata* and *P. membranacea* but poorly preserved goniatites including *Cravenoceras sp*. are present 1.16 m to 3.48 m above the base of the fossiliferous sequence which is taken as the base of E_{1a} and hence, by definition, as the base of the Namurian. Section SK 05 SE/22 includes about 6 m of tough calcareous silty mudstone, with darker fissile fossiliferous intercalations containing *C.* cf. *leion* in the basal 1.0 m. Below, some 10.34 m of partially exposed mudstone separate the beds with *C.* cf. *leion* from the highest Viséan goniatite horizon. The *C.* cf. *leion* Band is traceable south-eastwards to near Back o' th' Brook (SK 05 SE/23), but beyond here it may be absent due to overlap on to Dinantian strata (see p.34). To the south, however, *C. leion* and *E.* cf. *tornquisti* were recovered from a limestone bullion in the shale quarry at Cauldon Cement Works (SK 04 NE/31), indicating that the Dinantian–Namurian junction, inferred to lie a few metres below, is locally conformable here.

The *Eumorphoceras pseudobilingue* Band (E_{1b}) is exposed in the School House section (SK 05 SE/24) in the River Hamps at

Waterhouses (Morris, 1967b, p.344). This band is also recorded in the adjacent shale quarry section (SK 04 NE/31) where it lies about 44 m above the *C. leion* horizon noted previously.

The highest Pendleian goniatite band, that of *C. malhamense* (E_{1c}), is present in a small exposure [0686 5294] of weathered mudstone and calcareous siltstone at Martin's Low. Exposures of similar lithology containing abundant *P. corrugata* and *P. membranacea* together with poorly preserved goniatites occur at several localities west of Ford [e.g. 0560 5391] and are inferred to represent the *C. malhamense* Band. Near Moorside a faunal band from which *P. corrugata*, *P. sp.* and *Cravenoceras sp.* have been collected [0414 5457] is also inferred, from its position in the sequence, to be the *C. malhamense* Band.

The Minn Sandstones are represented on Morridge mainly by turbidites in their distal facies of mudstones-with-sandstones. They form mappable features from Moor Top [034 549] to Martin's Low [070 526], but the proportion of sandstone and siltstone diminishes towards the south-east and the outcrops can no longer be traced in the vicinity of Waterhouses. The lowest leaf is exposed in one of the gullies [0421 5476] at Moorside as 10 m of silty mudstone with many sharp-based bands of fine-grained protoquartzite up to 0.3 m thick. Above lie 4 m of mudstone with bands containing *Posidonia*. West of Ford about 4 m of the lowest leaf are exposed [0607 5388]; beds of fine-grained protoquartzitic sandstone up to 0.24 m thick with groove and bounce marks on the soles are interbedded with silty mudstone in roughly equal proportions. The relatively high proportion of sandstone accounts for this leaf extending farther towards the south-east than the others. The second leaf, exposed in part in a gully [0369 5500] near Moor Top, closely resembles the lowest leaf; the third leaf forms a rounded bench-like feature [as at 042 543] but is not exposed.

In the shale quarry at Cauldon Cement Works, two units of mudstone with thin sideritic ironstone bands containing silty basal laminae are probably the distal representatives of the two lowest leaves of the Minn Sandstones. The overlying third leaf, which forms most of the sequence between the *C. malhamense* and *C. cowlingense* bands, is not traceable south-east of the vicinity [071 519] of Ironpits. Here, numerous shallow excavations, now grassed over, are inferred to have been dug for the ironstone bands and nodules which characterise its distal parts.   NA,JIC

To the south-west of Morridge, occurrences of Pendleian strata are few. Miospores indicating the presence of the stage have been identified (MPA 2743) in mudstones exposed in Birchall Wood [9916 5443] but the strata are greatly disturbed here and cannot be related to those in neighbouring sections. No faunal bands of E_1 or E_{2a} age are known in the Combes area but the thickness of strata exposed below the *Ct. nititoides* Band [0076 5291] implies that the lowest 55 m of the generalised Combes valley section (Figure 14, column 2), exposed in the axis of an anticline [009 530], belong to the third leaf of the Minn Sandstones and are thus of Pendleian age. They are of turbidite facies, comprising fine-grained sole-marked sandstones in units up to 0.9 m thick with interbedded siltstones and mudstones. Similar sandstones in the axis of a sharp, faulted anticline at Roost Hill [006 538] are thought to lie at the same stratigraphical level, on the basis of their relationship to the supposed highest Minn Sandstones at Ballfields [009 534]. In a quarry [0059 5397], 8.2 m are seen, in sharp-based beds up to 0.5 m thick, with a few argillaceous bands.

South of Waterhouses, Pendleian strata thin markedly against an upstanding mass of Dinantian shelf-margin limestones at Caldon Low. A precise figure cannot be given, but the stage may be less than 30 m thick in this area (Figure 14, column 7) and may even be missing in places due to overlap by younger mudstones. There are no sandstone features, suggesting that the Minn Sandstones are absent. The lowest strata overlie the Kevin Limestones in sink-holes between Hoften's Cross [072 481] and Ribden [076 468]. Miospore assemblages indicate ages within the range P_2 to E_{2b}, probably E_1

(MPA 2751–53; SAL 5755–57). The best section [0761 4682], near Ribden, shows about 10 m of grey mudstone and siltstone with thin bands of sandstone and ironstone, dipping to the south-west at angles between 30° and vertical. A small gap separates these beds from the top of the limestone. Little is seen of the overlying mudstones.   JIC

East of Caldon Low, early Namurian mudstones are preserved in a small area around Thorswood House. The only exposure [1169 4726] consists of black mudstone yielding miospores that indicate a probable early Namurian age (MPA 550). Field relations imply that the mudstones lie conformably on the Widmerpool Formation to the north-east and south-west, unconformably on Milldale Limestones to the north-west, and pass beneath Triassic rocks to the south-east.   NA

An extensive but poorly exposed area of Namurian mudstone to the south-west of Parwich is inferred to be largely of Pendleian age. The only exposure [1768 5406] with age-diagnostic fossils consists of 0.15 m of dark calcareous mudstone yielding *C. leion* overlain by 0.50 m of mudstone with a thin bed of argillaceous limestone.   IPS

North of Ashbourne, the Lees Farm Borehole (SK 15 SE/12) proved the basal 9.4 m of the Namurian succession, consisting of mudstone with calcareous bands and a 0.46 m carbonate siltstone (at 11.80 m), lying conformably on Widmerpool Formation beds of similar but more silty lithology. The junction is taken at the base of a goniatite-bearing sequence which includes *Cravenoceras leion*, *C. sp.* and *Eumorphoceras involutum*. Nearby [1819 5006], slightly higher strata are exposed in a stream where 10 m of mudstone with thin beds of siltstone and sandstone overlie 21.3 m of mudstone and calcareous mudstone with a thin limestone; the lowest 4.20 m of the lower beds yield *P. corrugata* and *E.* cf. *tornquisti* (E_{1a} Zone). Numerous stream exposures [e.g. 1832 4794 to 1885 4897] are of turbiditic facies, mainly comprising silty mudstone with siltstone, sandstone and sideritic ironstone. Several exposures of interbedded fossiliferous mudstone [e.g. 1831 4910 and 1875 4844] contain *Cravenoceras* and *Eumorphoceras* of indeterminate species, indicating that the turbidites probably belong to the same E_{1b} to E_{2a} sequence recorded elsewhere in the Widmerpool Gulf (Frost and Smart, 1979, p.14).   NA,IPS

In the Carsington–Hulland outcrop, sections of proven Pendleian age are rare. The best are in Bradley Dumble near Banktop Farm (SK 25 SW/65) where about 21 m of dark mudstone are exposed, partly calcareous in the basal 5 m, and yielding *Cravenoceras sp.* about 5 m above the base. These mudstones are underlain by interbedded mudstones and thin limestones of the Widmerpool Formation (see p.31). Twenty five metres of probable E_{1a} strata were also proved in a borehole (SK 25 SW/10) near Upper Town. Grey friable mudstone in the uppermost 10.70 m passed down to harder dark grey fossiliferous mudstone, calcareous in part, with collophane patches and a few thin beds of argillaceous limestone. Faunas include fish scales, *P. corrugata*, *Cravenoceras sp.* and *Eumorphoceras* cf. *medusa*. A stream [2298 5183] WSW of Knockerdown exposes 13.1 m of dark mudstone with poorly fossiliferous bullions at two levels. An E_{1a} age is likely because down dip in the same stream [2281 5201] *E. pseudobilingue* occurs in dark calcareous mudstone, probably representing the basal faunal band of the E_{1b} Zone. This goniatite is also present in 1.9 m of ferruginous mudstone in a stream [2332 4757] north of Bradley Nook Farm. A few beds of turbiditic sandstone, interbedded with mudstone inferred to be of either E_{1b} or E_{1c} age, are exposed in streams around Hulland [e.g. 2336 4757 and 2448 4632].   NA

Arnsbergian strata, including highest Minn Sandstones and Hurdlow Sandstones

Arnsbergian strata crop out in anticlinal inliers at the western margin of the district and in an extensive tract from Leekbrook [986 539] to Ramshorn. Outcrops in the eastern area lie immediately north-east of Ashbourne and between Carsington and Hulland. The sequence reaches its maximum thickness of about 350 m around Morridge Side and Winkhill (Figure 14, columns 5,6) and is about 200 m thick north of Hulland; elsewhere it is incomplete or poorly exposed. Approximately half the thickest sequence comprises protoquartzitic sandy and silty turbidites of the Hurdlow and Minn Sandstones or their lateral mudstones-with-sandstones equivalent. Similar thin turbiditic sandstone beds are present in the east in the E_{2c} Zone between the three N. nuculum bands (Plate 6). The calcareous siltstones and mudstones that dominate the underlying Pendleian Stage persist into the E_{2a} Zone between the C. cowlingense and E. bisulcatum bands but above this level they are largely confined to the thick-shelled goniatite bands.

The successions of faunal bands and interbedded strata are similar to those described for the adjacent Buxton district (Aitkenhead and others, 1985, pp.70–76), and for the Duffield Borehole in the adjacent Derby district (Aitkenhead, 1977). The strata include a few laminae, generally 5–10 mm thick, of pale brown to white K-bentonite clay, and the distinctive cherty calcareous or dolomitic siltstone band ('the chert-bed') at the horizon of Ct. nititoides. This band of tough resistant rock, ranging from 0.30 m to 1.15 m thick, is exposed in the Combes valley section in the west and Carsington Reservoir site in the east. It normally yields a rich and varied fossil assemblage and shows incompetent folding in some exposures. Other hard carbonate-rich beds in the mudstones, such as the ankeritic limestones associated with the three N. nuculum bands in the E_{2c} Zone, tend to become decalcified on weathering.

DETAILS

The basal C. cowlingense Band (E_{2a1}) is exposed at Ironpits (SK 05 SE/26) (Trewin and Holdsworth, 1973, loc. 581) and at Lee Brook [0733 4969] near Cauldon (near locality 16 of Morris, 1967b, p.344). At the former locality, the fauna includes C. cowlingense and the band has a 5 mm intercalation of pale K-bentonitic clay in fissile mudstone 1.12 m below it. The fauna at the latter locality includes Eumorphoceras bisulcatum grassingtonense. The band was also exposed in a temporary excavation [0438 5410] near Moorside, where it contained C. cowlingense, P. corrugata and Streblopteria sp. in dark mudstone with calcareous siltstone bands.

The succeeding E. bisulcatum Band (E_{2a2}) is exposed in the railway cutting at Broomyshaw [0672 4980] and in the River Hamps near Waterhouses (SK 05 SE/27). At the latter locality it comprises about 2 m of thinly bedded tough calcareous mudstone and limestone with argillaceous partings; goniatites present include Cravenoceras gairense, E. bisulcatum and Kazakhoceras scaliger. Near Moorside, a band [0422 5411] containing P. corrugata and a 'ghost' of E. bisulcatum is probably the E. bisulcatum Band. The mudstones between and above the faunal bands are poorly exposed hereabouts but temporary pits near the last locality showed mudstone with ironstone bands, passing up to mudstone and siltstone with thin sandstone bands at the base of the highest leaf of Minn Sandstones. This leaf forms the crest of Morridge and is exposed in excavations for walling stone. The best section [0384 5413] shows about 2 m of fine- to coarse-grained sandstone in massive beds 0.3 to 0.5 m thick. The mudstones below the Hurdlow Sandstones are poorly exposed on Morridge and only partially exposed in the River Hamps section east of Winkhill, where fissile mudstone with sideritic ironstone and a few thin sandstone beds probably represents the highest leaf of Minn Sandstones. Above, fossiliferous beds exposed in a mudstone scar [0719 5040]

have yielded C. subplicatum (Morris, 1969, p.163, locality 48) indicating an E_{2b} age, and the main E_{2b} faunal band of Cravenoceratoides edalensis is exposed farther upstream (SK 05 SE/28) where it is underlain, in characteristic fashion, by two pale K-bentonitic clay intercalations. The Ct. edalensis Band was also proved in a site investigation borehole (SK 05 SE/14) near Winkhill.

The outcrop of the Hurdlow Sandstones is marked on Morridge by a complex of irregular ridges. Small exposures suggest that the formation consists mainly of mudstone and siltstone with sharp-based beds of protoquartzite up to 0.5 m thick, as seen, for example, in a ditch [0300 5423] near Town Field Farm, but lenticular bodies dominated by sandstone also occur, and form strong ridge features [032 539, 043 534]. The sandstones range from fine- to very coarse-grained; locally, as in the basal beds near Garstones [030 545], they contain quartz pebbles up to 2 cm in diameter. The formation has been penetrated by site investigation boreholes around Winkhill (SK 05 SE/8–15) and parts of it are well exposed in a deep gully near Pethills, in a disused quarry at Winkhill, and in a railway cutting at Broomyshaw. The Pethills section (SK 05 SE/25) comprises about 16 m of sandstone, in sole-marked beds up to 0.5 m thick, interbedded with mudstone with ironstone nodules. At Winkhill Quarry [0610 5148] about 4 m of fine-grained protoquartzitic sandstone are exposed in mainly massive amalgamated beds up to 0.93 m thick. The railway cutting [064 502] at Broomyshaw exposes about 27 m of similar sandstone with seams of mudflake cavities, and with thin ripple-laminated divisions forming the top part of some otherwise massive beds. Plant fragments are abundant on some laminae.

The mudstones above the Hurdlow Sandstones form a broad valley at Bottom House [041 527] but there are few exposures. The best section [047 523] shows a few metres of grey mudstone with diffusely-bounded siltstone bands. Miospores from these beds (MPA 2746) indicate an age within the range Pendleian to Arnsbergian as they do also (MPA 2745) for mudstone exposed in a railway cutting [0344 5182] adjacent to the faulted outcrop of turbiditic protoquartzites at Blakelow. These sandstones, and those of a neighbouring outcrop [026 522] are on this evidence referred to the highest part of the Hurdlow Sandstones. NA,JIC

To the west and south-west of Morridge, Arnsbergian strata are best exposed in the Combes valley (Figure 14, column 2) and south of Cheddleton (Figure 14, column 1). In Combes Brook south of Ballfields the 'chert-bed' that marks the Ct. nititoides horizon (highest E_{2b}) is exposed [0077 5292] as 0.3 m of lenticularly colour-banded sideritic and shaly chert on 0.5 m of dark fissile mudstone with wispy sideritic bands. The fauna includes Eumorphoceras rostratum (Bolton, 1978, locality 084). About 40 m of dark mudstone are seen in discontinuous exposures below, resting on a 20 m sequence of turbiditic sandstone interbedded with siltstone and mudstone. The turbidites are correlated with the highest Minn Sandstones (Figure 14, column 2).

Farther east, and across the Sixoaks Fault, Combes Brook runs obliquely across the strike of some poorly exposed mudstones with ironstone bands. Among these have been found a few fossiliferous beds including one [0188 5333] with Nuculoceras stellarum (E_{2c}) and another [0192 5334] with Actinopteria regularis. Both are known to lie close above the 'chert-bed' but this is not exposed here. Sandstones that crop out on the hill [010 536] north of Ballfields apparently underlie the mudstones, for which reason they are correlated, like the 20 m sequence described above, with the highest of the Minn Sandstones.

The Hurdlow Sandstones crop out at the northern end of the Combes valley, where they are identified by the presence of the underlying N. stellarum Band [0188 5333]. Two leaves can be distinguished. East of Apesford the top leaf, about 90 m thick, is exposed in the stream bed [0235 5354], where fine- to coarse-grained sandstone in graded beds up to 0.8 m thick is interbedded with siltstone and mudstone. Below, and also exposed in the stream [022 535], are some 50 m of mudstone with ironstone bands and sporadic layers of sandstone. The lower leaf, about 20 m thick, is made up of fine- to medium-grained sandstone in beds up to 0.4 m thick, with many mudstone and siltstone bands. Both leaves are of turbidite facies here, but farther to the south-west, near Padwick [013 526], only the upper leaf consists of undoubted turbidites. The lower leaf, seen in a 6 m crag [0108 5277], is of indeterminate facies, being composed of fine- to coarse-grained parallel- and ripple-laminated sandstone with mudstone clasts and much plant debris.

The mudstones above the Hurdlow Sandstones are estimated to be about 200 m thick (Figure 14, column 2). The lowest 65 m or so are of Arnsbergian age and contain ankeritic limestone bands with *Nuculoceras nuculum* (E_{2c}). Bolton (1978, localities 083, 082, 081) recognised three such bands in the Combes valley; the lowest, 0.6 m thick [0066 5292] is separated from the second, which is 0.1 m thick [0066 5285] by 8.0 m of mudstone with ironstone bands. The uppermost [0063 5269], 7 cm thick, lies some 33 m higher in the sequence; the intervening mudstone is incompletely exposed. Ankeritic beds with *N. nuculum* have also been found among the mudstones along the strike to the south-east, in Backhill Wood [010 524].

Arnsbergian rocks are represented among the folded and faulted strata north of the Combes valley. Blocks of the 'chert-bed', dug

from a trial pit [9974 5402] in Jackfield Plantation, indicate the presence of the *Ct. nititoides* Band. An overlying sandstone, 4.5 m thick, must represent the Hurdlow Sandstones. It is fine-grained, ripple-laminated and parallel-laminated, in sharp-based beds with grooved soles. Overlying fossiliferous mudstones are poorly exposed but near Middle Cliff a fauna indicating the highest of the *N. nuculum* bands has been collected from 0.1 m of black fissile mudstone in the stream bed [0002 5477] immediately below a prominent 2 m rib of hard calcareous mudstone. The fauna includes *E. bisulcatum*, *N. nuculum*, *Fayettevillea darwenense* and *Posidonia corrugata*. The underlying mudstones, about 40 m thick, are discontinuously exposed but contain *P. corrugata* at several levels. A sandstone exposed [0012 5491] below the mudstones is inferred to lie at the top of the Hurdlow Sandstones.

South-west of the Combes valley, around Cheddleton, no exposures of the Minn Sandstones are known, but some 13 m of grey siltstone with thin sandstone beds, with base at 128.6 m in the Cheddleton Paper Mills No.1 Borehole (SJ 95 SE/26), probably represent the top of them, since *N. stellarum* has been collected (Hester, 1932, p.38) from the overlying mudstone at a depth of 79.9 m. The strata below 128.6 m were not seen by a geologist but the driller reported 'no change' to the bottom of the hole at 176.8 m. Some 24 m of dark siltstone with thin bands of sandstone proved in the same borehole immediately above the *N. stellarum* Band rep-

Plate 6 Namurian turbidites, Carsington Reservoir site [2471 5087]

Typical mudstones-with-sandstones turbidite facies comprising sharp-based, graded, fine-grained protoquartzitic sandstones and siltstones interbedded with silty mudstone, here of E_{2c} age. The exposure was in a borrow pit for the reservoir dam embankment (MN 2640715)

resent some or all of the Hurdlow Sandstones. If all the Hurdlow Sandstones are present the sequence is unusually thin compared with those of adjacent areas; the alternative view has therefore been adopted (Figure 14, column 1), that the 24 m represent only a lower leaf of the sandstones. The top of the Hurdlow Sandstones is exposed in the bed of a stream [9773 5124] near Ashcombe Park, where up to 1 m of white siliceous fine- to medium-grained sandstone dips beneath dark grey mudstone from the lowest parts of which *N. nuculum* and *I. subglobosum* have been obtained.

South of Consall, and at the western margin of the district, the sequence in the Overmoor Anticline is poorly exposed. A degraded exposure [9612 4618] near the core of the anticline north of Heywood Grange has yielded *Cravenoceras* cf. *subplicatum* and *Eumorphoceras sp.*, indicating that the lowest beds seen are of E_{2b} age; they are protoquartzites and mudstones which must correlate in a general way with the Minn and Hurdlow sandstones.

South of Ipstones Edge only the Ipstones Edge Borehole (Figure 14, column 4; SK 05 SW/8) has provided any information on rocks of Arnsbergian age. At the bottom of the borehole 4.26 m of mudstone are overlain by 12.65 m of interbedded siltstone and fine- to medium-grained sandstone, taken to represent the top leaf of the Hurdlow Sandstones; they included a few graded beds. Above lie 2.58 m of mudstone with bivalves, separated by a fault from 11.94 m of mudstone with bivalves, *Lingula* and two *N. nuculum* bands. The fault is thought to cut out the lowest *N. nuculum* band and the throw, from a comparison with the Combes valley sections (Figure 14, column 2), is estimated at 40 m.

Arnsbergian strata are thinner over the Dinantian shelf limestone remnant at Caldon Low than elsewhere (Figure 14, column 7) but exact figures are not available. There are no exposures except in the south, where an excavation [0920 4598] near Kevin Quarry provided a section of the *E. bisulcatum* Band in brown decalcified silty mudstone, resting on grey silty mudstone and overlain by about 10 m of darker mudstone with ironstone bands. The absence of ridge features in this ground suggests that all the sandstone units have died out. JIC

At the eastern edge of the district the Arnsbergian sequence in the Carsington-Hulland area differs from that in the west, mainly in the absence of named, feature-forming turbiditic sandstones. Finer-grained turbidite units are present, however, both at the same levels as farther west and at higher levels (Plate 6). The generalised section (Figure 14, column 8) resembles that proved in the Duffield Borehole (Aitkenhead, 1977, figure 2), some 12 km to the south-east.

The basal E_{2a} *Cravenoceras cowlingense* Band is probably represented by a 0.94 m exposure of fossiliferous mudstone and argillaceous limestone near Knockerdown [2378 5212] and another small exposure near Atlow [2365 4839]. The overlying *Eumorphoceras bisulcatum* Band is exposed in a stream [2372 4843] near the last-mentioned locality and in two other stream sections near Hulland. The best of the latter [2460 4622] consists of 2.6 m of grey mudstone, platy in part, yielding a fauna comprising *Dunbarella yatesae*, *Obliquipecten costatus* (juv.), *P. corrugata*, *P. corrugata elongata*, *E. bisulcatum* and crinoid columnals. The succeeding turbiditic sequence is probably represented by a 5.15 m section (SK 24 NW/19) nearby in the same stream. The lithology comprises interbedded sandstone/siltstone and mudstone in a ratio of about 3:2. Parts of this sequence have been penetrated by several of the Carsington Reservoir site investigation boreholes (e.g. SK 25 SW/7, 9, 11, 13 and 14), 4 km to the north, which show an overall sandstone/siltstone to mudstone ratio of about 1:2. The highest faunal band of E_{2a} yielded *E. sp* (juv.) in boreholes SK 25 SW/7 and 14, and lay 2.19 m above the top of the turbiditic sequence in the latter borehole. In the outlier north-east of Ashbourne, E_{2a} faunas occur in two localities [1910 4815 and 1909 4807] in Punches Dumble, near Ashbourne Green (Charsley, 1979, p.239).

The *Cravenoceratoides edalensis* Band at the base of E_{2b} is exposed only in a deep ditch [2420 5236] south-west of Shiningford where platy partially decalcified mudstone forming the lowest 1.4 m of a 4.4 m mudstone section contains *P. corrugata*, *P. corrugata gigantea*, orthocone nautiloid, *Dimorphoceras* s.l. and *Ct. edalensis*. Elsewhere it is recorded in boreholes, as in SK 25 SW/7 where the band is 2.37 m thick. The middle E_{2b} band (*Ct. nitidus*) is recorded only in borehole SK 25 SW/30 at a depth of 17.65 m. The uppermost E_{2b} band, that of *Ct. nititoides* and *E. rostratum* with its distinctive cherty siltstone lithology, was found to be traceable from the section (SK 25 SW/66) near Shiningford to boreholes and temporary exposures at the Carsington Reservoir dam site. The band in the aforementioned section yielded the typical rich and varied fauna and shows incompetent folding similar to that found in other districts (Aitkenhead and others, 1985, p.74). Although exposure is poor and fossil recovery from boreholes incomplete, it is clear that the E_{2b} sequences between the main faunal bands are similar in this area to those proved in the Duffield Borehole (Aitkenhead, 1977, p.20). The *Nuculoceras stellarum* Band, at the base of E_{2c}, was proved in boreholes SK 25 SW/31, 43 and 69, and typically consists of a 0.20 m bed of hard grey carbonate siltstone or mudstone with abundant *Posidoniella* aff. *vetusta* and *N. stellarum*. The band was also seen in a temporary section (SK 25 SW/76) where the overlying sequence includes 5.43 m of grey pyritic mudstone with the bivalve *Actinopteria sp.*, lying 3.73 m below a 0.30 m band of brown platy carbonate mudstone with poorly preserved goniatites. The latter represents the lowest of the three main *N. nuculum* bands. The overlying sequence, up to the level of the middle *N. nuculum* band, is not completely proved but is probably similar to that in the Duffield Borehole. The strata include turbiditic siltstones and sandstones between the lower and middle *N. nuculum* bands, proved in the basal 4.0 m of borehole SK 24 NW/8. The same facies also occurs higher in this borehole, between the middle and upper *N. nuculum* bands. The unit is thicker (6.60 m) than its correlative in Duffield Borehole (4.80 m) and the turbidites are more proximal, containing a higher proportion of sandstone and siltstone (about 50 per cent) relative to mudstone. The *N. nuculum* bands themselves consist of single beds of hard grey ankeritic limestone up to 0.80 m thick. NA

Chokierian and Alportian strata, including Cheddleton Sandstones and lower part of Ipstones Edge Sandstones

In the western area the combined thickness of Chokierian and Alportian strata proved in the Ipstones Edge Borehole (SK 05 SW/8: Figure 14, column 4) is 131.83 m. The boundary between the two stages is poorly defined due to the absence of the *Hudsonoceras proteus* Band, here probably represented by mudstones with *Lingula*. A short distance to the east (Figure 14, column 6), the thickness may be twice as much due to the thick development of the Ipstones Edge Sandstones. In contrast, in the eastern area where the *Hd. proteus* Band is present and only thin sandstone beds occur, the thicknesses are 39.13 m for the Chokierian and a minimum of 8.78 m for the Alportian (Figure 14, column 8). Faunal bands are common here; the Alportian mudstones, in particular, are almost continuously fossiliferous.

DETAILS

The sequence in the eastern area, between Carsington and Hulland (Figure 14, column 8), is described first. The Chokierian (H_1) Stage is known only from boreholes SK 24 NW/8 and SK 25 SW/15, and from temporary sections, including SK 25 SW/75 in a 'borrow pit' that provided mudstone for the Carsington dam. The latter section extends from mudstones with bullions containing *Isohomoceras subglobosum* in H_{1a}, to the R_{1c} Zone. Borehole SK 24 NW/8 proved three levels with *I. subglobosum* in 7.53 m of strata compared with about 15 m of similar strata in a borrow pit [2473 5113] indicating the likely range of thickness for the H_{1a} Zone. The overlying H_{1b} Zone, some 32 m thick, contains calcareous mudstones with *Homoceras beyrichianum* and *Isohomoceras sp.* in the lower part, and mudstones with a few sandstone/siltstone turbidite beds up to 3 cm thick forming a 7.93 m sequence in the upper part. Borehole SK 25 SW/15 and section SK 25 SW/75 provide the best record of the zone, which is estimated to be 31.6 m thick. The borehole proved an *I. subglobosum* band, of uncertain zonal assignation, near the bottom. The H_{1b} Zone is certainly represented by the higher strata in this hole, including 0.18 m of brown decalcified mudstone with abundant *H. beyrichianum*. An isolated in-situ bullion in Scow Brook [2497 5093] yielded *Hd. proteus*, representing the basal faunal band of the Alportian (H_2) Stage. Nearby the whole Alportian mudstone succession, only 8.78 m thick, is recorded in the borrow pit section (SK 25 SW/75). It includes a basal lenticular-bedded limestone band up to 0.42 m thick, with *Hd. proteus*, and several bullion beds in fossiliferous grey-brown to dark grey mudstones with barren grey bands. A somewhat thicker (10.05 m) H_2 mudstone sequence proved in borehole SK 25 SE/61, about 0.5 km to the south-east, contains two thin beds of argillaceous limestone. The lower bed immediately underlies a faunal band containing *H. smithii* and therefore probably represents the *Hd. proteus* horizon. NA

In the western area the Ipstones Edge Borehole (SK 05 SW/8) provides an excellent section (Figure 14, column 4; Figure 15) through the Chokierian and Alportian beds. The lowest Chokierian mudstones, 16.75 m thick, contain several thin limestone bands and the fauna comprises bivalves, *Lingula* and goniatites including *I. subglobosum* and *H. beyrichianum*. The overlying 10.73 m of mudstone contain no limestones and the fauna consists of bivalves and *Lingula* only. Above the mudstone are 12.58 m of siltstone with bands of fine- to medium-grained sandstone, some of them graded; they make up the lowest leaf of the Cheddleton Sandstones here (Figure 15, D), but are perhaps also equivalent to the Lum Edge Sandstones of the district to the north (Aitkenhead and others, 1985, p.78) The overlying 25.41 m of siltstone and mudstone contain bivalves, *Lingula* and fish debris, but no goniatites; however, they are believed to be equivalent to the *Hd. proteus* Band and the boundary between Chokierian and Alportian is provisionally drawn at their base. Above lie 12.15 m of siltstone (Figure 15, C) with ripple-laminated sandstone bands, but no graded beds, and these are overlain by 6.86 m of unfossiliferous mudstone and siltstone, perhaps a representative of the lowest *H. undulatum* band. The overlying 43.61 m include the main Cheddleton Sandstones in two leaves (Figure 15, A, B), consisting of fine-, medium- and coarse-grained protoquartzitic sandstone in erosive-based units up to about 4 m thick, interbedded with siltstone. Scattered quartz pebbles up to 1 cm in diameter are present in some beds. All are apparently of shallow-water facies. The sandstone leaves are separated by argillaceous beds with *Lingula* and fish debris, perhaps equivalent to another *H. undulatum* band. The 3.74 m of mudstone above the Cheddleton Sandstones contain abundant fossils, including *Homoceratoides prereticulatus* in the lower part, and Kinderscoutian faunas above.

Chokierian and Alportian strata crop out some 2.5 km north-west of the Ipstones Edge Borehole, in the Combes valley. A thick sequence of mudstone above the *N. nuculum* bands (Figure 14, column 2) is presumed to be of Chokierian age, though no faunal bands are exposed. The overlying Cheddleton Sandstones are up to about 40 m thick and form a continuous ridge on the east side of the valley but to the west appear as disconnected lenses. They are of shallow-water facies, consisting of fine- to very coarse-grained, cross-bedded, parallel-laminated and ripple-laminated sandstone with rounded siliceous pebbles up to 5 cm in diameter. There is a lens of conglomerate locally at Sharpcliffe Rocks [015 520], with cross-

bedding in sets up to 2.5 m thick; foreset dip directions indicate local palaeocurrent flow from the north.

To the north some 75 m of striped unfossiliferous mudstone exposed upstream from Ashenhurst Mill [999 545] are believed to belong to the Chokierian Stage, because they appear to lie in sequence above an *N. nuculum* band exposed [0004 5478] near Middle Cliff. The section includes several small faults, one of which has probably cut out the *I. subglobosum* bands. West of the Combes valley, the basal mudstone with *I. subglobosum* is exposed [9771 5107] not far above the Hurdlow Sandstones near Ashcombe Park. The highest 33 m of the mudstone were proved in Cheddleton Paper Mills No.2 Borehole (SJ 95 SE/27), with *I. subglobosum* some 24.4 m below the sharp base of the overlying sandstones. The type locality of these, the Cheddleton Sandstones, is an old quarry [9816 5197] by the River Churnet near Churnet Grange, where 4 m of fine- to coarse-grained siliceous sandstone with rolling depositional dips are exposed. Small exposures to the north [980 521] show similar sandstone with scattered quartz pebbles up to 1 cm and large plant stems. All the sandstones are apparently of fluviatile facies. The highest 38 m of the Cheddleton Sandstones, interbedded with mudstone and siltstone, were proved at the bottom of Cheddleton Paper Mills No.16 Borehole (SJ 95 SE/35), where they are overlain by mudstone of Kinderscoutian age.

South-east of the Combes valley, the mudstone that contains the Kinderscoutian marine bands cannot be traced for more than 0.5 km east of the Ipstones Edge Borehole, so that on Ipstones Edge the Cheddleton Sandstones cannot be separated from the overlying Kniveden Sandstones. All are, therefore, referred to as Ipstones Edge Sandstones, which range in age from Chokierian to Kinderscoutian. The sandstones are best seen in an old cutting [0631 4802] near Windy Harbour, where 3 m of fine- to very coarse-grained poorly bedded sandstone overlie 10 m of fine-grained ripple-laminated sandstone with purplish siltstone bands. Rib and furrow structures indicate palaeocurrent flow to the NNE. From its maximum thickness of between 200 and 300 m, near Swineholes Wood [045 503] (Figure 14, column 6), the sequence thins to the south-east as individual sandstones die out until at Moorside [066 476] only the highest bed remains; another generalized section (Figure 14, column 7) has been drawn near here. South of Moorside, the sequence thickens up again by the addition of sandstones at progressively lower levels. At Ramshorn [082 452] the sandstones disappear beneath the Trias, but an isolated inlier of protoquartzite [093 445] in Wootton Park suggests that they continue in strength for some distance to the south-east.

Kinderscoutian strata, including Kniveden Sandstones and upper part of Ipstones Edge Sandstones

Kinderscoutian strata are between 40 and 80 m thick in the western area. Around Cheddleton, the Combes valley and Ipstones, fossiliferous mudstones of R_{1a} to R_{1b} age are overlain by the Kniveden Sandstones, but between Ipstones and Ramshorn the poorly exposed sequence is inferred to consist largely of sandstone and siltstone, the upper part of the Ipstones Edge Sandstones. In the eastern area, where the sequence reaches a maximum thickness of about 70 m, there is an almost complete record of the dominantly mudstone sequence from boreholes and excavations for the Carsington Reservoir scheme. Goniatite bands including those of *Hodsonites magistrorum*, *Reticuloceras eoreticulatum* and *R. reticulatum* (the last is the lower of two bands yielding this goniatite) are present, marking the bases of the R_{1a}, R_{1b} and R_{1c} zones respectively. Distal sandstone and siltstone turbidites occur mainly in the R_{1c} Zone but do not form a mappable unit. Three K-bentonitic clay bands are present in the R_{1a} Zone at the Carsington Reservoir site, at similar levels to occurrences in the adjacent district north-east of Leek (Ashton, 1974; Aitkenhead and others, 1985, p.80).

DETAILS

The best sections of Kinderscoutian strata are in the Combes valley. The mudstones responsible for large landslips in The Combes [004 524] contain several faunal marker bands in the lower part (Figure 14, column 2). Stratigraphically significant goniatites collected during the recent resurvey are *Reticuloceras circumplicatile* [at 0048 5243], *R.* ex. gr. *dubium* and *R. nodosum* [at 0041 5238], and *R.* cf. *reticulatum* [at 0038 5238]. Many of the mudstone exposures are landslipped, so that the exact relationships between the faunas cannot be determined; they do, however, indicate a range of ages from R_{1a} to R_{1c}. Morris (1967a) recorded faunas from part of this range as did Ashton (1974). The mudstone passes up into siltstone with bands of ripple-laminated sandstone, well exposed in crags [0031 5204 and 0017 5168]. All are of shallow-water facies, as are the overlying Kniveden Sandstones. These are about 20 to 25 m thick and comprise fine- to very coarse-grained rocks showing cross bedding, parallel and ripple-lamination. There are sporadic layers of small pebbles, and plant stems are common in places. Exposures on both sides of the valley are good, especially at [0044 5272], where some 10 m are seen, and at [0056 5229] where 7 m are exposed.

To the west of the Combes valley, near Cheddleton, fossiliferous mudstone 44 m thick was proved between the Cheddleton and Kniveden sandstones in Cheddleton Paper Mills No.16 Borehole (SJ 95 SE/35). Goniatites characteristic of the R_{1c} Zone, *R. reticulatum* and *Vallites striolatus*, were collected at levels below the base of the Kniveden Sandstones of 2.8 and 38.4 m respectively. The mudstone is not exposed in the area. The lowest 16.6 m of the Kniveden Sandstones, as proved in this borehole, contain a high proportion of interbedded mudstone. The main body of overlying sandstone forms a prominent feature [972 506] south of Ashcombe Park and the top part is well exposed in Felthouse Wood [978 500], where the steam runs along a strike section of the contact with the overlying Marsdenian mudstone; the sandstones are hard, white, siliceous and roughly flat-bedded.

The highest 25.27 m of mudstone in the Ipstones Edge Borehole (Figure 14, column 4; SK 05 SW/8) are of Kinderscoutian age. The lower half contains abundant goniatites that indicate the presence of the R_{1a} and R_{1b} zones, but the upper half contains only sparse bivalves and fish debris. Overlying unexposed mudstones and siltstones, with an estimated thickness of about 34 m, crop out to the south of the borehole and are succeeded by a small ridge [026 510] of protoquartzitic sandstone near New House. This is correlated with the Kniveden Sandstones by virtue of its position above the fossiliferous mudstones. These mudstones form a well marked slack between the Kniveden and Cheddleton sandstones, and can be traced by this means to near Crumwithies [033 509], where the slack dies out among the Ipstones Edge Sandstones.   JIC

At the eastern margin of the district Kinderscoutian mudstones with minor turbiditic sandstones, about 70 m thick, are inferred to crop out below the Ashover Grit escarpment [253 516 to 252 501]. Exposures are poor and the rocks are known mainly from borehole SK 25 SE/61 and the borrow-pit section SK 25 SW/75, the latter providing the best record of the lowest 42 m of the sequence, with most of the known goniatite horizons present (Figure 14, column 8). The R_{1a} Zone, 11.64 m thick, consists of dark grey to black fissile mudstone and blocky calcareous mudstone, with limestone bullion beds at the level of *R. circumplicatile* and just below the *R. todmordenense/R. paucicrenulatum* horizon. Three pale grey K-bentonitic clay laminae occur in the lowest part of the sequence, between the *Hodsonites magistrorum* and *R.* cf. *circumplicatile* levels. The R_{1b} Zone includes similar fossiliferous mudstones with scattered bullion bands but a few sharp-based turbiditic sandstone beds up to 6 cm

thick are also present in the top 3.37 m of the 12.60 m sequence. The lowest 17.76 m only of the R_{1c} Zone are present, including two goniatite bands lying at and 3.84 m above the base, both containing *R. reticulatum*. 9.70 m of grey silty mudstone with thickly interbedded sandstone, siltstone and ironstone occur above the higher *R. reticulatum* band; the total thickness is probably double that temporarily exposed. The arenaceous beds are of distal turbidite facies, are individually up to 0.1 m thick, and together form about 13 per cent of this mudstone-with-sandstone sequence. These beds are inferred to lie below the highest R_{1c} goniatite band (*R. coreticulatum*; equivalent to the Butterly Marine Band) recorded in the Derby district in the Callow Borehole (Frost and Smart, 1979, p.166b). They are, therefore, the stratigraphical equivalent of the Lower Kinderscout Grit / Shale Grit / Mam Tor Sandstones sequence (Stevenson and Gaunt, 1971, plate 17), though not necessarily derived from the same source area.   NA

Marsdenian strata, including Brockholes Sandstones, Ashover, Roaches and Chatsworth grits

The Marsdenian sequence does not vary greatly in the western outcrop area (Figure 14, columns 1 – 3, 6 – 7), where it is 125 to 170 m in thickness. Mudstone at the base contains a sequence of goniatite bands from *Reticuloceras gracile* (R_{2a}) to *R. metabilingue* (R_{2b}). In the south and west these are followed by protoquartzites, the Brockholes Sandstones, but in the east and north by a feldspathic sandstone, the Roaches Grit. Both appear to die out near Ipstones but exposures are poor and the relationship between them cannot be demonstrated; however, in a ravine [959 559] just beyond the north-west corner of the district (Sheet 110), near Great Longsdon Farm, sandstones of the two facies interdigitate (SJ 95 NE/19). The Roaches Grit predominates here, in four leaves spread over a thickness of 60 m; the Brockholes Sandstones are represented by 2 m of fine-grained siliceous sandstone with mudstone bands, overlain by a thin coal, between the top and second leaves of the Roaches Grit.

Above the sandstones of R_{2b} lie mudstones, with the *R. superbilingue* and *Donetzoceras sigma* bands (R_{2c}), which pass up into the thickest of the feldspathic sandstones, the Chatsworth Grit. Thin coals generally overlie the Roaches and Chatsworth grits and have been worked in places. In the east of the district the basal mudstone with R_{2a} to R_{2b} goniatite bands is overlain by thick turbidites belonging to the feldspathic facies and forming the lowest leaves of the Ashover Grit (Figure 14, column 8).

DETAILS

South of Cheddleton, the lowest mudstones are seen in a stream bed at Felthouse Wood [979 502], and R_{2a} and R_{2b} faunas have been collected from them. A limestone containing *R. gracile* preserved in solid form was recorded from here by Hester (1932, p.39), but without precise details of locality. Subsequently, though the limestone has not been located, the *R. gracile* Band has been found in mudstones [9799 5020] immediately above the Kniveden Sandstones. Ashton (1974, locality 114) assigned this fauna to the lowest leaf of the *R. gracile* Band but mistakenly believed that it lay beneath the Kniveden Sandstones. The overlying mudstones contain two other marine bands, the *R. bilingue* early form Band exposed [9798 5023] close to the last locality and the *R. bilingue* late form Band seen [9813 5043] some 250 m downstream. The mudstones pass up through siltstone into fine-grained siliceous sandstone on the east bank of the stream. The sandstone is the lowest of the Brockholes

Sandstones, and is better exposed in an old quarry nearby [9846 5057], where it is fine- to coarse-grained, in lenticular beds up to 0.5 m thick with partings of purplish-grey silty mudstone. The main leaf of the Brockholes Sandstones is poorly exposed in Consall Wood [983 502]; loose blocks of white siliceous sandstone are fine to coarse in grain, with some pebbly lithologies.

In the Combes valley the lowest mudstones are poorly exposed, but in one good section [0036 5145] *R. metabilingue* and *R. bilingue* early form (R_{2b}) occur in a 0.5 m band among mudstones faulted against sandstone. This, as seen in small exposures nearby, varies from very fine- to very coarse-grained and contains siltstone bands. It is believed to be one of the Brockholes Sandstones; the type locality of these [0115 5129] lies about 0.8 km to the east, where 5 m of parallel-laminated fine- to coarse-grained protoquartzitic sandstone are visible in an old quarry. To the south, some of the overlying mudstones are exposed in a small ravine, with *D. sigma* in a 5 cm band [0135 5101]. The Chatsworth Grit forms a strong escarpment above, at Coltstone [014 507], and is well exposed at Gog and Magog [006 504] where 16 m of very coarse-grained cross-bedded sandstone, with scattered quartz pebbles up to 2 cm across, can be seen. The cross bedding indicates palaeocurrent flow to the south-west. Nearby, in the Abovechurch Borehole (SK 05 SW/6), an upward-coarsening sequence from mudstone to sandy siltstone was overlain by the Chatsworth Grit, 44 m thick (Figure 14, column 3). A seam of coal, 0.86 m thick in the borehole, lies just above the grit and has been worked (Barrow, 1903, p.8) from adits and shallow pits, traces of which can still be seen along the outcrop [009 501, 019 507]. Shafts up to 45 m deep were sunk to the coal near Oddo Hall [013 501], and even deeper (about 60 m) near New House Farm [020 493]. Old workings in the seam are visible in a stream [0371 4941] at Ipstones Park, overlain by 5.6 m of dark mudstone below the *G. cancellatum* Band.

A stream section [026 502] at Lowtop, north of Ipstones, shows an upward-coarsening sequence below a thick, coarse-grained sandstone thought to be the Chatsworth Grit, but the section is bounded by faults and the sandstone could alternatively be the Rough Rock.

In the area south-east of Ipstones, the *R. gracile* Band is well exposed at Star Wood, Cotton Dell [0612 4608] and is in two leaves. The lower, a red-weathering ankeritic limestone 0.1 m thick lying 1.2 m above the top of the Ipstones Edge Sandstones, contains goniatites in solid preservation and has been described by Alkins (1923, pp.39–40), Morris (1969, p.169) and Ashton (1974, pp.308–310). The upper leaf, 1.7 m thick, consists of mudstone with a 0.2 m limestone near the centre and is separated from the lower leaf by 1.8 m of mainly barren mudstone.

The mudstones above contain several goniatite bands, including *R. bilingue* early form [0616 4635 and 0564 4740], and *R. eometabilingue* with *R. metabilingue* [0612 4577]. Ashton (1974, localities 153–155) also records *R. bilingue* 'sensu stricto' from Cotton Dell. Sections are not continuous, so that the exact levels of these bands in the sequence are not known and the arrangement shown (Figure 14, column 7) is somewhat conjectural. However, the total thickness of mudstone and siltstone present between the top of the Ipstones Edge Sandstones and the base of the Roaches Grit is about 43 m in a borehole (SK 04 NE/2B) at Cauldon Low Pumping Station, near Upper Cotton, and a similar thickness is probably present at Cotton Dell.

The Roaches Grit lies at the top of an upward-coarsening sequence. Cross bedded fine- to coarse-grained sandstone 2.9 m thick overlies 2.3 m of interbedded siltstone and fine-grained sandstone in a small ravine [0646 4630] below Cotton College, and underlying siltstones exposed in adjacent ravines pass down into mudstone [0632 4632]. The coarse-grained facies forms extensive dip slopes around Upper Cotton [055 476] and up to 3 m are exposed in an old railway cutting [054 480]. The full thickness is unlikely to exceed 10 m, and the Roaches Grit is absent in places, as in the Ramshorn Borehole (SK 04 NE/1). The top is seen in a ditch [0666 4665] near

the college, where it is interbedded with siltstone and overlain by a thin earthy coal. Small workings close to the outcrop of the seam are visible in Star Wood [062 455], by Bleach Farm [056 474] and by Longshaw Brook [069 449], but the thicknesses extracted are not known.

In Shirley Hollow (SK 04 NW/49; Figure 14, column 6), about 6 m of well bedded mudstone and siltstone are exposed below the Roaches Grit, which is about 15 m thick. The grit is made up mainly of fine-grained micaceous ripple-laminated sandstone, with interbedded siltstone and mudstone; a single bed of medium- to very coarse-grained cross-bedded sandstone up to 5 m thick is present towards the top. Discontinuous exposures of the sandstone in the sides of Shirley Hollow [043 487 to 031 479] extend over a distance of about 1.5 km. The unit was named after this locality by Morris (1969, p.166) but its identity with the Roaches Grit of the Leek area is now established beyond doubt. The sandstone forms extensive dip-slopes to the north and east of Shirley but to the north-west is faulted against Chatsworth Grit near Ipstones Park Farm [039 496]. Beyond the fault it appears to continue as a small ridge with exposures of red coarse-grained sandstone, and this can be traced north-westwards to a point [0302 5041] near Crowgutter, where it dies out. The top of the sandstone contains rootlets and is overlain in places by a thin shaly coal; this is 0.3 m thick where seen [0379 4809] in Shirley Hollow.

Fossiliferous mudstones above the coal are exposed at several places in Shirley Hollow. The best section [0379 4809] shows 6.7 m of mudstone, with *D. sigma* in two thin bands at 3.0 m and 3.8 m below the top and *R. superbilingue* in the lowest 1.1 m, resting on 2.7 m of silty mudstone; this in turn rests on the coal. Barren mudstone above the fossiliferous beds is exposed in a ravine [041 481] near Oldridge and passes up into siltstone [0370 4796]. The overlying Chatsworth Grit forms a strong escarpment and is well exposed, notably around Harston Rock [034 478] and at Garston Rocks [050 475]. It is cross-bedded and very coarse-grained. Cross bedding at Garston Rocks indicates palaeocurrent flow to the south-west. The total thickness of sandstone in this area is estimated at about 60 m, in a single leaf at Oldridge and Garston Rocks but in two leaves south of Foxt [035 485]. The coal above the Chatsworth Grit was worked around Gimmershill [033 473] from shafts, the thickness ranging from 0.5 to 0.9 m; crop workings have been seen in a ravine [038 477] near Oldridge and on the hillside [053 473] south-east of Garston Rocks.

Farther south, around Cotton and Oakamoor, the Chatsworth Grit is in two leaves, the lower up to 8 m thick and impersistent, the upper 25 to 35 m thick. Both are composed mainly of cross-bedded coarse-grained sandstone. The sharp base of the upper leaf rests on purple siltstone in Star Wood [0578 4546] and the highest 4 m, which are finer grained, are well exposed in a nearby ravine [0556 4540]. To the north of these exposures a coal, its presence revealed by crop workings [054 459], lies about two metres above the grit but to the south, as around Goldenhill Farm [060 450], about 15 m of reddened siltstone and fine-grained sandstone intervene between grit and coal. The seam has been worked from shallow pits around Beelow Hill [065 449], in Carr Wood [052 452] and to the south-east of Cotton [065 456]. JIC

In the Carsington–Hulland area, the outcrop of the lowest sandstones of the Ashover Grit just extends into the district south of Carsington. One borehole (SK 25 SE/62), of many drilled along the line of the Carsington Reservoir aqueduct, started in the sandstone and penetrated the base of the Marsdenian strata. It reached a depth of 90 m, proving the *R. gracile* Band in the basal 7.0 m, an *R. bilingue* band from 77.80 m to 80.10 m, and a band containing *R. eometabilingue* and *R. bilingue* from 64.97 to 65.90 m. The sequence containing the faunal bands is entirely of mudstone, pyritic in places and with a few thin sideritic bands. Above the highest band with *R. eometabilingue*, turbidite beds prevail, the lithology showing an overall gradual coarsening upwards from silty mudstone to fine-and medium-grained feldspathic sandstone, the latter predominating in the top 30 m where it forms the lowest leaf of the Ashover Grit. Sharp-based graded beds showing the Bouma (1962) sequence of internal sedimentary structures are common and the top 20 m consists largely of massive (non-laminated) divisions indicating a proximal position on the delta-front. This overall change illustrates the gradual prograding of the Ashover Grit delta into the Central Pennine Basin in late R_{2b} times (see Jones, 1980, figs. 1 and 13). NA

Yeadonian strata, including Rough Rock

Yeadonian strata are present only in the western area, where they crop out around the margin of the Cheadle Coalfield and on the western flank of the Overmoor Anticline. The succession is similar to that present over a wide area of the southern Pennines, comprising mudstones with the *Gastrioceras cancellatum* Band at the base and the *G. cumbriense* Band a few metres higher, overlain by a sandstone, the Rough Rock. The lower mudstone sequence generally totals about 37 m in thickness and the Rough Rock ranges from 5 m to 35 m, being thinnest along the western margin of the district.

Details

The best section of Yeadonian strata is provided by Ruelow Wood No. 3 Borehole (Figure 14, column 3; SK 04 NW/5). The *Gastrioceras cancellatum* Band, in two leaves, consists of mudstone with goniatites including *G. crencellatum* 0.10 m, below barren mudstone 0.66 m, below mudstone with *G. crencellatum* 0.71 m. Barren mudstone 1.98 m thick separates this from the overlying *G. cumbriense* Band, which is also in two leaves, the lower 0.61 m thick and separated by 2.01 m of barren mudstone from the upper, 8 cm thick. Much of the barren mudstone contains small nodules of pyrite. The marine bands lie close to the base of an upward-coarsening sequence from mudstone to sandy siltstone, the whole about 37 m thick and overlain by some 21 m of soft pink thickly bedded sandstone, the Rough Rock. A 2.7 m seatearth rests on the sandstone and is overlain directly by the basal Westphalian Subcrenatum Marine Band.

Plate 7　Rough Rock at Wetley Rocks [966 492]
View to the south along the strike of the steeply dipping, thickly bedded, coarse-grained sandstone unit. The ground to the left is underlain by Namurian strata in the Overmoor Anticline, and to the right by Westphalian strata in the Shaffalong Syncline (L2014)

The borehole sequence differs only in minor respects from that which can be built up from outcrop information and other boreholes in the area between Ipstones and Oakamoor. The basal beds are well exposed at Ipstones Park in a stream section [0371 4941] which shows 7.9 m of mudstone resting on the coal above the Chatsworth Grit. The *G. cancellatum* Band, 0.8 m thick, lies 5.6 m above the top of the coal. The band has also been identified in a small exposure [0139 5027] close to the Abovechurch Borehole (SK 05 SW/6). *G. cumbriense* has been collected from a temporary exposure [0662 4506] of mudstone at Beelow Hill. The overlying siltstones are poorly exposed [035 493] in Blackbank Wood. The Rough Rock forms a strong escarpment to the west of Ipstones and is well exposed as a medium-grained cross-bedded sandstone at Noonsun Common [0158 4976] and at Wetley Rocks [966 490] (Plate 7). It underlies the village of Ipstones and forms a large dip slope around Whiston.

At Moneystone Quarry [046 461] it is currently worked for silica sand and is exposed in faces up to 15 m high as a pink and white mainly medium-grained sandstone, with cross-bedding indicating palaeocurrent flow towards the south. The top of the underlying siltstone has been exposed in parts of the quarry floor. Boreholes show that the full thickness of sandstone in the area varies from 27 to 35 m, but that bevelling by erosion has left only a thin basal remnant of the sandstone at the top of the dip slope. South of Consall the Rough Rock decreases markedly in thickness (Figure 14, column 1), and in a stream section [9788 4806] it consists of about 5 m of siltstone with sandstone bands (SJ 94 NE/18; also Cope, 1946, p.4). Its identity is established by the presence of the *G. cumbriense* Band not far below [9764 4821]. Farther south its thickness and lithology are variable but it forms a small feature in places, as far as the Triassic boundary near Stansmore Hall [961 439]. JIC

CHAPTER 5

Westphalian

Coal Measures belonging to Westphalian A and the lower part of Westphalian B are present in the Ashbourne district. The base of Westphalian A is drawn at the Subcrenatum Marine Band, and that of Westphalian B at the Vanderbeckei Marine Band (Ramsbottom and others, 1978, plate 2). The strata are preserved in two synclines, one on each side of the Overmoor Anticline (for description of this and other structures see Chapter 10), at the western side of the district. The Cheadle Coalfield, east of the anticline, is partially concealed by an unconformable cover of Triassic rocks and extends beneath these to the south for an unknown distance. The smaller coalfield at Shaffalong lies west of the anticline, only part of it falling within the district.

There is little drift cover in either coalfield so that the existence of the coal seams has been known for a very long time and old workings near the outcrops are common. Some details of the early history of coal mining are given by Molyneux (in Plant, 1881) and by Barrow (1903). The sequence in the Cheadle Coalfield was first fully described by Barrow (1903); earlier geologists had thought that the Two Yard Coal was the same as the Dilhorne Coal and had in consequence failed to realise that the valuable Dilhorne seam lies beneath a large area south of the Dilhorne Fault. Since that time both the Dilhorne and Woodhead seams have been mined out as far south as the Callowhill Fault and the large collieries have closed down. The only potential that now remains for deep mining is in the unproved area south of the Callowhill Fault, where the seams lie at greater depths beneath thick Triassic rocks; an earlier attempt to reach them at Draycott Cross was defeated by the inflow of water from Triassic sandstones during the construction of the shafts. Opencast mining was carried out during the post-war years along the outcrops of several seams and some accessible reserves remain, but no workings are in existence at the present time. Small-scale mining by private operators continues, however, in areas where patches of coal close to the surface have been left between earlier workings.

The sequence of strata in the Cheadle Coalfield is shown in Figure 16, and lateral variations of the strata are shown in Figures 17 and 18. The sequence at Shaffalong includes only the strata below the Kingsley Sandstone, but is thicker than the equivalent part of the Cheadle succession. The coals are found among a cyclical sequence of grey mudstones, siltstones and sandstones, as in the other coalfields of the Pennine area (e.g. Magraw, 1957, p.17). Correlation with the nearby Potteries Coalfield was first established by Cope (1946); the equivalent seam names are shown in Table 4, together with some local synonyms for the Cheadle seams.

The Westphalian strata were folded and faulted by the Hercynian earth movements; they were then deeply eroded before the deposition of an unconformable cover of Triassic sandstones. The presence of these sandstones limited the extent of mining, in that large panels of coal had to be left in place as a barrier against an influx of water from them. The measures are reddened for a depth of 10 to 20 m below the unconformity and oxidation during the period of erosion appears also to have destroyed the coals to about the same depth, for boreholes through the Trias have proved the absence of several seams in this situation, even though in each case the horizon of the coal, as indicated by its roof measures and seatearth, was present. The sub-Triassic surface is locally uneven, as proved by boreholes at Cheadle Park, with a topography apparently controlled by pre-existing fault lines. Post-Triassic faulting along both north–south and east–west lines has affected the area to a small extent.

The revision of the maps has involved the tracing of sandstone ridge features and old coal and ironstone crop-workings, and an examination of all the natural sections. This information has been integrated with the records from the original survey, with details of faults and seam levels from the mine plans, and with the records of numerous boreholes, many of them drilled when the opencast prospects of the coalfield were being assessed. The BGS fossil collections from the Cheadle Coalfield have been made at intervals over a long period of time, the most useful being obtained from boreholes drilled by the National Coal Board. Selected faunal lists, based on recent determinations by M. A. Calver and N. J. Riley, are quoted in the text.   JIC

SANDSTONE PETROGRAPHY

Samples from the **Woodhead Hill Rock** are more feldspathic than the Namurian Chatsworth Grit and Rough Rock and verge upon an arkosic composition. Modal analyses were made of fine-, medium- and coarse-grained examples (Table 3). E 51329 is fine grained, with a high degree of compaction, shown by pressure solution and syntaxial quartz overgrowth textures. The analysis indicates a significant proportion of organic detritus, which represents a minimum for the component, because the sample also contains organic-rich laminae that were avoided in making the point-count. Accessories include zircon, rutile and tourmaline. E 51625 is a medium-grained grainstone which contains mainly subangular clasts and is not highly compacted in the Carboniferous context. Distinctive features include a coarse crystallinity of the authigenic clay, the presence of cataclastic texture in much of the interstitial 'matrix' although strained and polycrystalline quartz grains are not especially abundant, and the presence of a few felsic lithoclasts (chert and/or acid volcanic rock) such as characterise the protoquartzitic rather than the feldspathic sandstone suite. E 51624, a coarse-grained example of the Woodhead Hill Rock, is a poorly sorted grainstone with dominantly subangular clasts. Despite a high porosity there is evidence in the form of concavo-convex quartz grain junctions of quite strong authigenic compaction. Ferric oxide

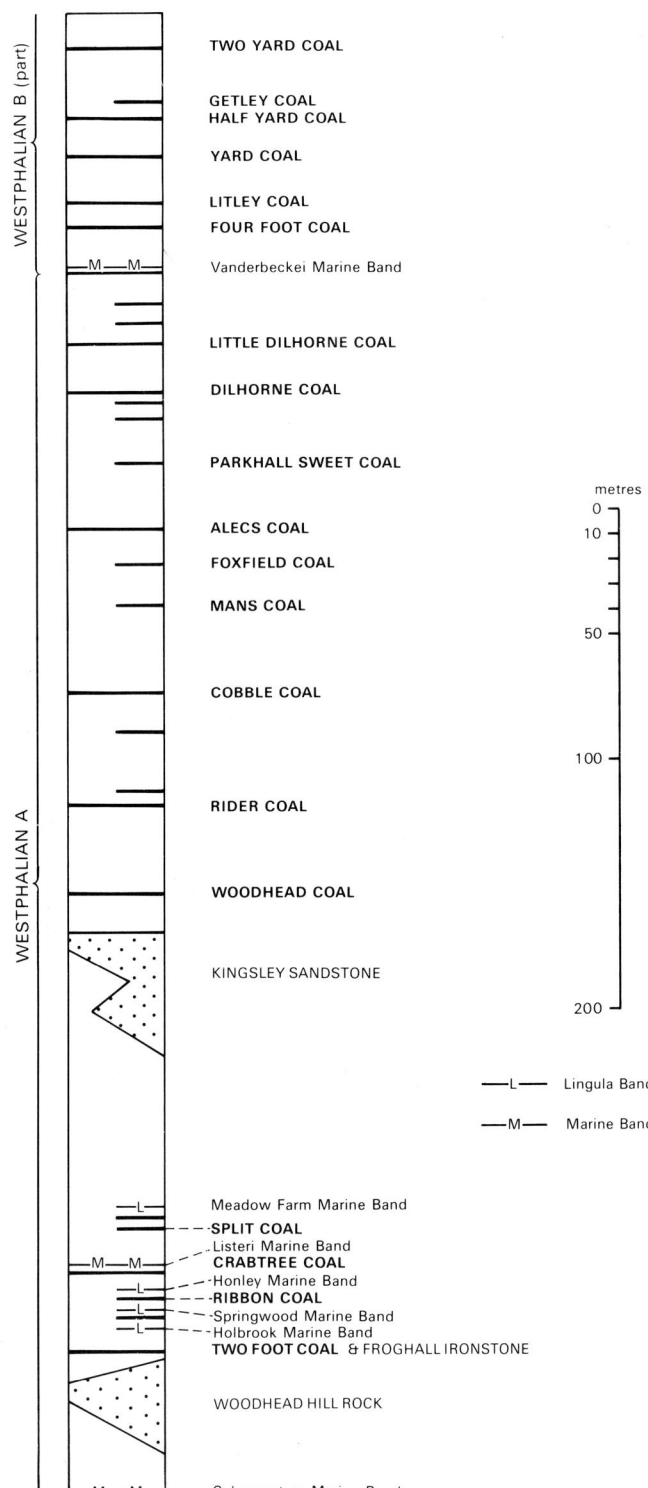

Figure 16 Generalised sequence in the Cheadle Coalfield

Figure 17 Comparative sections in the Cheadle Coalfield: strata below the Woodhead Coal

The name of each section, its number in BGS files and any reference in the geological literature, are as follows:
1. Park Hall Colliery, part of shaft with boring from shaft bottom (SJ 94 SE/22). Ward, 1890, pp.84–88.
2. Natural section, Out Wood, Consall (part of SJ 94 NE/18).
3. Natural sections, Consall valley (SJ 94 NE/20).
4. Natural sections, Consall valley (SJ 94 NE/19).
5. Natural section opposite Consall New Lock (SK 04 NW/29).
6. Natural section, Glenwood ravines (SK 04 NW/28).
7. Section of strata associated with the Froghall Ironstone, Booth's Wood (SK 04 NW/22). Binney, 1855, p.34.
8. Section at Gilmoor Mine (SK 04 NW/33). NCB plan 9500.
9. Section of Engine Pit, Cloughhead (SK 04 NW/21). Barrow, 1903, p.12.
10. Sinking near Foxt (SK 04 NW/31).
11. Key Wood Borehole (part of SK 04 NW/1).

Table 4 Correlation of coal seams at Cheadle with those of the Potteries: based on Cope (1946) and Barrow (1903). Synonyms given in brackets

Cheadle coalfield	Potteries coalfield
Two Yard	Ten Foot
Half Yard	Bowling Alley
Yard	Holly Lane
Litley	Hardmine
Four Foot	Stinkers
Little Dilhorne	Banbury
Dilhorne (Huntley)	Cockshead
Parkhall Sweet	—
Alecs (Stinking)	Bullhurst
Foxfield	Winpenny
Mans	—
Cobble (Lucksall; Eaves)	Diamond
Rider	Brights
Woodhead (Shaws)	King
Split (Sweet)	—
Crabtree (Stinking)	Crabtree
Ribbon (Sweet)	—
Two Foot Coal and Froghall Ironstone	Two Foot

have been altered by weathering and soil development prior to coal formation, however, and it is possible that the rock has attained its present composition by leaching of a more feldspathic sand. Nevertheless, the spectrum of lithoclastic types is similar to that of Namurian protoquartzites, in that metamorphic quartzite is dominant and fine-grained felsic rocks such as rhyolite, felsite and chalcedony (and/or chert) are also present, together with a small proportion of micaceous fine-grained sediments. The rock is a medium- to fine-grained highly porous grainstone with dominantly subangular clasts; in the Carboniferous context it is not highly compacted.

The **Kingsley Sandstone** (E 51626) is a silty fine-grained arkosic rock indicative of a feldspathic sediment source (Table 3). The abundant micaceous matrix appears to be mainly detrital in origin, although it is strongly stained by ferric oxide.

cement is patchily but, over larger areas, quite evenly distributed.

On the evidence of sample E 51627 the **sandstone beneath the Crabtree Coal** resembles the protoquartzitic facies, the modal analysis (Table 3) closely matching those of the early Namurian sandstones. The beds beneath this coal

NGB

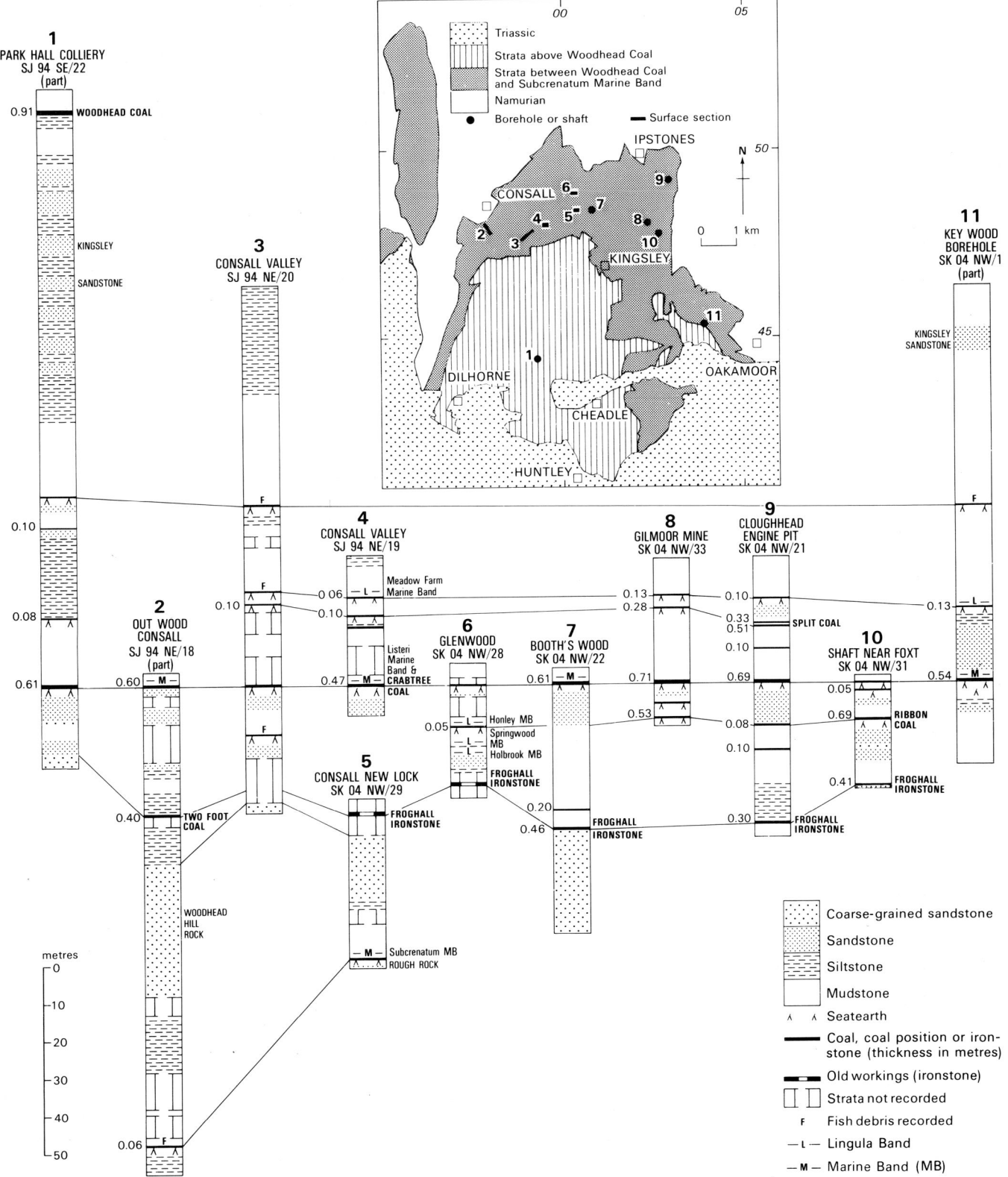

Figure 17 Comparative sections in the Cheadle Coalfield: strata below the Woodhead Coal. For details see opposite

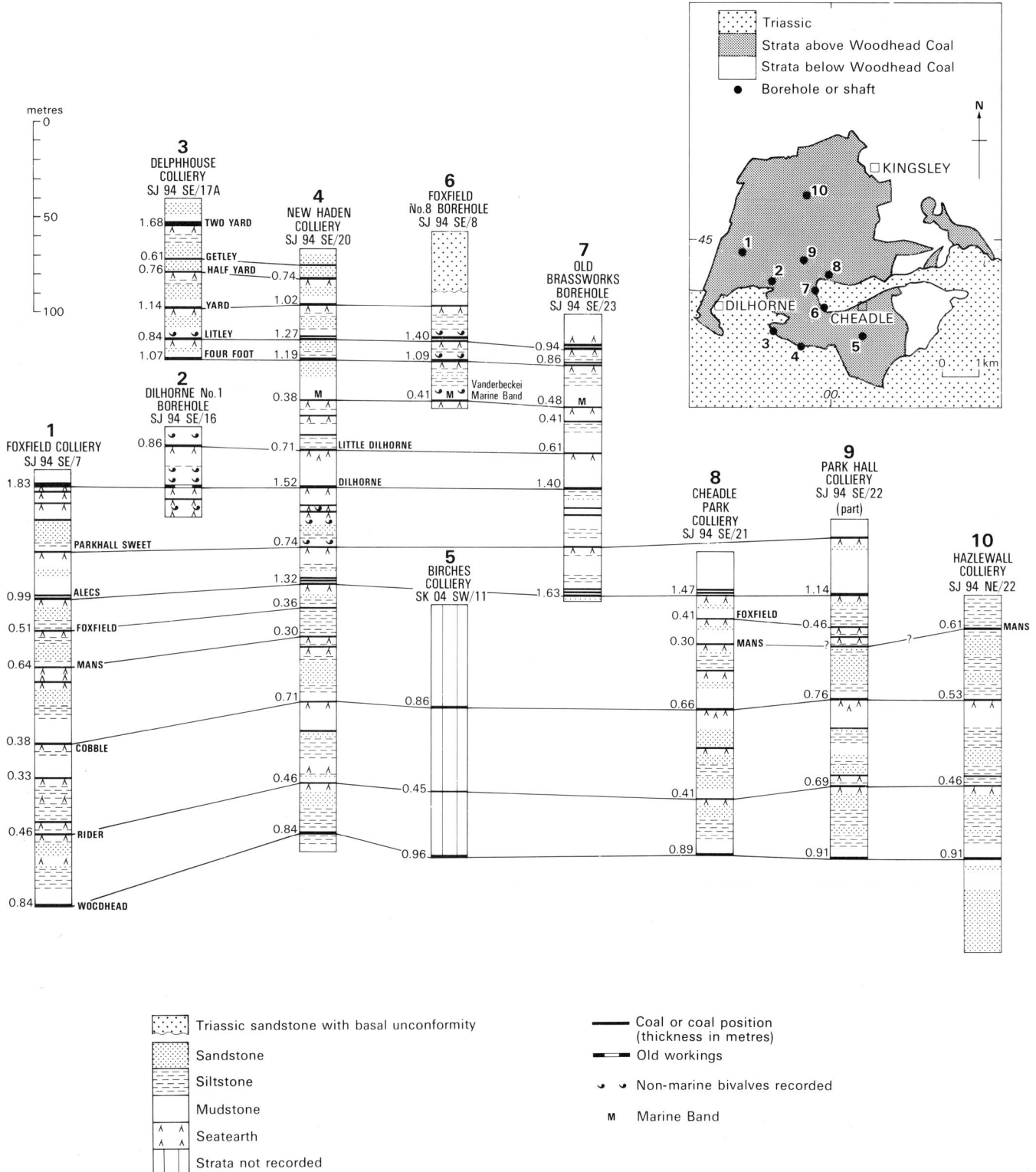

Figure 18 Comparative sections in the Cheadle Coalfield: strata above the Woodhead Coal. For details see opposite.

Figure 18 Comparative sections in the Cheadle Coalfield: strata above the Woodhead Coal

The name of each section, its number in BGS files, and any reference in the geological literature, are as follows:
1. Foxfield Colliery shaft (SJ 94 SE/7).
2. Dilhorne No. 1 Borehole (SJ 94 SE/16).
3. Delphhouse Colliery (SJ 94 SE/17A). Barrow, 1903, p.51.
4. New Haden (Draycott) Colliery, No. 8 shaft (SJ 94 SE/20).
5. Birches Colliery shaft (SK 04 SW/11). Molyneux *in* Plant, 1881, pp.297–298.
6. Foxfield No. 8 Borehole (SJ 94 SE/8).
7. Borehole near Old Brassworks, Cheadle (SJ 94 SE/23). Stobbs, 1905, p.510.
8. Cheadle Park Colliery shaft (SJ 94 SE/21). Barrow, 1903, p.54.
9. Park Hall Colliery, part of shaft (SJ 94 SE/22). Ward, 1890, pp.84–88.
10. Hazlewall Colliery, downcast shaft (SJ 94 NE/22). NCB plan 6056.

STRATIGRAPHY

Strata from Subcrenatum Marine Band to Crabtree Coal

The thickness of these strata varies from about 60 to 120 m in the Cheadle Coalfield (Figure 17) and is about 130 m in the Shaffalong Syncline. Five sedimentary cycles can be recognised (cf. Eden, 1954, p.85). The lowest contains the Subcrenatum Marine Band at the base and a coarse-grained sandstone, the Woodhead Hill Rock, at the top. The thickness of the cycle is normally about 40 m but this increases towards the north-west, being at least 64 m in a borehole (SJ 95 SE/2) just beyond the sheet boundary at Shaffalong, and about 88 m in a natural section (Figure 17, column 2) near Consall. The next cycle, with the Two Foot Coal and Froghall Ironstone at the base, contains an impoverished representative of the Bassy Mine non-marine

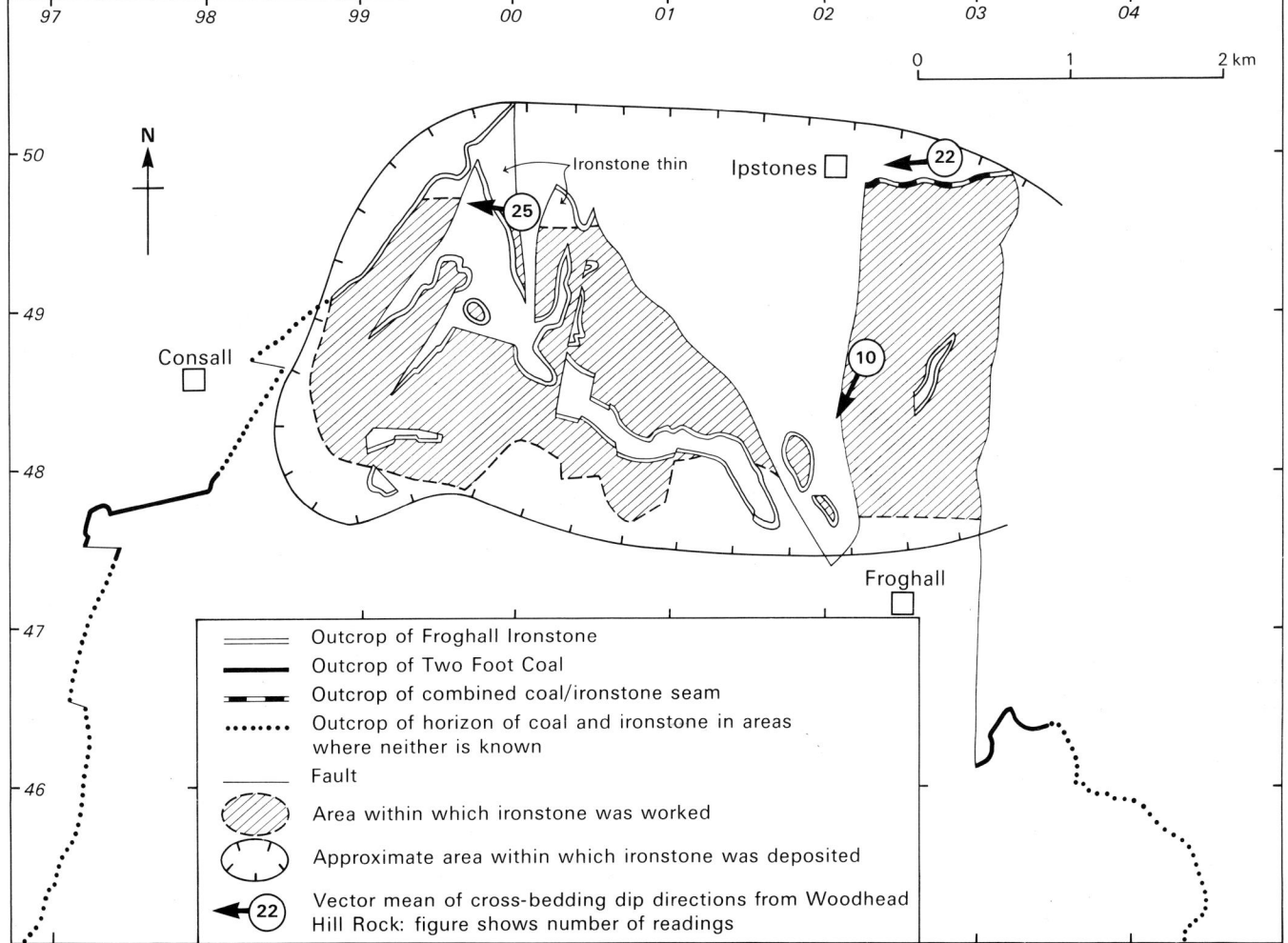

Figure 19 Distribution of Froghall Ironstone and Two Foot Coal, with palaeocurrent data for Woodhead Hill Rock

bivalve ('mussel') fauna of Lancashire. The three remaining cycles contain *Lingula* bands that are believed to represent the Holbrook, Springwood and Honley marine bands of the standard Westphalian sequence (Ramsbottom and others, 1978, plate 2). Accurate figures for the combined thickness, 27 to 38 m, of the top four cycles are given by the boreholes and shafts which have penetrated these strata in search of the Froghall Ironstone, but the records do not provide a detailed account of the lithological sequence. Such details, including the existence of the *Lingula* bands, are known only from surface exposures, mainly in the valleys of the Churnet and its tributaries (Figure 17, columns 2–6). However, all the natural sections are discontinuous and the correlation lines shown in Figure 17 are open to re-interpretation should new information become available.

Details

Subcrenatum Marine Band

The band generally lies on or just above a seatearth, locally with a thin coal, and consists of 0.1 to 0.6 m of mudstone. Marine bivalves and goniatites, including *Gastrioceras subcrenatum*, have been collected at the following localities:

a Excavation [9664 4944] at Wetley Rocks.
b Natural section by River Churnet opposite Consall New Lock (Figure 17, column 5).
c Natural section in Newhouse Wood [0177 4885], Ipstones.
d Ruelow Wood Borehole (SK 04 NW/5) at 10.05 m depth.
e Crowtrees No.8 Borehole (SK 04 NW/19) at 4.31 m depth (Anon, 1957, p.36).

The best of these sections is at Consall New Lock; the existence of a marine band here was first noted by Molyneux (1864, p.343). The details are:

	Thickness m
Mudstone, grey and purple, fissile at base	0.79
Mudstone, grey with *Dunbarella sp.*, *Gastrioceras subcrenatum* and *Anthracoceratites sp.*	0.55
Mudstone, purplish grey striped	0.30
Seatearth, purplish grey	0.70
Sandstone, white, fine- and medium-grained (Rough Rock)	1.00

At Out Wood, Consall (Figure 17, column 2) no marine fauna has been detected at the expected level in the sequence (Cope, 1946, p.78), the section there [9789 4805] being:

	Thickness m
Mudstone, grey, with ironstone bands	0.80
Mudstone, black, fissile, with fish debris	1.30
Siltstone, grey, argillaceous	0.04
Coal	0.06
Seatearth	0.40

The apparent absence of the marine band has not been satisfactorily explained.

Strata between Subcrenatum Marine Band and Two Foot Coal: Woodhead Hill Rock

The mudstone and siltstone above the marine band are rarely exposed, the best section being that opposite Consall New Lock

(section b, above). The overlying Woodhead Hill Rock is a pink or red-stained coarse-grained feldspathic sandstone; petrographic details have been given above. It varies from 0 to 45 m thick, the maximum figure being that recorded in a ravine [023 499] at Ipstones. Around the Churnet valley, where it is best exposed, the thickness is generally between 10 to 30 m. Cross-bedding (Figure 19) indicates palaeocurrent flow mainly from the east. In the past this bed was widely mistaken for the Rough Rock, which it closely resembles.

At the east side of the Shaffalong Syncline and along the western edge of the Cheadle Coalfield, where the dips are relatively steep, the Woodhead Hill Rock forms a discontinuous low feature with poor exposures, but round the northern and eastern sides of the coalfield gentle dips prevail and the bed forms a prominent feature, with good exposures in crags and quarries.

At Out Wood, Consall (Figure 17, column 2), 40 m of soft red coarse-grained sandstone are overlain by 12 m of siltstone and sandstone, and then by 0.4 m of coal (the Two Foot). North-east from here the sandstone forms a strong feature that can be traced to Mosslee Hall [000 506] beyond the Churnet valley. Between here and Cherryeye Bridge [014 481] the sandstone is well exposed in riverside crags, the outcrop being broken by several small faults. Crop workings in the overlying Froghall Ironstone serve to identify the sandstone almost everywhere, however. A cliff above the river at Consall New Lock (Figure 17, column 5) shows 18 m of pink coarse-grained feldspathic sandstone with a sharp base resting on 0.4 m of purple siltstone; crop workings in the ironstone lie about 5 m above the top of the sandstone. East and north of here the sandstone forms a prominent plateau at Hermitage [021 479] and a strong ridge near Ipstones, where there are good exposures in a ravine [023 499]. The sandstone attains its maximum thickness of 45 m here, and is overlain by purplish grey siltstones associated with ironstone crop workings. From Ipstones the outcrop is displaced by a strong fault southwards as far as Eavesford [034 467] from where it can be traced as a small feature, though with few exposures, south-eastwards to Oakamoor. The outcrop is there interrupted by east–west faults, but to the south of these a low ridge at the foot of the Triassic escarpment near Moss Fields Farm [027 426] is believed to represent the Woodhead Hill Rock. Old quarries [0280 4263 and 0248 4229] show degraded sections in pink and grey fine-grained micaceous sandstone, with moderate dips to the north-west.

Froghall Ironstone and Two Foot Coal

The Froghall Ironstone, at the same horizon as the Two Foot Coal, is a localised development of calcareous hematite with some black-band ironstone (Binney, 1855, pp.33–36; Smyth, 1862, pp.276–277, 291; Wardle *in* Sleigh, 1862, pp.234–239; Molyneux *in* Plant, 1881, pp.283–290). It lies about 5 m above the Woodhead Hill Rock and was extensively worked around Kingsley, Froghall and Ipstones. Plans of some of the workings exist but for many the only evidence is the spoil heaps of purplish siltstone and mudstone, with fragments of red ironstone, that still surround many old shafts and crop workings. The area where the bed was found is shown in Figure 19, which is based partly on mine plans and surface indications and partly on the account given by Barrow (1903, pp.16, 18–19). The thickness was up to 0.66 m (Smyth, 1862, p.278; Ward, 1890, pp.68–77) and in the nineteenth century the ironstone was worked from shafts up to 137 m deep, but since about 1900 it has only been got on a small scale, mainly for making red paint (Barrow, 1903, p.18). Working ceased in 1923 and its history has been described by Chester (1979). In the north, near Ipstones, the ironstone was interbedded with coal, a typical section being that at Radfields [0267 4967], where ironstone 0.10 to 0.23 m rested on coal 0.15 to 0.38 m. Coal has also been recorded from the area of ironstone workings near Lawn Farm [992 489]. South of a line from

Froghall to Consall (Figure 19) the ironstone thinned out and became unworkable.

The Two Foot Coal is also of localised occurrence (Figure 19), the only known developments (apart from those at Radfields and Lawn Farm, above) being to the south of Consall, where it was proved in shallow boreholes for about 900 m west of its exposure (Figure 17, column 2) in Out Wood, with a thickness of 0.4 to 0.8 m, and south of Eavesford, at the bottom of a shaft (SK 04 NW/23) at Ross Banks (Barrow, 1903, p.14), where it was 0.46 m thick. There is no associated ironstone in either of these areas. In the centre of the Cheadle Coalfield a borehole from the bottom of the Parkhall Colliery shaft (Figure 17, column 1) proved that neither coal nor workable ironstone is present at this horizon (Ward, 1890, pp.86–88).

Strata between Two Foot and Crabtree coals

In the Potteries Coalfield the mudstone above the Two Foot Coal contains a 'mussel' fauna which correlates with that above the Bassy Mine of Lancashire (Evans and others, 1968, p.99). This fauna has not been encountered during the resurvey of the Cheadle Coalfield, perhaps because the strata that overlie the Two Foot Coal and Froghall Ironstone, where now exposed, are commonly siltstones rather than mudstones; but faunas including 'mussels' and fish remains have been recorded from this level (Binney, 1855, p.34; Wardle *in* Sleigh, 1862, p.237; Molyneux *in* Plant, 1881, pp.290, 309–310; Ward, 1906, p.114). Fossils were rarely found in the ironstone itself (Barrow, 1903, p.19). The best section through this part of the sequence is at Out Wood, Consall [9800 4785] where about 6 m of grey well bedded sandy siltstone overlie the Two Foot Coal. At Ipstones, 2.5 m of a similar lithology are visible in a stream bank [0229 4977], but here the underlying Froghall Ironstone is not exposed.

The siltstone grades up into fine-grained sandstone, well seen in two ravines near Glenwood House, where it is about 2 m thick and overlain by dark mudstones, siltstones and paper-shales with *Lingula*, the supposed equivalents of the Holbrook and Springwood marine bands. A section in the northern ravine [0031 4890] is as follows:

	Thickness m
Mudstone, dark grey, with ironstone nodules	1.21
Shale, black, with fish debris and *Lingula* (Springwood Marine Band)	0.05
Mudstone, dark grey, with small pyrite nodules at top; silty at base; fish debris, *Carbonicola sp.* (could be *C. discus*) and cf. *Geisina arcuata*	0.18
Siltstone, dark grey, poorly bedded; ferruginous at base	0.23
Mudstone, dark grey, silty at top	0.35
Shale, black, with fish debris and *Lingula* (Holbrook Marine Band)	0.10
Siltstone, grey, argillaceous at top, sandy at base	0.92
Sandstone, buff, fine-grained, silty, flat-bedded	1.90
Siltstone, grey, sandy, flat-bedded	0.30
Gap with crop workings in Froghall Ironstone near base	c.11.00
Woodhead Hill Rock	—

Similar sections can be seen in the southern ravine (Figure 17, column 6) and in a steep bluff [0049 4866] not far away.

Above the beds just described lies an ill exposed sequence with the thin Ribbon Coal (Evans and others, 1968, p.106). This varies from 0 to 0.69 m in thickness and has been worked close to the outcrop locally, as at Gilmoor Mine (Figure 17, column 8) and Rake Edge [036 460], under the name Sweet Coal. The use of this name is liable to cause confusion, however, since it has also been applied to a higher seam (p.62) in the same area. Below the Ribbon lies a thin seatearth and sandstone, and above it lies a black shale with *Lingula*, believed to represent the Honley Marine Band. The best exposure of these strata is in the northern ravine [0035 4891] near Glenwood House, where the section is:

	Thickness m
Mudstone, dark grey, with ironstone nodules	0.53
Shale, black, with fish debris and *Lingula* (Honley Marine Band)	0.07
Mudstone, dark grey	0.08
Ribbon Coal, shaly	0.05
Clay, pale grey	0.10
Gap	1.98
Seatearth, grey	0.86
Siltstone, pale grey	0.10
Sandstone, pale grey, fine-grained, with bands of siltstone	0.80
Gap to top of section containing Springwood and Holbrook marine bands (see above)	1.90

The *Lingula* band and coal are also exposed in the southern ravine (Figure 17, column 6). An exposure in Cloughhead Wood [024 484] noted by Barrow (1903, pp.12–13), of a *Lingula* band in black shale above a thin coal, is no longer visible but was probably at this level in the sequence.

The overlying strata (Figure 17) contain a variable assemblage of sandstones (including ganister) and seatearths (Barrow, 1903, pp.12–17), locally with a thin coal, beneath the Crabtree Coal. Petrographic details of one sandstone sample are described above (p.56) and in Table 3. The sandstone forms a feature locally as in Out Wood [980 478], Lower Ladypark Wood [992 481], around the ravines [003 488] near Glenwood House, in Massey's Wood [023 489], at Park Farm, Ipstones [028 496] and from Rake Edge [035 460] to Key Wood [042 452]. It is exposed in many places in the valleys of the Churnet and its tributaries, as a buff coloured fine- to coarse-grained poorly bedded sandstone up to about 5 m thick, with buff and pale grey seatearth above. A typical section [9955 4812] in the Consall valley is:

	Thickness m
Crabtree Coal	0.47
Seatearth, pale grey	2.20
Sandstone, buff, fine- to medium-grained, coarse-grained at sharp undulating base; silty bands at top, massive below	4.50
Mudstone, grey	0.10

There are many other small exposures of the strata that lie between the Froghall Ironstone and Crabtree Coal in the Churnet valley and its tributary ravines, besides those described above. The most complete sections are near Consall (Figure 17, columns 2, 3) and near Ipstones [0230 4969 and 0314 4979].

Crabtree Coal

The Crabtree or Stinking Coal (the alternative name refers to its sulphurous quality) lies close to the surface over a wide area in the northern part of the Cheadle Coalfield (Figure 17; Barrow, 1903, pp.11–18) with a thickness in the range 0.46 to 0.86 m. It has been proved at depth in the centre of the coalfield (Figure 17, column 1), the thickness there being 0.61 m, and it is also present, though thinner, in the

Shaffalong Syncline. Working was formerly widespread in areas close to the outcrop. Plans of the workings are few, but waste tips can normally be identified by the presence of fragments of black shale with *Dunbarella* and goniatites, derived from the Listeri Marine Band that overlies the seam. Crop working continued on a small scale until 1930, and there was opencast working in 1955–56.

DETAILS

At the western margin of the coalfield the Crabtree has been proved only in boreholes near Banktop [970 462] and its outcrop is inferred from that of the surrounding strata. Around the northern edge of the coalfield the seam is well known and easily traced by borehole records, old workings and exposures, from Banktop to the Churnet valley near Belmont Hall [003 497] and throughout a triangular area that includes the Consall and Churnet valleys as far downstream as Cherryeye Bridge [014 481]. Within this area the dip is generally towards the south-east but the outcrop is repeated by several faults. Three small strips were worked opencast south-east of Consall, the largest at [984 480]. The average thickness of the seam here was 0.72 m, and 0.6 m of this is visible at outcrop (Figure 17, column 2) nearby. At Far Kingsley Banks [998 483], farther down the Consall valley*, sections in the stream banks show the following:

	Thickness m
Mudstone, dark grey; fissile in basal 0.25 with marine fossils (Listeri Marine Band)	6.00
Crabtree Coal	0.72
Seatearth and sandstone	5.80

In another section (Figure 17, column 4) not far away, the coal was only 0.47 m thick.

Along the north side of the Churnet valley, from the ravines [003 488] near Glenwood House to Hill House [011 486], the dip is low and the outcrop is marked by lines of waste tips, but on the south side there is little sign of surface workings, perhaps because the outcrop is partly concealed by landslips. A shaft record in this area (Figure 17, column 7) gives a thickness of 0.61 m.

East of here the seam is almost flat-lying in a fault-bounded strip dissected by the ravines south of Ipstones, and here too its outcrop can be traced by lines of workings. Exposures of the seam show incomplete sections but mining records (Figure 17, columns 8,9) give thicknesses of about 0.70 m.

To the south, faulting brings the seam to outcrop again in the Churnet valley at Ross Bridge [030 458], where the thickness recorded in a shaft (SK 04 NW/23; Barrow, 1903, p.14) is 0.61 m. The outcrop can be traced by surface indications east from here to Key Wood [041 456], where it is faulted off. The thickness in the Key Wood Borehole (Figure 17, column 11) is 0.54 m. South of Key Wood a seam of coal, perhaps the Crabtree, has been worked [0447 4471] near Oakamoor and there are shafts to the seam, identified by marine fossils in the tips, in Gibridding Wood [029 448]. From this point south to the Triassic escarpment at Rakeway [020 420] the existence of the coal has not been proved, though its outcrop can be conjectured from the trend of the adjacent strata.

* This term is used in this account for the valley running eastwards to join the Churnet from a point south of Consall.

Strata between Crabtree Coal and Woodhead Coal

These are is about 150 m thick (Figure 17). The lowest 50 m, known from shaft and borehole sections as well as surface exposures, contain several thin coals and two marine horizons. The highest 100 m, less well documented, consist of a thick upward-coarsening sequence with the Kingsley Sandstone near the top, overlain by finer beds and the Woodhead Coal.

The Listeri Marine Band, at the base, is well developed and easily identified by its characteristic fauna. Regional correlation of the overlying strata is based on comparison with the sequence proved in the Ridgeway Borehole (Magraw, 1957; Evans and others, 1968, pp.99–101), at the east side of the Potteries Coalfield (Sheet 123). On this basis the lowest coal, not present in all sections but represented in the Cloughhead shaft section (Figure 17, column 9), is equivalent to the Inch Mine of Lancashire and the overlying Split Coal is equivalent to the Upper Mountain Mine. The Split Coal consists of one or two leaves and attains a workable thickness locally. Its alternative name, Sweet Coal, is not used in this account, to avoid confusion with a lower seam (p.61) that was worked under the same name. The next overlying seam is correlated with the Cannel Mine of Lancashire and a *Lingula* band in its roof is therefore taken to be the Meadow Farm Marine Band of the standard Westphalian sequence (Ramsbottom and others, 1978, plate 2). The next higher cycle boundary, a rootlet bed, lies beneath a thick sequence of mudstones from the base of which a fish fauna has been obtained (Figure 17, columns 3, 11). It is believed to represent the Pasture Mine of Lancashire. No equivalent of the Amaliae (Tonge's) Marine Band was identified by Magraw (1957) in the Ridgeway Borehole and hence none is currently recognised in the Cheadle sequence.

The overlying thick mudstones and Kingsley Sandstone represent respectively the Accrington Mudstones and Old Lawrence Rock of Lancashire. The Daubhill 'mussel' fauna, which in Lancashire (Magraw, 1957, p.19) lies between the Old Lawrence Rock and the Arley Mine, is well represented at Cheadle, and serves to identify the immediately overlying Woodhead Coal, both with the Arley Mine and with the King Mine of the Potteries Coalfield.

DETAILS

Listeri Marine Band

Material from the band is commonly present on tips from shallow workings in the Crabtree Coal but good sections are few. In the Key Wood Borehole (Figure 17, column 11) it consisted of 0.79 m of mudstone containing *Lingula mytilloides*, *Ammodiscus sp.* and fish debris, on 0.35 m of mudstone with a rich fauna including *Gastrioceras listeri*, *Posidonia gibsoni*, *Caneyella multirugata* and *Dunbarella papyracea*, resting on or close above the coal. Exposures of the lower, richly fossiliferous, part of the band are to be seen in the Consall valley at Out Wood [9805 4781], where there are 0.3 m of black shale with *G. listeri* and fish remains; at [9955 4812], where 0.40 m of weathered brown shale with *Dunbarella sp.* can be seen, and at [9979 4831] where 0.25 m of black shale contain *G. listeri*, *C. multirugata* and *Dunbarella sp.* In the ravines south-east of Ipstones there are several poor exposures, the best [0298 4900] showing 0.22 m of black shale with *C. multirugata* and *Gastrioceras circumnodosum* overlain by 1.5 m of grey mudstone. Farther south, in Gibridding Wood [031 450] there are several old shafts to the Crabtree Coal, and fossiliferous material from the Listeri Marine Band, including calcareous 'bullions', can be collected on the tips (Barrow, 1903, p.15). The sequence of faunal phases in the band was first noted by Molyneux (*in* Plant, 1881, p.291) and has been described in detail by Ward (1906, pp.115–116) from a section in the Consall valley. The Listeri Marine Band has been recorded (Scott, 1927) in the Shaffalong Syncline, but no exposures are known there at the present time.

*Strata between Listeri Marine Band and Meadow Farm Marine Band :
Split Coal*

Mudstone with ironstone bands lies above the Listeri Marine Band and is exposed in a number of sections in the Consall valley, notably at Hollins Wood [9896 4775] and Far Kingsley Banks [9979 4831]. The mudstones pass up (Figure 17) into an alternation of seatearth, siltstone and mudstone with impersistent thin coals, capped by mudstone with a basal *Lingula* band at the supposed horizon of the Meadow Farm Marine Band. The best section through these beds is a landslip scar at Far Kingsley Banks (Figure 17, column 4) described by Barrow (1903, p.17) as the most complete natural section in the district. The following sequence is exposed:

	Thickness m
Siltstone, brown-grey, striped	3.00
Mudstone, dark grey, with a few ironstone nodules	7.50
Mudstone, dark grey, fissile, with fish debris, *Curvirimula* and ostracods	0.43
Ironstone, grey, pyritic, with fish debris and pale silt-filled burrows (*Teichichnus sp.*)	0.12
Mudstone, dark grey, silty, fissile, with fish debris and *Lingula* (supposed Meadow Farm Marine Band)	0.03
Siltstone, grey, full of plant debris	0.02
Coal	0.06
Seatearth, grey, mottled red in places, with hard siliceous bands at top and base	5.00
Mudstone, dark grey	0.03
Split Coal	0.10
Seatearth, pale grey	0.60
Siltstone, pale grey, poorly bedded	0.60
Sandstone, pale grey, fine-grained, silty	0.35
Siltstone, pale grey, poorly bedded, with laminated sandy bands in places	2.00
Mudstone, grey and silty at top, dark grey below; ironstone nodules up to 0.20 thick; sharp base	0.45
Siltstone, pale grey and brown; sandy, with sphaerosiderite at top; argillaceous below	0.60
Mudstone, dark grey, silty at top; a few ironstone nodules	4.00
Gap (estimated)	11.00
Crabtree Coal	—

The siltstone with sphaerosiderite resembles a seatearth and probably marks the horizon of the Inch Mine of Lancashire. The Split Coal is a single seam in the present section, although Barrow (1903, p.17) notes two seams about 0.9 m apart in the vicinity. Parts of the same sequence are seen farther upstream (Figure 17, column 3), but here only fish debris has been found at the horizon of the Meadow Farm Marine Band. The lower part of this section was formerly well exposed, and the sequence described by Barrow shows the Split Coal to consist of two thin seams 1.04 m apart, but at present only the top seam is visible. It was thick enough to be worked not far away, at Upper Ladypark Wood [985 479], as shown by surface evidence and borehole provings of 'gob', but boreholes in Out Wood [982 478], a short distance along the strike, show a single leaf of coal only 0.18 to 0.36 m thick. Ward (1906,

p.116) records sparse fish debris from mudstone associated with the Split Coal in the Consall valley.

In the ravines south of Ipstones, exposures of these strata were formerly more numerous (Barrow, 1903, pp.12–14) than at present. The Split Coal was 0.84 m thick, in two leaves, in the Cloughhead shaft section (Figure 17, column 9) and was worked in several places close to the outcrop. Surface evidence of workings can still be seen [028 492] near Park House Farm, in Moseymoor Wood [023 482] and in Foxt Wood [027 479]. A plan of a more recent working near here [0267 4812] gives the seam section as coal 0.30 m *on* dirt 0.05 m *on* coal 0.28 m. A sandstone close below the Split Coal forms a low feature to west and south of Cloughhead [027 489] and is exposed in the ravine [0295 4905] nearby.

In the Key Wood Borehole (Figure 17, column 11) a *Lingula* band is recorded at the horizon of the Meadow Farm Marine Band, underlain by a thin coal, but the strata between here and the Listeri Marine Band are mainly sandstone, perhaps the bed exposed at surface [0392 4546] nearby. The Split Coal is absent here, though its horizon is probably at the top of the sandstone.

In the Parkhall shaft section (Figure 17, column 1) this part of the succession is not easily correlated with the sequence just described, though a coal 8 cm thick and lying about 17 m above the Crabtree Coal, may possibly be the Split.

Strata between Meadow Farm Marine Band and Kingsley Sandstone

Between the Meadow Farm Marine Band and the seatearth at the supposed horizon of the Pasture Mine lie 20 to 30 m of mudstone and siltstone, best seen in a gully [9885 4765 to 9888 4771] in Broadoak Wood (Figure 17, part of column 3), where the section is:

	Thickness m
Mudstone, dark grey, with sparse fish debris at sharp base (?horizon of Pasture Mine)	—
Siltstone, pale buff-grey, hard, massive, with rootlets	0.10
Seatearth, buff and red mottled	2.00
Gap	1.50
Siltstone and silty mudstone, grey, well bedded in lower part	4.00
Gap	3.00
Mudstone, grey and silty at top, dark grey below with a few ironstone nodules; sparse 'mussels' 2.00 from top	12.00
Siltstone, dark grey with pale grey clasts derived from bed below (?horizon of Meadow Farm Marine Band)	0.05
Siltstone, pale grey, hard, massive, ganister-like	—

Farther up the Consall valley [9827 4767] a seatearth 1.7 m thick is overlain by about 10 m of dark grey mudstone. Barrow (1903, p.16) recorded marine fossils in the mudstone, but none has been found here during the resurvey. The horizon may be that of the Meadow Farm Marine Band, or possibly the Pasture Mine.

At the Key Wood Borehole (Figure 17, column 11) the interval between Meadow Farm Marine Band and Pasture Mine consisted of mudstone, with a sparse 'mussel' fauna including *Carbonicola bellula* and *Curvirimula* cf. *belgica*, passing up into siltstone and seatearth.

Above the Pasture Mine horizon lies a thick sequence of grey mudstones that pass gradually up through greenish grey siltstones into the Kingsley Sandstone (Figure 17, columns 1, 3, 11). Sparse fish debris has been collected at the base of the mudstone in the Broadoak Wood section (see below) and the Key Wood Borehole, but these measures are otherwise almost unfossiliferous. Good exposures are to be seen at intervals along the south side of the Consall valley, where the greenish colour of the siltstones has been altered to a purplish tint in places. The section at Broadoak Wood (Figure 17, column 3) shows:

	Thickness m
Siltstone, purplish grey	29.00
Mudstone and siltstone, greenish grey, discontinuous exposure	27.90
Mudstone, dark grey, with sparse fish debris in lowest 0.60; sharp base (?horizon of Pasture Mine)	3.00
Siltstone, pale buff-grey with rootlets	—

The top of this section is faulted against the Kingsley Sandstone. A sequence showing the upward passage into the latter is exposed near the top of a steep ravine [9967 4774] north-east of Hollins:

	Thickness m
Sandstone, buff, fine-grained, ripple-laminated, poorly exposed	c.1.00
Sandstone as above, with bands of siltstone	c.1.00
Sandstone, grey, fine-grained, poorly bedded, strongly erosive base	0.60
Siltstone, grey, sandy in places; parallel and ripple-lamination	6.00
Sandstone, grey, fine-grained, silty; parallel lamination	0.90
Siltstone, grey and greenish grey, sandy in places; parallel- and ripple-lamination	7.50

The mudstones and siltstones below the Kingsley Sandstone are also exposed in the Churnet valley, as at Ashbourne Hey [034 458] and Gibridding Wood [0310 4504], and there are small exposures in a stream east of Lightwood Farm [021 428].

Kingsley Sandstone

The bed is named after the village of Kingsley, which is built on the main outcrop. The alternative name Woodhead Sandstone (Barrow, 1903, p.19) is no longer used since it is liable to be confused with the name of a lower sandstone, the Woodhead Hill Rock (p.60). The Kingsley Sandstone consists of a series of lenticular fine-grained sandstones interbedded with siltstone, the proportion of sandstone in the sequence varying markedly from place to place. The harder bands form upstanding features and this has allowed the bed to be mapped through areas of poor exposure. The top is sharp and can be accurately mapped but the base is ill defined and the line shown on the map is in most places a notional one. Much of the sandstone is ripple-laminated, with subordinate parallel lamination and cross bedding. The palaeocurrent flow was from the south-west, the evidence for this being fourteen measurements of ripple-lamination directions ('rib and furrow' structures, as seen on surfaces parallel to bedding) from exposures in the Churnet valley between Bank Sprink [016 474] and Hawksmoor Wood [032 445]. Petrographic details of a fine-grained sandstone sample from the Churnet valley are given on p.56 and Table 3.

An account of the sandstone outcrop has been given by Barrow (1903, pp.19–22), and the following notes are intended to supplement this. At the west margin of the coalfield the ground is drift-covered and the outcrop of the sandstone is largely conjectural as far north as a roadside gully [972 454] near Whitehurst, where about 20 m of purplish sandstone and siltstone are exposed dipping steeply to the east. North of here the bed forms a low feature, with small exposures, as far as Blakeley Lane Farm [976 470], near where the strike swings round to an east–west trend. Boreholes [975 462] west of Dairy House Farm proved the local development of a thin coal on top of the Kingsley Sandstone. From Blakeley Lane the outcrop

continues, with strong features, along the south side of the Churnet valley as far as Hazlescross [005 478]. Faulting in this stretch gives rise to several displacements of the outcrop, notably around Broadoak [985 473]. Good exposures can be seen in a ravine [988 474] near here; the sandstone is fine-grained with bands of sandy siltstone and varies in colour from buff and grey to greenish and purplish. The trace fossil *Arenicolites carbonarius* has been collected here. The top of the sandstone is exposed [9878 4718], the section being:

	Thickness m
Mudstone, dark grey, with ironstone nodules; fissile at base	2.10
Mudstone, black, with coal laminae	0.25
Sandstone with siltstone bands; rootlets at top	4.60

At Hazlescross the outcrop widens and swings south to form a belt of slightly higher ground along the crest and flanks of a faulted north–south anticline that can be traced through Kingsley to Lockwood Hollow [016 455]. South of here the outcrop is cut off by the Woodhead Fault. There are many exposures in the sides of the Churnet valley, the most complete, by the river [0207 4726] near The Round Hill, showing about 40 m of buff fine-grained ripple-laminated sandstone with siltstone bands, dipping west at 10 to 50°. Disused quarry sections showing 10 to 20 m of similar rock can be seen just west of here [0156 4733] and at Banktop Wood [0255 4652]. Good exposures have been cut by streamlets flowing down to the Churnet at Hag Wood [026 462], Ochre Wood [029 466] and Lock Wood [028 453].

South of the Woodhead Fault and as far as the outskirts of Cheadle at Gibraltar [018 434], the outcrop is broken up into disconnected patches by faults and folds and is partially hidden beneath the Triassic outlier at Hales Hall [021 440]. South of Gibraltar, however, the harder bands form a series of good features, with gentle dip slopes defining the eastern edge of the Cheadle Coalfield as far south as Rakeway [020 420], where the main Triassic cover comes on. Exposures are poor.

Strata between Kingsley Sandstone and Woodhead Coal

Between the Kingsley Sandstone and the Woodhead Coal lie about 15 m of mudstone, silty sandstone and seatearth. The mudstones contain 'mussels', some preserved in ironstone nodules, that indicate a correlation with the Daubhill fauna of Lancashire (Cope, 1946, pp.9–10; Magraw, 1957, p.19). The only good exposure is in a ravine [9879 4719] in Brough's Wood, Kingsley Moor (Barrow, 1903, p.21; Cope, 1946, p.9), where the section is:

	Thickness m
Woodhead Coal: old crop workings	—
Seatearth, grey	0.6
Sandstone, grey, silty; ferruginous at top, with rootlets	1.3
Gap	1.3
Mudstone, dark grey, with large ironstone nodules; 'mussels' in upper part, including *Carbonicola torus* and variants approaching *C. bipennis*	13.5
Kingsley Sandstone	—

About 1.5 m of the same mudstone, with ironstone nodules containing *Carbonicola* cf. *bipennis*, is exposed in the stream bed [0124 4639] south of Kingsley. Exposure was formerly much better at this locality (Barrow, 1903, p.21; Ward, 1906, p.119).

Woodhead Coal

The Woodhead is the most widely worked of the Cheadle seams and reserves are now all but exhausted. It varies in thickness from 0.76 to 0.96 m, 0.86 m being an average figure. Working was limited by deterioration in quality in two areas, south-east of Cheadle and west of Boundary [981 425]. A thin lower leaf, the Ouster, lies close below the Woodhead in most sections. A curious feature of the seam is the local presence of isolated pebbles of quartzite (Stobbs, 1922). The roof is a hard black shale, or 'bass', containing fish debris (Ward, 1906, pp.117–119). The outcrop follows that of the Kingsley Sandstone round the edge of the coalfield, the line being marked in many places by uneven pitted ground, a relic of former crop workings. Good accounts of the seam have been given by Molyneux (in Plant, 1881, pp.296–304) and Barrow (1903, pp.19–23).

DETAILS

At the western edge of the coalfield the Woodhead Coal is not proved at outcrop from Cresswellford [962 430] north to Whitehurst [975 453]. Underground workings from Foxfield and New Haden collieries followed the seam westwards towards the outcrop but ceased well short of the surface, due in part at least to a deterioration in quality. The thickness at the limit of working is not known, but at the Foxfield shafts (Figure 18, column 1) it was 0.84 m.

From Whitehurst north to near Blakeley Lane [978 470] the outcrop is known in detail from boreholes, opencast workings, exposures and old crop workings. Deeper workings east of here have been patchy, however, and small drift mines continue to exploit areas of coal remaining between the deep workings and those along the outcrop. The thickness of the seam at one of these, Moorland Colliery [9772 4691] was 0.81 m. It was 0.86 m thick at Moorland opencast site [978 470].

East from Moorland Cottages the line of outcrop can be traced by old surface working as far as Hazlescross [006 477] where the strike swings north–south on the flank of the Kingsley Anticline. There are now no exposures of the full seam thickness in this area, though it was formerly visible, 0.84 m thick, in Brough's Wood [9879 4710] (Barrow, 1903, p.21). South of the outcrop it was 0.91 m at Hazlewall Colliery (Figure 18, column 10), and at Shawe Colliery [9994 4652] the section was: Woodhead Coal 0.86 m on black stone 0.20 m on grey seatearth 0.33 m on Ouster Coal 0.11 m.

From Hazlescross to Shawe Hall [008 460] the outcrop is complicated by faulting but can be inferred with reasonable confidence from surface indications and mining records. At Kingsley No. 2 Mine [0102 4661] the section was: Woodhead Coal 0.86 m on grey marl 0.61 m on Hooster Coal 0.08 m, and at Brocton Colliery [009 462] it was: Woodhead Coal 0.86 m on seatearth 0.23 m on Houster Coal 0.05 m.

On the east side of the Kingsley Anticline the coal crops out in several faulted patches, revealed in part by old surface working, between Kingsleybanks [020 472] and Gibridding Wood [031 451] and its presence may also be inferred across the Whiston Fault south of the Kingsley Sandstone outcrop at Jackson Wood [034 455]. At Kingsley Holt No. 2 Mine [0236 4563] the section was: Woodhead Coal 0.89 m on dirt 0.15 m on Ouster Coal 0.15 m. The top 0.4 m of the coal are exposed [0299 4575] near Ross Bridge, overlain by black shale with fish debris.

Returning to the west side of the Kingsley Anticline, at Shawe Hall, the position of the seam can be traced by outcrop workings southwards to the Woodhead Fault [011 449] near Broadhay. South of this fault the outcrop of the coal, like that of the Kingsley Sandstone beneath, is broken by faults and folds and concealed in part by

Triassic rocks. Old shafts prove that the seam is present around Woodhead [011 443] from which locality the seam takes its name (Molyneux in Plant, 1881, p.296), but it is cut off by faulting before reaching the surface. East of here a complex outcrop around Woodhead Hall [025 448] is known from surface evidence (Barrow, 1903, p.22). West of Woodhead, at depth, seam thicknesses of 0.89 and 0.91 m were recorded at Cheadle Park and Parkhall collieries respectively (Figure 18, columns 8, 9). It was in the Parkhall workings that several isolated quartzite pebbles up to about 0.3 m in diameter were encountered, mainly in the Woodhead Coal but also in beds immediately above and below (Lister and Stobbs, 1917, 1918; Stobbs, 1920, 1922).

South of Cheadle, old crop workings reveal the surface position of the coal from Cheadlemoor [016 433] south to the Triassic escarpment near Rakeway [020 420]. At depth the seam has been worked beneath parts of Cheadle; at Birches Colliery (Figure 18, column 5) it was 0.96 m thick but not far to the south, at Rakeway Colliery [0152 4223], the quality was poor. No workings are recorded south of Rakeway. Westwards and northwards the Cheadle workings stopped at faults, leaving reserves untouched, though doubtless much faulted, between here and the workings documented at New Haden, Parkhall and Cheadle Park collieries.

At New Haden Colliery (Figure 18, column 4) the Woodhead Coal was 0.84 m thick and was worked southwards to the Callowhill Fault, a large WNW-trending fracture that forms the limit of mining up to the present time. Eastwards the workings ended among a group of north–south faults near Scarletlake [000 418] and to the west they extended across the axis of the main syncline beyond Boundary [981 425] but, as stated earlier, the quality deteriorated west of there and the workings finished well short of the outcrop.

Strata between Woodhead Coal and Vanderbeckei Marine Band

These strata are about 250 m thick (Figure 18). Sandstones are more common below the Alecs Coal than above it, being especially prevalent at the northern outcrop, where they underlie the high ground of Kingsley Moor. They are fine-grained rocks, commonly grading into siltstone, and form low rounded ridge features at the surface. Many of the mudstones contain non-marine faunas, the most notable of these being the fish beds above the Woodhead and Cobble coals (Ward, 1906, pp.117–121; Ward and Stobbs, 1906) and the series of mussel bands in the strata above and below the Dilhorne Coal (Ward, 1906, pp.122–123; Cope, 1946, p.14). The latter (p.68) belong to the cristagalli and regularis faunal belts in the early part of the Modiolaris Zone.

There are seven workable coals. Of these the Rider, Mans and Foxfield seams are thin and have only been worked locally near outcrop. The Cobble is thicker and has been worked along much of the outcrop, with local deeper mining in the area of maximum thickness near Cheadle. The Little Dilhorne Coal is of similar thickness and has also been widely worked near the outcrop. At depth, small areas have been got beneath Dilhorne Common [978 433] and at New Haden Colliery. The Alecs seam is thicker than these but is sulphurous and is split by numerous mudstone partings. Shallow workings at and near the outcrop are common and there has been some deep mining beneath Dilhorne Common. The Dilhorne Coal is the best in this part of the sequence. It was first worked at outcrop north of the Dilhorne Fault but due to a miscorrelation with the Two Yard Coal (p.72) its presence south of the fault was not recognised until about 1900 (Barrow, 1903, p.28). Since then the seam has been extensively worked in the synclinal area between the Dilhorne and Callowhill faults from New Haden and Fox-field collieries and only small patches have been left, for safety reasons, near the eastern and western outcrops. There has been opencast mining of the Cobble, Mans, Foxfield, Alecs, Dilhorne and Little Dilhorne seams.

DETAILS

Strata between Woodhead and Rider coals

The black shale above the Woodhead Coal contains a well documented fish fauna (Ward, 1906, pp.117–119). A section [9877 4711] at Brough's Wood shows part of this bed, but the base has collapsed into old workings. The lowest 0.2 m can be seen, resting on the coal [0299 4575] near Ross Bridge.

Above lies a variable sequence of mudstones, siltstones and sandstones (Figure 18), poorly exposed. The sandstones form low features at intervals along the east side of the coalfield, as at Barnfields [006 466], Shawe Hall [008 460], east of Long Croft Farm [007 455], west of Woodhead Hall [025 448] and south of Lightwood [017 430].

Rider Coal

The seam consists of about 0.3 m of coal resting on a similar thickness of 'cannel-shale' (Barrow, 1903, p.30). In the several shaft sinkings that encountered it (Figure 18), the thickness is recorded as ranging from 0.41 to 0.69 m, but it is uncertain how much of the cannel was included in these figures. So far as is known the seam has never been worked at depth, but there is evidence of minor outcrop working in places, as between Kingsley and Hollins [993 474]. At present the only good section [0178 4490] is in the bed of a stream east of Broadhay:

	Thickness m
Mudstone, grey	1.40
Coal	0.25
Cannel and blackband ironstone	0.35
Clay, grey	0.20
Sandstone, silty at top	1.50

Barrow (1903, p.26) recorded 'mussels' in the cannel at this locality. A stream section [0145 4619] south of Kingsley, showing 0.29 m of coal overlying 0.10 m of hard black shale with coal laminae, may also be in the Rider. A trial pit [0076 4561] dug in 1949 for opencast working in the Rider Coal near Long Croft Farm revealed the following section:

	Thickness m
Mudstone	1.80
Coal	0.33
Cannelloid shale with *Carbonicola pseudorobusta*	0.38
Seatearth	—

The position of the outcrop north and south of here was proved by drilling but the seam was not worked. Provings of a similar nature were made north-west of Kingsley [at 006 475], where the coal was recorded as 0.3 m thick, and west of Dairy House Farm [at 976 461] where it was recorded as 0.3 to 0.8 m. A seam between the Woodhead and Cobble outcrops, possibly the Rider, was proved as an opencast prospect in boreholes [002 467] west of Barnfields, with a thickness of 0.6 to 0.8 m, and west of Shawe Hall [003 462] with a thickness of 0.6 to 0.9 m. A seam formerly exposed at the bottom of a brickpit [000 472] west of Kingsley is also thought to be the Rider;

an exposure, recorded nearby by Barrow (1903, p.26) and incorrectly described as the Cobble Coal, is no longer visible.

Strata between Rider and Cobble coals

The lower two thirds of this interval is generally an alternation of sandstone, siltstone and mudstone with up to three coal horizons; the upper third is generally mudstone. The coals are too thin to work. The following section can be pieced together from exposures in ravines [987 469 and 988 469] in Brough's Wood:

	Thickness m
Mudstone, pale grey with rootlets at top, darker below; discontinuous section	8.80
Coal	0.12
Coal and black shale, interlaminated	0.27
Sandstone, white, hard	0.04
Seatearth, pale grey	c.0.50
Siltstone, grey; sandy at top, argillaceous at base	c.2.00
Sandstone, pale grey, silty	c.1.00
Mudstone, grey, silty; darker band 0.2 at 2.5 above base	c.6.00
Mudstone, dark grey, with fish debris	0.25
Coal	0.05
Seatearth, grey	0.40
Sandstone, buff, fine-grained, with siltstone and mudstone bands	1.20
Mudstone, grey, silty; sandstone bands at top	2.00

The outcrop of the Cobble Coal (not exposed but proved in boreholes) lies a few metres beyond the upper limit of this section, suggesting that the top mudstone item is that which normally lies immediately below the Cobble (Figure 18). The bottom of the section is separated from the outcrop of the Woodhead Coal by a large strike-fault, which cuts out the Rider Coal.

There are small exposures of the beds between Rider and Cobble in a stream [978 462] just west of Dairy House and the sandstones form features between Moorside Farm [000 463] and Booth's Farm [006 452]. A coal horizon above one of these can be seen at Stone Hole [0072 4582], where the section is:

	Thickness m
Mudstone, grey	0.80
Shale, black, with fish debris	0.07
Clay, black	0.12
Seatearth, grey	0.20

South of Cheadle, fragmentary exposures of these measures in stream banks between Cecilly Bridge [013 435] and The Eaves [011 417] suggest that they are mainly mudstone and siltstone, with few sandstones, although the record of Birches Colliery given by Molyneux (*in* Plant, 1881, pp.297–298) shows a thick sandstone at this level in the sequence.

Cobble Coal

The seam is generally of good quality and reaches 0.86 m in thickness. The seatearth is said to be unusually hard (Cope, 1946, p.11). At the western margin of the coalfield the seam has been identified with certainty only at the Foxfield Colliery shaft (Figure 18, column 1), where it was 0.38 m thick, and in boreholes at Whympney Wood [974 439], where it was 0.10 m. A seam formerly exposed [9686 4402] north-west of Dilhorne was considered by Barrow (1903, p.30) to be the Cobble and an outcrop has been conjectured to north and south of here. A seam formerly exposed [9650

4291] near Cresswellford is also thought to be the Cobble. There are no records of working in the western outcrop area.

Around the north side of the coalfield the thickness varies between 0.3 and 0.5 m. The outcrop of the seam can be accurately mapped by the presence of old surface workings, together with evidence from boreholes and opencast workings. No deep workings are known. North-east of Dairy House the seam was 0.41 m thick at an opencast pit [980 463] worked during the 1950's. Between Greenhead [984 467] and Silverdale Wood [007 465] the line of outcrop can be traced from old surface working, and the thickness, as proved in opencast trial pits, varies from 0.30 to 0.46 m. No opencast working has taken place here, however. A small exposure [0053 4648] in Silverdale Wood shows the following section, believed to be in the Cobble Coal:

	Thickness m
Mudstone, grey, loose	—
Coal	0.05
Siltstone, pale grey, hard	0.02
Mudstone, dark grey	0.04
Coal	0.35
Seatearth, grey	0.90

South of here, between Waste Wood [000 461] and Booth's Farm [006 452], patches of the coal have been worked opencast, the thickness increasing from 0.43 m in the north to 0.52 m in the south. At Hazlewall Colliery (Figure 18, column 10) it was 0.53 m thick, but no workings are recorded.

From the region of Booth's Farm south to where the outcrop runs beneath the Triassic cover near Plantation House [016 417], the seam is thick enough to have been worked at moderate depth and, though few detailed records remain, there is evidence of mining throughout this area (Barrow, 1903, pp.29–30), from Rimmon's Shaft [0036 4497] and others nearby, through Birches Colliery (Figure 18, column 5), where it was 0.86 m, to an engine shaft [0087 4155] at Mobberley, where it was between 0.46 and 0.61 m thick. At a trial pit [0063 4439] near Harewood Park it was 0.66 m. The line of outcrop is marked in many places by pitting. Farther west, and at greater depths, the seam was encountered at New Haden, Cheadle Park and Parkhall collieries (Figure 18, columns 4, 8, 9), the thickness ranging from 0.66 to 0.76 m. Limited areas were extracted close to the shafts at New Haden and Cheadle Park.

Strata between Cobble and Mans coals

The roof of the Cobble Coal has yielded a notable fish fauna at Cheadle Park Colliery, where the following section is recorded (Ward and Stobbs, 1906):

	Thickness m
Dark grey mudstone	—
Dark mudstone with fish remains	0.10
Grey mudstone with plant remains	0.76
Cobble Coal	—

'Mussels' were recorded from the roof of the Cobble Coal at New Haden Colliery (Cope, 1946, p.11). The only exposure of this part of the sequence is in a stream [9781 4608] near Dairy House, where the details are:

	Thickness m
Mudstone, dark grey, fissile	0.40
Mudstone, dark grey	0.08
Cobble Coal	0.15 +

Above these mudstones lies a variable series of sandstones which form low ridge features from Dairy House to Greenhead [983 467] and thence to Shawe Colliery [999 465]. Farther south, Booth Hall [002 454] and Hammersley Hayes [011 446] stand on ridges of sandstone at the same horizon. Exposures are few, the best being in Cartwright's Drumble [971 445] where a few metres of purplish grey siltstone and silty sandstone lie some distance above a seatearth believed to be that of the Cobble Coal.

Mans Coal

A variable group of rooty beds, with thin coals in places, overlies the sandstones just described. The name Mans Coal is generally applied to the thickest seam present in this interval. As thus defined it varies up to 0.69 m in thickness, and may be in one or two leaves.

A seam 0.3 to 0.6 m thick proved in boreholes [966 430] east of Cresswellford is believed to be the Mans, as is a thin seam formerly exposed [9696 4384] west of Dilhorne, although the records of boreholes in Whympney Wood [974 439], not far away, showed no coal at this level in the sequence. The seam was 0.64 m thick, in two leaves, at Foxfield Colliery (Figure 18, column 1). North-east of here the seam has been worked opencast in a series of pits along the outcrop from Dairy House to near Longhouse Colliery [002 458], the thickness ranging from 0.25 to 0.69 m in one or two leaves. A typical section [9966 4611] shows coal 0.34 m *on* black shale 0.21 m *on* coal 0.15 m. North of these opencast workings the sequence is repeated by faulting and the seam was proved as an opencast prospect around Victoria Cottages [992 466] but was not worked. The thickness was about 0.5 m, generally in two leaves. Farther south the seam is recorded at Cheadle Park and Hazlewall collieries (Figure 18, columns 8, 10). At Parkhall Colliery a 0.46 m seam called Mans by Barrow (1903, p.55) is now believed to be the Foxfield (Figure 18, column 9); a thin seam below is probably the Mans. Between Meadow Farm [001 451] and Harewood Park [005 442] the seam, in one or two leaves, was proved as an opencast prospect but was not worked. A trial pit [0038 4428] showed the thickness as 0.33 m. South of Cheadle the seam is 0.30 m thick at New Haden Colliery (Figure 18, column 4) but the outcrop has not been identified with certainty. Coal debris dug out in the stream bank [0105 4215] near Dandillions may possibly be the Mans seam, however.

Strata between Mans and Foxfield coals

Sandstone, siltstone and mudstone can be seen in discontinuous section in a stream [9785 4583] south of Dairy House and sandstone is exposed in small streams on a dip-slope [988 461] west of Hazlewall Farm. Fish debris is recorded from the roof of the Mans Coal at New Haden Colliery.

Foxfield Coal

The seam varies up to 0.58 m in thickness, everywhere as a single leaf. At the west margin of the coalfield the outcrop has not been located and no coal was recorded at the appropriate level in the boreholes in Whympney Wood [974 439], but at Foxfield Colliery (Figure 18, column 1) it was 0.51 m thick and small areas, mainly close to the shafts, were mined. It was formerly exposed near here (Barrow, 1903, p.29). The seam has been worked opencast along the outcrop west and east of Hazlewall Farm and a larger area was extracted east of Leafields. The thickness varied between 0.42 and 0.53 m. Exposures in a small mass of coal remaining near the outcrop [9972 4563] east of Leafields showed loose siltstone, *on* coal 0.48 m, *on* seatearth. The seam was also at one time exposed, 0.46 m thick, in a brickpit [992 462] close to Hazlewall Colliery. North of here the outcrop is repeated by strike faulting and a small area of the seam has been proved by drilling, at Kingsley Moor [996

464]. The thickness was 0.53 to 0.58 m. South of Leafields an area of the seam was proved close to the surface midway between Harewood Hall [000 447] and Harewood Park [005 442], with a thickness of 0.38 to 0.41 m, but no opencast working resulted. An exposure [0030 4451] in a stream nearby shows the lowest 0.15 m of the seam resting on seatearth. Down dip the seam was proved with similar thicknesses at Cheadle Park and Parkhall collieries (Figure 18, columns 8, 9) but was not worked. South of Cheadle a coal formerly exposed in a stream bank [0100 4186] near The Eaves is believed to be the Foxfield, in view of its position relative to the outcrop of the Alecs Coal. The Foxfield Coal was proved at depth at New Haden Colliery (Figure 18, column 4) but was not worked.

Strata between Foxfield and Alecs coals

At the west side of the coalfield these strata are poorly exposed but are recorded as mainly sandstone in boreholes in Whympney Wood [974 439] and at Foxfield Colliery (Figure 18, column 1). The sandstone, interbedded with siltstone, is exposed in the stream [979 457] south of Dairy House, and can be seen at intervals around the northern outcrop, as at Hazlewall Farm [9905 4606] and in streams [995 459 to 997 452] north of Little Harewood Farm. South of here sandstone is subordinate to finer-grained lithologies at New Haden, Cheadle Park and Parkhall collieries (Figure 18, columns 4, 8, 9); there are small exposures of mudstone in this part of the sequence in a stream [001 445] south-east of Harewood Hall and in another [009 417] west of The Eaves.

Alecs Coal

The seam has a sulphurous character and consists of a variable alternation of coal and argillaceous layers. The total thickness of coal (including shaly coal) varies from 0.38 to 2.43 m, spread through 0.68 to 8.07 m of strata. It has been mined at and near the outcrop from an early date and has been opencast in recent times. There has also been localised extraction by deep mining.

At the western outcrop the coal was worked near Oaklea, close to the Callowhill Fault, from a shaft [9706 4280] reported to be about 46 m deep (Barrow, 1903, p.28), and the outcrop has been proved by boreholes just to the west of here. The section in one of these was: coal 0.61 m *on* bind 0.15 m *on* coal 0.38 m. At depth to the east of this outcrop the seam was worked from Foxfield Colliery. A rectangular area of about 0.75 sq km, south of the Dilhorne Fault and stretching across the centre of the syncline, was extracted, the thickness taken out varying from 0.7 to 1.3 m. North of the Dilhorne Fault the outcrop is marked by old workings in Whympney Wood [973 441] and old boreholes record the section as: coal 0.46 m *on* grey rock and bind 1.37 m *on* coal 0.30 m *on* brown bass 0.61 m *on* coal 1.14 m *on* bass or shale 3.66 *on* coal 0.53 m. Molyneux (*in* Plant, 1881, p.294) records the working of a 1.5 m seam of sulphurous coal, probably the Alecs, in this area. The lowest leaf of the seam, 0.30 m thick, is exposed in a gully [9734 4485] in Pearcroft Wood and the full section was proved not far away in the shaft at Foxfield Colliery (Figure 18, column 1): coal 0.38 m *on* pricking 0.15 m *on* coal 0.61 m. However, the only known workings in this area are at outcrop.

Along the north outcrop the seam has been worked in opencast pits, especially around Leafields [993 455]. The section was very variable but in general the lowest part, 0.84 to 1.35 m thick, contained the fewest shale partings and was extracted. In the areas not exploited by this means there are extensive old workings along the outcrop, which is twice repeated by faulting, between Lower Above Park [987 460] and Harewood Kennels [992 453]. There is a small exposure [9874 4567] of coal and black seatearth in a stream about midway between these two points. West of Harewood Kennels the seam was proved as an opencast prospect at relatively shallow depth but was not worked. A typical borehole section [9879 4534] showed:

coal 0.08 *on* fireclay 0.15 m *on* coal 0.15 m *on* fireclay 0.15 m *on* dirty coal 0.15 m. Immediately north and east of Harewood Hall [000 447] the ground is pitted by old workings in the Alecs Coal, the outcrop of which is repeated by faulting. A borehole [0008 4503] here proved 1.5 m of shaly coal. South of Harewood Hall the approximate position of the outcrop is known as far as the Dilhorne Fault, but beyond is concealed beneath the Triassic outlier of Cheadle Park. An area immediately north of Cheadle Park Colliery [000 441] has been worked opencast; a trial pit dug prior to working showed: coal 0.08 m *on* coal and dirt 0.10 m *on* coal 0.19 m *on* grey shale 0.03 m *on* coal and black shale 0.30 m *on* dark shale 0.05 m *on* carbonaceous shale 0.18 m *on* pyrite 0.03 m *on* coal 0.30 m *on* shale 0.05 m *on* coal 0.77 m (Cope, 1946, p.16). Only the two lowest leaves were worked. Sections recorded in the colliery shafts nearby (Figure 18, columns 8, 9) appear to have been generalised, but a borehole (Figure 18, column 7) gives details similar to those described above, from the opencast site. Attempts to work the seam at Parkhall Colliery were abandoned due to swelling of the seatearth (Barrow, 1903, p.28).

South of the faulted Triassic at Cheadle the outcrop is known from near Birches Colliery [008 424] to the main Triassic escarpment. The seam was proved in boreholes south of Dandillions [008 421] with a thickness of about 1.2 m, generally in two leaves and overlain by black shale, and was worked at a depth of 6.4 m from a shaft [0086 4143] near Mobberley (Barrow, 1903, pp.28–30). West of Cheadle the seam was reached in a shaft near Majorsbarn [0036 4269]; the thickness recorded was 1.83 m, but it was apparently too deep to work (Barrow, 1903, p.28). At New Haden Colliery (Figure 18, column 4) there were 1.32 m of coal in three leaves, but only a small patch close to the shaft was worked.

Strata between Alecs and Dilhorne coals

There are numerous sections of these strata in streams between Hatchley [982 454], Leafields [993 455] and Parkhall Farm [992 438]. The continuity of sequence is broken by many small sharp folds and associated faults and it has only proved possible to identify in a general way the individual horizons exposed in these sections with those known in the borehole and shaft sections of Figure 18.

A sandstone above the Alecs Coal (Figure 18) is exposed in the stream [9797 4551] west of Hatchley, but at this general level in the sequence in the streams below Lower Above Park [987 460] the exposures are of sandy siltstone. Above lies the Parkhall Sweet Coal (Figure 18, columns 1,4,7,9), of variable thickness up to 0.74 m, but nowhere worked. At New Haden Colliery a fauna of 'mussels', fish and ostracods is recorded from the overlying black shale. Strata at about this level in the sequence are exposed in the streams west of Hatchley, where they consist of mudstones with one or more thin coals and several fossiliferous bands. A typical section [9813 4556] is:

	Thickness m
Mudstone, dark grey, with ironstone bands and 'mussels'	0.40
Ironstone, carbonaceous, fissile	0.20
Mudstone, dark grey	0.25
Coal	0.10
Seatearth, grey	0.10+

'Mussels' including *Carbonicola rhomboidalis* and *C. cristagalli*, the ostracod *Carbonita humilis* and fish debris have been collected from a similar section [9802 4534] in the main stream nearby. Black shale with ostracods has been noted in the same area, but the exact number and sequence of beds is obscured by folding and discontinuous exposure. In the next stream [9879 4553] a 0.1 m coal overlain by siltstone is thought to lie in the same part of the succession. Black shale with 'mussels' exposed in the stream [9912 4491] by Parkford and black shale with ostracods exposed about 230 m downstream from here, are also thought to lie at about this level, as is a section [9922 4439] by Parkhall Colliery showing about a metre of dark grey mudstone with ironstone bands containing 'mussels'. Thin coal seams are exposed at several points in this stretch of stream, but their exact stratigraphical relationship to one another and to the Parkhall Sweet Coal, which is named from its occurrence in the nearby colliery shaft (Figure 18, column 9), is unknown.

A sandstone not far above the level of the Parkhall Sweet Coal forms a low feature that can be traced from the stream section west of The Bates [984 452], where it is exposed over a distance of about 350 m, south to the Dilhorne Fault near Parkhall Farm [992 438]. There are small exposures of the sandstone in a stream near here, with a thin coal above. A section [9920 4407] shows:

	Thickness m
Mudstone, dark grey	0.17
Coal with black shale laminae	0.10
Shale, black, with coal laminae	0.16
Coal with black shale laminae	0.10
Seatearth, soft	0.30

The Dilhorne Coal, its outcrop revealed by old surface working, lies not far away but the intervening strata—mainly mudstone with thin coals (Figure 18)—are cut out by faulting. However, the missing strata are exposed in a discontinuous strike section in the stream that runs south of The Bates and past Godleybarn [983 445] towards Parkhall Farm. Small-scale folding and faulting make it impossible to equate the various coals and faunal bands seen in these exposures with those shown in Figure 18. The lowest beds, probably at the same horizon as those in the measured section detailed above, are exposed south of The Bates. The best section [9829 4510] shows:

	Thickness m
Mudstone, pale grey; ironstone bands near base	1.00
Shale, black, with ostracods, fish debris and 'mussels'	0.07
Mudstone, grey, slickensided	0.15
Siltstone, black, hard	0.05
Coal with black shale laminae	0.05
Seatearth, grey; passage at base	0.25
Sandstone with siltstone bands	—

Strata at about the same level, including at least one thin seam of coal, are exposed at intervals for about 400 m downstream from here and are overlain by siltstone and sandstone exposed [984 446] near Godleybarn. Downstream from the latter the beds immediately below the Dilhorne Coal are exposed. Sections [9863 4427] in folded strata show the following composite sequence:

	Thickness m
Coal with a few shale partings (base of Dilhorne)	0.54
Siltstone with rootlets	0.18
Mudstone, silty; rootlets at top; irregular ironstone nodules	c.2.20
Sandstone, buff, fine-grained	0.35
Mudstone, grey, silty at top; ironstone bands in lower part	1.60
Mudstone, dark grey, fissile	0.25
Cannel with bright coal laminae in lower part	0.17
Seatearth, grey	0.20 +

Exposures of siltstone, sandstone and mudstone between here and the Dilhorne Fault near Parkhall Farm lie in the same part of the sequence. South of the Dilhorne Fault these measures are recorded in a shaft and two boreholes (Figure 18, columns 4,6,7) but there are no good exposures. During the deepening of the New Haden shaft, faunas were collected from the strata between the Dilhorne and Parkhall Sweet coals, including *Geisina arcuata, Carbonicola* aff. *oslancis, Naiadites flexuosus* and fish remains. A fauna recorded by Ward (1906, p.122) 19.5 m below the Dilhorne Coal at Cheadle Park Colliery is probably from about the same horizon. In a cutting [004 425] near Cheadle Station a section below the Dilhorne Coal formerly extended down to a seam of 'cannel shale' (Barrow, 1903, p.27), but only the seatearth of the Dilhorne can be seen now.

At the west side of the coalfield there are several small exposures of the strata between the Alecs and Dilhorne coals in gullies in Foxfield Wood [974 448], but correlation of individual beds with those recorded in the shaft nearby (Figure 18, column 1) has proved impossible. Feature-forming sandstones have been mapped south from here as far as Whympney Wood [974 439].

Dilhorne Coal

The Dilhorne Coal is thickest (1.83 m) in the north-west and thinnest (0.60 m) in the south-east; it is now almost worked out. Over most of the area from which it has been extracted it ranges between 1.4 and 1.6 m in thickness and is of good quality.

At the western outcrop the seam has not been seen south of the Dilhorne Fault and its surface position has been inferred there from levels underground. The thickness beneath Dilhorne Common [977 433] ranged from 1.4 to 1.6 m and in a borehole (SJ 94 SE/1) it was 1.52 m thick. North of the Dilhorne Fault the outcrop swings round the north end of the main coalfield syncline; the seam was worked from shallow pits and has probably all been taken out (Barrow, 1903, p.27) though no detailed records have survived. The line of outcrop is pitted by old surface workings from Foxfield Wood [975 448] to Godleybarn [983 445]. The thickness at Foxfield Colliery shaft (Figure 18, column 1) was 1.83 m, of which 0.3 m, shaly at the top and overlain by grey clay, is visible by the colliery sidings [9761 4454]. The lowest 0.54 m of the seam, resting on seatearth, is exposed in the stream bank [9863 4427] below Godleybarn. East of here the coal is twice repeated by north-south faults; old surface workings reveal a small outcrop 450 m south of Parkhall Colliery [993 444], though there are no exposures, and a narrow fault-bounded strip about 350 m east of the colliery was proved by drilling and then worked opencast. The thickness in a trial pit [9959 4470] near the north end of this working was 1.43 m.

South of the Dilhorne Fault the seam has been worked eastwards as far as a fault at the western end of the hill of Triassic sandstone at Cheadle Park [006 436]. A borehole (Figure 18, column 7) drilled in 1903 at the foot of the hill here proved the coal to be 1.40 m thick and confirmed its stratigraphical position beyond any doubt (Barrow, 1903, p.28). A heading through the fault at the limit of working proved the existence of the seam beneath Cheadle Park but it was never worked, probably for fear of tapping the water in the overlying Triassic sandstones. South of Cheadle Park the seam crops out again and is exposed in a railway cutting [0047 4256]: black shale *on* coal 1.30 m *on* black shale 0.02 m *on* seatearth. It was worked in this area, and farther south, as the Huntley Coal until its true identity was established by Barrow (1903, p.27). South of the railway cutting the seam can be traced by surface indications until it is cut off by a fault near the Triassic escarpment at Mobberley [007 413]. Trial boreholes near Dandillions [007 421] showed the seam to be between 0.6 and 1.0 m thick but full of old workings. To the west of here the seam has been worked at depth from New Haden Colliery across the centre of the syncline and as far south as the Callowhill Fault. The thickness at New Haden shaft (Figure 18, column 4) was 1.52 m.

Strata between Dilhorne and Little Dilhorne coals

These are about 20 m thick, mainly mudstone (Figure 18), though with a sandstone south of Majorsbarn [002 429]. The sandstone can be seen at the west end of the railway cutting [0036 4255] by Cheadle Station. The roof-measures of the Dilhorne Coal are exposed at the east end of the cutting [0046 4256], where the section (*see also* Barrow, 1903, p.27) is:

	Thickness m
Mudstone, grey, with ironstone bands	0.80
Shale, black, with ironstone bands; a cannelloid band at top contains *Anthracosia regularis*, *Carbonicola venusta*, *Geisina arcuata*, fish debris and *Spirorbis*	0.50
Mudstone, grey, with a few ironstone bands	1.85
Shale, black	0.06
Dilhorne Coal	—

A list of the fish species is given by Ward (1906, p.123).

A higher faunal band, with abundant 'mussels', was encountered about 7 m above the Dilhorne Coal in a borehole (Figure 18, column 2) and a thin coal overlain by black shale with fish debris was found 14.7 m above the Dilhorne in a borehole (SJ94SE/1) on Dilhorne Common. The beds immediately below the Little Dilhorne Coal are exposed in a deep ditch near Foxfield Colliery, a typical section [9783 4466] being:

	Thickness m
Little Dilhorne Coal	—
Seatearth, grey, argillaceous	1.0
Siltstone, grey, with ironstone nodules and some rootlets	0.3

Little Dilhorne Coal

The seam is of good quality but owing to its small thickness (0.61 to 0.86 m) has only locally been worked. North of the Dilhorne Fault its existence was recorded by Barrow (1903, p.27) in a shaft at Oldengine Farm [983 441] and a recent borehole nearby (Figure 18, column 2) has proved its thickness to be 0.86 m. North of Godleybrook [978 445] the seam lies very close to the surface and a considerable area is covered with old pits. A section of the coal, probably part of a pillar left to support the workings, can be seen in a ditch [9773 4484], the thickness being 0.50 m. Just south of Godleybrook an area at the centre of the syncline was worked opencast in 1951, with a thickness of 0.66 m. The seam was also worked opencast, with the Dilhorne Coal, in a narrow fault-bounded strip east of Parkhall Colliery. The thickness recorded in a trial pit [9973 4436], dug prior to working, was 0.65 m.

South of the Dilhorne Fault two small areas of the seam beneath Dilhorne Common have been mined from Foxfield Colliery; in one of these, near Blake Hall [983 430], the thickness was 0.74 m. Elsewhere on Dilhorne Common a borehole (SJ 94 SE/1) proved the coal absent though there are no plans of workings at this point. Farther south, small areas were exploited close to the shafts at New Haden Colliery, the thickness there being 0.71 m (Figure 18, column 4). At the eastern outcrop the existence of the seam was noted by Barrow (1903, p.27) and there are signs of outcrop working [005 415] near Mobberley, but no reliable records of thickness exist.

Strata between Little Dilhorne Coal and Vanderbeckei Marine Band

These are about 25 m thick and consist of two or three cycles, each capped by a thin coal or seatearth (Figure 18). There are no exposures. At the base, the roof-measures of the Little Dilhorne Coal, proved in a borehole (Figure 18, column 2), are mudstones with cannelloid bands and a fauna of 'mussels', fish debris and ostracods. The highest of the coals, at the top of the subdivision, is the thickest (normally 0.38 to 0.53 m but only 2 cm in a borehole (SJ 94 SE/1) at Dilhorne Common) and has been found wherever this part of the sequence has been drilled. The other two seams are only locally present. Above the upper one a fauna of 'mussels', ostracods and fish debris was recorded in the borehole at Dilhorne Common.

Vanderbeckei Marine Band

Prior to the survey by Barrow (1903, p.29) the Dilhorne Coal was confused with a higher seam, the Two Yard. As a consequence of this the strata between the Four Foot and Alecs seams were thought to be about 36 m thick and devoid of workable coals (Molyneux *in* Plant, 1881, pp.293–294, 300; Ward, 1890, pp.80–81). The drilling of a borehole in 1903 (Figure 18, column 7) near the Old Brassworks proved the true nature and thickness of these measures for the first time and revealed the existence at Cheadle of a richly fossiliferous band (Stobbs, 1905, p.510) later correlated (Cope, 1946, p.11) with the Seven Feet Banbury Marine Band of the Potteries Coalfield and hence (Ramsbottom and others, 1978, plate 2) with the Vanderbeckei Marine Band. The band is taken by international agreement as the boundary between Westphalian stages A and B.

DETAILS

The band has been proved in three boreholes and a shaft section (Figure 18) but is not exposed at surface. Following the initial discovery in the borehole near the Old Brassworks a section and faunal list were recorded by Stobbs (1905, p.511) at New Haden (Draycott) Colliery (Figure 18, column 4). In a recent borehole (Figure 18, column 6) the section was:

	Thickness m
Mudstone, pale grey, with ironstone bands	—
Mudstone, grey, with ironstone bands and abundant non-marine fauna including *Anthracosia aquilina*, *A. aff. lateralis*, *A. ovum*, *Naiadites quadratus*, *Carbonita inflata*, *C. evalinae*, *C.* cf. *bairdiodes*, and *Spirorbis sp.*	5.54
Mudstone, grey, with fragments of *Anthracoceratites sp.*, *Lingula mytilloides*, arenaceous foraminifera, *Naiadites sp.* and *Anthracosia sp.*	1.24
Mudstone, dark grey, with rich marine fauna including *Anthracoceratites vanderbeckei*, *Dunbarella papyracea mut.* γ and *Holinella* cf. *claycrossensis*	0.49
Mudstone, dark grey, silty, with fish debris	0.05
Coal	—

Strata between Vanderbeckei Marine Band and top of proved sequence

These measures are about 105 m thick and consist of seven cycles, with five workable coals (Figure 18). Of the latter the Yard Coal was considered to be the best (Barrow, 1903, p.32) and was the most extensively mined, but all have been worked, both along the outcrops and at depth. Plans of a few mines exist but for most of the workings there is now no evidence other than the widespread uneven topography of subsidence and the remains of old waste tips. The extent of old workings has made these seams a poor prospect for opencast mining and only small areas of the Four Foot, Litley and Two Yard coals have been won by this means. Several sandstones are recorded in shaft sections (Figure 18) but none has been mapped, due to the lack of surface features. Many of the mudstones contain non-marine faunas of 'mussels', ostracods, fish debris and *Spirorbis*, notably above the Vanderbeckei Marine Band and above the Four Foot, Litley and Half Yard coals. The faunas are typical of the ovum and phrygiana belts, from the higher part of the Modiolaris Zone.

DETAILS

Strata between Vanderbeckei Marine Band and Four Foot Coal

Mudstones about 7 m thick, with a rich fauna of 'mussels', overlie the marine band (see above). These are succeeded by barren mudstone, siltstone and sandstone; some small exposures of siltstone in the stream bank [0033 4184] north of Huntley are believed to lie in this part of the sequence.

Four Foot Coal

The coal is only present south of the Dilhorne Fault. It was described by Barrow (1903, p.33) as of inferior quality and by Cope (1946, p.12) as containing 4 per cent of sulphur and many dirt partings. It was worked all along the outcrop but only in patches at depth. The thickness ranges from 0.58 to 1.27 m, with 1.08 m as an average. On the west side of the syncline the seam incrops on the base of the Triassic sandstones along a north–south line through Dilhorne Common [976 433] and Callowhill [975 427]. Plans exist of workings not far west of Boundary [981 425] and there may have been other workings north of here for which no records remain. Thus at Dilhorne Common a borehole (SJ 94 SE/1) proved coal absent at the appropriate level, though in this instance the lack of coal could be due to pre-Triassic oxidation. Plans of Delphhouse Colliery show workings in two areas, one [987 427] near the centre of the syncline (Figure 18, column 3) and one [994 428] on the eastern flank near Brookhouses, but there is no doubt that uncharted workings are widespread to the north of here, for there are shafts reported to have been sunk to the Four Foot Coal near Newclosefield [984 436], Parkhall Farm [992 437] and Brookhouses [995 430]. The coal was unusually thin and shaly in the borehole (Figure 18, column 7) near the Old Brassworks, but was a normal thickness, 1.09 m, in another (Figure 18, column 6) nearby. The seam does not reach the surface in the area north of Brookhouses, being cut off by a north–south fault that runs beneath Cheadle Park close to the borehole last mentioned. East and south of Brookhouses the seam crops out in a heavily faulted area where several patches have been worked, with the overlying Litley Coal, in opencast pits. The thickness in these generally was about 1.1 m, with a pyritic band recorded in the lower part. West of the outcrop area plans of deeper workings exist, with records of older unmapped workings, at New Haden Colliery; the thickness in the main shaft there (Figure 18, column 4) was 1.19 m.

Strata between Four Foot and Litley coals

The thickness of strata between these seams is normally 9 or 10 m (Figure 18) but may locally be as little as 6.72 m (see below). Immediately above the Four Foot Coal lies a band with 'mussels' and plant remains, recorded by Ward (1906, pp.126–127) from the New Haden shaft sinking. A borehole (Figure 18, column 6) has also encountered the band and it was seen during opencast operations near Majorsbarn in 1964, where the section [000 428] was:

	Thickness m
Litley Coal	—
Sandstone, pale grey, ganister-like	1.83
Mudstone, pale grey, with siltstone bands	2.74
Mudstone, dark grey, with ironstone bands and abundant 'mussels' including *Anthracosia* cf. *ovum*, *A. phrygiana* and *Anthracosphaerium turgidum*	0.91
Mudstone, grey, with ironstone nodules and sparse 'mussels' including *Anthracosia subrecta* and *Anthracosphaerium affine*	1.14
Shale, black	0.10
Four Foot Coal	—

The sandstone at the top of the cycle is also prominent in the shaft sections (Figure 18, columns 3, 4) but nowhere does it form a mappable surface feature.

Litley Coal

The seam is generally in two leaves (Figure 18), the thickness of coal varying from 0.79 to 1.55 m, with an average value of 1.20 m. In the west the sub-Triassic incrop lies close to that of the Four Foot, described above. The horizon was identified a few metres below the unconformity in the borehole (SJ 94 SE/1) on Dilhorne Common but there was no coal, doubtless as a result of pre-Triassic oxidation. No plans exist of workings in this area but some of the shafts [978 425] west of Boundary are reputed to have been sunk to the Litley, and farther north some sunk to the Four Foot near Newclosefield [984 436] must have intersected the seam. East of here, likewise, there are shafts to the Four Foot near Parkhall Farm [992 437] and near Brookhouses [995 430], with a possibility of workings in the Litley. A borehole (Figure 18, column 6) at Cheadle Park showed coal 0.84 m *on* mudstone 0.15 m *on* shaly coal 0.08 *on* pyritous coal 0.48 m. The older borehole nearby (Figure 18, column 7) gave a similar section, though with less coal. An exposure of coal, dipping steeply into the Dilhorne Fault in a stream bank [9918 4393] near Parkhall Farm, may be of the Litley. The section shows grey clay *on* coal 0.25 m *on* coal and black shale 0.27 m *on* coal 0.29 m *on* grey clay. Otherwise the outcrop of the Litley Coal is restricted to the area south and east of Brookhouses; an isolated exposure of part of the seam can be seen in a stream bed [9923 4268] near Haden House Farm. Opencast operations have removed several patches of the seam, together with the underlying Four Foot Coal. A section [000 428] measured during the excavation showed coal 0.23 m *on* clay 0.13 m *on* coal 1.09 m. At a deeper level, to the south-west of the outcrop area, there have been minor workings at New Haden Colliery (Figure 18, column 4), where the seam section was: coal 0.81 m *on* clunch 0.30 m *on* coal 0.46 m. A shaft [9990 4203] near Litley is reputed to have been sunk through the Triassic sandstones to the Litley Coal, but no seam plan exists. Similarly, at Delphhouse Colliery, where shaft sections (for example, Figure 18, column 3) show the seam to be 0.84 m thick, in a single leaf, workings are known to exist, though no detailed records remain.

Strata between Litley and Yard coals

The thickness of these strata is about 16 m (Figure 18). The mudstone roof of the Litley Coal contains a fauna of 'mussels' with fish debris and *Spirorbis* (Ward, 1890, pp.92–93; 1906, p.127; Barrow, 1903, p.31). The bed was exposed during opencast mining near Majorsbarn, the section [000 428] being:

	Thickness m
Mudstone, pale grey and pink	3.05
Mudstone, dark grey, with ironstone bands and 'mussels' including *Anthracosia* aff. *beaniana*, *A.* aff. *lateralis* and *A. phrygiana*	0.25
Mudstone, pale grey with pink bands	0.30
Litley Coal	—

The overlying sandstone recorded in some shaft sections (Figure 18) forms no surface feature and cannot be mapped.

Yard Coal

The seam is of good quality and is probably almost worked out (Barrow, 1903, pp.32–33). The thickness varies between 0.76 and 1.14 m, the average being 0.99 m. The sub-Triassic incrop from west of Boundary [980 427] to the Dilhorne Fault has been calculated from old shaft records that quote depths at which the seam was reached and from levels in the Dilhorne Coal workings below. Plans of some Yard Coal workings in this area exist but the cover is not complete. On the eastern flank of the syncline the seam crops out west of Adderley [992 435], the line being fixed precisely from borehole evidence. The ground is very uneven with old outcrop workings. East of Adderley the seam is repeated by faulting but the outcrop position is not well documented. East of this outcrop the seam is again repeated by faulting and a sub-Triassic incrop below Cheadle Park can be inferred from a borehole section (Figure 18, column 6). The borehole proved the horizon of the seam, about 8 m below the unconformity, but there was no coal, its absence being attributed to pre-Triassic oxidation. South of Brookhouses the outcrop is shifted west by a fault to Lower Delphhouse Wood [990 427], whence it can be traced by old surface workings to the edge of the made ground associated with New Haden Colliery. The seam was formerly exposed in a railway cutting [993 422] below the colliery (Barrow, 1903, p.32) and is displaced by a north–south fault there. The thickness in the shaft (Figure 18, column 4) was 1.02 m. From the fault just mentioned to the foot of the Triassic sandstone scarp the outcrop is known from boreholes. The workings are said (Barrow, 1903, p.31) to have extended south beneath the Trias to Huntley Wood [998 416], but no plans exist. There are, however, plans of extensive workings west of here, especially at Delphhouse Colliery, but the limits of working are nowhere known in detail and there may be some coal left in a strip north of the Callowhill Fault. The thickness at Delphhouse (Figure 18, column 3) was 1.14 m.

Strata between Yard and Half Yard coals

The strata between these coals vary in thickness from 12 to 18 m. A fish fauna was recorded by Ward (1906, p.128) from a bed of dark shale resting on the Yard Coal at Delphhouse and in the railway cutting [993 422] by New Haden Colliery. The overlying sandstone forms no surface feature and is not exposed.

Half Yard Coal

The seam is of fair quality and has been widely worked (Barrow, 1903, p.32) but plans exist of workings in only two small areas, at Delphhouse Colliery [986 427] and Madgedale Colliery [981 437]. The average thickness is 0.77 m. West of Boundary [980 427] the incrop at the base of the Triassic sandstones has been calculated from that of the Yard Coal. On the east side of the syncline, likewise, the outcrop is conjectured largely by calculation from the position of the Yard Coal, for there are no unequivocal signs of crop working by which it can be traced. Its position is independently fixed by borehole evidence locally, however, as at Lower Delphhouse Wood [989 427], where the thickness in a trial pit was 0.79 m, and in the railway cutting [993 422] by New Haden Colliery (Barrow, 1903, p.32). The thickness in the shaft here (Figure 18, column 4) was 0.74 m.

Strata between Half Yard and Two Yard coals

These measures are 22 to 25 m thick. A band of hard shale with fossils that forms the roof of the Half Yard Coal was formerly exposed in the railway cutting (see above) by New Haden Colliery (Barrow, 1903, pp.31–32). It was also recorded by Ward (1906, pp.128–129) from a shaft sinking at Delphhouse Colliery, where it contained fish debris, abundant 'mussels' and bands with abundant *Spirorbis*. The overlying sandstone, not exposed, contains a thin coal locally, the Getley Coal, which was described as 'useless' (Barrow, 1903, p.31).

Two Yard Coal

The seam is described by Barrow (1903, p.32) as of poor quality. The thickness varies from 1.68 to 2.16 m, in one or two leaves. Workings in the seam north of Bull Pit [9860 4282] at Delphhouse, and at Surprise Pit [9900 4197], are recorded in mine plans, but uncharted workings near the outcrop were proved by boreholes about 400 m east of Blake Hall [983 430] and in an opencast excavation [986 426] at Upper Delphhouse Wood; such workings are doubtless present wherever the seam lies close to the surface. The thickness recorded in the opencast site was 1.83 m, and in the area drilled east of Blake Hall a typical section was: coal 1.37 m *on* dark shale 0.46 m *on* coal 0.46 m. The incrop of the seam at the base of the Trias has been calculated from seam levels in the Dilhorne workings below; in the outcrop area the same procedure has been followed but with fixed points provided by information from boreholes, opencast workings and old records of exposures (Barrow, 1903, p.32).

Strata above Two Yard Coal

Strata proved above the Two Yard Coal in shafts at Delphhouse Colliery are the highest for which details are known. They consist of mudstone and sandstone capped by a coal 'smut' 13.5 m above the Two Yard Coal. The beds immediately above the Two Yard Coal at Wonder Pit [9901 4204] were recorded by Ward (1906, p.129) as a thin black shale with fish debris, overlain by mudstone with 'mussels'.

Unproved higher strata

An additional 60 to 70 m of unrecorded strata are estimated to lie above the coal 'smut', in the centre of the syncline north of the Callowhill Fault and largely concealed by the Triassic cover. South of the Callowhill Fault no details are known, for the only attempt to mine coal here was abandoned due to the great flow of water when shafts [988 412] near Draycott Cross were being sunk into the Triassic sandstones.

JIC

CHAPTER 6

Dolomitisation of Dinantian limestones

SURFACE DOLOMITES

Secondary dolomitisation is extensively developed in the limestones of the north-east corner of the district between Ballidon and Brassington while smaller outcrops are present to the west around Tissington and Parwich (Figure 24). All the occurrences lie within an irregular belt that extends into the Buxton (Aitkenhead and others, 1985), Chesterfield (Smith and others, 1967) and Derby (Frost and Smart, 1979) districts. Much of the existing information has been summarised by Aitkenhead and others.

The secondary dolomitisation is characterised by its irregular and cross-cutting relationship to the stratigraphy and by its disappearance at depth. The dolomite/limestone interface is in most cases quite sharp though minor dolomitisation is widespread along joints outside the dolomite outcrop. Aitkenhead and others draw attention to the close overall association between secondary dolomitisation and the occurrence of Pocket Deposits, though the latter have a slightly wider distribution. In the present district both occur in the north-eastern outcrop though in the Weaver Hills only Pocket Deposits are present.

The dolomitisation has been attributed to the action of downward-percolating brines from the Zechstein sea in late Permian times (Parsons, 1922, p.63; Dunham, 1952, p.415). There is direct evidence that it pre-dates the mineralisation at Golconda Mine (Aitkenhead and others, 1985, p.121) and elsewhere. The last authors (1985, p.102) consider that, in view of the absence of proved Permian deposits around the area of secondary dolomitisation, alteration by Triassic groundwaters is a possibility; but in either case, control of the process by an impermeable Namurian cover, subsequently removed, is considered to account for the patchy distribution of the dolomites.

The dolomite probably reaches a maximum thickness of about 100 m in the present district, to the north-east of Carsington. At outcrop the rock is buff, medium to coarsely crystalline and vughy. In places the rock contains undolomitised bioclasts and, on a larger scale, less-altered masses of limestone also occur.

Just north of the district a sharp but irregular contact at the base of the dolomite was formerly exposed in Manystones Quarry [2359 5506] (Aitkenhead and others, 1985, p.103). Around Brassington the rock forms a number of characteristic tors (see also p.110); in one of these, Rainster Rocks [2190 5483] about 40 m of massive partly cavernous dolomite is exposed. The irregular base of the dolomite is well seen in the valley [211 545] west of Black Rocks. A quarry [2124 5084] north-east of Kniveton (see also p.26) shows a partially dolomitised knoll-reef in the Milldale Limestones; the lower contact of the dolomite is sharp and undulating.

DEEPER DOLOMITES

Other surface occurrences, mostly small isolated outcrops in the Hopedale Limestones, are less likely to be attributable to sub-Permo-Triassic alteration. More probably they are surface outcrops of the second main type of dolomitised limestone, which is interstratified either with unaltered limestones or with other sediments; this is known mainly from boreholes. The most notable occurrences (Figure 24) are in boreholes at Lees Farm (SK 15 SE/12), Rusheycliff Barn near Tissington (SK 15 SE/8), Bradbourne (SK 25 SW/18) and Caldon Low (SK 04 NE/36). The diagenesis of these dolomites has not been studied and they may prove to have a complex history.

In the Lees Farm Borehole, the dolomitised limestones are a subordinate component of the mudstone-dominated turbidite sequence of the Widmerpool Formation that also contains basaltic volcaniclastic rocks. In the laterally equivalent carbonates of the Hopedale Limestones, proved in the Rusheycliff Barn Borehole, about one third of the sequence is dolomitised (Figure 12; Bridge and Kneebone, 1983, p.53). Dolomite is also predominantly present between depths of 17.32 and 55.76 m in the Hopedale Limestones proved in the Bradbourne Borehole, interstratified with unaltered or partially dolomitised limestone (Cox and Harrison, 1980, p.130).

The dolomites in these boreholes are either interbedded with, or in an area marginal to, the predominantly argillaceous sequence of the Widmerpool Gulf. This suggests that the dolomitisation is analogous to that in the lower part of the Woo Dale Limestones, recently described by Schofield and Adams (1986). These authors conclude that much of the magnesium and iron available for dolomitisation came from formation-waters expelled from surrounding basinal sediments during deep burial in late Carboniferous times, and from decomposing volcanic rocks.

In the Caldon Low Borehole (Figure 6), the Rue Hill Dolomites include very fine-grained finely laminated dolomites or dololutites that commonly show brecciation probably indicative of the former presence of evaporites (Plate 2.2a). The dolomitisation in this sequence may therefore be very early, associated with periods of hypersalinity in an intertidal/supratidal sabkha environment. The dolomitisation is not confined to this facies, however, but also affects the fully marine bioclastic limestones both intercalated and overlying; its present distribution is thus mainly of later diagenetic origin.

At Wardlow Quarry (p.29) the presence in the Caldon Low Conglomerate of pebbles of dolomite set in a limestone matrix, indicates that some dolomitisation of the Milldale Limestones had already taken place prior to deposition of the conglomerate, which is of Asbian age.   NA, JIC

CHAPTER 7

Triassic

Triassic rocks crop out over most of the southern half of the district and in the Leek outlier in the north-west. The main outcrop forms the northern edge of the Needwood Basin (Stevenson and Mitchell, 1953, p.68). The strata are classified according to Warrington and others (1980) into two major units, the Sherwood Sandstone Group below and the Mercia Mudstone Group above. These replace the 'Bunter' and 'Keuper' units which carried an invalid implication of chronostratigraphic equivalence with the sequence in Germany. The Sherwood Sandstone Group is distinguished by a dominance of sandstone over finer-grained sediments, and the Mercia Mudstone Group by that of mudstone and siltstone over sandstone. The sequence (Charsley, 1982) in the Ashbourne district has been classified into formations and members (see Table 5). The current view on the age of the various units is also shown. The rocks were deposited as continental red beds in a mainly semi-arid climate, and rivers transporting the sediment flowed from south to north across the area.

The Triassic rocks lie on an eroded surface of Carboniferous strata, ranging from Dinantian to Westphalian in age, that were folded and faulted during the Hercynian orogeny (see p.117). The period of erosion that followed removed a great thickness of strata and the resulting landform, controlled to a large extent by the Hercynian structure, was one whose relief was similar to that of the present day (see Figure 20).

The structure-contour map of the base of the Triassic (Figure 20) shows two main valleys, one in the west near Oakamoor and the other farther east aligned in part at least with the present River Dove. A number of embayments, probably the sites of tributaries, occur on the flanks of the Carboniferous highlands. Locally the pre-Triassic landscape is clearly evident, for example at Limestone Hill [136 463], which is a Dinantian knoll-reef where the base and top of the hill have been partly exhumed from beneath a Triassic sandstone cover. The orientation of a pre-Triassic valley at Cheadle was apparently controlled by the east-west trend of faults in the Westphalian, but this early topography, and the drainage system implied in the figure, was later buried by sediments carried across the area from south to north (Figure 21).

The Triassic rocks of the Leek outlier rest with marked unconformity on folded and faulted Carboniferous rocks, but are themselves only slightly deformed; tectonic dips are generally low (Figure 22) and only one fault is known. Around the margins of the outlier the basal contact dips inward at angles of up to 34° and boreholes nearer the centre confirm that the structure is an elongate closed hollow, with about 200 m of sandstone preserved in the deepest part. Approximate contours on the basal surface are shown in Figure 22. The structure is not a simple north-south syncline, for the dips observed at surface are much less than those inferred, or seen, at the marginal contacts; the steeply

Table 5 Classification of the Triassic in the Ashbourne district

Lithostratigraphic Subdivision			Stage
Mercia Mudstone Group	Undivided		Ladinian
			——?——
	Denstone Formation		Anisian
			——?——
Sherwood Sandstone Group	Hollington Formation		
	Hawksmoor Formation	Lodgedale Member	Scythian
		Freehay Member	
	Huntley Formation		

dipping east and west flanks of the hollow must represent the sides of a buried valley in the pre-Triassic landscape, as was recognised at an early date (Wardle in Sleigh, 1862, pp. 232, 288; Hull and Green, 1866, p. 62). Later tectonic warping has isolated the outlier (Aitkenhead and others, 1985, p.99).

PRE-TRIASSIC SURFACE

The surface of unconformity beneath the Triassic rocks can be seen at three localities: Hawksmoor Wood [0420 4458], Ordley Brook [1373 4628], near Stanton, and in a road-cutting in the Leek outlier near Basford Green (SJ 95 SE/62; see also Hull and Green, 1866, p.62 and fig.19). The basal unconformity here dips at 34°, with several metres of concordantly dipping sandstone above. The dip in the sandstones decreases away from the contact, and in a stream section [9950 5123], about 300 m distant, is almost flat. Several boreholes in the Triassic sandstones have penetrated the basal unconformity and have provided evidence of the form of the pre-Triassic surface (Figure 22).

Although elsewhere in the country the rocks of the sub-Triassic surface are commonly red-stained to a considerable depth, this is not the case in all parts of the present district, for there are many places, both at outcrop and underground in boreholes, where there is no reddening at all. Shallow depths of reddening are commonly observed close to the Triassic outcrop, however, and some of the Carboniferous

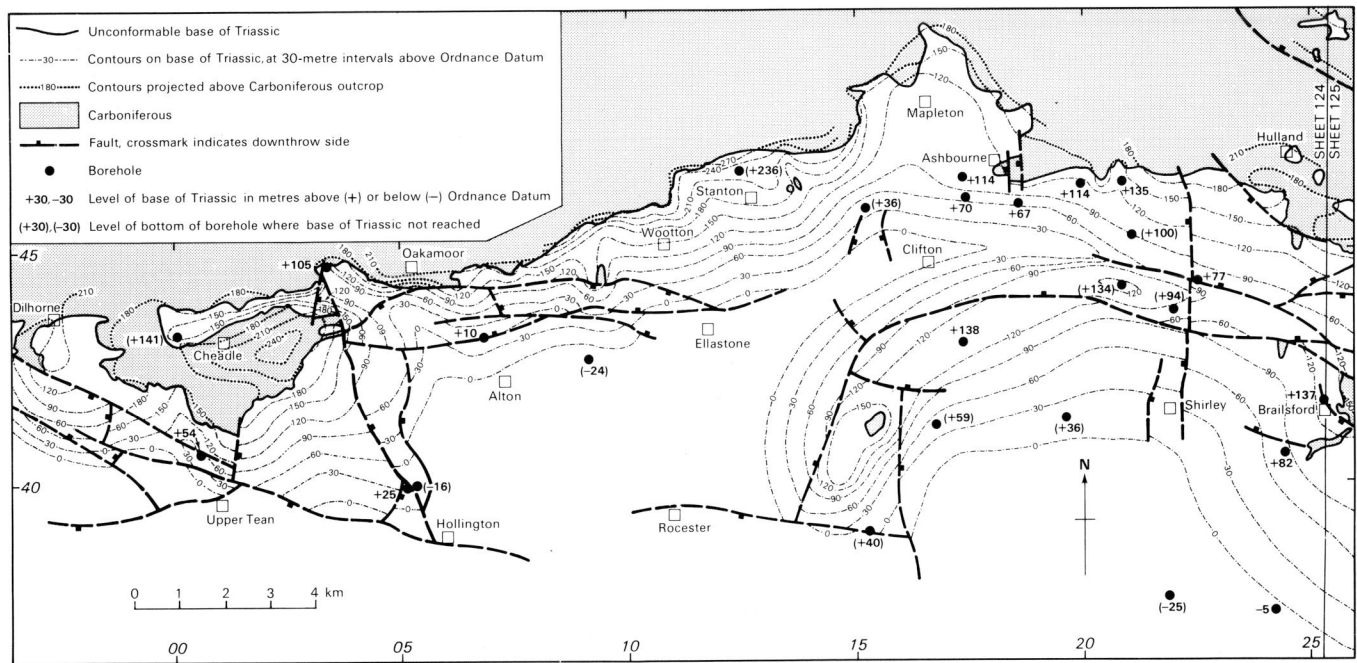

Figure 20 Structure contours on the base of the main Triassic outcrop; contours above Ordnance Datum only

rocks well away from the Trias are also reddened, an effect attributed to the former more widespread cover of Triassic rocks (Aitkenhead and others, 1985, p.99). TJC, JIC

Neptunian dykes of red siltstone and sandstone occupying fissures in the Dinantian limestones are believed to be of Triassic age on account of their colour. Such dykes are particularly common in the Caldon Low area, where they are up to 0.5 m wide, and occupy fissures partly filled with sparry calcite and hematite. The deepest encountered was in the Caldon Low Borehole (SK 04 NE/36), at a depth of 292 m below the surface. An example (E 51370) from Caldon Low could be termed an arenaceous limestone (see modal analysis, Table 3) but it is clear from microscopic evidence that much of the calcite replaces former terrigenous grains. The original sediment was probably a fine- to medium-grained moderately well sorted grainstone, possibly containing a proportion of limestone clasts that are now difficult to distinguish from the pervasive dominant sparry matrix; in its present form the rock would not appear to be grain supported. The replacement of clastic grains by calcite appears to be concentrated on feldspar and fine-grained lithic lithologies, thus enhancing the proportions of resistant grains such as quartz, quartzite and acidic volcanics. Like the samples from the Huntley Formation (p.76) this rock has grains coated by primary pellicles of ferric oxide. Accessory grains include opaque oxides, zircon, garnet and a local clot of kaolinite. JIC, NGB

Some of the Pocket Deposits (p.88) in collapse-hollows in the limestone may be of Triassic age. The best example is at Sallymoor [083 464], where 10 m of pebbly sandstone are overlain by 20 m of red and green siltstone and mudstone. The sequence resembles that of the nearby Triassic outcrop, where the Denstone Formation overlies the Hollington Formation. JIC

SHERWOOD SANDSTONE GROUP

In the district the group consists of sandstones, pebbly in part, and conglomerates which form a large part of the sequence locally. The rocks are in the main poorly cemented and soft or friable at outcrop, except for the Hollington Formation, which is for the most part moderately well cemented. Mudstones and siltstones occur as beds or intraclasts and are more common in the upper part of the sequence, where they are also more persistent. The dominant colour of the sediments is red-brown, but they are also yellow or brown in places and yellow-mottling is widespread. The red-brown colour is due to the presence of hematite either surrounding the sand grains or in the intergranular matrix. The hematite was probably deposited by circulating groundwater at an early stage, while many of the yellow or brown bands and mottles are of secondary origin, formed by the leaching or reduction of iron minerals by mineralising fluids.

The pebbles consist mainly of well rounded quartzite and quartz derived from outside the depositional area, with rarer pebbles including igneous rocks and fossiliferous sandstones, which point to a provenance between south-west England and north-west France. Local lithologies, including Carboniferous-type limestone, chert, sandstone and siltstone are abundant in places in the basal sandstones and are usually present in minor proportions throughout. Age determination of micas from the Stockport–Macclesfield area (Fitch and others, 1966) indicates a Hercynian age and also points to a source in a pre-existing Hercynian mountainous region between England and France. Cross-bedding measurements (Figures 21, 22) confirm that the sediments entered the district from a generally southerly direction, and this and the other evidence is in accord with the palaeoenvironmental reconstructions of Warrington (1970) and Wills (1970).

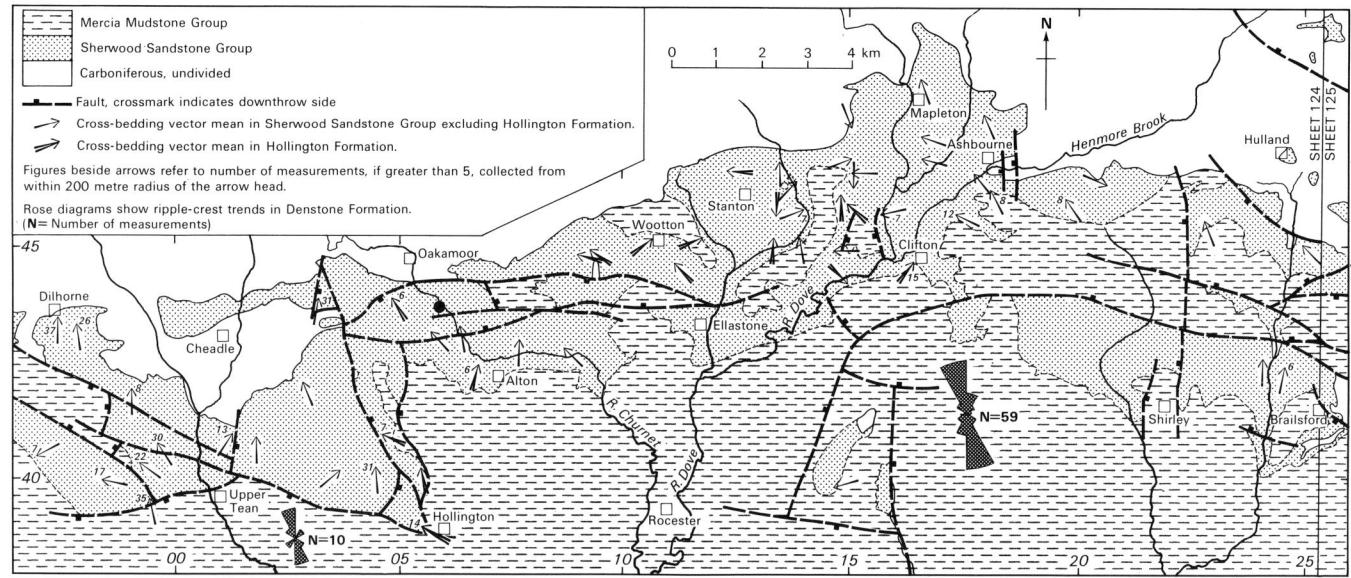

Figure 21 Generalised map of main Triassic outcrop, showing palaeocurrent data from Sherwood Sandstone Group and Denstone Formation

The mainly arenaceous lithology of the group is attributed to the effect of continental conditions in a fluvial environment. The lack of faunal or floral remains or traces in all but the youngest parts of the sequence points either to rapid deposition or to intensely oxidising conditions, and both were probably operative during most of the deposition of the group.

The Sherwood Sandstones give rise to poor soils and in many areas where they are pebbly no agricultural use has been made of the land. Many of the commons and woods of the district lie on steep slopes underlain by pebbly sandstones and conglomerates, as at Huntley Wood [998 416], Hawksmoor Nature Reserve [035 443], North Plantation [026 401] and Bradley Wood [200 462]. A characteristic topography consisting of closely spaced short narrow rounded dry valleys and interfluves occurs on the more homogeneous poorly cemented parts of the sequence; this is probably a periglacial feature (see p.111). A good example occurs in the Hawksmoor area [037 438].

In the south-western part of the district, and in the Leek outlier, the Sherwood Sandstone Group has been divided into formations (Charsley, 1982; Table 5); in the remainder of the district, however, subdivision has not proved possible and the Group itself has been mapped as a single unit.

The thickness of the Sherwood Sandstone Group varies from a feather edge on the flanks of the Weaver Hills and near Bradley [220 465], where it is overlapped by the Mercia Mudstone Group, to the maximum recorded thickness of at least 325 m in Cresswell No. 1 Borehole (SJ 93 NE/1). Comparative vertical sections of some of the thicker sequences are shown in Figure 23.

Details of the areas where the group is subdivided are given first and the undivided areas are separately described.

Huntley Formation

The Huntley Formation is present locally at the base of the Sherwood Sandstone Group where it overlies the sub-Triassic surface. The formation has been mapped in the area between the Weaver Hills and Cheadle, and typical sections occur close to the village of Huntley [003 412] (Charsley, 1982, p.2). Away from this area and as far east as Ashbourne the formation has been found locally at outcrop and is also recorded from a number of boreholes; owing to its extreme thinness it has not been mapped. Traces of its presence have also been detected in the Leek outlier (*see also* Aitkenhead and others, 1985, p.99).

The formation is defined on the basis of its distinctive lithology which consists predominantly of very coarse-grained pebbly sandstone or poorly sorted matrix-supported conglomerate containing a large proportion of locally-derived sub-rounded to angular clasts of granule to pebble size. The matrix is either red or yellow in colour and consists of silt to sand-sized grains commonly well cemented by calcite or dolomite. It is argillaceous locally where the formation overlies Carboniferous mudstone. TJC

The sandstones contain a much higher proportion of non-quartz lithoclasts than do the sandstones higher in the sequence (Table 3). Two samples (E 51368 and E 51369) from near Cheadle are strongly cemented by mostly sparry calcite and contain grains coated by primary pellicles of ferric oxide. Both are lithic grainstones containing a wide variety of lithoclast types including bioclastic limestone, chertified limestone, ferric-oxide cemented sandstone, metavolcanic rocks (commonly of intermediate composition), quartzose granulites and gneisses, and coarse granitic igneous rocks. One sample, E 51368, shows poor sorting without any obvious dominance of a particular grain size. However, in E 51369 there is a strong suggestion of bimodal grain distribution: the rock consists of a fine-grained lithic grainstone (clasts of 0.06 to 0.3 mm diameter) containing prominent pebbles up to 20 mm diameter. Many of the groundmass grains are subangular, a feature enhanced by partial calcitisation in many cases.   NGB

In the type area the formation varies in thickness between 4 m near Huntley and about 15 m in the disused railway tunnel [992 420] 2 km south-west of Cheadle, where Barrow (1903) noted two beds of conglomerate each 25 feet (7.6 m) thick separated by a thin red marl . Away from the type area there is a range in thickness between absence or 'feather edge' development to about 15 m.

No evidence for the age of these beds has yet been found, but together with the similar Moira and Hopwas breccias of neighbouring areas they are regarded as a basal facies of the Sherwood Sandstone Group, believed to be of Triassic age in the present district. However, the possibility of a Permian age for the Huntley Formation cannot be entirely ruled out.

Various lithological aspects of the formation, such as the angularity and local origin of the clasts and the nature of the bedding, point to a near-source origin within alluvial fans or as wadi-infills deposited by flash floods. Locally some of the deposits may be fossil screes infiltrated by water- or wind-borne fine-grained sediment. They are distinct in respect of their predominantly local origin from the rest of the Sherwood Sandstone Group.

DETAILS

In a cutting at the type section near Huntley an almost continuous exposure up to 2 m thick can be seen along the railway line for about 160 m [0037 4156 to 0024 4177]. The rock is typically a very coarse-grained pebbly sandstone, granular in texture, with a predominance of subrounded to subangular clasts of Carboniferous limestone, sandstone and siltstone. Exposures in the banks of a stream [014 437] which flows through Cheadle show up to 2.5 m of pebbly sandstone which is conglomeratic in part. Carboniferous-type clasts are abundant and included a bullion containing *Gastrioceras listeri*, the nearest exposure of which lies about 2 km to the north-east, a direction from which the beds were apparently derived according to cross-bedding directions measured at the Cheadle exposure.

On the flanks of the Weaver Hills east and south-east of Softlow Wood [109 462] four small outcrop areas occur consisting of a well cemented conglomerate made up mainly of subrounded to angular limestone clasts. Conglomerates of a similar type have been seen in small exposures in Ordley Brook near Stanton [1372 4628], near Mapleton [1641 4891] and as a line of large boulders beside a small stream north of Okeover Hall [1571 4859].

To the south, where the formation is overlain by an increasing thickness of Triassic rocks, a similar facies has been recorded in boreholes at Ashbourne and at Greatgate: for example about 3.7 m at the Nestlé Factory, Ashbourne (SK 14 NE/5A) and 13.7 m in Greatgate No. 1 Borehole (SK 03 NE/17).

In the Leek outlier, angular clasts of local derivation are present in the lowest part of a section [9701 5307] near the base of the Trias in the grounds of Cheddleton Hospital but elsewhere the Hawksmoor Formation appears to rest directly on the pre-Triassic surface.

Hawksmoor Formation

The formation takes its name from Hawksmoor Wood [035 443] 2.5 km ENE of Cheadle (Charsley, 1982, fig.2). It consists of red-brown, sporadically yellow-mottled, very fine- to coarse-grained sandstone which is commonly cross-bedded. Pebbles, predominantly of quartzite and quartz, are common in places, and in the area between Hawksmoor and Hollington (Staffs) the formation includes two conglomeratic units which have been separated as members (see below). A feature of the formation is that it is typically poorly cemented and friable, in marked contrast to the overlying Hollington Formation.

The formation commonly rests on the sub-Triassic unconformity, but locally it overlies the Huntley Formation. In the latter case, its base is taken at the point in the sequence where conglomerate or sandstone containing abundant locally-derived clasts gives way to a similar lithology but with few such clasts.

The thickness varies from a feather edge on the southern flanks of the Weaver Hills to a maximum development of about 156 m around Greatgate [052 400] with a similar thickness in the area of the Crumpwood No. 1 Borehole (SK 04 SE/11).

Outside the type area the formation has been mapped in an area south of the Carboniferous outcrop between Cheadle, Hollington (Staffs) and the River Dove, and in the Leek outlier. No evidence of age has been found, but it is correlated in a general way with the Pebble Beds division of Hull (1869).

The nature of the beds, and in particular of the conglomerates, indicate deposition in a high-energy fluvial environment, probably from braided rivers with only sporadic developments of overbank or floodplain deposits. Cross-bedding measurements indicate flow from a general southerly direction (Figures 21, 22).   TJC

DETAILS

In the west, Triassic escarpments at Cheadle Park [005 435] and from Huntley Wood to Dilhorne are composed largely of soft red sandstone, pebbly in part, the best exposures being in the sides of a dry valley [974 434] south of Dilhorne.   JIC

Sections in the Hawksmoor Nature Reserve include about 11 m of conglomerate and sandstone [0392 4422] and 2.8 m of trough cross-bedded sandstone with large mudstone clasts [0396 4467]. Exposures are common in the steep sides of the Churnet valley and its tributaries between Oakamoor and Crumpwood and include a section in the roadside [0720 4245] below Alton. The uppermost part is overlain by the Hollington Formation at Rainroach Rock [0631 4299] (see p.83). Farther east, good sections are present in Ordley Brook, east and south-east of Stanton. In particular, exposures of up to 8 m of cross-bedded, soft, red-brown, commonly yellow-mottled, fine- to medium-grained sandstone can be seen underlying hard pebbly sandstone of the Hollington Formation [between 1397 4587 and 1387 4510]. An exposure in a small waterfall [1382 4617] in the same stream shows an unusual lithological variation, more than ten discrete mudstone bands up to 48 cm thick being interbedded with sandstone.

A narrow stream section in Upper Mayfield shows about 29 m of soft red-brown and yellow fine- to medium-grained sandstone with sporadic pebbles [1504 4655 to 1514 4666].   TJC

In the southern half of the Leek outlier (Figure 22), up to about 100 m of soft sandstone are preserved in a valley in the pre-Triassic landscape. The sandstones are red, pink or buff, with scattered siliceous pebbles and a few conglomeratic bands. Red mudstone beds are rare. Flat bedding, low-angle wedge bedding and trough cross-bedding are all common, the last-named indicating a consistent palaeocurrent flow from south to north. The sandstones are

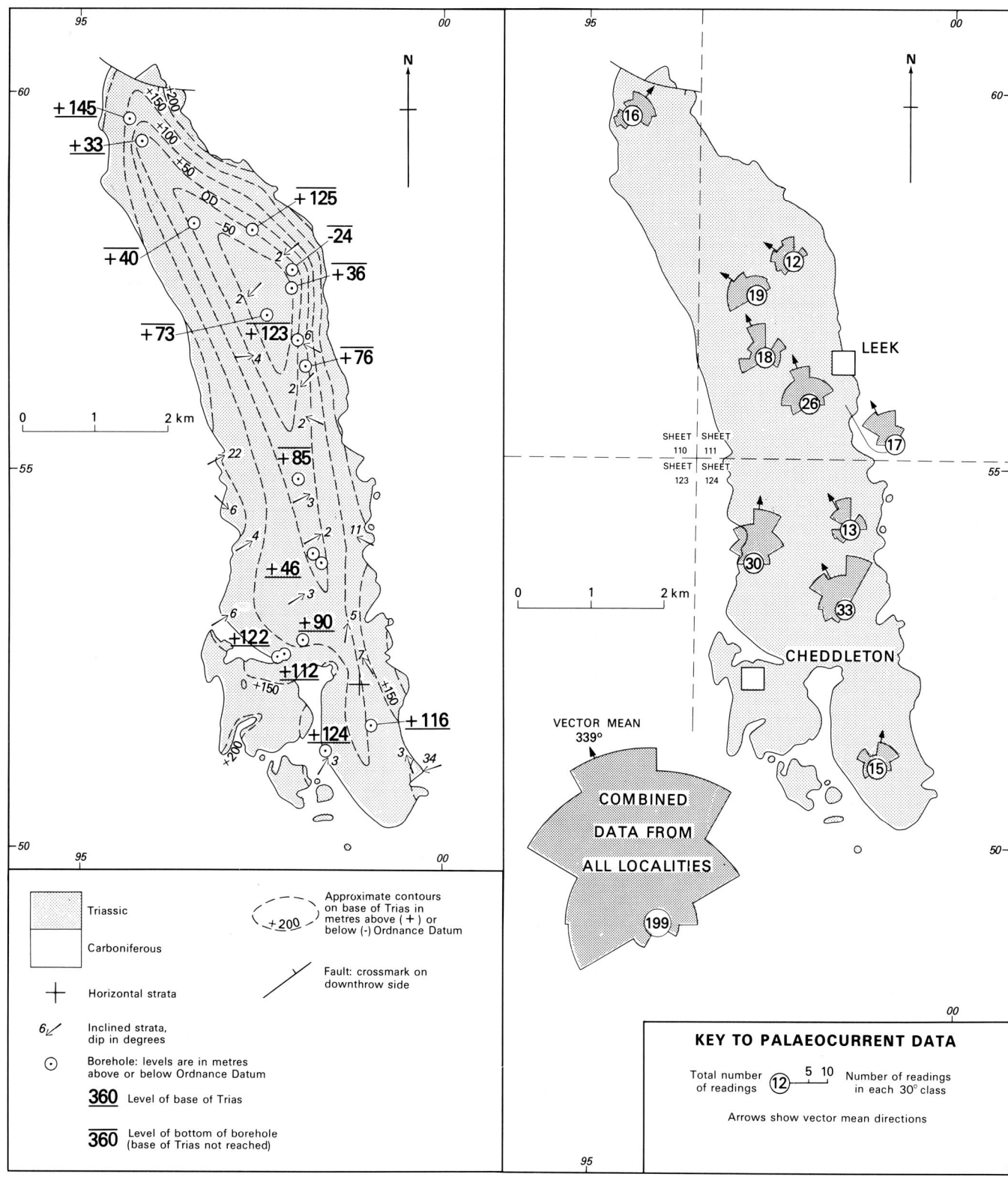

Figure 22 Structure, thickness and palaeocurrent data for Triassic rocks of the Leek outlier

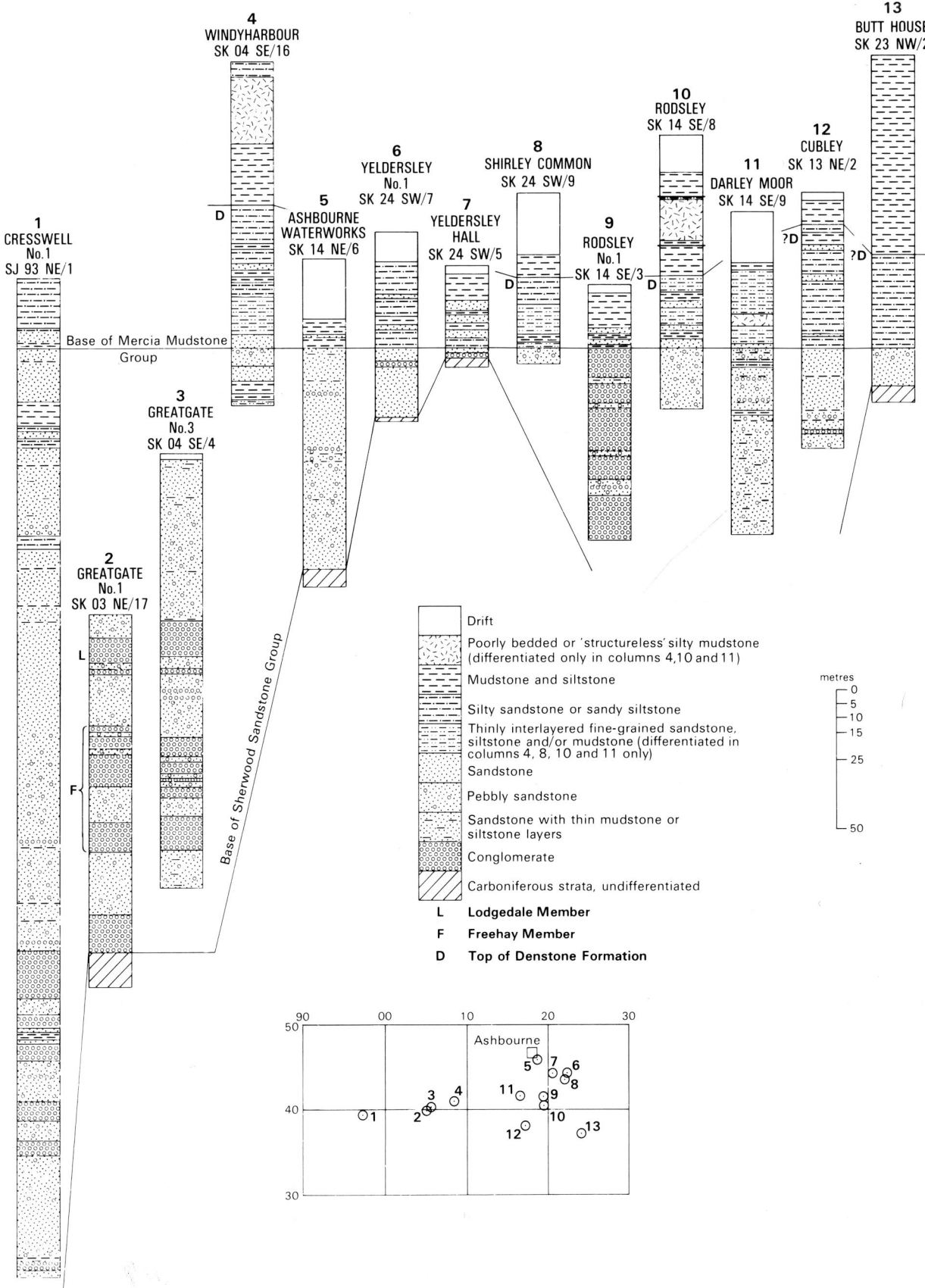

Figure 23 Comparative vertical sections of boreholes in the Sherwood Sandstone and Mercia Mudstone groups

mainly of Hawksmoor Formation lithologies, with only local traces of the Huntley Formation at the base (Aitkenhead and others, 1985, p.99).

The basal beds are best seen near Basford Green (SJ 95 SE/62) where a thin bed of red mudstone rests unconformably on the Chatsworth Grit. The overlying metre of Triassic strata is obscured but 3.3 m of soft red sandstone with scattered pebbles and a thin mudstone bed are seen above.

Exposures in the main mass of sandstone are common, the best being in railway and road cuttings. At Cheddleton Heath one of these [981 528] shows 23 m of sandstone and another [9810 5335] 17 m. Sections up to 15 m are seen north of Cheddleton Hospital [9730 5383], by Sheephouse Farm [9878 5413], and in a tunnel entrance by Leek Golf Course [9817 5456]. JIC

Freehay Member

To the east and south-east of Cheadle, between Freehay, Winnothdale and the Cheadle-Alton road, a persistent conglomeratic body up to 56 m thick has been separately mapped as a member within the Hawksmoor Formation. It has been extensively worked and sections showing up to 40 m can be seen in working and disused quarries, for example at Mobberley Quarry [012 409], Freehay Quarry [017 414] and Muddale Quarry [036 414]. A number of small natural sections can also be seen in Hawksmoor Nature Reserve [039 442].

The member consists of conglomerates with subordinate sandstones and sporadic mudstone beds or intraformational clasts. The conglomerates are either clast-supported or matrix-supported, and the two types may form alternating thin beds. Cross-bedding in the conglomerates in sets up to 2 m thick occurs in many places. The sandstones commonly occur as impersistent lenses which tend to be relatively well cemented compared to the poorly cemented conglomerates, and stand out as resistant ribs in the quarry faces.

Away from the type area, the member loses its identity as the proportion of sandstone increases. In Greatgate No. 1 Borehole (SK 03 NE/17), for instance, 3.5 km ESE of Freehay, a number of separate conglomerate units are present, with a total conglomerate thickness of only about 26 m (Figure 23). The unit has not been traced beyond the boundaries of Sheet SK 04 except in the area of Huntley Wood [993 416].

This member, with the Lodgedale Member (see below), may together be correlated with a conglomerate unit which Barrow (1903) noted south and east of Cheadle.

DETAILS

The principal sections in the Freehay Member occur in working and disused gravel quarries and complete sections have been proved in a number of boreholes (Rogers and others, 1981).

One of the best sections was in Muddale Quarry [038 417] and showed 41.5 m of interlayered conglomerates and partly pebbly sandstones, in the proportion 13 of conglomerate to 6 of sandstone. Maximum thicknesses of individual lithologies were 4.25 m and 2.3 m for conglomerate and sandstone respectively. Comparable figures were obtained from a 15.6 m section in Highshutt Quarry [032 439] with a maximum conglomerate thickness of 2.9 m.

Good quarry sections up to 39 m occur in Freehay Wood Quarry [017 414], and in Mobberley Quarry [012 409] where faults cut off the conglomerates along the east (Plate 8) and south sides. In Huntley Wood Quarry [995 415] up to 25 m of loose conglomerate

are visible, with subordinate beds of sandstone up to 1 m thick. A section in Hawksmoor Nature Reserve shows about 11 m of loose conglomerates and sandstones, while other small sections occur elsewhere in the Reserve (Charsley, 1982, fig.2).

Lodgedale Member

The member has been recognised only in an area between Winnothdale and Greatgate. It has been named after Lodgedale Farm [046 395] near Hollington (Staffs). A typical section of 5 m of crudely stratified poorly cemented conglomerate is present in a small gravel pit 270 m northeast of the farm.

The Lodgedale Member comprises pebbly sandstones and conglomerates. The latter, though locally predominant, are impersistent over the area as a whole.

To the north of Lodgedale Farm the unit is about 32 m thick, while an analogous conglomerate 17 m thick was recorded in the Heath House Borehole (SK 03 NW/2), 1.6 km to the west. To the east, in Greatgate No. 1 Borehole (SK 03 NE/17), the member is represented by about 13 m of conglomerate (see Figure 23).

DETAILS

The upper boundary of the member was seen in a small excavation at Lodgedale Farm [0467 3957] where 1.5 m of conglomerate were overlain by 1.7 m of very thinly bedded red-brown and yellow sandstone with scattered pebbles. A good section can be seen in the disused gravel pit at Intake Plantation [045 403]: about 15 m of poorly-cemented conglomerates are interlayered with sandstones, well cemented in part, in the proportion of about 10 of conglomerate to 3 of sandstone.

Hollington Formation

This is typically developed between Hollington (Staffs) and Alton (Charsley, 1982, p.7) where it is well seen in several disused and working quarries.

The formation consists mainly of cross-bedded red-brown and yellow sandstones, commonly arranged in finingupward units. A typical unit is composed of sandstone, sometimes with a basal pebbly part, overlain by finer grained sandstone which may be succeeded in turn by a mudstone or 'marl' band. The pebbles include mudstone intraclasts in places, and the 'marl' band is commonly an interlayered sequence of mudstone, siltstone and very finegrained sandstone.

Locally the 'marl' bands have been mapped, but most are too laterally impersistent for this. Between Alton, Wootton and Denstone a prominent mudstone lies at a constant horizon close to the top of the formation. It was penetrated in the Windyharbour Borehole (SK 04 SE/16) 11.37 m below the overlying formation and was at least 8.97 m thick. To the north, around Alton, what is probably the same mudstone is about 8 to 10 m thick.

In areas of faulting or folding the mudstones assisted in channelling or trapping mineralising fluids which leached iron from the sandstone and later deposited an intergranular cement of calcite, baryte or, less commonly, dolomite. The resulting well cemented sandstones, commonly pale coloured due to leaching, contrast with the underlying poorly-cemented red-brown or orange, finer-grained sandstone of

Plate 8   Fault in Triassic sandstones and conglomerates at Mobberley Quarry near Cheadle [0133 4088]

The fault, which has a throw of about 15 m, downthrows soft brown and yellow mottled sandstones of the Hawksmoor Formation against conglomerates of the Freehay Member (L2017)

the Hawksmoor Formation, and stand out as lines of crags. These crags are well seen in the Churnet and its tributary valleys, for example at Alton Castle [073 424] (Plate 9). The basal part of the Hollington Formation commonly consists of pebbly or conglomeratic sandstones, with an erosional base in places; these pass upwards into planar sets of sandstone separated by distinct bedding-plane partings or thin mudstones. The cemented character of the sandstones has also made them suitable locally as building stones, still worked at four quarries in the district (p.131).   TJC

One thin section has been examined, E 51371 from near Ramshorn (see Table 3). The sandstone is a moderately well sorted medium-grained subarkosic grainstone comparable to Carboniferous feldspathic sandstones in its microcline content but bearing a much larger proportion of non-quartzite lithic grains and smaller proportions of detrital and authigenic clay matrix than its nearest Namurian equivalents. It contains a high proportion of syntaxial quartz cement, but lacks calcite; this kind of cementation may not be typical of the formation as a whole.   NGB

The sometimes patchy cementation and the presence of mudstone bands produces a characteristic topography. Barrow (1903) described this as 'nubbles or small hillocks', and these are well seen at Threapwood [043 427]. Around Blake Low [117 465] there is a step-like topography with small scarps formed by spring-sapping above persistent mudstone horizons.

The formation is present in the same area as the underlying Hawksmoor Formation, between Cheadle, Hollington and the River Dove. It is highly variable in thickness, with rapid variations apparent over short distances. For example, a borehole at Wootton (SK 04 SE/15), commencing a few metres below the top of the formation, terminated at 45.72 m in a hard conglomerate presumed to lie near the base. About 500 m to the south, at Waste Farm [098 434], and south of two faults (see below), the formation has a calculated thickness of only about 20 m.

Elsewhere, the thickness varies from a feather edge development on the flanks of the Weaver Hills, where it overlaps the underlying Hawksmoor Formation, to a maxi-

Plate 9   Junction of the Hollington and Hawksmoor formations below Alton Castle [0730 4240]

Hard off-white cross-bedded pebbly sandstone at the base of the Hollington Formation overlies friable pale brownish red cross-bedded sandstone with scattered pebbles, the Hawksmoor Formation (L1652)

mum of about 50 m in the Hollington (Staffs) area. The maximum variations occur, however, in the faulted area close to the Carboniferous outcrop between Hawksmoor and Wootton. It is quite possible that the geological structure, the pre-Triassic surface, or both factors, exerted control on sedimentation here.

The Hollington Formation has yielded the majority of the macrofossil remains and trace fossils known from the Triassic of the district. Probably the most important find was a skull of a labyrinthodont, amphibian, *Cyclotosaurus stantonensis* (Woodward), found in Stanton Quarry [123 466] (Ward, 1900), and referred by Paton (1974) to *C. leptognathus* (Owen).   Footprints have been recorded from Townhead Quarry, Alton [076 424] and quarries in Hollington (Staffs) (Anon., 1919; Beasley, 1892; 1907; Sarjeant, 1974; 1985).

Plant remains have also been noted from Townhead Quarry (Beasley, 1914; Cummins, 1965) and from Greatgate Quarry [055 402] (Anon., 1919).

The formation is similar in its macrofossil remains and traces, and in its general lithology, to units referred to as 'Keuper Sandstone' or 'Keuper Building Stone' elsewhere in the Midlands and can be broadly correlated with these. Although no diagnostic palynomorph assemblages have been recovered from the Hollington Formation (Warrington *in* Charsley, 1982, p.15) it pre-dates the overlying Denstone Formation of Anisian age and is perhaps best considered as early Triassic in age.

In view of the lithology, sedimentary structures and fossil evidence there is little doubt that the Hollington Formation was deposited in a continental fluvial environment. The presence of a number of persistent mudstone and siltstone bands points to a change in depositional conditions from those of the Hawksmoor Formation. The change is believed to have resulted from the establishment of meandering channel systems with associated overbank or floodplain deposits which became increasingly important. Cross-bedding measurements indicate that the direction of river flow, while being locally somewhat more variable than at earlier times, remained reasonably constant overall from south to north across the area (Figure 21).

DETAILS

Beds at the base of the formation tend to be better exposed than those above; they can be seen in a number of places in the area between Hollington (Staffs), Oakamoor and Alton. At Rainroach Rock [0631 4299] the following section is exposed overlooking the Churnet valley:

	Thickness m
Sandstone, red-brown, medium- to coarse-grained, cross-bedded, well cemented, with scattered pebbles	8.90
Sandstone, red-brown, pebbly, conglomerate in part, cross-bedded	2.50
Mudstone, dark red-brown, micaceous	0.04
Sandstone, red-brown, medium- to coarse-grained, with rare pebbles	0.20
Interlayered cross-bedded pebbly sandstone and conglomerate; erosional base	4.75
Sandstone, bright red-brown, in places yellow mottled, medium- to coarse-grained, cross-bedded, with scattered pebbles and red-brown siltstone clasts; well cemented in basal 1.35; erosional base	3.45
Interlaminated dark red-brown siltstone, very fine-grained sandstone and mudstone	0.03

Hawksmoor Formation

Sandstone, red-brown, with some yellow mottling, fine- to medium-grained, cross-bedded, soft, with rare pebbles	0.95
Sandstone, red-brown, medium- to coarse-grained, cross-bedded, well cemented, with rare pebbles	0.60

Similar sections can be seen at Toothill Rock [0679 4251] and Mickleton Rock [0464 4102] where 16.25 m and 9.6 m respectively of cross-bedded hard pebbly sandstone and conglomerate overlie softer sandstone of the Hawksmoor Formation.

Typical sections from the middle part of the formation are exposed in quarries at Hollington and Greatgate. The following, in relatively well cemented sandstone, is generalised from Oldham's Quarry, Hollington (Staffs) [0558 3902]. A graphic section is given by Charsley (1982, fig. 3).

	Thickness m
Sandstone, fine- to coarse-grained, in five sharp-based units	5.95
Sandstone, fine- to coarse-grained, with mudstone parting above; pebbles in basal part	2.54
Mudstone with rare siltstone and sandstone laminae	0.39
Sandstone, medium- to coarse-grained in two sharp-based units	2.83
Mudstone and sandstone, the latter in a 0.15 m band at 0.03 from base	0.21

Sandstone, fine- to medium-grained, with micaceous partings in three sharp-based units	3.35

Another section in this part of the succession is exposed in the southern part of Fielding's Quarry, Greatgate [0552 4020] (see also Charsley, 1982, fig. 3):

	Thickness m
Sandstone, fine- to coarse-grained, laminated in upper part, cross-bedded in basal 0.3	1.25
Mudstone, with silty sandstone laminae in middle	0.07
Sandstone, fine- to coarse-grained, cross-bedded in part with mudstone clasts on foresets	1.50
Sandstone, fine- to medium-grained, micaceous partings throughout	0.85
Mudstone; silty in part, micaceous	0.26
Sandstone, fine- to medium-grained, micaceous partings in top 5 cm	1.00

A section of just over 8 m of sandstone and mudstone in the upper part of the formation was formerly visible in Townhead Quarry, Alton [076 424]; here Cummins (1965) recorded sole structures, including groove and flute casts, on the undersides of some of the sandstone beds.

Small exposures in the thick mudstone which occurs towards the top of the formation can be seen in the Alton area, generally in the sides of disused marl pits. At Threapwood Farm, about 4 m of red silty mudstone are exposed in one of these [0450 4311]. In Windyharbour Borehole (SK 04 SE/16) a mudstone 8.97 m thick was proved, overlain by 11.37 m of cross-bedded sandstone typical of the formation (Figure 23).

Other good sections can be seen at Moss Banks Quarry, Alton [0490 4388] (18.28 m exposed); below Alton Castle (Plate 9) [0720 4245] (c.10 m); Stanton Quarry [1233 4661] (6.3 m); Mayfield Quarry [1481 4609] (12 m); also in a road cutting at Clifton [1649 4482 to 1642 4465].

Sherwood Sandstone Group, undivided

To the east of the River Dove and in the south-west and north-east corners of the district, the Sherwood Sandstone Group has not been subdivided. This is due to differences in lithology in these areas and to the relatively poor exposure that results from the greater thickness and extent of the superficial deposits.

In general the rocks consist of poorly cemented sandstones though conglomerates crop out locally in the area between Osmaston, Shirley and Brailsford in the south-east and near Hulland in the north-east. Mudstones occur only rarely.

DETAILS

In the east of the district the base of the Triassic is commonly obscured by head or downwash. The only place it can be observed is in Birchwoodpark Quarry, Snelston, where sandstones with pebbles lie on an eroded limestone surface and fill fissures in it. At the southern end [1534 4101] of the quarry about 1 m of a medium- to coarse-grained quartzitic sandstone is seen and is very similar to hard baryte-cemented pebbly sandstone exposed in a quarry [1465 3988] 1.4 km to the SSW near Woodhay. The sandstone fissure-fillings at Birchwoodpark Quarry were the subject of a petrographical study by Arnold-Bemrose (1904) who believed them to be of Triassic age and similar to the 'Keuper Sandstone' of neighbouring areas.

Sandstones typical of the main part of the sequence can be seen in a road cutting and quarry [1810 4627] south of Ashbourne; this shows about 26 m of yellow and red-brown fine- to medium-grained sandstones with scattered pebbles, cross-bedded in part. To the east, 9.75 m of sandstones and conglomerates are exposed in a disused quarry in Bradley Wood [1971 4604]. At a nearby exposure [1974 4596] the conglomerates contain a number of subangular pebbles of Carboniferous-type sandstone as well as the more typical well rounded quartzite and quartz pebbles.

Similar sandstones and conglomerates were quarried in a number of places west of Brailsford, including 12.5 m of cross-bedded sandstone and conglomerate exposed in a quarry by Slack Lane [2470 4234]. The large working gravel quarries of the Ravensdale Park–Mercaston–Mugginton area lie almost entirely within the Derby District (Frost and Smart, 1979). An exposure of 0.2 m of laminated micaceous siltstone and mudstone of Triassic type overlain by sand and gravel in the disued gravel pit at 'Blackwall' [2493 4968], near Mill Fields, casts doubt on the previous identifications of the sand and gravel outcrop there as being entirely of Pleistocene age (Deeley, 1886; Clayton, 1953a).

Near the western edge of the district, several good sections occur in railway cuttings between Cresswell and Cheadle. At the disused railway station at Totmonslow [9946 3970] a fault throws down trough cross-bedded red sandstone with rare pebbles and mudstone clasts, to the north-east, against 7 m of conglomerate with lenticular sandstone beds up to 0.4 m thick. Another faulted exposure occurs to the north [9931 4037] and here about 4 m of well laminated buff sandstone with some mudstone and siltstone clasts is faulted against about 2 m of cross-bedded red sandstone with rare quartz pebbles and mudstone clasts. Nearer Cheadle, cross-bedded red sandstone is exposed [996 408] in a cutting, with a 0.5 m pebbly bed and a 0.1 m siltstone at the eastern end. At the south end of Draycott tunnel [9898 4136] 8 m of soft red sandstone with scattered pebbles are exposed.   TJC

MERCIA MUDSTONE GROUP

The Mercia Mudstone Group comprises mudstone and siltstone with subordinate sandstone (Warrington and others, 1980). It is widely distributed in the southern half of the district (Figure 21). On the flanks of the Weaver Hills [103 457], near Bradley [220 465] and on Snelston Common [155 414] it overlaps the underlying Sherwood Sandstone Group and lies directly on Carboniferous rocks. Elsewhere it succeeds the lower group conformably, the change being gradual, with rocks of mixed facies at the boundary.

Throughout the district a basal unit, the Denstone Formation, has been recognised, but the remainder of this group has not been further subdivided. In southern Nottinghamshire, however, the equivalent Colwick Formation (Warrington and others, 1980, p.57), formerly called the Waterstones Formation, is overlain by strata in which six formations have been distinguished (Elliott, 1961), in ascending order, the Radcliffe, Carlton, Harlequin, Edwalton, Trent and Parva formations. The lowest four of these have been recognised in the adjacent Derby sheet (Frost and Smart, 1979, p.86). These formations can be recognised in a general way in some of the boreholes in the district and the characteristic lithologies are discussed on p.86. However, no subdivisions above the Denstone Formation have proved to be mappable at the surface, the only differentiation in the beds above the Denstone Formation having been in the delineation of harder feature-forming bands ('skerries').

The undivided part of the Mercia Mudstone Group is thus equivalent to the 'Keuper Marl' of previous geological maps. The 'Keuper Marl' was usually taken as that part of the Triassic sequence between the 'Lower Keuper Sandstones', including the Waterstones, and the Rhaetic, and was referred to as 'New Red Marl' in Hull's original classification (1869). Details of the undivided part of the Mercia Mudstone Group are given below (p.85).

Denstone Formation

The formation (Charsley, 1982, p.10 and fig. 4) has its type section in Windyharbour Borehole (SK 04 SE/16), near Denstone, between 51.57 and 103.16 m (Figure 23); much of the following description is based on this.

The formation consists of a succession of mainly red-brown siltstones, thinly interlayered with subordinate fine-grained sandstones and mudstones (Charsley, 1982, fig. 5). It is characterised by the presence of ripple-marked surfaces, mica-covered bedding-planes, pseudomorphs after halite, calcite-encrusted vughs and mudcracks. For the most part these rocks are thinly bedded, though poorly bedded, homogenous or 'structureless' parts occur. The siltstone and sandstone beds are well cemented in part, mostly by calcite or less commonly by baryte or dolomite; gypsum occurs in places as thin beds or as small nodules.

The base of the formation is taken at the point where the arenaceous Sherwood Sandstone Group gives way to a finer-grained facies of alternations of siltstone, sandstone and mudstone. This was at a depth of 103.16 m in Windyharbour Borehole. The upper boundary of the formation is referred to below (p.86).

The Denstone Formation occurs throughout the district. To the west of the River Dove, it has a fairly constant thickness of about the 52 m, proved in the Windyharbour Borehole, though surface and borehole evidence at the western margin of the district around Cresswell [975 393] suggest an increase to some 57 m. East of the Dove, the formation thins from about 35 m at Norbury [123 422] to the 26 m recorded in the Shirley Common (SK 24 SW/9) and Rodsley (SK 14 SE/8) boreholes (Figure 23).

No faunal remains or traces have been noted, other than a few probable worm-trails recorded from the Windyharbour Borehole. Miospore assemblages have, however, been recovered in samples from a number of localities, and indicate a middle Triassic age for the formation, within the Anisian Stage (Warrington in Charsley, 1982, p.15).

Most of the formation is attributed to a fluvial flood-plain environment, either as overbank or, less commonly, as shallow channel deposits. Occasional subaerial exposure and drying out is proved by the presence of pseudomorphs after halite and mudcracks, while some of the poorly bedded siltstones or very fine-grained sandstones may be loessic deposits. The lack of macrofossil remains or trace fossils and the presence of miospore assemblages provides additional evidence in favour of a non-marine environment.

The crestal trends of straight-crested ripple-marks from the Denstone Formation show a strong NNW–SSE alignment (Figure 21). Most appear to be current rather than wave ripples, but few were found with an asymmetry pronounced enough to determine current directions, and internal structure was rarely determinable.

The formation is lithologically similar to the Waterstones (Formation) of the Midlands and Cheshire basins (Charsley, 1982). The 'Waterstones' have been shown (Warrington, 1970) to be diachronous across the country on a broad scale, so that chronostratigraphic equivalence with similar units may be only partial.

The rocks of the Denstone Formation produce a red-brown loamy soil, commonly finely sandy, with fragments of siltstone or fine-grained sandstone. In most places the rocks form an unbroken slope above a bench formed by the more resistant sandstone below. Low topographic features have been produced locally by harder bands, as at Bradley in the Moors [059 410], where a 2 m hard sandstone band can be traced over a distance of 700 m along the hillside.

DETAILS

A detailed graphic log of the Denstone Formation which was passed through between 51.57 and 103.16 m in the Windyharbour Borehole (SK 04 SE/16) is given by Charsley (1982, figure 4). Complete sections were also proved in the Rodsley and Shirley Common boreholes (SK 14 SE/8 and SK 24 SW/9), while that in the Darley Moor Borehole (SK 14 SE/9) was almost complete (see Figure 23).

The formation is moderately well exposed throughout the district in stream sections and cuttings, and details of many of the smaller sections are given on the six-inch geological maps. Some of the more extensive sections are given below.

In a small stream just west of Upper Tean [0069 3946 to 0050 3931] sections of up to 3 m include one [0058 3936] with a 1.44 m fine-grained sandstone. A number of sections occur in Broadgatehall Drumble, 2 km WSW of Hollington (Staffs). A typical example [0438 3795 to 0435 3783] is:

	Thickness m
Interlayered siltstone, very fine-grained sandstone and mudstone, red-brown	0.80
Sandstone, brown, fine-grained, thin-bedded	0.60
Mudstone, red-brown, silty, with subordinate beds of siltstone and very fine-grained sandstone with ripple-marks	4.25
Interlayered siltstone and mudstone, grey-green	0.48
Mudstone, red-brown, silty, with siltstone beds	3.00

Numerous sections up to 1.5 m thick in red-brown mudstones with a few sandstone beds can be seen in the banks of a stream north of the Alton-Denstone road [0805 4178 to 0940 4131].

In the Snelston area, good exposures occur in Brookfarm Dumble, south-east of the village where there are a number of sections up to 4.5 m thick. A typical example [1587 4260] shows red-brown, buff and green mudstone, part fissile, silty and micaceous in places and with a 0.12 m sandstone at 0.1 m from the base, 2.14 m. At a small waterfall [1595 4237] in the same stream the following section was exposed:

	Thickness m
Siltstone, yellow, finely sandy, thin bedded, micaceous	0.35
Sandstone, pale yellow, fine-grained, silty	0.13
Sandstone, pale yellow, fine- to coarse-grained, with	

conglomeratic base erosional into the unit below in a channel aligned E–W	0.18–0.31
Mudstone, red-brown, mottled yellow and green in part, silty, a few impersistent siltstone and fine-grained sandstone layers; ripple-marks at base	c.3.5

In the road cutting east of Snelston [1586 4322] a section shows interlayered ripple-marked red-brown and yellow micaceous siltstone and mudstone totalling 0.95 m. Farther to the east, the cover of superficial material is extensive and there are few exposures. Around Shirley, however, the Denstone Formation is again exposed; the village owes its elevation to the presence of resistant fine-grained sandstone and siltstone beds. On the edge of the village there is a sequence of 4.23 m of interlayered red-brown and buff siltstones and mudstones with rare fine-grained sandstone layers exposed in a road cutting [2182 4175]. Ripple-marks are common on siltstone surfaces, many of which are also mica-covered. Mudstone with flaggy beds of fine-grained sandstone and siltstone up to 0.16 m thick is exposed beside the road on the south side of the village [2180 4132].

Mercia Mudstone Group, undivided

These, the youngest solid rocks in the district, crop out in a nearly continuous strip across the southern part of the district; a few outliers occur farther north, around Forsbrook [969 416], Farley [072 441] and Yeldersley Hall [209 441], and these are partly fault-bounded.

The lowest of the formations established by Elliott (1961) in south Nottinghamshire (see p.84) can be recognised in a general way in some of the boreholes and sections. In the Windyharbour Borehole (SK 04 SE/16), for instance, 'Radcliffe-type' beds are overlain by 'Carlton-type' beds (see below) with a skerry, a possible equivalent of the Plains Skerry, at the top (Charsley, 1982, figure 6). A comparison of thicknesses between the Windyharbour Borehole and the Nottinghamshire sequence is given in the following table:

	Southern Nottinghamshire (after Elliott, 1961)	Windyharbour Borehole (based on approximate correlations)
Plains Skerry	1	5
Carlton Formation	21	23
Radcliffe Formation	12	23
Waterstones/Denstone Formation	34	52

It is thought likely that equivalents of Elliott's Harlequin Formation, the Cotgrave Skerry, and the basal part of the Edwalton Formation are present along the southern margin of the district; however, exposure is poor and no detailed borehole logs are available from these areas. The calculated thickness of the part of the Mercia Mudstone Group above the Denstone Formation which is present in the district is about 90 m. This thickness must include some 39 m of the Mercia Mudstone Group lying above the top of the Windyharbour Borehole section.

The rocks consist of three distinct lithologies, all of which are commonly calcareous or dolomitic; firstly, thinly interlayered red-brown siltstone and mudstone (typical of the Radcliffe Formation); secondly, poorly bedded or homogeneous red-brown silty mudstone (typical of the Carlton Formation); and finally, thin- to medium-bedded grey-green to buff siltstone ('skerry').

The thinly interlayered siltstone and mudstone lithology is characterised by the presence of pseudomorphs after halite, ripple marks, cross-lamination and numerous micaceous surfaces. Grey-green beds are common and their primary nature is indicated by the sporadic occurrence of palynomorphs. The lithology is most commonly developed in the basal part of the succession, and occurs in the Windyharbour Borehole (SK 04 SE/16) between 28.58 and 51.57 m.

A variation of this lithofacies occurs at the base of the sequence, where about 0.7 m of mudstone and siltstone thinly colour-laminated in shades of red-brown, pink and grey-green marks the boundary with the Denstone Formation. This horizon has been located at a number of places in the district and its distinctive nature and widespread occurrence indicate that it is a chronostratigraphic marker band, the only one known in the Triassic of the district.

Poorly bedded, homogeneous or 'structureless' beds overlie the interlayered beds in the Windyharbour Borehole and predominate between 6.38 and 28.58 m. They consist of red-brown micaceous calcareous silty mudstones which are commonly blocky in texture or more rarely nodular or brecciated. Grey-green mottling is common, either as a vein-like network or as 'fish-eyes' consisting of small round mottles, some with dark nuclei.

The thin- to medium-bedded pale grey-green siltstones, the third main lithology, are commonly cross-laminated and contain convolute bedding, although in some places they are more massive and rubbly in appearance. Dolomite occurs either as grains or as a secondary intergranular cement, but calcite is more common. Well cemented siltstones, which are relatively hard, are referred to locally as 'skerries'. They give rise to resistant landscape features characterised by low scarps capped by the 'skerry'. Extensive dip slope features are more rarely developed. Where these 'skerry' features are laterally persistent and small exposures have proved the presence of siltstones, they have been mapped and provide a guide to structure.

Other less common lithologies include laminated or very thinly bedded mudstones and rare fine- to medium-grained sandstones, some of which consist of uncemented well rounded quartz grains of probable aeolian origin.

Palynological data (Warrington *in* Charsley, 1982, fig. 7) have not provided sufficient evidence to enable direct biostratigraphic correlations to be made with sequences from neighbouring areas. However, the overall age of the succession can be established from the palynomorph assemblages as middle to late Triassic, with a range between the Anisian and Carnian stages.

Other than miospores and a few microplankton there is a marked lack of faunal or floral remains or traces in the succession. The fine grade and interlayering of the sediments point to deposition either on a flood plain or in a shallow lake. There is abundant evidence in the form of pseudomorphs after halite, mudcracks, and penecontemporaneous disruption of layering that the environment was subject to periodic drying out and so it seems likely that most of the deposition took place in a shallow ephemeral lake basin. Some of the more homogeneous beds may possibly be of loessic origin. Infrequent marine incursions are suggested by the presence of organic-walled microplankton (Warrington *in* Charsley, 1982, pp.15–16).

The origin of the red-brown and grey-green colours of the rocks has been discussed in the adjacent Derby district (Frost and Smart, 1979, p.77). So far as the present work is concerned the preservation of palynomorphs in the grey-green beds points to a primary origin, though green mottling and spotting caused by reduction of red-brown beds is also obvious in places. The red-brown colours are believed to be early diagenetic in origin.

The alternation and recurrence of the two main lithofacies through the Mercia Mudstone sequence occurs elsewhere and has been reviewed for the Cheshire–Shropshire basin by Arthurton (1980) who related the structureless or blocky facies and the laminated facies to emergent and flooded conditions respectively. Possible modern analogues of these facies have been described by Glennie (1970), Glennie and Evans (1976) and Arthurton (1980, p.55). Of the few other modern analogies reported in the literature, the most striking is that in Turkestan, where Huntington (1905) recorded a series of Quaternary lacustrine deposits around Lake Sistan. These consisted of an alternating sequence of pink to brown and green or white clays, silts or, more rarely, sands. From a study of the sedimentary features and contained plant material, Huntington concluded that the beds all had a similar source but that the pink to brown beds were deposited by rivers in a flood basin or temporary playa lake and subjected to subaerial oxidation, while the green beds were deposited subaqueously when the lake was more permanent. A similar situation may have existed when the Mercia Mudstone Group was deposited, the only variations being in the lack of preserved plant material and the evidence of incursion of marine waters into the lake basin.

The characteristic 'skerry' features of this part of the Mercia Mudstone Group can be well seen in the area between Croxden Abbey [066 397] and Denstone, and in the area south-east of Rocester, to the east of the River Dove. Another aspect of the landscape is the presence of numerous disused marl pits, usually sited on the steep slope under the lip of a 'skerry' feature; some were undoubtedly dug for clay for brickmaking, but the vast majority appear to have been dug for 'marling' or enriching light sandy or gravelly soils, especially for wheat growing. The land is now mostly used as pasture.

DETAILS

In addition to the section in the Windyharbour Borehole (for detailed log see Charsley, 1982, fig. 6), 37.25 m and 6.07 m respectively of this part of the succession were cored in the Rodsley (SK 14 SE/8) and Shirley Common (SK 24 SW/9) boreholes (Figure 23). In all three boreholes the basal colour-laminated beds overlie a sequence of siltstones, sandstones and mudstones belonging to the Denstone Formation.

These distinctive basal beds have also been recorded from a number of exposures in the district. In the south-west they are well exposed in a stream bank [0042 3920] south-west of Upper Tean: grey-green, yellow and red-brown interlaminated mudstone and siltstone 0.56 m *on* interlaminated yellow and red-brown micaceous siltstone and mudstone 0.18 m. A section exposed in a stream bed [0444 3820] 1.9 km south-west of Hollington (Staffs) was as follows:

	Thickness m
Interlaminated siltstone and mudstone, red-brown and grey, with ripple marks	0.60
Siltstone; grey-green, mottled red, with grey mudstone laminae	0.25
Mudstone; red-brown, silty, with one thin siltstone bed	0.52
Interlaminated red-brown and grey-green mudstone and siltstone	0.79

Denstone Formation

Interlaminated mudstone and siltstone, grey-green	0.18
Interlaminated silty mudstone and siltstone, red-brown, with calcite in vugh at top	0.80

To the north, in the fault-bounded outlier near Farley, interlaminated red-brown and green mudstone are exposed in the bank of a lane [0725 4411] north-east of the village. The same beds are exposed in a number of places in a stream which traverses a faulted outlier on the Denstone Formation outcrop about 1.5 km south-east of Snelston. One section [1610 4205] shows a 0.12 m colour-laminated mudstone overlying a 6 cm fine- to medium-grained sandstone which in turn overlies 0.32 m of interlayered siltstone and mudstone.

Above the basal beds, the succession consists of interlayered mudstone and siltstone overlain by poorly bedded, commonly blocky, mudstones as in the Windyharbour Borehole. Both lithologies are widely distributed throughout the area, as are harder siltstone 'skerries'.

The thinly interlayered 'Radcliffe-type' (see p.86) beds that form the lower part of the sequence are particularly well exposed in small streams and disused marl pits on the steep slopes above the east bank of the River Dove, south-east of Rocester. A typical exposure in Sedsall Rough [1143 3822] showed interlayered red-brown and green mudstone and grey-green siltstone with some ripple-marks and pseudomorphs after halite, 4.17 m.

To the west small exposures in this part of the succession occur in the upper part of Broadgatehall Drumble [e.g. 0378 3887], and an excavated face [0997 3954] at Messrs J. C. Bamford's factory in Rocester revealed an 11 m section of the same lithology; material from this locality yielded miospores (Warrington *in* Charsley, 1982, pp.16–17).

The poorly bedded 'Carlton-type' (see p.86) mudstone lithology is also well developed in the area south-east of Rocester, but as these beds are readily weathered, exposures are not common. The following representative section can be seen in a disused marl pit [1138 3584] just west of Upwoods Farm:

	Thickness m
Soil	0.25
Mudstone, dark red-brown, blocky, homogeneous above basal 10 cm, with green spots throughout	1.27
Siltstone, pale grey-green, blocky, with a few thin irregular mudstone beds	0.44
Mudstone, dark red-brown, blocky, homogeneous, with green spots throughout	1.20
Siltstone, pale red-brown with green spots, grey mottled in lower part, with a few flakes and laminae of mudstone; cross-laminated in part	0.78
Siltstone, pale grey-green, with a few green and red-brown mudstone laminae; part with ripple-marks and cross-lamination	0.20
Mudstone, dark red-brown, blocky, homogeneous	1.00

Elsewhere, small exposures show the blocky texture and green spotting, in disused marl pits along the southern boundary of the district between Upper Leigh and Osleston.

Although the 'skerry' lithology is rarely well exposed, small blocks and fragments are common in the soils and disused marl pits of the district. In the area south and west of the Windyharbour Borehole, dip-slopes underlain by 'skerries' are extensive, but exposures are rare. The village of Hollington (Derbys) [230 398] also lies on a 'skerry' proved in auger holes and shallow excavations. To the south-west of Upper Tean several 'skerries' occur on the hill slopes but there are few exposures; however, a disused marl pit [0023 3797] west of Tean Leys shows 2 m of siltstone. The siltstone, which is grey-green, is interlaminated in part with red-brown mudstone. Ripple-marked surfaces, convolute bedding and cross lamination are common, and rare pseudomorphs after halite also occur. 'Skerry' features are also common in the area to the east of the River Dove, south-east of Rocester, and a section there [1312 3772] shows 0.2 m of a grey-green to pale brown siltstone with ripple-marks, cross-lamination and pseudomorphs after halite.

Skerry features are also formed by poorly bedded siltstones which have few of the characteristic sedimentary structures of the thin-bedded types. This lithology occurs at a depth of 1.52 m in the Upwoods Farm section quoted above and in the same skerry in a marl pit to the west [1129 3594]. At the latter locality 0.2 m of blocky rubbly poorly bedded grey-green siltstone with irregular small voids occurs in a sequence of blocky red-brown mudstones.

In the south-eastern corner of the district, where the youngest Triassic rocks occur, a number of thin sandstones have been mapped. These are mainly poorly cemented and do not generally form pronounced features. At Osleston [247 368], however, sandstone forms a well-marked dip slope.

Exposures are rare and most sandstones were located by hand-augering, but one band at Croppertop is exposed in two places. At Croppertop Farm [2374 3629] a section in the pond bank shows: red-brown mudstone, blocky, with green spots and scattered siltstone laminae 1.0 m *on* pale grey-green to white, medium-grained sandstone, irregularly bedded 0.1 m. To the south-west, in the banks of a disused marl pit [2341 3599], fine- to medium-grained sandstone, red-brown with grey spots and with buff siltstone laminae at the base, 0.50 m, overlies red-brown mudstone 0.30 m.

TJC

CHAPTER 8

Pocket Deposits

Deposits trapped and preserved by collapse into solution cavities in the limestone and dolomite have been collectively termed 'Pocket Deposits'. They include materials of various ages from Carboniferous to Pliocene. Pleistocene deposits commonly overlie them but have not, in general, been affected by collapse.

The geological importance of the Pocket Deposits is out of proportion to their size, for they provide information on the otherwise little-known Mesozoic and Tertiary history of the region. They owe their economic importance mainly to their content of quartz-rich refractory sand (Boswell, 1918, p.127; Howe, 1920, pp.168–175), though the clays have also been used (Green and others, 1887, p.163). Most of the workings are now abandoned and many have been filled in.

The distribution of the pockets is shown in Figure 24. They occur in two separate groups, which do not necessarily have the same history. The north-eastern pockets, around Brassington, are part of an extensive series, most of which lie in the Buxton district (Aitkenhead and others, 1985, pp.105–108). The majority of these contain Tertiary deposits now referred to the Brassington Formation (Boulter and others, 1971). The south-western group, in the Weaver Hills, contains soft clays and pebbly sands that may belong to the Brassington Formation, but some pockets also include lithified deposits that resemble those of the nearby Triassic outcrop. The pockets are mainly found in the thickly bedded limestones of the Dinantian shelf provinces though a few are known in the adjacent thinly bedded limestones (Figure 24). The shelf limestones of the Brassington area are widely dolomitised, but those of the Weaver Hills area are not.

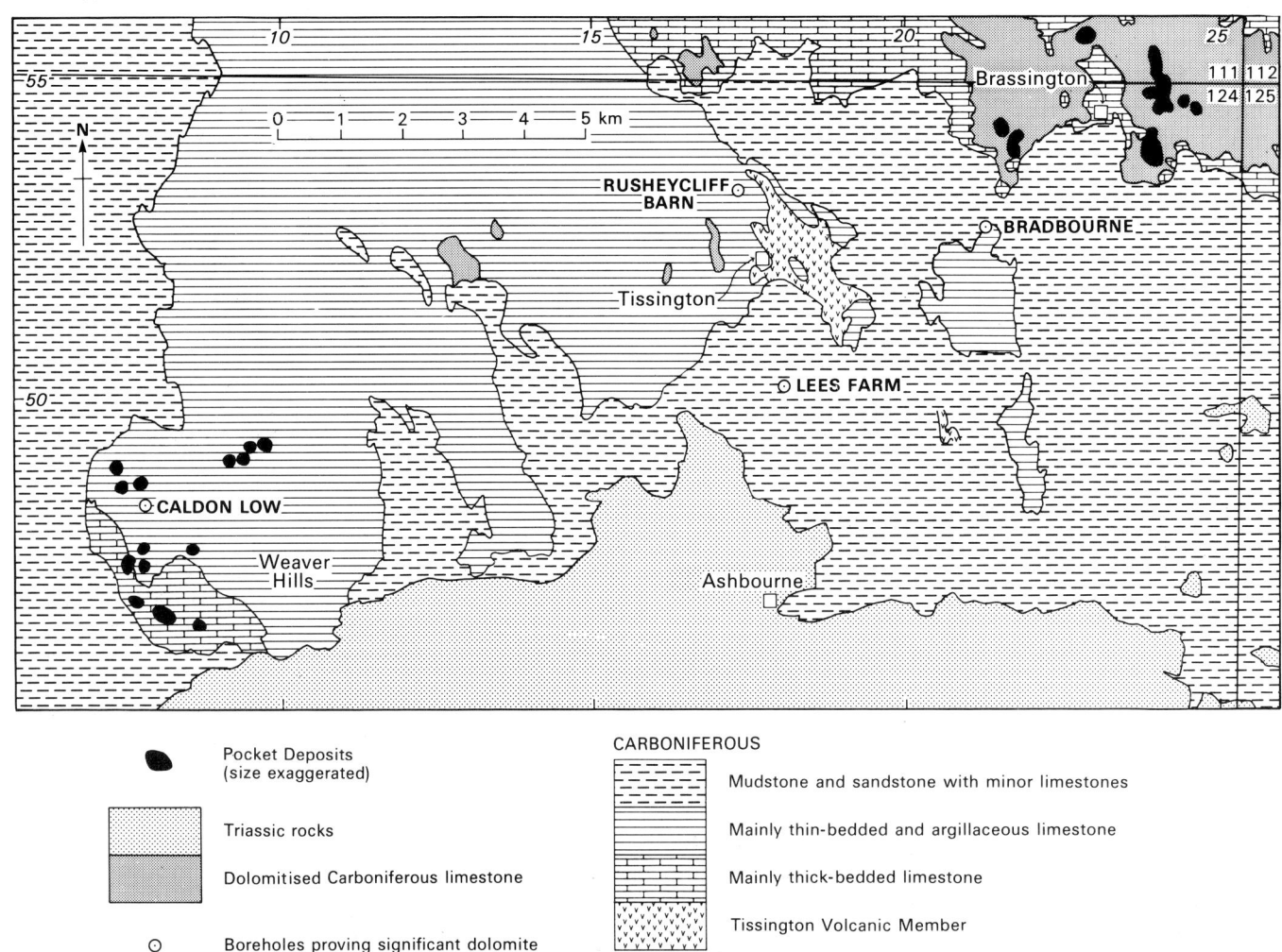

Figure 24   Distribution of Pocket Deposits and secondary dolomite in the Ashbourne district

BRASSINGTON AREA

The sequence of deposits at the Bees Nest Pit [241 545] appears to be typical of the north-eastern group. The sequence (modified from Walsh and others, 1972, pp.532–533) is:

5   Pleistocene deposits (till and head)
4   Brassington Formation
3   Black Namurian mudstone
2   Chert breccia and clay
1   Wall rocks

The relationships between these deposits, and their significance to the geological history of the region, are matters of debate; a discussion and summary of current views has been given by Aitkenhead and others (1985, pp.105–106). The following remarks are based on that account.

Wall rocks

The walls, of limestone or dolomite, are commonly steep, and detached masses are locally incorporated in the Pocket Deposits.

Chert breccias

These are now believed to be residues of limestone solution, but their age is uncertain. Their position between the wall rocks and the slabs of Namurian mudstone does not necessarily indicate that they are of pre-Namurian age, for they could have formed by intrastratal solution; Walsh and others (1972, pp.552–553) believe that they are of Tertiary age.

Namurian mudstone

Slabs of steeply dipping black mudstone have been recorded near the margins of several of the pockets, resting against the chert breccias or the wall rocks. Where overlain by the sands of the Brassington Formation the mudstone is commonly altered to a lilac colour. The slabs are believed to represent remnants of the surface on which the Brassington Formation was laid down (Walsh and others, 1972, p.525).

Brassington Formation

White, pink and yellow siliceous pebbly sands, with some brightly coloured silts and clays, make up the main fill of the pockets. Where bedding is present, it dips steeply or is otherwise disturbed; a basin-like structure has been detected in some of the pockets, notably at Bees Nest. The youngest deposits, at the centres of the basins, are plant-bearing clays of Tertiary age, but those underlying are unfossiliferous and their age has not been established with certainty. The pebbly sands are similar to the Triassic sandstones (p.75) that crop out widely around the southern Pennines, and some authors have inferred from this that they are of Triassic age (Kent, 1957; Yorke, 1961). More recent authors (Ford and King, 1969, p.60; Walsh and others, 1972, 1980) have suggested, however, that the deposits are all of Tertiary age and that the

pebbly sands are made up of derived Triassic material. A study of the surface features of quartz grains (Wilson, 1979) suggests that the sands are only slightly modified from their Triassic source rocks.

Detailed studies by Walsh and others (1972, p.522) have led to the recognition that a tripartite sequence of deposits is consistently present in the larger pockets and that this probably represents the remains of a widespread sheet of sediment. The deposits are believed to have accumulated in a terrestrial environment, in which sands and gravels, laid down by rivers flowing mainly from the south, were overlain by silts and clays of lacustrine or swamp origin (Walsh and others, 1972, p.523; 1980, p.57).

The name Brassington Formation is applied to the whole sequence and its type locality is at Bees Nest Pit [241 545]. Three members have been recognised (Boulter and others, 1971):

3   Kenslow Member (grey clays)
2   Bees Nest Member (coloured clays)
1   Kirkham Member (sands and gravels)

The Kirkham Member comprises siliceous pebbly sands of orthoquartzitic composition. The pebbles are mainly of quartzite and are well rounded; they are very similar to those in the Triassic sandstones (p.75) of neighbouring areas.

The Bees Nest Member consists of poorly bedded red, green and yellow, partly mottled, silt and clay. The base and top are apparently conformable in all sections (Walsh and others, 1972, p.523; Ford, 1972).

The Kenslow Member, up to 6 m thick, is a grey clay with plant remains. Extensive studies of these (Boulter and Chaloner, 1970; Boulter, 1971) indicate a Miocene to Pliocene age for the member.

Pleistocene deposits

Till has been recorded in only a few of the pockets, but overlying head is present almost everywhere. It consists of red-brown unstratified silt or clay, generally with chert fragments (see pp.108–109).

Origin of the pockets

The age and origin of the solution hollows (dolines) in which the deposits are found is still in some doubt. Walsh and others (1972, pp.524–530) have summarised the evidence and conclude, in the light of experimental data of their own, that the majority of the deposits have been preserved in cavities that formed, after the deposition of the Brassington Formation, by gradual solution rather than by sudden collapse of cavern roofs.

DETAILS

Harboro' Farm, Brassington

A series of deposits, inferred to belong to a single pocket elongated north–south, lies west and south of Harboro' Rocks [242 554] (Sheet 111). The southern part of the pocket lies within the district, with good sections in the Green Clay and Bees Nest pits (see below). Refractory sands and clays have been worked here over a long period (Howe, 1897, pp.146–147; Boswell, 1918, p.128, 'Harborough'; Howe, 1920, p.173, 'Brassington pit'; Yorke, 1961, 'Brassington pits'; Ford, 1972).

The Bees Nest Pit [241 545] provides the type section of the Brassington Formation and of its middle part, the Bees Nest Member. Photographs showing steeply dipping strata are included in the account by Yorke (1961). A detailed map and measured section given by Boulter and others (1971, fig. 1) show that dolomite wall rocks, chert breccias and blocks of Namurian mudstone are all present, with a central basinal fill of pebbly sands (about 37 m thick), coloured clays (about 6 m) and grey clays with lignite (about 2 m). A short account, with a map, is given by Walsh and others (1972). A detailed structural analysis by these authors shows a series of steeply dipping synclinal sags similar to structures produced by them in experimental models. Plant remains from the grey clays have provided evidence for a Miocene/Pliocene age for the Kenslow Member at the Bees Nest and Kenslow Top pits (Boulter and Chaloner, 1970; Boulter, 1971).

The Green Clay Pit [240 548] lies some 300 m north of the Bees Nest Pit (Ford and King, 1969, fig. 2). Dolomitic wall rocks are visible on the west side. Walsh and others (1972, p.533) recorded a Brassington Formation sequence similar to that at Bees Nest Pit, with chert breccia and black Namurian mudstone at the edges. Yorke (1961) includes several photographs and notes the presence of old lead mine shafts sunk through the sands.

Carsington Pasture

Two small pits about 0.5 km east of Bees Nest Pit are shown by Ford and King (1969, fig. 2) as lying in a possible extension of the Harboro' pocket. Boswell (1918, p.128) includes a reference to a pit here, as does Howe (1920, p.173). The western pit [2446 5460] contains traces of buff sandy clay and pebbles; the other [2462 5453] shows poor exposures of pale pebbly sand.

Wester Lane

A low-lying area about 0.5 km south of Bees Nest Pit contains evidence of pocket deposits; sandy soil with pebbles at the east side and a small pit [2388 5401] showing 1.7 m of brown loam with scattered pebbles overlying 1.9 m of off-white pebbly sand. Howe (1920, p.169) noted that lead mines here were dug in sand to depths of between 33 and 59 m. The deposit was also recorded by Ford and King (1969, fig. 2).

'Kirkham's pits'

An irregular pocket in the dolomite about 1 km west of Brassington contains 'Kirkham's pits' [217 540] (Ford and King, 1969, fig. 2). The wall rocks are visible in several places, and masses of Namurian mudstone are also present. Sections showing up to 10 m of yellow, buff and red sand, partly pebbly, were visible at the time of survey, with smaller sections in the coloured clays and grey clays. Boulter and others (1971) chose this as the type section of the Kirkham Member, on account of the complete section then visible, including the basal contact on Namurian mudstone and the upper contact with the Bees Nest Member. An account by Ford (1972, p.233) notes the lilac staining of the Namurian mudstone and records the presence of grey clays with plant debris, the Kenslow Member.

'Spencer's pits'

Two small pits in pockets about 0.4 km north-west of Kirkham's pits are called 'Spencer's pits' by Ford and King (1969, fig. 2). The western [2141 5421] shows dolomite walls with traces of sand adher-

ing; the other [2149 5417] is 5 m deep, in buff and brown sand with red and green clay partings at the south side.

Sandhurst Farm

Traces of pebbly sand were mapped by Ford and King (1969, fig. 2) in small pits by Sandhurst [216 532] and at Ochre Pits [210 539]. Neither pocket can be larger than a few tens of metres across.

WEAVER HILLS

The pockets in the south-western group are scattered over an area of some 6 square km around Caldon Low, mainly in the Kevin Limestones. A few penetrate the underlying Milldale Limestones. Pockets range from a few metres to about 300 m in diameter, with near-vertical, irregularly fluted sides and a flattish or rounded base. Most now contain little but remnants of pebbly sand, although some, especially the larger ones, also contain blocks and larger masses of red and buff pebbly sandstone of Triassic aspect. One pit, at Sallymoor [083 464] contains laminated siltstone reminiscent of the Triassic Denstone Formation. Older records of pits in the Weaver Hills (Maw, 1867; Green, 1867; Brown, 1867; Green and others, 1887, p.164; Howe, 1897; 1920, p.174; Scott, 1927) indicate the presence of white sands and clays, partly bedded, with pebbly bands. Also recorded are blocks of sandstone of Triassic type and a single mass of Carboniferous mudstone. No chert breccias have been recorded in this area.

It is likely that these pockets have had a somewhat different history from the northern group, with collapse of Triassic cover rocks, as well as material derived therefrom (Brassington Formation) into solution cavities formed close to the margin of the Triassic outcrop as it existed in Tertiary times. The threefold division of the Brassington Formation has not been applied to the Weaver Hills pockets.

DETAILS

Ribden

The largest of the Weaver Hills pockets is about 300 m across at its widest part, with irregular steep limestone walls exposed at the north end of Ribden Pit [077 473]. The pit was formerly worked for refractory clay and sand (Howe, 1920, p.174) but at the time of survey only patches of pebbly sand, with blocks of pebbly pink and cream sandstone resembling the Hollington Formation, were still to be seen. The pit is about 10 m deep. An old borehole (SK 04 NE/32) in the floor of the pit proved some 30 m of gravel and boulders without reaching limestone. The contents of two small pits within the area of the present excavation were described by Howe (1897, pp.143–144: Weaver pits 2 and 3). In pit 2, white and yellow sand with pebbles, yellow sand with thin clay beds, and pinkish clay were seen, dipping roughly north at angles between 40° and vertical. Blocks of pebbly sandstone were seen in pit 3. A pit at Ribden was earlier described and illustrated by Brown (in Maw, 1867, figs. 6, 7).

Another pit [079 475], now filled, lies about 200 m north-east of the Ribden pocket. Howe (1897, p.143: Weaver pit 1) recorded the presence of pebbles, white and yellow sand and thinly bedded sand and clay. The pocket is situated in a dry valley and a deposit of valley-bottom head (loam with limestone rubble) up to 9 m thick was present above the pebbly sands.

Two other small pockets of sand occur in the Ribden area, one [0798 4729] known from surface indications, the other [0871 4752] known from a borehole (SK 04 NE/7) which proved sand, clay and pebbles to a depth of 54 m without reaching the bottom of the pocket. Small pockets of pebbly sand, up to 5 m across, have also been revealed in the limestone workings at Wardlow Quarry [083 473].

Sallymoor

This locality is named on older editions of the six-inch Ordnance Survey map. A pocket at least 200 m across is mainly till-covered but a pit [083 464] some 10 m deep exposes a sequence of clastic sediments dipping south-west at 35 to 45°. These comprise some 20 m of red and green mudstone and laminated siltstone, resting on about 10 m of pale buff sandstone with rounded siliceous pebbles. The colours have been altered by bleaching but the lithologies otherwise resemble those of the Denstone and Hollington formations of the Triassic outcrop, some 1.5 km distant, rather than those of the Bees Nest and Kirkham members of the Brassington Formation. Thirty feet (9 m) of lignite recorded by Ludford (1940, p.217) may have been part of the Kenslow Member, but no trace of it now remains.

Pebbly sandstone has also been seen in pockets nearby; blocks of yellow sandstone with pebbles, sand and red mudstone, were seen beneath 3 m of till in a pit [0786 4673] to the west of Sallymoor Pit, and blocks of red sandstone were present, with yellow pebbly sand,

in pockets [0884 4636 and 0870 4622] exposed during developments at Kevin Quarry. Small pockets [085 461] close to the limestone-mudstone boundary at Kevin Quarry contained dark grey Namurian mudstone and yellow-brown earth, but no pebbly sands.

Caldon Low

On the north-west side of Caldon Low, near the Waterhouses road, Howe (1897, p.144) recorded a pocket containing red, yellow and mottled clay and sand, a mass of black 'limestone-shale' with *Posidoniella minor*, and large blocks of pebbly sandstone. Its exact location is not known. A pocket 'at the Caldon Hill Limestone Quarry', illustrated by Binney (*in* Maw, 1867, fig. 5), may be the same one. During the present survey, small pockets have been revealed in the limestone workings at Caldon Low Quarry [076 486]; they contained red and yellow pebbly sand, with red sandstone blocks also present in a few cases. All were relatively short pipe-like structures with near-vertical sides and rounded bases. None exceeded 10 m in diameter.

Huddale

Four small pockets around Huddale Farm [098 490] contain brown and yellow sand, pebbles, and red and grey clay. All are less than 50 m across. White 'china clay' noted at Milk Hill Gate (Maw, 1867, p.247) probably came from here.   JIC

CHAPTER 9

Quaternary

Superficial or drift deposits of Quaternary (Pleistocene and Recent) age are widespread in the district (Figures 25 and 26). The Pleistocene deposits had been investigated by a number of geologists (Deeley, 1886; Green and others, 1887; Anon. 1899; Barrow, 1903) before any distinction between older and younger glacial deposits was recognised (Jowett and Charlesworth, 1929; Wills, 1937). More recently the Quaternary chronology of the north Midlands has been refined by integrating evidence from deposits such as river terraces with that from the glacial deposits and from geomorphological studies (Clayton, 1953a; Posnansky, 1960; Jones and Charsley, 1985). Several reviews, which refer mostly to a much wider area, have also been published (King, 1966; Rice, 1968; Gemmell and George, 1972).

The Quaternary deposits of the district are here divided into glacial, fluvial and periglacial; peat and landslips are described separately (Table 6). Reference is also made to landforms and structures that can be related to glacial or periglacial processes and a separate section deals with the denudation chronology.

The glacial deposits were all formed in association with melting masses of ice, either directly without water transport and sorting (tills or boulder clays), or from water flowing within the confines of the ice (glacial sands and gravels). Two distinct groups of glacial deposits are present; the older are now preserved mainly on high ground, particularly on interfluves, and the younger tend to occur in valleys and on lower ground, close to the western margin of the district. It is now generally accepted that the younger deposits were laid down by the late-Devensian Irish Sea ice-sheet, whereas the age of the earlier deposits is less well established, partly because they are outside the range of radiocarbon dating but mainly because of outstanding problems of regional correlation. In the present account, stage names for the earlier deposits have been avoided where possible, but if used they follow the correlations proposed by Mitchell and others (1973).

The oldest Quaternary fluvial deposit in the area is the Ashbourne Gravel, which was laid down and cemented by calcite prior to the deposition of the 'older' glacial deposits. More widespread fluvial deposits were laid down both before and during the Devensian ice-advance (higher and lower terraces). Incision of the terrace deposits and deposition of alluvium followed the retreat of the ice and still continues in the main valleys of the district.

During the glacial episodes a periglacial environment, in which frozen ground was widespread, prevailed outside the glacier limits. At times when ground ice in the surface layers was able to melt due to increased insolation or other climatic factors, solifluction was widespread. The main product of this process was 'head', a poorly sorted and poorly stratified mixture of drift and bedrock material. Head mantles many of the slopes in the district and fills many small valleys. Where the valleys contained active water-courses the head

was sorted and incorporated in the fluvial terrace system. Most of the head now preserved is of late-Devensian age since it can be linked closely to the lower terrace deposits, but some appears to be related to the higher terrace deposits and is thus older.

Other effects of periglacial conditions seen in the district include superficial folds and faults and rare vertical stone orientation and involutions. Silty loam (p.109), of probable aeolian origin, has been noted in a number of soil profiles across the district; it is thought to have been deposited under periglacial conditions during the late Devensian. The mapping of this deposit falls outside the scope of the present survey. Screes occur in the limestone dales and are believed to have formed mainly during the late Devensian when frost-shattering was common.

Landslips have occurred in areas underlain by mudstones and siltstones of Carboniferous age. They are common in places where the tectonic dip is close in direction and angle to valley-side slopes. They are also very common close to the Devensian ice-margin where meltwater has deepened pre-existing valleys; the Churnet valley, between Consall Wood and Oakamoor, is probably the best example (Figure 26). Landslips in Triassic rocks are uncommon, but have been noted near Stanton.

Peat is not common in the district and almost all the deposits which have been mapped are confined to valley bottoms. No great thicknesses of peat have been observed and most peat appears to be of recent origin.

GLACIAL DEPOSITS

Glacial deposits, mostly in the form of till ('boulder clay'), are widely distributed throughout the district (Figure 25). The till, which was deposited directly from melting glacier ice, is typically a poorly sorted unstratified mixture of rock fragments up to boulder size in a matrix of clay to sand-size material. Its composition, which varies considerably from place to place, is closely dependent on the nature of the bedrock or superficial deposits over which the ice mass moved. The tills appear to be part of a complex which locally includes layers of stratified sand and gravel. In places the latter are believed to have been deposited along an ice margin, but it is possible that some, particularly those in the Dove and Henmore valleys close to the limit of the 'eastern' ice, may be glaciofluvial outwash deposits. Locally, as around Yeaveley [186 403], a distinct gravelly till with a sandy matrix, presumably derived from the Sherwood Sandstones, can be distinguished and has been shown separately on the 1:10 000 maps.

Older and newer glacial deposits, with different distributions, have been recognised (Figure 25). The older deposits are preserved mainly on interfluves and as remnant patches on valley sides and are obviously dissected or

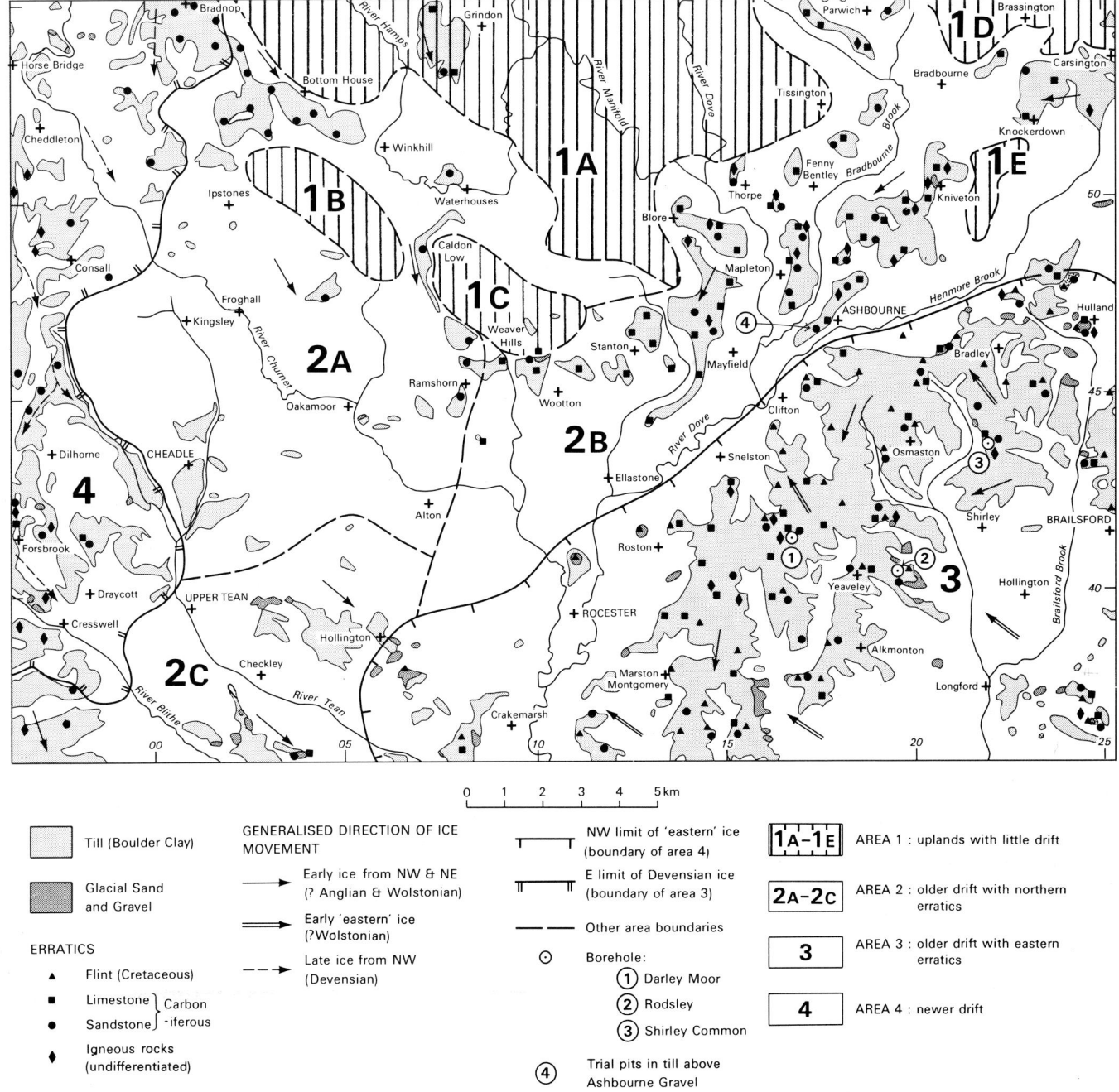

Figure 25   Distribution of glacial deposits in the Ashbourne district; with ice-movements, ice limits and area boundaries partly defined by the distribution of erratics

degraded. They are commonly covered by solifluction deposits and, in places where these are derived from the glacial deposits, the dividing line between the two has proved difficult to draw. The newer glacial deposits, which occur only in the western part of the district, are identified by their less degraded nature, by their common occurrence as valley fills, by their close association with anomalous drainage patterns and by the presence within them of many north-western igneous erratics. The absence of fresh glacial landforms in the district is believed to be due to erosion by meltwaters from the retreating ice front.

The newer glacial deposits are considered to have been deposited by the Devensian Irish Sea ice-sheet which advanced southwards across the Cheshire and Staffordshire lowlands at least as far as Four Ashes near Wolverhampton, from where a maximum age of 30 500 years B.P. has been obtained (Morgan, 1973). Evidence from near Stafford (Morgan and others, 1977) indicates that the mid-Staffordshire area was ice-free from 13 490 (± 375) years B.P., so that the period of late-Devensian ice-advance is fairly well defined.

To the east of the area affected by the Devensian glaci-

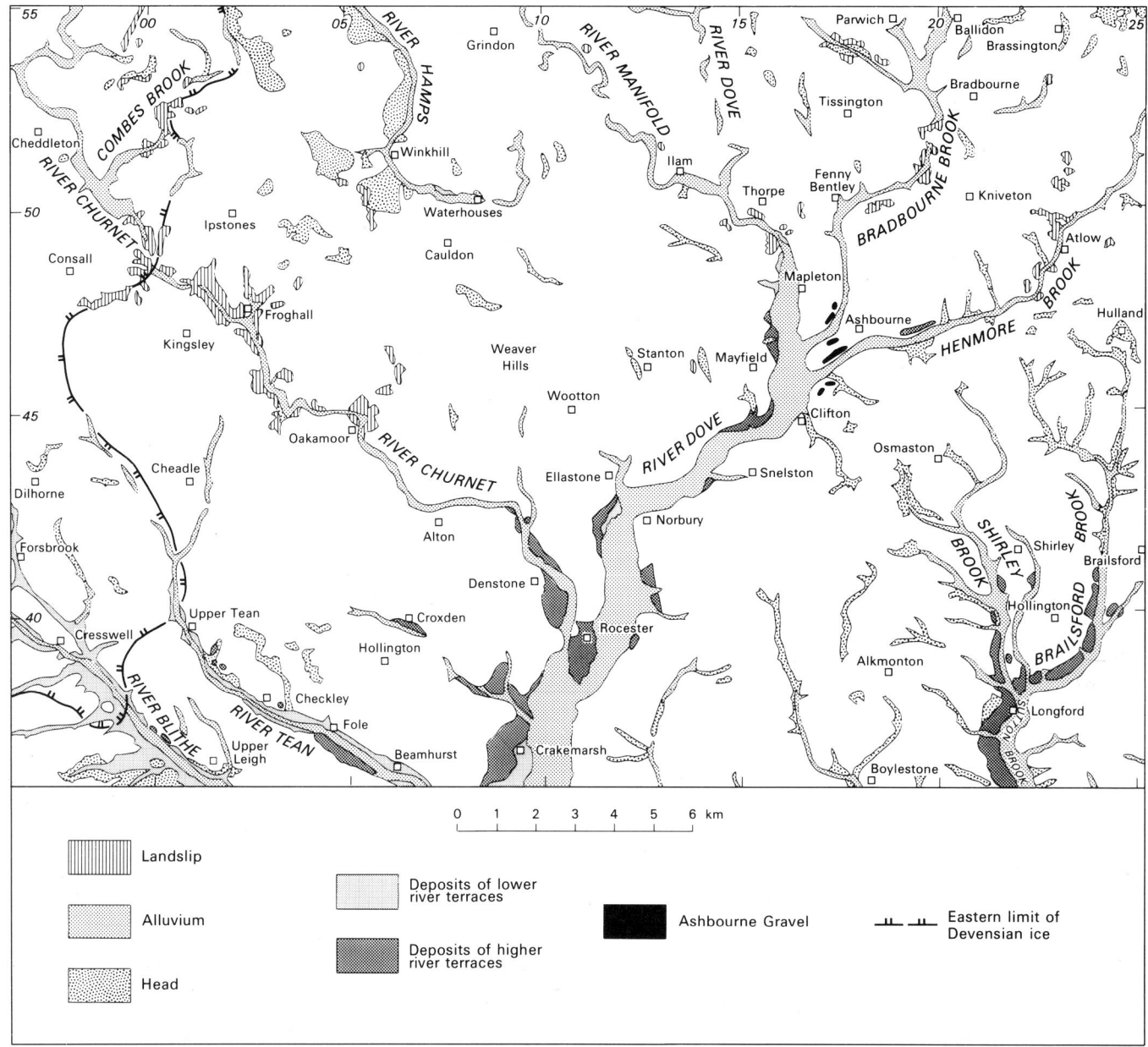

Figure 26 Distribution of fluvial deposits, head and landslips in the Ashbourne district

ation, the older glacial deposits appear to have been laid down during two episodes in which variations in flow directions occurred both in space and time. Generalised ice-flow directions can be arrived at by analysis of the distribution of certain erratics across the district (Figure 25), while some information on variations through time has been obtained locally from boreholes and sections. Only selected types of erratics have been plotted and these were recorded either from sections of tills or glacial sands and gravels or as single erratics of cobble size or greater found loose at the surface. Pebbles of quartz and quartzite believed to be derived from the Sherwood Sandstones, the so-called 'Bunter' pebbles, are ubiquitous in the glacial deposits and no significance has been attached to their occurrence. The igneous erratics have not been classified though many appear to have a prov-

enance in north-west England while some come from the Carboniferous volcanic rocks of the Peak District.

For description, the district has been divided into areas with distinct characteristics, including differing erratic suites (Figure 25). Areas 1 to 3 contain 'older' glacial deposits; area 4 contains 'newer' deposits.

Area 1: Uplands with little drift

The area comprises ground lying above the extensive till-covered tracts of relatively low relief. It consists of a number of sub-areas (1a to 1e in Figure 25) and includes most of the higher ground, from above 305 m (1000 ft) in the west of the district to above 229 m (750 ft) in the east. The area is mostly till-free, although an extensive till deposit occurs on gently

Table 6 Drift deposits of the Ashbourne district

Stage	Glacial deposits (Areas 1–4 as described in text)	Fluvial deposits	Periglacial and other deposits
Flandrian		Alluvium	Peat, Landslips
Late-Devensian	Area 4: 'newer' drift	Lower terrace deposits	Head, Landslips, Aeolian deposits, Screes
Late-Wolstonian – Ipswichian – Middle Devensian		Higher terrace deposits	Head, Landslips
Glacial (?Wolstonian)	Areas 2 and 3: 'older' drift		
Interstadial or interglacial (?Hoxnian)		Ashbourne Gravel	
Glacial (?Anglian)	Area 1: uplands with little drift		

sloping ground to the west of Grindon [087 543] and small patches occur on the Weaver Hills and north of Carsington at [252 543].

The wide scatter of erratics (Jowett and Charlesworth, 1929) and the distribution of the till which, though patchy, extends on to the highest ground in the district, for example that near Grindon at approximately 360 m, are regarded as evidence of the former existence of a cover of glacial deposits over most, if not all, of the district. These deposits are thought to be distinct from those which form more extensive sheets flanking the high ground (in areas 2a, 2b and 4), and which have a well defined upper altitudinal limit. If this distinction is valid, separate ice advances and probably separate glaciations are involved, an early episode marked by a complete ice-cover of the district and a less intense later episode with ice locally reaching an altitude of 305 m. This conclusion is in general agreement with that of various authors who believed they had found evidence for an early Pennine glaciation on the basis of glacial and fluvial sequences to the south of the present district (Deeley, 1886; Wills, 1937; Posnansky, 1960). The gravels at 'Blackwall' (see p.97–98), however, are now believed to be relict after glacial gravels or gravelly till of the later glacial episode rather than an earlier one as suggested by Deeley (1914, p.70) and Clayton (1953a).

No deposits that can be related to the early glaciation have been noted away from the high ground and this is due either to removal by the succeeding glaciation or to the difficulty of distinguishing them from later deposits. The presence of Lake District erratics in Dovedale and on the high ground to the north of the district (Jowett and Charlesworth, 1929) is in agreement with the view (Posnansky, 1960; King, 1966; Gemmell and George, 1972) that this ice advanced across the district from a general north to north-west direction. In spite of doubts regarding the validity of correlations across the country, it seems most likely that this early Pennine glaciation is of Anglian or earlier age.

DETAILS

Although a large spread of boulder clay occurs to the west of Grindon [087 543] in area 1a, exposures are rare; however, sink-holes up to 4 m deep are entirely in till. In the southern part of this tract, an excavation [0791 5318] near Oldfield's Farm showed 1.3 m of grey-brown till with common Carboniferous sandstone erratics, mainly quartzitic, about 25 per cent 'Bunter' and 5 per cent limestone pebbles. No sections were seen in the small patches of till on the Weaver Hills (area 1c), but hand-augering shows them to consist of yellow and brown silty clay, with fragments and small pebbles, at least 1.3 m thick over most of the outcrop. The till north of Carsington (area 1d) consists of brown sandy clay with many 'Bunter' pebbles and scattered chert and dolomite pebbles.

Area 2: 'Older' drift with northern erratics

The areas designated 2a to 2c lie between the lower altitudinal limits of area 1 on the north, by the limit of Devensian ice (area 4) in the west and by the limit of 'eastern' ice (area 3) in the south-east (Figure 25). Spreads of till of relatively low relief generally flank the high ground, their upper limits showing a consistent fall from about 320 m in the west to about 260 m in the east. The deposits at the highest levels lie in well defined cols or gaps at Bottom House [041 527], south-west of Caldon Low [079 486] and Knockerdown [231 515]; elsewhere the maximum altitude is commonly considerably lower.

Evidence that the deposits of area 2 are related to a separate glacial period to those on higher ground (area 1) is provided by:

1 the apparent strong control of till distribution around the high ground by altitude

2 the presence on the flanks of the Weaver Hills of gravel [1007 4587] believed to be a lateral moraine (p.96; Taylor, 1917); this is at an altitude of about 290 m and lies on the upper margin of a related till sheet. It appears to mark a local ice margin.

3 the erratics (Figure 25), which indicate derivation of some of the area 2 deposits from the north-east (see also p.96).

Three separate sub-areas have been defined on the basis of the distribution of certain erratics (Figure 25).

Area 2a: 'Older' drift with north-western erratics

In this area Carboniferous sandstones are the preponderant erratics, even adjoining the limestone of Caldon Low. Ice movement appears to have been from the north-west, along the western side of Morridge; the ice was then split by

Ipstones Edge (area 1b) into two streams, the southern moving south-east towards Oakamoor, while the northern crossed the gap at Bottom House and deposited till in the low ground north of Waterhouses. The northern stream was then diverted through the gap south-west of Caldon Low by the high ground of Caldon Low and the Weaver Hills (area 1c). It is possible that the northern stream divided again and a part passed through a gap at Caltonmoor north of the Weaver Hills, but no glacial deposits are known here and the eastern end of the gap may well have been blocked by a contemporaneous stream of ice from the east.

DETAILS

The till to the west and south of Bottom House consists of yellow and grey clay with sandstone blocks and 'Bunter' pebbles, up to 0.1 m long. The deposit is known to be at least 4 to 5 m thick over extensive areas and may be considerably thicker in places. There is commonly a thin layer of clay with angular sandstone debris, probably head, overlying the till and major spreads of the same material occur to the north and south of the gap. A section [0253 5390] near Park Farm shows about 4 m of stiff grey and brown clay with sandstone blocks, many of which are rounded, and another, in a gully [0505 5157] west of Winkhill, about 5 m of sandy clay with angular to subrounded sandstone pebbles and a few 'Bunter' pebbles. To the east, on the northern side of the Hamps valley at Waterhouses, a stiff mottled brown and grey clay with a similar clast content was seen to a depth of 1.57 m in a temporary excavation [0787 5062].

Till up to 16.44 m thick was found in boreholes (SK 04 NE/33–35) near Moorend Farm [070 487], to the west of Caldon Low; in the same area stony clay is exposed in sink-holes, one of which [0726 4842] shows 3 m of brown clay with sandstone blocks and 'Bunter' pebbles overlying massive limestone. In the sides of a pit [0830 4644] at Sallymoor, 3 m of brown and yellow boulder clay with sandstone blocks and rare 'Bunter' pebbles rest on Pocket Deposits (p.91).

Patches of boulder clay between Ramshorn and Oakamoor consist of red and brown sandy clay with sandstone blocks and 'Bunter' pebbles; two patches north of Whiston [041 472] are very similar. An isolated mound of gravel [0552 4453] apparently overlies the boulder clay just south of Oakamoor.

Excavations [0135 4410], on the north side of Cheadle, showed about 1 m of red, yellow, brown and grey clay, with sparse 'Bunter' pebbles but otherwise resembling weathered Carboniferous mudstone. The deposit forms a thin veneer over a wide area north and south of the town and is provisionally classified as till, though it may consist partly or wholly of soliflueted bedrock material.

Area 2b: 'Older' drift with north-eastern erratics

That the ice from the north-east was part of a major stream is inferred from the erratic suite in this area (Figure 25). The suite is mixed, with limestone somewhat more common than sandstone and igneous erratics scattered throughout. The common occurrence of Carboniferous sandstone erratics in till flanking the limestone hills is evidence that the ice did not come directly off the limestone. The local presence of Triassic rock fragments also supports this conclusion; for example, the presence of large baryte-cemented Triassic sandstone blocks in till on the Carboniferous outcrop south-east of Swinscoe [1433 4742] excludes the possibility of ice flow from the north-west. The presence of scattered Lake District erratics suggests the contrary, but these may have been derived from earlier glacial deposits of north-western origin,

or have been carried into the area via the Derwent and Wye valleys.

A two-fold subdivision of the till north of Ashbourne Hospital was indicated by excavations [1742 4668 to 1744 4662] made in an investigation of the Ashbourne Gravel (p.103). A lower red-brown till with a mixed suite of erratics including Carboniferous and Triassic sandstone, siltstone and mudstone pebbles, numerous coal fragments, and rare limestone, chert and igneous pebbles underlay a brown till with many large limestone blocks and scattered Carboniferous sandstone, ironstone and chert pebbles. This implies that an early ice-stream from the ENE was followed by one from a general northerly direction. This is in keeping with the idea that the ice, as it advanced, eventually overrode the interfluve at Knockerdown and veered in a south-westward direction across the edge of the limestone outcrop before proceeding southwards.

DETAILS

The boulder clay which occurs south and east of the Carboniferous limestone outcrop in the Weaver Hills–Swinscoe area commonly contains large blocks of limestone set in a brown or reddish-brown clay matrix, with pebbles of Carboniferous and Triassic sandstone, chert and igneous rocks abundant in places. Close to Stanton the boulder clay lies on dip-slopes of Triassic sandstone and does not appear to be more than a few metres thick. To the west and north-west of Mayfield and to the east of Blore, the thickness is probably 15 m or more.

Sections are not common and at the time of survey were mostly confined to freshly dug ditches or shallow excavations. In a roadside ditch [1433 4742] south of Swinscoe, 1.3 m of a reddish brown stony clay loam, with erratics including Carboniferous limestone, sandstone and chert, Triassic baryte-cemented sandstone and Triassic-derived quartzite and quartz pebbles, and one of an andesitic tuff, were exposed. Farther south, in another roadside cutting [1497 4645], 1.5 m of stony clay contained several large rounded ice-scratched limestone blocks as well as scattered quartzites. East of Blore a count of erratics in a ploughed field [146 491] showed about 60 per cent Carboniferous limestone, 35 per cent Carboniferous sandstone, 4 per cent of 'Bunter' pebbles and two andesite pebbles. A borehole (SK 14 NE/4) in this area proved 4.57 m of 'gritty marl', presumably boulder clay, overlying interbedded limestone and shale.

On the steep south-facing slope of the Weaver Hills, sections up to about 1.5 m in a partly cemented gravel can be seen in a pit [1007 4587] (Plate 10). It is a poorly sorted, unstratified deposit consisting of subangular to subrounded limestone boulders (up to 1.1 m long), cobbles and pebbles in a matrix of angular to subrounded grains and granules of limestone, with rare scattered 'Bunter' quartzites and Triassic sandstone blocks up to 0.23 m long. A variety of limestone types occurs; many cannot be matched with nearby outcrops. Down slope the gravel appears to pass into a gravelly till and then into a stony clay till. The lithology of the deposit is typical of an unsorted morainic gravel and it is interpreted as a lateral moraine.

Several cuttings in boulder clay were made during the construction of the Ashbourne to Buxton railway (Arnold-Bemrose, 1899). Trial holes along the proposed line had already indicated a considerable thickness of drift in places (Barke, 1894). One of these trials on the high ground to the north of Ashbourne was stopped in clay with limestone and sandstone boulders at a depth of about 11 m. In the same area, the record from a well (SK 14 NE/7) at Ashbourne Hospital showed 9.6 m of clay with boulders. The excavations (p.104) north of the hospital proved that a till with limestone boulders overlay another with a mixed suite without

Plate 10 Cemented limestone gravel in disused gravel pit, Weaver Hills [1007 4587]

Unstratified and unsorted calcite-cemented gravel believed to be a morainic deposit emplaced at the margin of the ?Wolstonian ice sheet. The clasts consist of a variety of limestone types together with some well rounded quartz and quartzite pebbles. The rule is 1 m in length (L2030)

limestone and indicated that the two tills were together about 18 m thick on the crest of the hill.

To the north, cuttings [1752 4793] opposite Sandybrook Hall, [1730 4903] near Alder's Farm, [1652 4981] west of Ashes Farm and [1700 5060] west of Bentley Hall all showed deposits of boulder clay with limestone blocks (commonly striated) and sandstone, shale, chert and igneous pebbles (Arnold-Bemrose, 1899). Reddish brown fine-grained sand with scattered quartzite and quartz pebbles, which occurs in the Ashes Farm cutting, is believed to underlie the boulder clay, but is probably part of the till complex. These deposits, which are all on high ground, form cappings to interfluves and are likely to have a maximum thickness of about 20 m.

A large spread of boulder clay occurs on the high ground to the east of Bentley Brook, although towards Kniveton an area around Rowfield [196 493], close to the highest point, is apparently drift-free.

A section [1818 4831] at Pool Close, in till typical of this area, showed 3.3 m of reddish brown clay with blocks and fragments of Carboniferous limestone (many with polished ice-scratched surfaces), Carboniferous sandstone and mudstone, a few small quartzite, quartz and volcanic pebbles. In Kniveton glacial deposits oc-

cupy the low ground and must have filled a pre-existing valley. The road from Ashbourne to the village passes through a 4 m cutting [2063 5009] in boulder clay with many limestone blocks, while close by in the village there is an area of glacial sand. A small section [2077 5027] in this deposit showed cross-laminated sand with lenses of brown clay, but the relationship of the sand to the till was nowhere seen.

The areas of boulder clay to the south and east of Tissington and around Parwich are featureless and devoid of sections and the drift is not likely to be thick.

An extensive area of boulder clay occurs south-west of Carsington and occupies the interfluve at Knockerdown. Sections are rare, but Carboniferous limestone, sandstone and chert and 'Bunter' pebbles are moderately common in the soil. A borehole (SK 25 SW/4), beside the road just south of Knockerdown and near to the edge of the deposit, proved 8.07 m of dark red-brown stony clay with Carboniferous cherty limestone, dark mudstone and sandstone fragments overlying dark mudstone.

The gravels at 'Blackwall', near Mill Fields, have been regarded either as fluvioglacial outwash (Deeley, 1886; Clayton, 1953a) or as weathered Triassic conglomerates (Frost and Smart, 1979).

Although sections are not now common in the pits, a small one was seen [2493 4968] in micaceous siltstones and sandstones of undoubted Triassic type. The surface material in the vicinity of the section was, however, an ill sorted and unstratified gravel consisting mainly of quartzite and quartz pebbles obviously derived from Triassic conglomerates, but with scattered small blocks and fragments of Carboniferous sandstone and one small Carboniferous limestone block. The deposit is reinterpreted as Triassic sandstone overlain by glacial gravel.

Area 2c: 'Older' drift with Triassic pebbles

In this area quartzite and quartz pebbles derived from the Sherwood Sandstones make up the greater part of the erratic suite. Triassic conglomerates that crop out extensively around Cheadle are believed to be the source of the pebbles. The deposits south of Checkley [028 380] appear to be dissected remnants of a formerly more extensive cover. Channels in bedrock, elongated in a general north-west to south-east direction, have been proved in two places. A borehole (SK 03 NW/13) north-west of Brookfieldhead [024 370] which showed 11.8 m of sand and gravel below 2.7 m of boulder clay, and a well at the farm said by the farmer to be in sand at 7.5 m, both indicate glacial deposits on a narrow interfluve at a considerably lower level than the surrounding Mercia Mudstones. A similar situation was found in an excavation at Nobut Hall [0380 3594] where a bedrock hollow occurs, filled with more than 7.4m of sand and gravel with cross-beds inclined to the ESE. A spring [0412 3594], northeast of the hall where the base of the sand and gravel crops out above Triassic mudstone, indicates an eastward slope into the hollow and confirms the conclusion that it is a channel scoured by sediment-laden waters or ice flowing from the north-west. The sands and gravels are either proglacial outwash laid down during the advance of ice from the north-west or may have been deposited subglacially.

DETAILS

The high ground to the west of Hollington (Staffs) is mantled by a mixture of gravel and reddish brown stony loam. Where sand is the sole constituent of the matrix the deposits have been mapped as glacial gravel; elsewhere clay and silt are important constituents and the deposits are regarded as till. The pebbles are almost entirely Triassic with only a few of Carboniferous sandstone and limestone. A temporary section in the till at Paradise Cottage [0397 3966], near Hollington, showed 0.4 m of stony soil overlying 0.5 m of unstratified and ill-sorted bright red-brown gravelly silty sand with some clay. Although no sections were visible at Hollington during the present survey, glacial striae, trending WNW-ESE, on a Triassic sandstone surface underlying boulder clay, have been noted in a quarry (Lamplugh, 1899).

Glacial sand and gravel is relatively common on the high ground between the Blithe and Tean rivers; in addition, much of the boulder clay is gravelly in composition, and the glacial deposits seem to be part of a complex which includes true tills and well-sorted glaciofluvial deposits. In a small gravel pit [0205 3761], at Leighbank Farm, the section shows 3 m of crudely stratified gravel, with a few well-sorted bands and some thin sand layers, grading laterally into poorly sorted clayey sand and gravel which in turn grades into a red-brown and yellow clay till. Relationships between the lithologies are disturbed and the whole deposit is considered to be a complex melt-out sequence, the stratified sand and gravel being deposited sub or englacially prior to the final ice melt which deposited the till.

In the south-western corner of the district the boulder clay on the high ground consists of brown, grey or red-brown stony clay with predominant 'Bunter' pebbles but also with Carboniferous sandstone, limestone and chert, rare igneous rocks and Lower Palaeozoic mudstone clasts. The till is gravelly locally and in places includes small sand bodies, for example in a ditch [9842 3681] south of New House. A feature of this area is the mantle of soliflucted boulder clay on all slopes below the till spreads; in many places it is only in the lower parts of old marl pits that the solid rock can be seen and in the area as a whole the boundary between till and head is difficult to determine. Sections are mostly confined to shallow ditches but north of Blakelow a deep ditch [9761 3680] has provided a 3.25 m section in brown and grey stony clay with 'Bunter' pebbles and Carboniferous sandstone and coal fragments.

Area 3: 'Older' drift with eastern erratics

This area, in the south-east of the district, is characterised by the occurrence of Cretaceous flints. The largest continuous spread of boulder clay in the district occurs in this area, covering most of the high ground between Bradley and Marston Montgomery (Figure 25); the surface of this shows little relief. It has a denticulate margin due to stream incision of a once more extensive till sheet. The glacial deposits, which consist mainly of a mixture of gravel and clay tills, underlie a number of marked 'flats', as at Darley Moor [170 418], Yeaveley [186 403] and Bentley Hall [178 381], previously regarded as erosion surfaces on 'solid' rocks (Clayton, 1953b), but now believed to have reached their present form by periglacial processes (Jones and Charsley, 1985).

The precise source of the flints is still in doubt and, although one from Ashbourne [1910 4545] yielded Upper Cretaceous foraminifera, few others have been examined. Though flints have been recorded from the north-west of the district (Jowett and Charlesworth, 1929), these are rarities of probable Irish Sea origin and it must be presumed that those found abundantly in the south-east of the district originate in the Chalk of eastern England.

Many of the flints are pale grey to yellow, rather than dark grey to black, and many show evidence of wear, but not of rounding; this suggests derivation from an older 'chalky boulder clay'. Chalk fragments have been recorded locally in auger holes, for example [2418 3648] near Cross Close, Osleston and in Lower Thurvaston [2253 3706]. No Jurassic fragments were found during the survey; their absence, together with the colour and state of the flints and the scarcity of Chalk fragments, supports the suggestion that the till is derived from an older 'eastern' till.

Except for the presence of flint, the erratics of this area are similar to those to the north (area 2b), consisting mainly of Carboniferous limestone and sandstone with scattered igneous pebbles. However, there is an extra element, as shown by pebble counts on till cores from the Darley Moor Borehole (Figure 27). These indicate early deposition from the north-east, with a change to deposition from the north marked by a change in colour and erratics at 15.50 m depth. Flints were not recorded in the hole, but their presence in surface soils nearby shows that the provenance of the ice again changed, with a second incursion of 'eastern' ice, at the end of the glacial episode. Elsewhere, flints are also common in the surface soils but less so in sections, and it seems

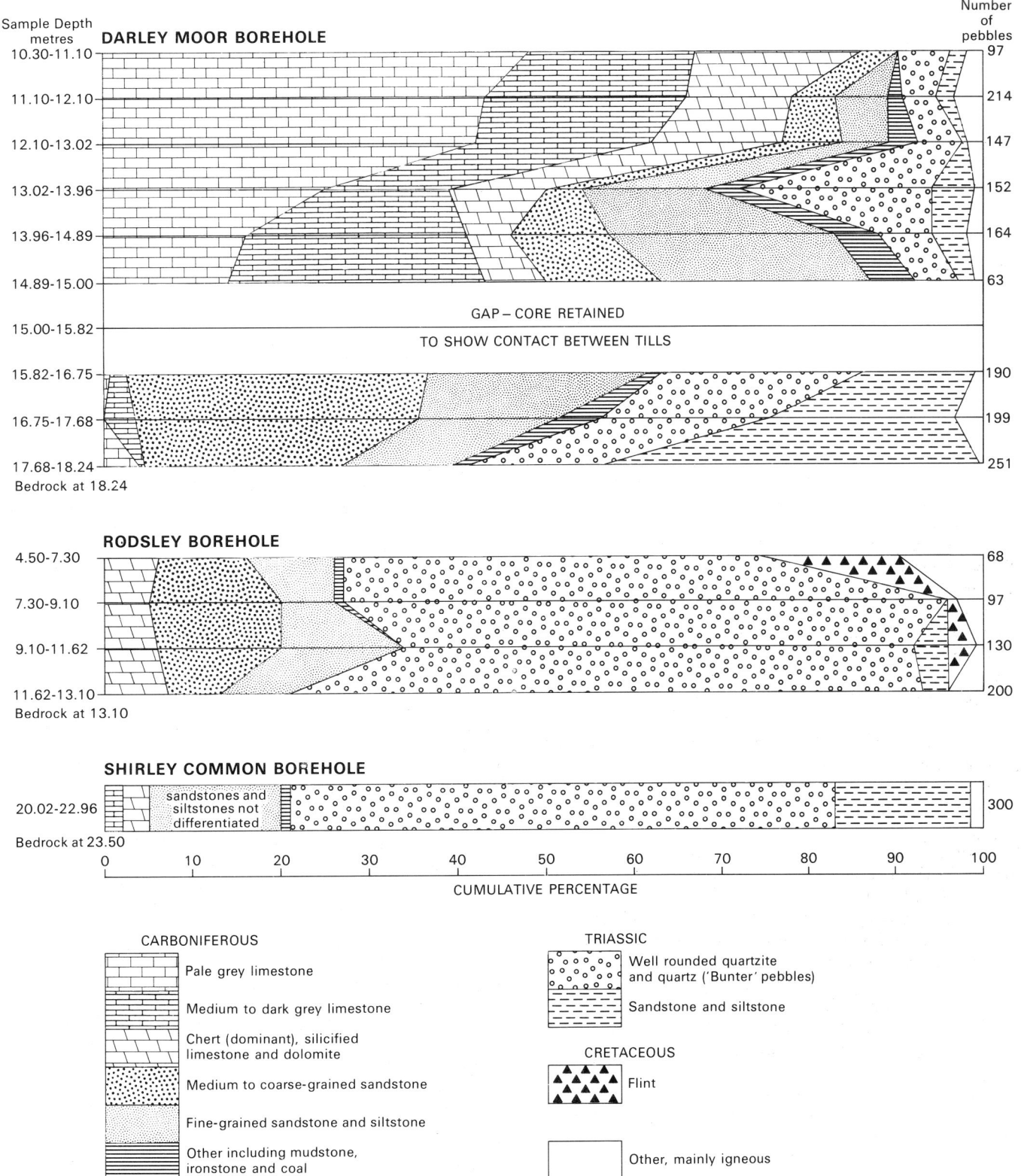

Figure 27 Pebble counts from borehole cores in till

likely that the final overriding by 'eastern' ice was widespread. The earlier incursion of ice from the north appears not to have reached the sites of the Rodsley or Shirley Common boreholes (Figures 25, 27). The sequences in both the Shirley Common and the Darley Moor boreholes include sands and gravels; in the former, about 3 m of laminated sand and silt were recorded from within the glacial sequence.

Thus in this area (area 3) and in that to the north and west (area 2) till deposition, probably of lodgement type, was initiated by ice from the north-east followed in the west and north by deposition from the north. 'Eastern' ice then overrode part of the area and the melting of this produced the complex fluvial/glacial sequences seen in the Darley Moor and Shirley Common boreholes, and deposited flinty tills and gravels. Flinty gravels are common just inside the supposed limit of the 'eastern' ice, which corresponds closely to the line of Henmore Brook and the River Dove between Atlow and Norbury.

The westward advance of the 'eastern' ice on to relatively high ground in the district indicates a weakening of the flow of ice from the north-west and north-east, but whether the ice from these directions was still active, was wasting, or had melted altogether at the time, is uncertain. There is, however, no evidence to suggest that there was a marked break in time, involving interglacial or interstadial conditions, between any of these events. On the contrary, the similar heights, topography and state of dissection of the till both north and south of the 'eastern' ice limit suggest an origin as part of a single continuous glacial event.

Given that the glacial deposits of areas 2 and 3 were laid down during a single glaciation, the following evidence indicates that this predated the Devensian:

1   the deposits commonly occur on interfluves and are extremely rare on low ground
2   they are covered in places, for example south of the Weaver Hills [101 466], by silty loam of probable aeolian origin
3   they have many similarities to deposits underlying proven Ipswichian terrace gravels at Boulton Moor (Jones and Stanley, 1974)
4   terrace deposits, unaffected by glaciation and correlated with the Ipswichian terrace gravels at Boulton Moor, occur in the area.

The relative youth of the deposits is indicated by:
1   the preservation of extensive interfluve plateau-like areas of low relief with little dissection except at the margins
2   both Henmore and Bradbourne brooks are deeply incised in places, probably by meltwater from the glaciation, but although the valley sides have been extensively modified by landslips (Figure 26), only very limited valley widening has occurred
3   the deposits are not commonly deeply weathered.

Considering the above evidence, which is more in keeping with survival through one interglacial and glacial period rather than two, the deposits are believed to date from the penultimate glaciation (?Wolstonian), (see Table 6).

DETAILS

Between Hulland and Bradley the glacial deposits are highly variable and include sands and gravels, gravelly and stony tills and clay tills with rare stones. The sands and gravels have been separately mapped. A section in the till occurs north of Bradley in a disused gravel pit [2265 4742] which shows sections up to 1.3 m in gravel with a matrix varying from sand to clay, but with no sorting or stratification. Blocks of Carboniferous sandstone up to 0.6 m occur and cobbles of quartzite and quartz are common; other erratics include pebbles of flint, Carboniferous chert and ironstone, black chert and microgranite; above the pit the gravel gives way to a stony clay. West of Bradley a disused sand pit [2095 4610] in an area of glacial sand and gravel showed 0.35 m of poorly stratified coarse-grained pebbly sand, argillaceous in part, overlying 0.55 m of cross-bedded coarse-grained sand with scattered small pebbles, mainly of 'Bunter' quartzite and quartz but including sandstone, chert and rare Carboniferous limestone and mudstone. The thickness of the deposits around Bradley and Hulland does not appear to be great since they have a rather patchy distribution and in a number of places the higher ground is drift-free, for example around The Knob [237 457] and near Irongate House [215 464]. To the south and west the thickness is known to increase considerably.

A major spread of boulder clay extends southwards from Bradley towards Shirley; it is sandy and gravelly in the south where it overlies Triassic sandstones and conglomerates. The deposit is probably thicker between Shirley Common and Yeldersley, and the Shirley Common Borehole (SK 24 SW/9) recorded 23.5 m of variable glacial deposits indicating a filled-in bedrock hollow. Recovery of the drift was poor but the approximate section was:

	Depth m
No core (probably stony clay)	to 3.0
Sand, clayey	to 9.50
Clay, stony	to 12.24
Sand, silt and clay, laminated	to 15.32
Sand	to 17.98
Clay, stony	to base of drift at 23.50

Just to the north, the Yeldersley Borehole (SK 24 SW/7) proved stony clay to 3.35 m, on sand and gravel to 7.32 m.

Glacial deposits are also widespread to the east of Brailsford Brook; a thin gravelly loam, with flints abundant in places, commonly overlies stony clay. The deposits are variable in thickness, but reach 12 m in a borehole (SK 24 SE/4) just outside the district.

To the west, the area of low relief on which the former Ashbourne Airfield was built is underlain by a considerable thickness of glacial till, sand and gravel. A borehole at Ashbourne Waterworks (SK 14 NE/6) proved 16.61 m of boulder clay on 5.26 m of sand above Triassic strata. Near the borehole site a temporary excavation [1859 4572] exposed 3 m of stiff brown and grey clay with scattered limestone fragments, while shallow excavations at the edge of the airfield [1909 4544] showed sandy clay with numerous quartzite and quartz pebbles, flints and some Carboniferous limestone and sandstone pebbles. To the north, near Nether Sturston, a narrow ridge of Triassic sandstone is capped by glacial sand and gravel. A section [1984 4644] showed 0.75 m of crudely stratified gravel with a clayey sand matrix containing many Triassic conglomerate blocks and common flints.

Boulder clay covers all the high ground south of Ashbourne, towards Osmaston and Edlaston. Sections are rare, but evidence from soils indicates that the composition varies from sand to gravel to stony clay over very short distances and few areas of glacial sand and gravel proved separable. The whole deposit is regarded as a till complex in which much of the sand and gravel reflects its Triassic source material rather than sorting by meltwater. The variation is shown in a disused gravel pit [1939 4343] west of Osmaston, where 1.5 m of gravel and pebbly sand grades into a gravelly till with a sandy clay matrix.

The former Darley Moor Airfield is another drift-covered area of low relief, and the Darley Moor Borehole (SK 14 SE/9) proved 19.24 m of glacial deposits overlying Triassic bedrock. The drift sequence in the borehole was:

	Depth m
Clay, sandy	to c.1.00
Sand, yellow, coarse-grained	to c.2.00
Sand, fine-grained, and clay	to c.3.00
Clay, brown	to c.6.00
Clay, brown with scattered pebbles	to 10.00
Clay, pale to dark yellow-brown, stony	to 15.50
Clay, red-brown, stony	to 18.24

The colour change at 15.50 m is abrupt and coincides with a change in erratic content (Figure 27), implying the superposition of two separate tills. The clasts in the lower are derived mainly from Triassic and Carboniferous sandstone outcrops, indicating ice flow from the north-east; those in the upper include a high proportion of Carboniferous limestone and indicate ice flow from the north. On the north side of the airfield, a section [1772 4280] in a small stream shows 3 m of a basal red sandy clay till with many Triassic fragments and rare limestone and flint pebbles. To the south of the airfield a 3 m cutting [1711 4079] shows yellow-brown till resting on red-brown till.

To the west of Darley Moor the boulder clay thins against the Carboniferous limestone inlier at Snelston Common [154 412] and it is likely that part of the limestone outcrop was drift free prior to quarrying. The glacial deposits form a continuous spread on the high ground and underlie further 'flats' at Yeaveley [186 403], Alkmonton [186 385] and Bentley Hall [178 381]. The boulder clay is very gravelly in places and has been distinguished locally on the six-inch maps as gravelly till. From the mapped occurrence of till, both north and south of Yeaveley, it is probable that in general the gravelly facies underlies the more argillaceous facies in this area and where present it commonly forms a steeply rising feature at the junction with the underlying Triassic mudstones. The relationship between gravelly and clay tills is more complicated locally than suggested above, as seen in ditches north-west of Bentley Hall. One section [1705 3878 to 1703 3883] showed pebbly clay grading downwards into sand and gravel and back into pebbly clay, with a further gravelly band below resting on Triassic mudstones. Here and in other sections in this area, flints and Carboniferous limestone and sandstone are common. In Rodsley Borehole (SK 14 SE/8) boulder clay was recorded directly overlying the Triassic at a depth of 13.10 m, sand or gravel being absent.

The main spread of glacial deposits is continuous to the west and south of Snelston Common and forms a capping to the interfluves to and beyond the southern margin of the district, south of Marston Montgomery. Traced southwards the deposits become increasingly arenaceous and gravelly and one of the largest patches of glacial sand and gravel in the district occurs to the south-west of Great Cubley. In addition to the patches of sand and gravel, gravelly till has been shown separately on the six-inch maps. A typical section in this deposit occurs in a disused gravel pit [1523 3659] north of Vernon's Oak Farm, where 2 m of an ill sorted, unstratified gravel with a matrix varying from red clay to sand grades into stony clay in places; quartzite and quartz pebbles are abundant here while other erratics include pebbles of flint, sandstone, limestone, chert and Triassic siltstone. The clay till hereabouts is mainly a yellow-brown or brown stony clay with abundant 'Bunter' pebbles and common flints. The only evidence of thickness is in a borehole for coal (SK 13

NE/3), made in 1835 south-west of Sandhills Farm, Cubley, the record of which showed brown soil and yellow clay to 0.53 m with 'marl, flintstone etc. conglomerate' (presumably till and gravel) to 12.34 m over light brown Triassic marl.

Several patches of glacial deposits occur to the west of the main spread. Some consist of glacial sand and gravel with flints, thought to have been deposited by meltwaters at the margin of the 'eastern' ice. In one such patch south of Norbury a section [1282 4163] in a disused gravel pit showed 1.8 m of a flinty gravel. North of Rocester, glacial gravel forms a mound on an area of pebbly boulder clay and a section [1113 4092] in a gravel pit exposed 3m of gravel with common 'Bunter' pebbles and flints, and minor yellow sand pockets. Almost in alignment with these two patches are five separate gravel deposits south-east of Hollington (Staffs): most of these occupy hill-top positions. Flints occur in a rather poorly sorted gravel overlying pebbly clay north of Hollywood [0655 3802], indicating an eastern source.

To the south-east, several areas of glacial deposits occur on the sides of the Dove valley. Two boreholes north of Creighton Park showed 3.66 m (SK 03 NE/1) and 5.49 m (SK 03 NE/2) of 'drift' over red marl.

The two areas of boulder clay on the high ground to the east of the Dove are regarded as dissected remnants of the main spread at Marston Montgomery, to the north-east. The boulder clay is generally brown or red-brown and contains mainly 'Bunter' pebbles and flints, with a few Carboniferous sandstone and chert erratics. A fine-grained sand which appears to pass laterally into gravel and till can be seen in a small pit [1183 3750] near Eaton Barn; the glacial deposits here are about 7 m thick. A borehole at Upwoods Farm (SK 13 NW/2), on a patch of boulder clay at the southern margin of the district, showed 11.58 m of clay and 'drift' overlying red marl.

In the south-eastern corner of the district the glacial deposits occur as isolated patches, some of which bear no obvious relationship to topography, occurring both on hill tops and valley sides. The boulder clay is dark brown or grey when fresh and contains flints as well as 'Bunter' pebbles; chalk fragments were seen in a number of auger samples. The deposit at Cross Close [240 364], south-west of Osleston, has an outcrop which, when related to local relief, suggests that it occupies a channel in bedrock; an uneven bedrock surface may explain the somewhat random outcrop pattern of many of the deposits in this area. Sections are rare, but a small exposure [2479 3656] east of Osleston Cottage showed 1.1 m of red-brown to dark brown stony clay with common 'Bunter' quartzites and flint, other erratics including Carboniferous limestone, sandstone and ironstone, Triassic mudstone and siltstone, and tuff.

Area 4: 'Newer' drift

This area lies on the western margin of the district and contains deposits related to the Devensian ice. These are characterised by a mixed suite of erratics with Carboniferous sandstone most abundant in the north, but 'Bunter' pebbles are dominant in other places; igneous rock and Lower Palaeozoic erratics are more common than elsewhere in the district. A further feature of this area is that the deposits have no consistent relationship with topography and occur both on interfluves, for example [966 470] south of Wetley Rocks, and in valley bottoms, as [993 435 and 968 434] around Dilhorne.

The deposits consist mainly of red-brown stony clays. Within the Devensian limit around Cresswell they are sandy with numerous 'Bunter' pebbles, and may be partly of glaciofluvial origin, but in other areas the stony clays are regarded as true tills either of lodgement or melt-out types. Glacial sands and gravels are rare and form only minor features closely associated with spreads of till. Some of the glacial deposits, especially those on the highest ground, may be relics from an earlier glaciation, either overridden by ice or lying on high ground above glacier level; the gravelly clay on the Huntley Wood ridge [988 418] is regarded as such a relic, only the till on the lower ground flanking the ridge having been deposited by Devensian ice.

The apparent lack of glaciofluvial deposits both inside and marginal to the area is believed to be due to the nature of the ground to the north and west. To reach the headwaters of the Churnet and the Dilhorne area the ice would either have had to surmount high ground or passed through narrow cols. Once wasting set in, ice in these areas would have become isolated relatively rapidly while the main melting ice-margin would have been to the west in the Cheshire–north Staffordshire lowlands.

Outside the ice limit, head has been mapped over large tracts of ground (Figure 26) and is also widespread where it is not thick enough to map. Close to the limit, many of the valleys, including that of the Churnet, are deeply incised, probably by meltwater. That this process took place relatively recently is indicated by extensive landslipping: in places, for example in the Churnet valley [012 481] north-west of Froghall, the valley is underlain entirely by landslip debris (see p.112).

Within the limit in the north-west many of the topographic features of the Churnet valley and drainage modification to the north and west of the district are thought to relate to the Devensian ice advance. The belief that many of these features were overflow channels associated with ice-impounded lakes (Jowett and Charlesworth, 1929; King, 1960) has been questioned in view of the lack of lacustrine features or sediments (Johnson, 1965). Meanders of the Churnet and the moundy valley bottom topography north and west of Cheddleton Heath indeed appear to be best explained as relict subglacial meltwater features.

Prior to the 'Newer Drift' glaciation, the Churnet was possibly divided into an upper course above a Froghall col [around 005 483], flowing north into the upper Trent, and a lower southward-flowing course. The breaching of this col was believed to have been caused either by overflow from a proglacial lake (Jowett and Charlesworth, 1929; King, 1960) or solely by proglacial meltwater (Johnson, 1965). There is, however, a lack of fluvial deposits in the lower reaches of the Churnet attributable to such an important erosive event at this time. The Churnet contains very limited areas of low terrace (see Figure 26) while those just above its junction with the Dove are similar to and continuous with Dove terraces regarded as correlatives of the Ipswichian Boulton Moor terrace (Jones and Stanley, 1974). The contrast with the Blithe valley, where deposits containing abundant north-western igneous erratics form a very extensive low terrace, is marked.

Some incision probably took place in the Churnet Valley in Devensian times and the higher terrace at Rocester has erosive features [107 390] relatable to this period but, given the lack of the large volumes of sediment that would have been produced by the breaching of the col and the incision of the river, it seems more probable that the southward flow of the Churnet from Horse Bridge to Rocester dates from a retreat stage of an earlier ice lobe, probably of Wolstonian age.

The headwater valley of Combes Brook, which runs almost parallel to Morridge [020 550 to 023 536] and is regarded as a submarginal meltwater channel, may also relate either to the Devensian or to the earlier (?Wolstonian) ice limit (Figure 26).

Evidence that the Devensian ice overran Wetley Rocks [966 495] (see also Barrow, 1900) is provided by the smoothed-off form of the steeply dipping Namurian sandstones, which contrasts with the more obviously frost-shattered outcrops at The Roaches, to the north, which were then ice-free. This ice stream is regarded as being responsible for the valley-floor tills (see p.101), which occur to the east and west of Dilhorne (Figure 25).

DETAILS

Boulder clay is patchy on the higher ground to the east of the Churnet south of Bradnop, and its distribution is determined to a great extent by the position of Namurian sandstone ridges, many of which are drift-free. The boulder clay is typically a brown or reddish brown sandy clay with 'Bunter' pebbles and blocks of Carboniferous sandstone, the latter commonly somewhat rounded. Weathered sections up to 1.5 m are common in ditches. Exposures of bedrock within the spreads of boulder clay indicate that the deposits are not more than about 10 m thick.

The glacial deposits on the flanks of the Churnet valley north of Cheddleton consist of a mixture of till, sand and gravel; their arenaceous nature probably reflects the local bedrock of soft Triassic sandstone. In general the till is a brown or red-brown sandy pebbly clay, gravelly in places, the pebbles consisting mainly of quartzite and quartz of Triassic derivation. Small mounds of glacial sand and gravel, of possible constructional form, occur around Leekbrook [985 539]; some appear to overlie sandy till. A section [9834 5424] in one mound shows 1m of cross-bedded buff sand and gravel.

To the south and south-west of Cheddleton, boulder clay is widespread in the hollows between Namurian sandstone ridges. In places the latter extend beneath the boulder clay but retain their form, indicating the blanketing effect of the drift and the absence of a planed-off subdrift surface. Exposures are not common, but where seen, the boulder clay is mainly red-brown or yellow and locally grey and brown. It commonly consists of sandy clay with scattered subrounded Carboniferous sandstone blocks, 'Bunter' pebbles and igneous erratics. A typical section in a clay pit [9832 4932] north-east of Consall shows 1 m of red and yellow sandy clay with sandstone debris and scattered 'Bunter' pebbles.

Boulder clay occurs in the low ground on the west side of the stream that flows from Blakeley Lane [972 470] to [990 440] near Parkhall Farm and from there southwards on both sides of the stream towards Huntley. A spur of boulder clay also extends to the south-west and occupies the col [968 435] between the Triassic sandstone hills at Dilhorne and Blakeleybank. It consists of brown, yellow, pink or red pebbly clay with rare sandstone fragments, but few exposures occur and its presence is generally recognised by the numerous 'Bunter' pebbles in the soil. Mapping indicates that the deposit is mainly thin.

Small cappings of boulder clay also occur on the highest ground. One, south of Dilhorne, consists of gravelly clay, a section [9755 4293] showing 1.5 m of unbedded pink and red gravelly clay beneath 0.3 m of sandy pebbly soil, with many of the pebbles in the clay having their long axes vertical. To the south-east, boulder clay also caps the Triassic at Huntley Wood, and in Huntley Wood Quarry [994 415] numerous small sections up to 2 m can be seen.

The deposit consists of a pink and brown pebbly silt or red pebbly clay, sandy in part, with pebbles predominantly of Triassic derivation. These cappings on the higher ground are probably relics of older, pre-Devensian, glacial deposits and the pebble orientation in the patch south of Dilhorne can be explained as a Devensian periglacial effect, as can the solifluction-induced crude layering seen in places at Huntley Wood.

South of the col at Dilhorne, the boulder clay becomes sandy and very pebbly, probably reflecting the change to Triassic bedrock. In the area around and to the east of Forsbrook and south and west of Cresswell it is patchily distributed, thin and occurs both on high and low ground. The soil is mainly a stony loam, but ploughing and a few sections show that the underlying material is mainly clayey. A road cutting [9687 4162] at Forsbrook provided a 2.75 m section in brown stony sandy clay with 'Bunter' pebbles, Carboniferous sandstone and coal fragments and a subrounded granite block 0.5 m in diameter. South and west of Cresswell the boulder clay is again patchily distributed and is differentiated from the more uniform spread on the high ground to the south, which is regarded as 'older' drift (area 2c). Patches of gravel forming small mounds [969 398] on the north side of the River Blithe appear to overlie the boulder clay and may be remnants of constructional glacial landforms, possibly kames. Around Saverley Green [965 388] the boulder clay is sandy, with sand bodies locally, and contains common igneous erratics, mainly granite and 'north-western' volcanic rocks. A borehole (SJ 93 NE/10) south of Saverley Green proved a drift sequence consisting of stony sandy clay to 2.0 m on sandy gravel to 3.05 m with a stony silty clay to 5.10 m, while one just to the north (SJ 93 NE/12) recorded stony sandy clay to 4.2 m overlying sandy gravel to 4.6 m. These boreholes show the variable nature of the glacial deposits and explain why so many of the surface soils in this area are sandy or gravelly. Just to the east, closer to the inferred Devensian ice-limit, the deposits show a general increase in sand and gravel, which may indicate a degree of glaciofluvial sorting in these ice-marginal areas.

FLUVIAL DEPOSITS

The distribution of these is shown in Figure 26. The earliest deposit, the Ashbourne Gravel, underlies tills referred to the penultimate glaciation (?Wolstonian), but due to subsequent erosion and glacial deposition few exposures can be seen.

When the ice sheet melted during the latter part of the ?Wolstonian glaciation, till was deposited over much of the district but no fluvial deposits were laid down, other than the glaciofluvial material intermixed with the tills (pp. 95–101). Fluvial outwash sediments are probably lacking because the meltwater was dominantly erosive in the present district and deposition only occurred to the south, in the lower Dove and Trent valleys; the Hilton terrace or terraces are related to this episode (Clayton, 1953a; Stevenson and Mitchell, 1955; Posnansky, 1960; Straw, 1963).

However, as the climate ameliorated (Ipswichian Interglacial), alluvial gravels were deposited in most of the main valleys in the district, by the reworking of earlier deposits. This process was brought to a close by a climatic deterioration, and periglacial conditions were re-established (Devensian) giving rise to further fluvial aggradation. Dissection of the alluvial deposits during the latter part of this cold period left them as relict features, the higher terrace deposits, on valley sides. Although the height of the top of these deposits above the recent alluvium varies from river to river, they are all at least 3 m, and in places up to 8 m, above

the alluvium. They are also distinguishable by their height above the lower terrace deposits wherever the two are juxtaposed, as in the Dove valley at Crakemarsh [093 365].

Following the period of dissection, melting ice (late Devensian) in the Tean and Blithe valleys produced outwash deposits. These are included in the mapped lower terrace deposits. It is probable that much of the material underlying the modern flood plains of the main rivers was also deposited at this time although it is now covered by recent silts and sands. The lower terrace deposits are commonly between 1 and 2 m, but exceptionally up to 3 m above the recent alluvium.

Recent reworking of pre-existing deposits has produced alluvium along most of the major streams and larger rivers, such as the Dove. The relationships of the fluvial to the glacial and periglacial deposits has enabled an approximate stratigraphy for the district to be established (Table 6).

Work on the Trent and lower Dove terraces in adjacent districts has been reviewed and interpreted by Mitchell and others (1973), whose findings were partly confirmed by the discovery of an Ipswichian fauna in the Allenton (Beeston) Terrace near Derby (Jones and Stanley, 1974). The suggested chronology is as follows:

Deposit	Stage
Floodplain Terrace	Devensian
Beeston Terrace	Ipswichian
Hilton Terrace	Wolstonian

The higher terrace deposits in the Ashbourne district provide a link with this chronology for they can be traced southwards along both the Dove and Sutton Brook valleys into deposits mapped as 'first terrace' in the Burton upon Trent district, (Sheet 140). On a regional basis the latter has been correlated with the Beeston Terrace (Clayton, 1953a; Posnansky, 1960), and the Ipswichian age of this has allowed a chronology for the deposits of the Ashbourne district to be formulated (Table 6). It should be noted that elsewhere in the Burton upon Trent district, deposits labelled 'first terrace' are the southward continuation of both 'higher' and 'lower' terrace deposits of the Blithe and Tean valleys of the present district.

Ashbourne Gravel

Six outcrops of the Ashbourne Gravel have been located, aligned in a general north–south direction over a distance of about 2 kilometres, on the west side of Ashbourne (Figure 26). Two further small outcrops occur west of the River Dove near The Orchards [154 471]. The alignment of the outcrops at Ashbourne is almost normal to the local drainage pattern, but parallel to both the River Dove at this point and to Bentley Brook between the northernmost exposure and Fenny Bentley. Most of the deposits occur with their upper level on the lip of a marked bench cut into Triassic sandstone above a 10–15° valley-side slope and at an average height of about 15m above the alluvium of Henmore and Bentley brooks, tributaries of the Dove. The deposits decline in level from about 140 m above OD in the north to about 128 m in the south, a gradient of approximately 1 in 200, comparable to that of the present alluvium of the Dove. Up slope from the deposits there is either till or a thin (unmapped) veneer of head on Triassic bedrock.

The deposits consist mainly of angular to rounded cobbles and pebbles of Carboniferous limestone (more than 55 per cent) with subordinate (8–29 per cent) Carboniferous sandstone and minor quartzite and quartz of Triassic derivation, together with chert and igneous rock. To the south the proportion of quartzite and quartz increases, so that in the southernmost outcrop [1708 4549], near Halfway House, these make up about 17.5 per cent of the clasts.

The gravels are strongly cemented by coarsely crystalline calcite and have an openwork structure with fines falling mostly in the coarse sand to small pebble range. They have been worked for gravel locally, in spite of the presence of the cementing calcite. Quartzose sandstone lenses up to 0.13 m thick and 0.4 m in width, with horizontal bedding, occur in the outcrop at Halfway House. Poorly developed horizontal bedding or cross-bedding and crude sorting are present in the gravels in places, but on the whole they are poorly stratified and ill sorted. In the northernmost outcrop [1743 4759], near Haywood Farm, the base of the gravel is erosive in the underlying Triassic sandstone.

An excavation [1742 4668] on the hill north of Ashbourne Hospital proved 0.4 m of brown stony silty loam on 3.26 m of red-brown stony clay (till) which in turn overlay 0.61 m of calcite-cemented limestone gravel; the till contained a detached block of cemented gravel at its base. The sequence suggests that both deposition of the gravel and its cementation predated the till, making it pre-?Wolstonian in age. The sedimentary features of the deposits indicate high-energy river deposition, while cross-bedding and imbrication of pebbles at the Old Grammar School outcrop confirm the lithological evidence of a derivation predominantly from the north and north-west. It thus seems likely that the deposits were laid down during a pre-?Wolstonian fluvial phase, probably during late ?Anglian or ?Hoxnian times.

Plate 11   Section in Ashbourne Gravel, Old Grammar School, Ashbourne [1766 4657]

The section shows poorly sorted calcite-cemented gravel consisting of subangular to rounded pebbles and cobbles, mainly of Carboniferous limestone and sandstone, up to 11 cm long. In the hill behind this locality, the gravels underlie tills of possible Wolstonian age (L2528)

DETAILS

The largest outcrop occurs at the Old Grammar School in Ashbourne [1766 4657] where up to 2.8 m of cemented gravel occur over a horizontal distance of about 25 m (Charsley, 1979). The deposit (Plate 11) contains 70 per cent Carboniferous limestone pebbles up to 0.14 m in length, 24 per cent Carboniferous sandstone up to 0.19 m, the remainder being quartzite, quartz, chert and volcanic rock. Most pebbles are between 2 and 4 cm in length. In one place cross-bedded sets 0.4 m and 0.54 m thick are separated by a horizontal layer of fine gravel; the foresets are inclined to the SSW. Imbrication of flat pebbles indicates deposition by a current from the north-west.

In a small pit [1743 4759], south of Haywood Farm, 0.85 m of cemented gravel is exposed, consisting of angular to rounded clasts of Carboniferous limestone and sandstone, up to 0.23 m in length, in a coarse-grained matrix; large clasts are common and are mainly subangular. Quartzite and quartz are rare. The deposit is very poorly sorted and its base is erosive in Triassic rocks.

To the south of Clifton, 1.3 m of gravel with thin sandstone lenses occurs in a small pit [1708 4549], near Halfway House. The gravel is strongly cemented by calcite and contains clasts consisting of 58.5 per cent Carboniferous limestone, 20.5 per cent Carboniferous sandstone, 17.5 per cent Triassic quartzite and quartz, and 3.5 per cent chert and other pebbles. The maximum length of pebble is 0.15 m, but most are 2–4 cm in length.

Small exposures near The Orchards [154 471], west of the River Dove, are generally similar to those described above.

Higher terrace deposits

Higher terrace deposits occur in all the main valleys but are best developed in those of the Dove, and Sutton and Brailsford brooks (Figure 26). Small terrace remnants occur in the Blithe valley north-west of Upper Leigh, and in the Tean valley between Tean and Checkley, while a large patch occurs in the latter valley to the south of Fole. In the Churnet and Henmore valleys higher terrace deposits are only present within a few kilometres of their confluence with the Dove valley.

A feature of these deposits is that their surface is commonly uneven and in many places slopes at a low angle away from the river. The height of the terrace given below is that of the flat at the top of the bluff above the recent alluvium.

The presence of a broad lower terrace in the Blithe and Tean valleys, regarded as outwash from Devensian ice, indicates an early or pre-Devensian age for the remnant higher terrace patches in those valleys. In addition, the presence of flints in deposits in the Dove valley indicates partial derivation from 'eastern' till of ?Wolstonian age. The deposits must then have been laid down in the period between the ?Wolstonian and Devensian glacial maxima. No faunal evidence has been obtained during the present survey but correlation on morphological grounds is possible with the Ipswichian Beeston Terrace of the Trent (see above).

DETAILS

Dove, Churnet and Henmore valleys

Higher terrace deposits occur in the Dove valley between Okeover Park [157 473] and the southern margin of the district south of Crakemarsh [092 364], the broader expanses being in the south. The height of the terrace above the alluvium declines from just over 6 m south of Okeover to 3–4 m at Crakemarsh. The lithology varies, being a clast-supported gravel in the north, a sandy gravel at Combridge [095 375] and a clayey gravel at Crakemarsh. The pebble content also varies, being mainly limestone in the north but quartzite and quartz of Triassic derivation in the south, reflecting to a large extent the rock type 5–10 km upstream of the deposit; other constituents include Carboniferous sandstone and, in the south, flints. A small exposure [1596 4626] 500 m north of Hanging Bridge, Mayfield, showed gravel with pebbles predominantly of Carboniferous limestone with some Carboniferous sandstone and quartz. An exposure in the river bank [1585 4522] south of Hanging Bridge showed 2.2 m of a poorly sorted crudely stratified gravel with a few sand layers, on 3.9 m of Triassic sandstone with pebble layers. The pebbles in the gravel consisted of Carboniferous limestone, sandstone and quartzite of Triassic derivation and in the basal layers included blocks up to 0.3 m long. The upper 0.6 m of the gravel was partially iron-cemented and showed signs of cryoturbation. In a disused gravel pit [0958 3751] 250 m north of Brookend Farm, Combridge, 4.2 m of gravel with sand lenses was seen. The gravel was poorly sorted with pebbles mainly of quartzite, minor Carboniferous sandstone and a few of limestone and chert. This locality is probably the site of a feature regarded by Pocock (1929) as a moraine, but now believed to be a dissected part of a broad terrace which extends southwards to beyond Crakemarsh. At Brookend the terrace is cut by Nothill Brook which itself has terrace deposits along its length as far upstream as Croxden [065 397].

In the Churnet valley there are higher terrace deposits above the confluence with the Dove as far as Crumpwood Weir [094 425]; they vary from about 5 m in the north to 3–4 m above the alluvium north of Rocester. South of Rocester and close to the confluence, the terrace form is not well preserved, apparently due to degradation by a later period of erosion by the Churnet. The deposits consist of coarse gravels with a sand matrix and clayey layers in places. The pebbles are mainly quartzite and quartz of Triassic derivation, with limestone, Carboniferous sandstone, ironstone and volcanic rocks. A small exposure [1005 4094] south of Quixhill Bridge showed 1.1 m of gravel and sand beneath 0.5 m of silt and clay. The pebbles were mainly of Carboniferous limestone and quartzite with a few of Carboniferous sandstone, ironstone and volcanic rocks.

A strip of gravel lies on a terrace-like bench at Paper House [193 469] 6–7 m above the alluvium of Henmore Brook. Although the gravel is not exposed, pebbles in the soil indicate that it is composed mainly of quartzites, with scattered flints and rare pebbles of Triassic conglomerate and igneous rock.

Sutton, Brailsford and Shirley valleys

Higher terrace deposits occur, along Brailsford Brook and Sutton Brook, between Edlaston House and the southern boundary of the district, and along Shirley Brook as far upstream as Shirley Mill [213 408]. The terrace surfaces decline from about 6 m above the alluvium in the north to 3.75 m in the south near Mammerton [214 368]. North of Longford the deposits are somewhat degraded and commonly form narrow ridge-like features. Remnant patches on a narrow interfluve [217 388] north-east of Longford Hall indicate a former broad flat-bottomed river valley in that area, while just to the west of Longford a patch of head on the slope above the terrace points to a possible genetic link between the two.

Surface evidence indicates that the deposits are gravels with a sandy matrix. Quartzite and quartz are the commonest pebbles, with sporadic flints, Carboniferous sandstone, limestone and chert.

Tean valley

Small patches of gravel occur between Upper and Lower Tean and to the east of Checkley. The terrace surfaces are mainly convex with their highest points 7–9 m above the alluvium, and the deposits consist mainly of sandy gravel with predominant quartzite and quartz pebbles and a few of Carboniferous sandstone.

To the south a large spread of gravel occurs south of Fole [044 368]. The surface of this is dissected in part and forms an elongate low ridge rising to about 8 m above the alluvium although at its edge the height is only 4–5 m. A borehole (SK 03 NW/4) at Fole Farm indicated gravel to 5.79 m, while a shallow excavation nearby [0457 3669] showed the gravel to have a variable dark red-brown sandy clay or clayey sand matrix. A section in a small pit [0547 3622] to the south-east, near Overfole, showed 1.8 m of very poorly sorted sandy gravel with clay layers in the basal part. The pebbles, up to 0.3 m long, were mainly quartzite, with scattered chert, quartz and rare sandstone.

Blithe valley

Small patches of gravel and sand with irregular convex surfaces occur north-west of Upper Leigh. A spread [999 372] north-east of Dairy House Farm appears to lie on a bench and its surface is about 6.25 m above the alluvium. The gravel consists mainly of quartzite and quartz, and Carboniferous limestone.

Lower terrace deposits

Lower terrace deposits are well developed in the Blithe and Tean valleys and south of Crakemarsh in the Dove valley; minor occurrences are present elsewhere in the latter and in the Hamps and Churnet valleys. Lower terrace deposits are not developed along Sutton, Brailsford or Shirley brooks, but head occurs widely as a valley-fill material in their upper courses. This close association of valley-fill and lower terrace deposits is widespread throughout the area and suggests that they were formed at the same time. It is thought probable that a gradation exists between ill sorted solifluction deposits (head *sensu stricto*) and better-sorted and commonly stratified fluvial material. Deposits in the upper and middle courses of many of the rivers and streams of the district appear to be of this mixed type.

The surface of the lower terrace is commonly flat and similar in form to that of the alluvium, evidence of its relatively young age. The presence in the deposits of the Blithe valley of many 'north-western' erratics indicates a connection with the Devensian ice; the morphology of the deposits, especially around Forsbrook, where they appear to fill an anomalous drainage network, also indicates a close relationship with Devensian glacial deposits, which form fresh glacial topography not far to the west of the district. As the postulated Devensian ice-limit traverses both the Blithe and Tean valleys (Figure 26), the lower terrace deposits in this area are regarded as outwash from melting Devensian ice. Downstream and in small tributaries solifluction probably also supplied sediment to these rivers, forming a mixed fluvial-solifluction deposit. The low terrace deposits elsewhere in the district are also, on the grounds of their relations to the higher terrace deposits, thought to be Devensian in age.

DETAILS

Blithe valley

Lower terrace deposits are developed along the Blithe valley. They lie at an average height of 1.75 m above the alluvium. The thickness of the deposits is known from a series of boreholes (SJ 93

NE/26–34) about 2.5 km south of Cresswell, which showed sandy gravel between 2.45 m and 4.4 m thick overlying Triassic mudstones and siltstones. Elsewhere, exposures are confined to small ditch sections; one of these [9829 3882], south-east of Cresswell, showed 1.4 m of ill sorted and unstratified gravel with an orange-brown clayey sand matrix, silty in part. Gravel from a ditch [9689 3937] west of Cresswell contained, in addition to many quartzites, a great variety of other pebbles including 'north-western' granitic, volcanic and Lower Palaeozoic types together with Carboniferous sandstone and shale.

Tean valley

Lower terrace deposits occur in the Tean valley between Mobberley [007 413] and the southern margin of the district. The surface varies from 3.25 m near Croft Mill [005 401] to 2.9 m above the alluvium at Lower Tean [015 385]. No sections were seen at the time of survey; however, a borehole (SE 03 NW/1) at Fole Creamery recorded the following:

	Depth m
Soil	to 0.91
Marl	to 2.13
Gravel and boulders	to 3.66
Sand	to 3.96
Gravel	to 5.03
Triassic sandstone, siltstone and mudstone	to bottom of hole at 21.95

Dove, Hamps and Churnet valleys

Small patches of these deposits occur in the Dove valley from just north of Mapleton to the southern margin of the district, but the main developments are the spreads south of Ellastone and at Crakemarsh. North of Mapleton the terrace deposits form low features 1–1.4 m above the alluvium. A small area of terrace about 2 m above the alluvium occurs just west [142 432] of Snelston Rectory and appears to consist mainly of pebbly sand.

Both the terraces south of Ellastone and at Crakemarsh lie about 1.5 m above the alluvium and, from the appearance of the soils, consist of sand and gravel; the latter is made up mainly of Triassic-derived quartzites, but near Crakemarsh blocks of Carboniferous limestone, sandstone and ironstone up to 0.3 m were recorded.

Two small areas of terrace occur in the Hamps valley at Waterhouses; they lie at about 1.5 m above the alluvium and consist largely of gravel.

The Churnet valley contains only one small patch of lower terrace 1.3 m above the alluvium just east of Crumpwood [0923 4257].

Recent alluvium

Alluvium is present along all the main rivers and streams in the district (Figure 26). Alluvial flats up to 1 km wide occur in the Dove valley at Mayfield and north and south of Rocester. Other major spreads are present along the upper part of the Churnet, near Cheddleton, and in the upper tributaries of Bradbourne Brook, south of Parwich and Ballidon.

The alluvium typically consists of an upper layer of silt and/or fine-grained sand and an underlying poorly sorted gravel. In places where stream activity and sediment supply have been low for a long period a waterlogged organic-rich clay layer, or more rarely peat, overlies the gravel. The upper layer is commonly 0.4–1.2 m thick, except in the Dove valley where it exceeds 2.6 m in places. The thickness of gravel is known only in the few localities where boreholes have penetrated the underlying bedrock. The surface of the alluvium is uneven in places and commonly shows evidence of former river courses or subsidiary channels. A large number of boreholes in the Churnet valley, near Cheddleton, proved up to 25 m of alluvial deposits, mainly sands and gravels, whereas farther downstream at Crumpwood [0909 4271] a borehole (SK 04 SE/11) proved 0.76 m of gravel below silty and sandy clay.

The gravels of the lower layer of the alluvium are believed to have been brought into the valleys during the Devensian glaciation either as a mixed fluvial/solifluction deposit or as outwash from melting ice and snow. Downcutting since the end of the glacial period left part of the deposit as the lower terrace, while the rest was either buried by recent alluvium or reworked into it. Alluvial fan deposits are thought to have been laid down largely in the Devensian period and hence are probably best correlated with the lower terrace deposits rather than with alluvium.

DETAILS

Dove, Manifold and Hamps valleys

A thin strip of alluvium occurs in the Dove valley near Thorpe. The valley also contains a number of small alluvial fans. Wider spreads of alluvium occur in both the Dove and Manifold valleys just above their confluence. An exposure in the river bank [1396 5070] just to the east of Ilam showed 2.2 m of dark brown silty loam overlying thinly bedded limestone. Farther upstream, where the Manifold is deeply incised, alluvium occurs impersistently in the valley floor. To the west, the River Hamps is also deeply incised where it traverses the limestone outcrop and only a narrow strip of alluvium is present; upstream where the river crosses Namurian mudstones and sandstones the alluvial flat is broader. A borehole (SK 05 SE/14), on the alluvium just north of Winkhill, proved brown silty loam to 0.91 m overlying sand and gravel to 1.37 m with bedrock below.

South of Thorpe the Dove valley widens considerably, the main change in width coinciding with the unconformity between soft Triassic sandstones to the south and Carboniferous strata to the north. The alluvium consists of silty loam over gravel which commonly forms the bed of the river. At Church Mayfield a section was seen in a river bank [1564 4465]:

	Depth m
Brown silt with small pebbles	0.35
Pink to orange-brown loam with sandstone and mudstone fragments	0.06
Clayey gravel with pebbles mainly of Carboniferous limestone	0.10
Brown silt	0.77

Two exposures south of Middle Mayfield [1435 4369 and 1395 4339] showed the more usual sequence, with 1.5 m and 1.3 m respectively of brown silty sand over a gravel containing Carboniferous limestone and sandstone pebbles. An excavation at Swinholm [1191 4108] was said to have shown 0.6 m of loam over 2.3 m of coarse gravel.

In the banks of the Dove around Rocester, silt and fine-grained sand up to 2.65 m thick overlie gravel, of which 2.0 m are exposed [1145 3872] south of Rocester Bridge. Just above the confluence with the Churnet an exposure in the bank of the Dove [1037 3761]

showed a 1.2 m alternating sequence of silt and fine- to medium-grained pebbly sand in beds up to 9 cm thick. In this part of the valley there are a number of low banks and terraces up to 1m above the alluvium but they commonly merge into the main alluvial flat and are probably related to former channels or meanders.

Churnet valley

The Churnet valley and its main tributaries between the northern margin of the district and Consall Wood [000 489] contain an alluvial tract up to about 300 m wide. The surface material consists of silt and clay up to 2 m thick and overlies sands and gravels. Boreholes indicate that the valley is incised to a depth of about 25 m in solid rock. The Cheddleton Paper Mills No.2 Borehole (SJ 95 SE/27) proved:

	Depth m
Soil	to 0.46
Clay	to 0.91
Loam	to 3.35
Gravel	to 7.92
Sand and gravel	to 19.51
Sand and gravel with clay bands	to 24.89
Carboniferous	to bottom of hole at 67.97

South-east of Consall Wood and as far south as Oakamoor the valley is considerably narrowed by landslips and the alluvium is here discontinuous. Farther south, where the valley is cut in soft Triassic sandstones, the alluvial tract is wider and consists of silt or fine-grained sand overlying gravel, as in the Crumpwood borehole (see p.106). Towards Rocester, several sections in the river bank were seen with up to 2.2 m of silt and sand, while others south of Rocester show gravel underlying the upper layer.

Bradbourne and Henmore valleys

The alluvium in the upper part of Bradbourne Brook south of Parwich and Ballidon forms a broad flat with a brown loamy soil. To the west of Fenny Bentley, a borehole (SK 15 SE/12) close to the edge of the alluvium proved 1.20 m of 'soil' overlying 2.10 m of gravel on bedrock. Farther south, near Sandybrook Farm, 1.9 m of brown loam was seen in the stream bank [1764 4881].

A narrow strip of alluvium occupies the valley of Henmore Brook between Ashbourne and the eastern margin of the district. A section [2045 4712] to the east of Sturstonmill Bridge exposed 2.6 m of brown loam over impure gravel.

Blithe and Tean valleys

A thin strip of alluvium occurs along the River Blithe within the district. To the south-east of Cresswell it consists of a thin peaty soil over gravel, and peaty soil is common elsewhere; but most exposures in the river banks to the south are silt or fine-grained sand up to about 1m overlying gravel with a sandy or clayey matrix. A borehole (SJ 93 NE/33) south-east of Paynsley Hall proved:

	Depth m
Soil	to 0.40
Gravel, sandy	to 2.00
Clay, gravelly, silty	to 5.50
Triassic mudstone and siltstone	to bottom of hole at 14.60

Alluvium also occurs along the Tean valley, gradually becoming better developed to the south so that at Beamhurst Bridge [062 359] on the southern boundary of the district it is 200 m wide and consists of more than 1.6 m of silt and fine-grained sand over gravel.

Brailsford, Shirley and Sutton valleys

Brailsford and Shirley brooks, and their tributaries as far south as their confluence, flow along alluvial strips consisting largely of 0.3–1.3 m of waterlogged peaty silt and clay overlying poorly sorted gravel with a sandy clay matrix. South of the confluence the alluvium forms a flat which broadens to about 450 m at the southern boundary of the district. In this stretch, the northern part of Sutton Brook, the alluvium consists typically of up to 1.3 m of silty clay overlying poorly sorted coarse gravel.

PERIGLACIAL DEPOSITS, PROCESSES AND LANDFORMS

Periglacial conditions affected ice-free areas during the glacial episodes. The main effect was solifluction (the flow of rock and soil material down slope) of the 'active layer' affected by repeated freezing and thawing. Head is the main deposit produced by this process. Rockfalls and creep of frost-shattered angular fragments also give rise to deposits (scree or talus) below steep slopes, but no large accumulations occur in the district. The common lack of vegetation in the periglacial zone allowed particles of fine-grained sand, silt and clay to be transported by the wind and then deposited as loess. Silty loams of possible aeolian origin occur locally in the district in the soil profile but, due to their thinness and common admixture with other deposits, have not been mapped. Superficial folds and faults are common in valley bottoms underlain by the Mercia Mudstones but also occur in Carboniferous mudstones and are regarded as periglacial features. Frost action in the regolith has given rise locally to involutions and to vertical stone orientation, but these structures were rarely observed. Dry valleys are a feature of areas underlain by Carboniferous limestone and Triassic sandstones and conglomerates and are believed to have formed as run-off channels in the active layer overlying frozen ground. Surfaces of low relief in the south-eastern part of the district, for example the areas of the former Ashbourne and Darley Moor airfields, are believed to have developed from till plains by periglacial planation processes (Jones and Charsley, 1985).

Although a periglacial environment existed during each glacial episode, almost all the deposits and effects now seen in the district are believed to relate to the most recent (Devensian) glaciation. Deposits and surface effects of earlier periods are likely either to have been destroyed or to be present at deeper levels in later deposits, such as river terraces and slope deposits, and are not now distinguishable.

Head

Head is widespread in the district and is more extensive than shown in Figure 26 as it is commonly too thin or patchy to map; in places it is difficult to distinguish from underlying deposits.

Two closely related types occur. Slope deposits form extensive sheets in many places, but appear to be thickest close to the eastern limit of Devensian ice west and north-west of Waterhouses and west of Upper Leigh. Head also occurs as a valley-fill deposit in the tributaries and upper courses of most of the rivers and streams in the district, many of which are dry at present. In places it has been partially reworked and incorporated in fluvial deposits; much of the material making up the higher and lower terrace deposits and the present alluvium may have been originally derived by solifluction from the valley sides.

Head commonly consists of a heterogeneous mixture of angular fragments set in a finer-grained matrix, not dissimilar to glacial till. This similarity, and the problem of differentiating the two, is most marked in the south of the district, since the head deposits here have been derived largely from the mass wasting of glacial tills and gravels. An important local difference, however, is that head is often somewhat porous whereas till is usually well compacted and consolidated except in weathered exposures.   TJC

In the undifferentiated Namurian outcrop, the bedrock consists largely of mudstones, thinly interbedded with siltstone and sandstone, and is deeply weathered to a stiff clay in the top few metres. Head that normally overlies this weathered material originates from and closely resembles it. This head can be distinguished from the parent material by its more homogeneous and structureless appearance, particularly the absence of variegated lamination, and by the presence of dispersed, mainly angular, rock fragments. Another characteristic is the presence of relict shear planes. These were revealed in a trench [2445 5071] dug in undisturbed ground during investigation by Soil Mechanics Ltd (personal communication, D. Norbury, 1984) and BGS into the failure in 1984 of the almost-completed Carsington Reservoir dam embankment (Coxon, 1986). Such shears were probably formed during the original periglacial solifluction movements and they are of engineering significance because they may drastically affect the shear strength of the head.   NA

The thickest head occurs in the north-west where in some exposures it exceeds 4.5 m in thickness. In most areas the head is only a metre or so in thickness but many of the valley-fill deposits may be considerably thicker. Almost all the head in the district is believed to have been deposited during the Devensian cold stage; however, periglacial conditions certainly existed in previous cold periods and some of the deposits may relate to these stages.

Details

Waterhouses, Winkhill and Ipstones

Head is extensive in places between the Hamps and Churnet rivers. The deposits consist of angular blocks and smaller fragments of Namurian sandstone, with rare 'Bunter' pebbles, in a clay matrix; they are clearly derived from the local bedrock of Namurian sandstones and mudstones with a small drift component. Scattered exposures occur in ditches and gullies throughout the area and thicker deposits were seen locally, for example 4.5 m was exposed in a gully [0617 5048] south of Winkhill and 3 m of grey-brown stony clay with subangular pebbles, cobbles and rare boulders in another gully [0551 5468] north-west of Ford.

Head partially fills many small valleys, including two north-west of Ipstones that are regarded as ice-marginal or subglacial channels. In the southern valley up to 3 m of sandy clay with sandstone debris were seen in stream banks [007 506], while to the north-west another anomalous valley [000 534] is filled with sandstone blocks in a clay matrix. The appearance of the valley suggests that the latter deposit may be mainly derived from the settlement and partial reworking of older landslip material; the newer landslip debris mapped along the valley appears to overlie the head.

Dilhorne, Upper Tean and Upper Leigh

Head fills a number of narrow valleys around Dilhorne and farther to the south it occupies the upper course of a stream near Draycott-in-the-Moors; no sections were seen, but the deposit appears to be pebbly loam or gravel. South of Cresswell, the dissection of a former till sheet has exposed Triassic mudstones and siltstones on the valley sides, and these are almost everywhere covered with a thin veneer of head, many small gullies being completely filled with the deposit. This consists of a stony clay loam, a mixture of till and Triassic material; it has been mapped only where there is no surface evidence of the underlying strata.

Close to the southern boundary of the district the head is a gravelly clay. South-east of Blakelow a section [9808 3613] showed 1.75 m of red-brown stony sandy clay. To the north-west of Blakelow [9696 3715] the following was exposed:

	Depth m
Clay loam, red-brown, silty, with pebbles	0.4
Clay loam, yellow-brown, pebbly, silty	0.4
Gravel, red-brown, sandy	0.5
Clay, red-brown, with pebbles	0.2
Clay, red-brown, with siltstone fragments (weathered Triassic)	0.2

Stanton and Cauldon

Head consisting mainly of soliflucted till occurs to the east of Stanton; a section [1396 4632] north-west of Harlow Farm proved 1.9 m of pale brown stony clay loam overlying Triassic siltstone and mudstone. Just west of Stanton, head forms a slope deposit [122 464] of large Triassic sandstone blocks in a sandy matrix.

Head occurs on the Weaver Hills south-east of Cauldon, as a narrow valley-fill deposit [094 489] at Huddale, and a sheet-like spread in an area of low ground near Rue Hill. Exposures in the sides of sink holes in the latter deposit [080 480] show up to 1.5 m of brown silt with scattered 'Bunter' pebbles, the high silt content indicating probable derivation from local loessic material (see below).

Tissington, Brassington and Kniveton

The head in this area consists of brown silty loam with chert fragments, or more rarely 'Bunter' pebbles. Sections are rare but east of Brassington there are exposures in the sides of disused silica sand pits: in Bees Nest Pit, for example, a section [2419 5458] showed 1.8 m of brown loam with scattered quartzite and chert pebbles overlying sand of the Brassington Formation.

Ashbourne, Hulland, Brailsford and Alkmonton

The south-east corner of the district is characterised by valley-fill head, although locally, as at Hulland [246 468], it forms slope deposits. A major source of the head in this area is the till on the high ground and much of the head is stony or gravelly in consequence.

The head in the valleys commonly forms ill drained slightly moundy ground with a thin peaty clay cover locally. East of Ashbourne, at Nether Sturston [194 464], head fills a broad marshy area of low ground flanking the alluvium of Henmore Brook and consists of clayey gravels and sands. The alluvium in the upper parts of Brailsford Brook and its tributaries is flanked almost everywhere by, and probably overlies, head. Fresh sections are rare but, where seen, the deposits consist of impure, ill sorted and unstratified gravels. In a head-filled valley at Clifton, 2.3 m of unsorted sand and gravel were seen in a river bank [1686 4439].

In the southern part of the district, where till is less extensive, the Mercia Mudstones form the main bedrock. This is reflected in the composition of the head in the valleys, which commonly consists of structureless red-brown clay loam with scattered pebbles. In the banks [1836 3647] of a stream north of Boylestone such a deposit was more than 2 m thick. Elsewhere comparable sections up to 1 m in the banks of streams are common.

Extensive areas of head are developed near Hulland, down slope from high-level deposits of Triassic pebbly sandstones overlying Carboniferous mudstones, and from glacial gravels. The head consists of unstratified gravels with a variable clayey or sandy matrix; exposures are rare.

Similar deposits occur down slope of gravelly glacial deposits [226 473] north of Bradley Nook Farm, along Wyaston Brook [194 424] and [191 402] east of Yeaveley. A similar slope deposit at Longford appears to be genetically linked to the Longford higher terrace indicating that it may be of a similar age (pre-Devensian). A section [2120 3759] showed 1.3 m of brown pebbly loam overlying weathered mudstone.

Scree

In the Ashbourne district the only rocks which are hard enough to have produced scree are the Dinantian limestones in the north; however, few scree deposits of mappable proportions occur, probably because all but the latest have been removed by flood waters flowing through the narrow dales and gorges during earlier humid periods. Most of the screes appear to be stabilised and many are partly covered by vegetation, leading to the conclusion that they were formed in the later part of the Devensian under periglacial conditions.

DETAILS

Small screes occur in Dovedale at Ravens Tor [141 538], near Tissington Spires [146 521] and in Nabs Dale [145 535]. A long strip occurs on the south-east flank [144 512] of Bunster Hill, while just to the west [1395 5123] a small patch of cemented scree up to 2.4 m in thickness overlies reef-limestone. Small screes also occur in the Manifold valley near Ilam Hall [128 504] and in the Hamps valley [095 533] north-west of Soles Hill.

Silty loam

Silty loam is widespread as a surface deposit in the Ashbourne district, particularly in the limestone areas, but it does not appear to be anywhere much more than a metre thick and it is commonly admixed with other superficial deposits, making its delineation difficult. Analytical work carried out on material from north of the present district (Pigott, 1962; Cazalet, 1969; Bryan, 1970) indicates that when pure it has size gradings consistent with an aeolian origin. The mapping of the deposits falls outside the scope of the current survey; however, mapping in the Onecote area by the Soil Survey (Hollis, 1975) distinguished two soil series, the Crwbin and the Malham, which consist of silty clay loam, of probable aeolian origin, over limestone.

The silty loam is especially noticeable on the Carboniferous limestone, where it forms a major part of the deposits mapped as head. In places it provides a well drained soil cover in areas which otherwise might have only a thin residual clayey soil or a bare limestone pavement. Away from the limestone the mixing with other, more easily disaggregated, parent rock types makes recognition of the silty loam fraction more difficult. A silty drift, probably of similar origin, commonly overlies Triassic sandstones and conglomerates, however. The porous nature of silty loam makes its preservation unlikely where it overlies impermeable mudstones or siltstones, since in this situation excess rain or snow-melt would be dispersed as run-off, taking the surface material with it. The extent of aeolian silt on the Derbyshire Dome is uncertain since work by Bryan (1970) indicated that the finer fraction of many soils on the limestone is residual, except on plateau areas; this contrasts with the earlier views of Pigott (1962).

DETAILS

Small exposures of silty loam are common in soil profiles, but in most cases the deposit is mixed with other materials and few details of such exposures have been recorded. A section in the side of a disused gravel pit [1013 4588] on the flanks of the Weaver Hills showed 0.20 m of dark brown silty loam overlying a partly cemented openwork limestone gravel. A sample of the silty loam contained over 70 per cent of silt and very fine-grained sand. To the north, in an area [103 471] of low relief near Weaver Farm, auger holes proved up to 0.85 m of red-brown silty loam overlying bedrock.

Superficial structures

Superficial structures as described here include non-diastrophic folds and faults as well as cryoturbation structures. Folds and faults not attributable to tectonic causes occur in mudstones or siltstones of both Triassic and Carboniferous age. They tend to occur in narrow steep-sided valleys where till occupies the high ground. The folds are mostly asymmetrical and their trend almost invariably lies parallel or subparallel to that of the valley. Minor faulting, with little displacement of beds away from the fault plane, is commonly associated with the folds.

Similar valley bulge structures are well known from the Mesozoic rocks of the Midlands (Hollingworth and others, 1944) and their origin and mode of formation have been discussed by a number of authors (Shotton and Wilcockson, 1951; Kellaway, 1972). Superficial folds in the Namurian near Derby have been described by Jones and Weaver (1975) who concluded that the folding was developed as a result of the growth and decay of ground ice under periglacial conditions during the Devensian.

The structures seen in the present district are due to compression acting roughly at right angles to the valley trend, but these forces were not necessarily produced by the growth and decay of ground ice; a more simple mechanism involves the phenomenon of 'heaving' (Hills, 1972, p.74) following the removal of a superincumbent load during rapid valley incision. A periglacial climate would aid this process since permanently frozen ground would impede natural drainage and maintain a higher (perched) water table in the active layer, leading to a reduction in frictional and cohesive forces.

Although cryoturbation has disturbed many soil and weathered rock profiles, few examples of oriented structures were noted in the district. Involutions were seen at one locality in Triassic sandstones, while vertical stone orientation was seen in two places in weathered sections.

DETAILS

Small-scale folds probably of superficial origin, subparallel to the valley trend and at a large angle to the regional folds, occur in Namurian mudstones and siltstones in a number of streams north of Ashbourne. A tight anticline plunging downstream was seen in a stream section [1915 4869] south-east of Herdsman's Close Farm, while farther upstream folds with steep dips occur [1923 4876] just below the till cover. In similar strata in the Scow Brook valley [24 50] east of Hognaston, irregular folds and faults, attributed to periglacial cryoturbation processes, were revealed in several pits and boreholes associated with the Carsington Reservoir scheme (Aitkenhead and others, 1984).

Tight folds were seen in many of the deeper valleys in Mercia Mudstones overlain by till; the evidence being confined in places to small exposures of vertical strata in areas of generally low dip. In a deeply incised stream west of Headlow Fields Farm, folded and faulted strata occur in a succession of mudstones and siltstones of the Denstone Formation; a small anticline with a faulted limb was seen in Lower Brookfarm Dumble [1592 4242]. To the south, small disturbed sections occur in a stream south-east of Cubleycommon Farm, small folds in one exposure [1659 3862] having a wavelength of about 7 m.

Involutions were present in a temporary excavation [2373 4582] at The Knob Farm. Evidence of cryoturbation was seen in another cutting [2371 4575] in sandstone at the farm. Well developed vertical stone orientation occurs south of Dilhorne in a pit [9749 4290] in gravelly boulder clay and at Winnothdale the following section was exposed in a gravel pit [0312 4074]:

	Depth m
Loam, dark brown, sandy, pebbly (soil)	0.30
Loam, brown, silty, sandy, pebbly, with random pebble orientation (soliflucted layer)	0.45
Sand, red-brown, fine-grained, silty, with many vertically orientated pebbles (cryoturbated sandstone)	0.55

Tors

Tors are upstanding residual masses of rock isolated by differential weathering and erosion from their parent formations. Three types of tor are present in the district, only two of which are believed to have reached their present form under periglacial conditions.

The first type is that formed by the retreat of a sandstone scarp, leaving isolated masses of rock. They are not common, but examples are known from the Namurian Chatsworth Grit and the Triassic Hollington Formation, both thick-bedded coarse-grained sandstones, well cemented in part. Tors in the Chatsworth Grit include Gog and Magog rocks [0068 5045 and 0062 5037] near Ipstones and Harston Rock [0348 4785] near Foxt, all of which have slipped slightly down-slope out of their original position, and Hopestone Rock [0360 4983] near Ipstones. The Peakstone Rock [0514 4217] west of Alton consists of baryte-cemented pebbly sandstone, and stands clear of a low sandstone escarpment of the Hollington Formation; it was figured by

Hull (1869, p.92). This type of tor appears to have formed by differential weathering of irregularly cemented sandstone followed by the down-slope removal of the weathered debris.

The second type occurs in the north-east of the district, near Brassington, where residual dolomite masses form several tors. Good examples occur at Black Rocks [214 548] and Rainster Rocks [219 548]. Differential removal of calcite by waters percolating along fracture planes in the massive dolomites is believed (Ford, 1963) to have initiated tor formation as long ago as the Tertiary. Repeated warm humid episodes during Pleistocene interglacials continued the weathering process, while colder periods were characterised by erosion of the tors or by removal of the weathered debris around them. These tors lie outside the supposed Wolstonian glacial limit (Figure 25, area 1d) and so can be presumed to have been exposed to two periglacial episodes.

The unifying process in the formation of these first two types of tor is the removal of the weathered debris around the upstanding rock masses, which is believed to have taken place by mass wasting under periglacial conditions.

The third type of tor occurs in Dinantian limestones in the Dove and Manifold valleys, and appears to be the result of mainly solutional processes aided by glacial meltwaters. Examples such as Beeston Tor [1057 5408] and Ravens Tor [1412 5384], consist of knolls of massive reef-limestone surrounded by less resistant bedded limestones; others such as Pickering Tor [1428 5225] are limestone pillars isolated by karstic solution along intersecting vertical joints in massive reef limestones (Plate 1).

Dry valleys

Dry valleys, misfit streams and deeply incised valleys are common in the district and indicate hydrological conditions different from those operating at present. These features form part of a well developed dendritic drainage network (Warwick, 1964; Jones, 1979) which is not confined to any one rock type.

Dry valleys are best known in the limestone areas but are also common in Triassic sandstones. Even in areas of Triassic mudstones and siltstones some valleys are dry and many others contain only small misfit streams. The dry valleys of this part of the Midlands may have been superimposed from a former impermeable cover and now made dry by a falling water table (Linton, 1956; Warwick, 1964; Burek, 1977), or may be a product of a periglacial environment when run-off from melting snow and ice readily eroded channels in the active layer over permanently frozen ground, with high rates of mass wasting as a contributory factor (Jones, 1979).

The present work has tended to confirm the finding of Jones (1979), that in areas of Triassic strata many of the dry valleys contain head of probable periglacial origin. This, together with the fact that the valleys are commonly incised in till of Wolstonian age, implies that the dry valley network in these areas is a relatively young feature and as such is not likely to have been superimposed from a cover of sedimentary rocks. Although it is possible that a few of the dry valleys may be superimposed relict features, most are more convincingly explained as part of a late Pleistocene drainage network, formed by meltwater from periglacial ice or snow, and of late Wolstonian or Devensian age.

The best examples of dry valleys in the limestone area are the tributary valleys of the Dove: Hope Dale, Hall Dale and Nabs Dale.

Dry valleys are common in areas of Triassic sandstones, either as rounded ridge and gully features on steep slopes, as occur in the Hawksmoor [038 438] and Leek [985 533] areas, or as deeper broader valleys having an infill of head. A good example of the second type occurs in Osmaston Park [208 433].

A dry valley [045 376] near Fole starts in mudstones and siltstones of the Mercia Mudstone Group and then crosses the outcrop of the Denstone Formation. A similar pattern occurs north of Greatgate [057 404].

Dry valleys also occur solely on glacial deposits, and in the area between Rodsley and Wyaston examples occur on both clayey and gravelly tills. West of Wyastoncommon Farm a broad dry valley [190 417] starts in an area of pebble clay till and, before joining Brown's Brook, traverses an area of head over Triassic mudstone.

Surfaces of faint relief

A number of near-planar surfaces occur in the district (see also p.114); those at Darley Moor [16 41] and Ashbourne [19 45] were extensive enough to be used as wartime airfields. Similar surfaces occur around Yeaveley [18 40] and Bentley Hall [17 38]. These surfaces were regarded (Clayton, 1953b) as planation surfaces related to intermittently falling base levels of the River Trent and were believed to be mainly early Pleistocene in age.

Work in the present and the neighbouring Derby (Frost and Smart, 1979) districts has enabled a reappraisal of these surfaces to be made (Jones and Charsley, 1985). Most of the so-called planation surfaces have proved to be covered by thick deposits of till and other glacial deposits. The Shirley Common Borehole (SK 24 SW/9) revealed 24.0 m of glacial deposits below the level of Clayton's 'Yeaveley Surface', while 18.8 m of glacial material, mainly till, occurred in a borehole (SK 14 SE/9) on the 'Darley Moor Surface', 5 km south of Ashbourne.

The surfaces must be younger than the deposits of the penultimate (?Wolstonian) glaciation that underlie them, and in view of this relationship they are now regarded (Jones and Charsley, 1985) as having resulted from periglacial smoothing processes such as frost action, nivation and solifluction during the late ?Wolstonian or Devensian cold periods.

OTHER DEPOSITS

Landslips

Landslips are common in the northern half of the district (Figure 26), most occurring along the flanks of steep-sided valleys cut into mudstones of Carboniferous age. Examples of such valleys are the Churnet and its tributaries between Cheddleton and Oakamoor, the Dove between Thorpe and Mapleton, and Bradbourne and Henmore brooks and their tributaries. Exceptionally, landslipped areas have also been noted in well bedded limestones or Triassic mudstones and siltstones.

Almost all the landslips are rotational slides or slumps and have an upper slumped part with scarp features and a lower flow part with a hummocky surface, forming the toe of the slide. In most cases failure apparently occurred by a combination of rupture along a concave surface and bedding-plane slip, the latter being especially important where the bedding was inclined in the direction of the local ground slope.

The occurrence of hummocky slipped material in the toe of a number of landslips up to 250 m from the foot of the slumped part, for example north-west of Littlepark [159 491], indicates that at the time of failure the bedrock was in a weakly cohesive water-saturated state. Although the landslips are now covered in vegetation they show relatively fresh surface forms such as scarps and ridges, which are unlikely to have survived a long period of erosion. In addition, some landslipped masses in the Churnet valley [012 482] have been incised, but not reworked or covered by alluvium, indicating a late-Devensian or post-glacial age. A slightly greater (through still Devensian) age is indicated in the Atlow area where landslipped material has been incorporated locally in a valley-fill head deposit [230 492] which has been incised by the present stream. Two recent landslips noted during the survey were a small slip [228 492] in mudstones of the Widmerpool Formation on the eastern flank of Madge Hill, and a small ungrassed scarp [1842 4915] 1.85 m high in Namurian mudstones at the junction of two tributaries of Bentley Brook.

It thus appears that the landslips of the district are relatively young features and that slipping has occured from Devensian times to the present, most taking place under late Devensian periglacial conditions, probably in the saturated active layer overlying permanently frozen ground.

DETAILS

Churnet valley

Landslips are present in the Churnet valley and its tributaries from Oakamoor to north of Cheddleton, where they cut across Westphalian and Namurian mudstones or siltstones. Where sandstones are also involved, for example in the Churnet valley [031 454] south-east of Kingsley Holt and in The Combes [004 524], the slides appear to have been initiated in underlying mudstones.

The largest landslip in the district is about 0.75 km² in extent and occurs in the Churnet valley north-west of Froghall. For a short stretch [010 481 to 013 481] the river is incised in landslip and has not developed an alluvial strip as it has to the north and south.

The concentration of landslips along the Churnet valley and its tributaries is due in part to overdeepening by meltwaters from both the ?Wolstonian and Devensian ice sheets (see p.102), the last of which is believed to have reached a marginal position north-west of Froghall (Figure 26).

Hamps, Manifold and Dove valleys

Small landslips occur in the Hamps valley between Ford and Waterhouses, where it crosses Namurian mudstones and sandstones. Larger areas are present south-west of Winkhill, where mudstones below a ridge of Namurian Ipstones Edge Sandstones have slipped extensively.

In the Manifold valley three small landslips were noted in an area underlain by Hopedale Limestones. The largest occurs on the north bank of the Manifold [111 539], north of Cheshire Wood, in a place where the local dip is 12°–15° in the same direction as a ground slope of about 17°. A few mainly small landslips are present to the south in the outcrop of the Widmerpool Formation.

Several landslips occur in the Dove valley south of the confluence with the Manifold in mudstones of the Widmerpool Formation. In a large landslip [159 491], just north of Littlepark, flow material from several slides has formed a single hummocky area. In the upper part of Ordley Brook, small landslips occur in Widmerpool Formation mudstones, while to the south along the valley, west of Harlow Farm, areas of landslip [138 460] were noted in mudstones and sandstones of the Hawksmoor Formation. Farther south, mudstones and siltstones of the Mercia Mudstone Group form a narrow ledge [115 406] of landslip near Dovecliff.

Bradbourne Brook

Landslips occur in the valleys of Bradbourne Brook and its tributaries where they are underlain by mudstones either of the Widmerpool Formation or Namurian. Clays from the weathering of igneous rocks in the Widmerpool Formation may also have contributed locally to slipping, as at Woodside Farm, where a small exposure [1956 5069] of igneous material was found within an extensive landslip.

Elongate areas of landslip occur along the sides of the valley of Bletch Brook which is aligned close to the axis of a syncline in Namurian mudstones. The beds dip into the valley from both sides at 10°–15°, facilitating landslipping. The underlying Dinantian rocks are also involved.

Several small landslips occur along Havenhill Dale; most are in the Widmerpool Formation, but south of Bradbourne a landslip [212 523] lies wholly within the Hopedale Limestones.

Henmore Brook

Landslips occur along the valley of Henmore Brook and some of its tributaries where they flow across mudstones. The most extensive area [230 494] is close to Atlow Mill. On the eastern flanks of Madge Hill the dip is in the same direction as the hill slope and an area of recent landslip [2280 4925] and an incipient slip [2287 4915] were noted. A similar situation exists on the slopes [232 504] above Hognaston where landslips straddle the Dinantian-Namurian boundary and the tectonic dip is down slope.

Peat

Although peaty or organic-rich clays are moderately common in the alluvium of many valleys in the district, deposits of peat of mappable extent or thickness are rare. Most occur in valleys where stream activity is low, and in some places it appears that peat is still forming. No peat was found within any glacial or fluvial sequences in the district.

DETAILS

A patch of hill peat [033 526] up to 1.5 m thick overlies till just west of Bottom House.

Small deposits of peat occur in a number of the valleys in the district but the larger are confined to the eastern side, in areas underlain by Triassic strata. In the ill drained upper part of the small valley [176 434] which joins the Dove valley at Clifton, peat of unknown thickness extends for just over 300 m along the valley.

The valley of Shirley Brook is floored for most of its length by peaty clay soil up to 1.3 m thick overlying gravel and clayey sand,

Table 7   Relationships between deposits, faunas, floras and archaeology in two sections in Elder Bush Cave, together with comments on their environment of deposition (after Bramwell, 1964; see also Bramwell and Shotton, 1982)

Layer	Lithology — Main Cave	Lithology — Final Chamber	Fauna and flora	Archaeology	Comments
12	Brown loam with limestone fragments		Various bones	Various Mesolithic to Romano-British artefacts	Post-glacial
11B	*(layer not present in section)*	Travertine 'flakey stalagmite'			Considered contemporaneous – late-glacial cold and temperate climates represented
11A	Limestone gravel	*(layer not present in section)*	Bovid species, water vole, amphibians		
10	Transitional		Grouse, mallard, reindeer, bear, fox	?Palaeolithic flint tool and flakes with charcoal	Cold climate-?full glacial (?late-Devensian)
9	Red cave earth (red clay with subangular limestone fragments)		Reindeer, bear, fox	Palaeolithic artefact (shaped reindeer bone)	Cold phase
			Red deer, wild pig		Mild phase
			Hyaena, lion, bison, horse, woolly rhinoceros, cave bear, reindeer, lemming		Warm becoming colder (?early Devensian)
8	Travertine 'flakey stalagmite'	*(layer not present in section)*	Maple leaf and insect wing impressions; rodents		Warm to mild humid conditions (but see also Bramwell and Shotton, 1982)
7	Sandy cave earth	*(layer not present in section)*	Lion, hyaena, wolf, giant deer, bison, hippopotamus		Warm dry conditions (?Ipswichian interglacial)
6	Grey fine-grained sand	*(layer not present in section)*			Layers 5 and 6 are probably related deposits formed by run-off water, seepage, or stream-flood entry into cave in periglacial environment (?Wolstonian)
5	Laminated grey clay (average 5000 laminations where best developed)				
4	Travertine 'massive stalagmite'				Stable temperature conditions – cave above water table
3	*(layer not present in section)*	Breccia of gritstone and limestone, some rounded clasts			Probable contemporaneous deposits introduced by melt water, solifluction or mud flow under glacial or periglacial conditions (?Anglian)
2	Yellow sandy clay with ?calcareous concretions	*(layer not present in section)*			
1	White clay	*(layer not present in section)*			?Residual deposit

Note: Only selected parts of the fauna are noted

   Layer not present in section

and three areas of peat are present west and south-west of Shirley. Similar peaty soils, with peat locally, occur along the valley of Brailsford Brook, as east of Yeldersley Hollies where peaty soils with patchy peat overlie head, with peat about 0.7 m thick in one place [2372 4371].

Cave and fissure deposits

Deposits have been documented from four separate caves or fissures in the district but, except at Elder Bush Cave, excavations were carried out in the 19th or early 20th century and stratigraphic relationships are difficult to work out from the accounts published.

Work in Thors Cave [0986 5496] in 1864 (Brown, 1865) indicated a sequence of fine-grained sand or clay overlain by a breccia of subangular gritstone blocks with '2 to 4 feet' of red clay above forming the floor of the cave. The breccia has subsequently been found to contain an assortment of bones, mainly of birds and small mammals, indicating a late-glacial (Devensian) age (D. Bramwell and M. F. Stanley, personal communication). Excavations in the adjoining Fissure Cave (Wilson, 1937) revealed laminated (?glacial) clays at the base, overlain by deposits containing mammalian bones and human artefacts of Palaeolithic to Romano-British age.

A fissure fill or swallow-hole deposit was formerly visible in a quarry, believed to be Brownend Quarry [090 502] at Waterhouses, and mammoth remains were identified in a limestone breccia (Brockbank, 1864). The sides of the fissure were lined with stalactitic calcite and it was filled with angular limestone fragments and rounded sandstone boulders in a red loamy clay matrix (Brown, 1865). A record (Ward, 1902) of elephant, rhinoceros and hippopotamus remains from this deposit cannot be substantiated.

Quarrying has destroyed all traces of the cave discovered at Caldon Low [082 488] during early quarrying operations (Barke, 1906). It was floored by limestone fragments cemented by stalagmitic calcite, and bones found scattered 'under the floor' were subsequently identified as those of fox, bear, woolly rhinoceros, bison and deer (Barke, 1907).

Excavations between 1935 and 1952 at Elder Bush [0978 5489], in the Manifold valley near Wetton, have revealed a complex sequence of deposits, with faunal remains at a number of horizons. A summary of the main results (Bramwell, 1964; Bramwell and Shotton, 1982) is given in Table 7. A marker horizon is provided by the sandy cave earth (layer 7), with a fauna and flora indicating warm dry conditions, similar to those from Ipswichian sites elsewhere. Layer 8, above, has a mixed flora and fauna that may also be Ipswichian (Bramwell and Shotton, 1982). Below layer 7, two cold periods are indicated by a laminated clay (layer 5) and a breccia (layer 3), separated by a stable temperate period of stalagmitic calcite formation (layer 4). The area is not believed to have been ice-covered during the penultimate (?Wolstonian) glaciation (see p.95), but seasonal snow melt in a periglacial environment could account for the varve-like laminated clay and overlying sand (layers 5 and 6). Glacial deposits related to an earlier glaciation (?Anglian), when ice cover is believed to have been complete over the district, occur on high ground to the north, east and west of the area, and the breccia and sandy clay (layers 2 and 3) were probably deposited at this time by meltwater, solifluction or mudflow into the cave following its opening to the surface by glacial erosion. Above the supposed Ipswichian deposits (layers 7 and 8) the sequence of deposits and their fauna appear to show fluctuating climatic conditions during the onset, peak and decline of the last (Devensian) glaciation and through the ensuing post-glacial period.

DENUDATION CHRONOLOGY

An understanding of the development of the present drainage pattern is linked to that of various surfaces of low relief in the southern Pennines.

The first surface to have been recognised was the '1000-foot' surface (Swinnerton, 1935) or 'Peak District Upland Surface' (Linton, 1956). Fearnsides (1932) suggested that this originated in Permo-Triassic times and this suggestion has been recently revived with some modification by Frost and Smart (1979, p.94), who regard part of it at least as an exhumed sub-Permo-Triassic erosion surface. Exhumation of this surface is still taking place at the margins of the Triassic outcrop, as at Limestone Hill [136 463] near Stanton. Dolomitised limestone near Brassington may provide supporting evidence for the former proximity of this surface (p.73). However, in the Ashbourne district the sub-Permo-Triassic surface appears to be uneven and of similar relief to that of the present day, rather than a planation surface like that proposed by Frost and Smart (1979, fig. 56) in the Derby district.

A Tertiary age for the Upland Surface was first suggested by Linton (1956, p.34) and later refined to Mio-Pliocene (Kent, 1957). A much younger age is implied by the work of McArthur (1977) on denudation rates and Pitty (1968) on limestone solution rates. Both authors consider that, even given conservative erosion rates, no surface now visible could be older than middle- to late-Pleistocene in age.

The sequence in the Pocket Deposits (p.88) offers a possible key to the age of the Upland Surface since many of the dolines in which they are preserved have developed at or just below that surface. These deposits suggest that some erosion of the limestone occurred prior to the deposition of the Namurian mudstones and that, thereafter, periods of erosion followed by deposition occurred in Namurian, Permo-Triassic, Tertiary and Pleistocene times. During any erosional period the limestone surface may locally have been cleaned of earlier deposits and subjected to further planation by various processes, including solution (Pitty, 1968, pp.16–175).

Several surfaces below the Peak District Upland Surface were recognised in the district by Clayton (1953b). These descended from a 'Middle Surface' at a little over 700 ft (210 m) to about 460 ft (140 m) above OD and they were regarded as pre-glacial in age. The upper altitudinal limit of the 'Middle Surface' is now recognised as corresponding closely to the upper 'fill-line' of till-covered surfaces of low relief which occur all around the edge of the upland part of the district (pp.95–98; Figure 25, areas 2a and 2b). The lower surfaces are also till-covered plateau-like areas, whose surface form is now attributed to periglacial processes (Jones and Charsley, 1985).

Many authors have followed the views of Linton (1951) that the drainage network was initiated on a Chalk cover following late-Cretaceous and early Tertiary uplift. However, the evidence provided by the Pocket Deposits indicates a widespread cover, at least on the limestone uplands, of continental sediments in late Miocene or early Pliocene times (see p.90) and it is possible that the basis of the modern drainage pattern was established during the dissection of those sediments.

An alternative approach is to examine the relation of the drainage network to the present and earlier landscapes. Several features of the present network are relevant to a discussion of drainage development:

1 The network has a dendritic form (Warwick, 1964; Burek, 1977) which is still not fully established in the plateau-like areas of till, such as Darley Moor [175 423], thought to have been deposited from ice-melt during the waning stages of the penultimate (?Wolstonian) glaciation. These features imply immaturity in geomorphological terms.

2 Many dry valleys, some filled by head, are included in the network, indicating changed hydrological conditions since it was established. This (p.111) is believed to reflect formation of these valleys under (?Devensian) periglacial conditions.

3 The deeply incised parts of the Dove, Hamps and Manifold valleys contain neither glacial deposits, nor any other deposits regarded as older than Devensian (Ford and Burek, 1976, p.65). This implies that they were formed, or re-excavated to their present state, after the antepenultimate (?Anglian) glaciation. Warwick (1953), however, regarded the capture of a north-flowing Dove by a tributary of the Manifold as pre-glacial, a view based on his interpretation of halt stages in the downcutting of the rivers.

4 The incised parts of the Dove, Hamps and Manifold valleys appear to have developed irrespective of bedrock

structures and their position is difficult to explain except by superimposition. The suggestion (Pitty, 1968, pp.167–168) that they may be unroofed underground water courses is difficult to support in view of their obviously meandering form.

5 Anomalous drainage networks, both in the Churnet catchment and on the western margin of the district, are closely related to the supposed limit of the Devensian ice (p.102).

6 South of the upland area the drainage network has been incised through what must have been a widespread sheet of glacial deposits belonging to the penultimate (?Wolstonian) glaciation. This sheet may have simply draped over a similar landscape to that now existing, and the drainage network may have re-established itself on previous lines, as appears to have taken place in the Derwent valley near Derby, where till underlies terrace deposits (Jones and Stanley, 1974). However, there is evidence, including the pattern of the buried channels south of Checkley (p.98) and the distribution of the Ashbourne Gravel (p.103), that the drainage pattern on the sub-till surface was somewhat different from the present one.

The above evidence suggests that much of the drainage network, particularly in the higher-order tributaries, is of relatively recent (post-?Wolstonian) origin. The evidence for the age of the main river valleys is more equivocal, though some, such as the Churnet, may be of a similar age or only slightly older. There is no reason to regard the incision of the gorges of the Dove, Hamps and Manifold as a preglacial event; on the contrary, sediment-charged meltwaters could have caused rapid vertical incision. The actual drainage pattern of the main river valleys may, however, be a very old feature and could conceivably have been superimposed from a meander pattern established in late-Tertiary or early-Pleistocene times on pre-existing cover-rocks of Namurian to Tertiary age. TJC

CHAPTER 10

Structure

The Carboniferous rocks in the northern half of the district were folded and faulted mainly during the Hercynian orogeny. The southward tilting affecting the Triassic rocks to the south was largely the result of Alpine movements in mid-Tertiary times. The pattern of faulting that affects the Triassic rocks probably resulted from intermittent movements over a longer period of time, partly along existing Hercynian lines in the underlying Carboniferous.

The deeper structure of the Pennine region has been the subject of recent debate (Leeder, 1982; Miller and Grayson, 1982; Smith and others, 1985), with the application of theoretical models based on evidence from better-explored sedimentary basins. Leeder, applying the lithospheric stretching model of McKenzie (1978) has suggested that the sedimentary basins formed initially as rifts bounded by growth faults, and subsequently developed (in Namurian and Westphalian times) into broader sag-like structures. Seismic reflection evidence (Smith and others, 1985) has revealed the presence of such growth faults, which appear to have broken up the lower Palaeozoic basement into large blocks that tilted, and thereby affected sedimentation, particularly in early Dinantian times.

PRE-CARBONIFEROUS BASEMENT

The Caldon Low Borehole, the only direct evidence in the district of the rocks present below the Dinantian limestone sequence, proved 170.30 m of ?Devonian sediments, the Redhouse Sandstones of 'Old Red Sandstone' facies. The junction with the limestones appeared to be conformable and these beds are not regarded as basement in the same sense as the cleaved Llanvirn mudstones proved in the Eyam Borehole (Dunham, 1973) or the volcanic rocks of early Devonian or older age proved in the Woo Dale Borehole (Cope, 1979). Basement, as defined here, consists of rocks formed prior to the Caledonian orogeny.

The structure of the basement is uncertain. Miller and Grayson (1982) considered that the basement of the south Pennine region is broken up into tilt-blocks which are inclined to the north-east as a result of movements that accompanied Dinantian sedimentation. They also suggested that there is no necessary link between the location of Dinantian apron-reefs and the position of fault-scarps in the basement. Smith and others (1985) have modified the tilt-block hypothesis to account for differences in thickness and stratigraphy between the Eyam and Woo Dale boreholes, differences that were thought by Miller and Grayson to reflect the north-eastward slope of a single tilt-block. Smith and others cite seismic evidence for south-westward tilting of basement blocks and suggest that a north-east facing growth fault lies between the boreholes. A similar fault is postulated beneath the Weaver Hills [095 463] in the present district, on the supposition that the conglomerates in the Redhouse

Sandstones of the Caldon Low Borehole indicate the proximity of a fault scarp. The mid-Viséan unconformity at Caldon Low (see below) is also explained by this fault. Movement of the growth faults is thought to have ceased in late Chadian to Arundian times and neither is found at outcrop.

INTRA-CARBONIFEROUS MOVEMENTS

Within the district there is evidence for non-sequences within the Carboniferous succession at several places. A mid-Viséan break is evident at Caldon Low in a local angular unconformity between formations (p.28). The presence of siliceous pebbles scattered through the limestone above the unconformity may indicate (p.13) that the Redhouse Sandstones were exposed locally by tectonic movements at this time and that the inferred movements were associated with the creation of the Staffordshire shelf, for the margin of this sedimentary province was located in the Caldon Low area during Asbian times (p.7). The unconformity provides evidence for the existence of the growth fault suggested by Smith and others (1985).

Farther north, there is evidence (p.24) of a dramatic westerly increase in the thickness of strata overlying the Chadian knoll-reefs of Beeston Tor and Thors Cave that lie respectively to the east and west of the Manifold Valley Fault plexus (p.120). The net throw of the plexus is to the east, opposite to that expected for a growth fault associated with thickening to the west; however, there is no direct evidence of the nature of the displacement, and reactivation of the fault as a result of Hercynian compressive stress may have reversed the fault movement to produce an apparent easterly downthrow. In the district to the north (Aitkenhead and others, 1985, pp.51, 113), evidence supporting this hypothesis is provided by the presence of large blocks of reef-limestone in Ecton Limestones of Arundian age in the Manifold valley near Swainsley Farm (Sheet 111) [0927 5754], which could indicate a nearby synsedimentary fault. One fault in the Manifold Valley Fault plexus west of Manor House [0939 5593 to 1024 5802] (Sheet 111) is probably a high-angle reverse fault.

Around Ilam and Kniveton there is local overstep of the Widmerpool Formation. Near Ilam, limestones of this formation, of probable late Asbian age, are in contact with the Chadian knoll-reefs of Bunster Hill and Thorpe Cloud. North-east of Kniveton, field relations suggest that the Widmerpool Formation oversteps on to knoll-reefs and inter-reef beds of the Milldale Limestones; the contact is not exposed. This disconformity, though probably pre-late Asbian, has not been dated precisely owing to the lack of fossil evidence. The sequence on the Derbyshire shelf was apparently complete during this period except for minor breaks reflecting short emergences in late-Holkerian times.

A pre-Namurian disconformity is proved mainly by the absence of Brigantian strata along the Dinantian shelf margins. At Waterhouses (p.45) the off-shelf sequence is apparently complete, but a hiatus develops rapidly southwards and from Hoften's Cross [072 480] to Kevin Quarry [090 460] the basal Namurian mudstones rest directly on Asbian limestones (p.46). There is no evidence for tectonic movements at this time, however, and the disconformity may be attributed to either erosion or non-deposition at the Staffordshire shelf margin, during a period of lowered sea-level.

Similar relationships have been recorded along the margin of the Derbyshire shelf (Frost and Smart, 1979, p.7; Aitkenhead and others, 1985, pp.109–110) in adjoining districts. In the present district basal Namurian mudstones rest directly on Asbian apron-reef limestones between Brassington and Parwich, and Brigantian rocks are missing.

HERCYNIAN STRUCTURES

The Hercynian movements produced different effects in different parts of the district, with the result that, as in the adjoining Buxton district (Aitkenhead and others, 1985, p.109), strongly folded 'mobile' areas can be distinguished from weakly folded 'stable' areas. Figure 29 shows how the Ashbourne and Buxton districts are related structurally, with the approximate boundaries between stable and mobile areas. The boundary lines are based partly on the structural style and partly on the location of the Asbian apron-reefs; the main mobile zone here corresponds with the off-shelf province of Dinantian sedimentation and the stable zones with the shelf provinces. In the Namurian outcrop the bounding lines are based entirely on the nature of the structures.

The mobile zone trends ESE across the district with a projection extending down the west margin. Within it (Figure

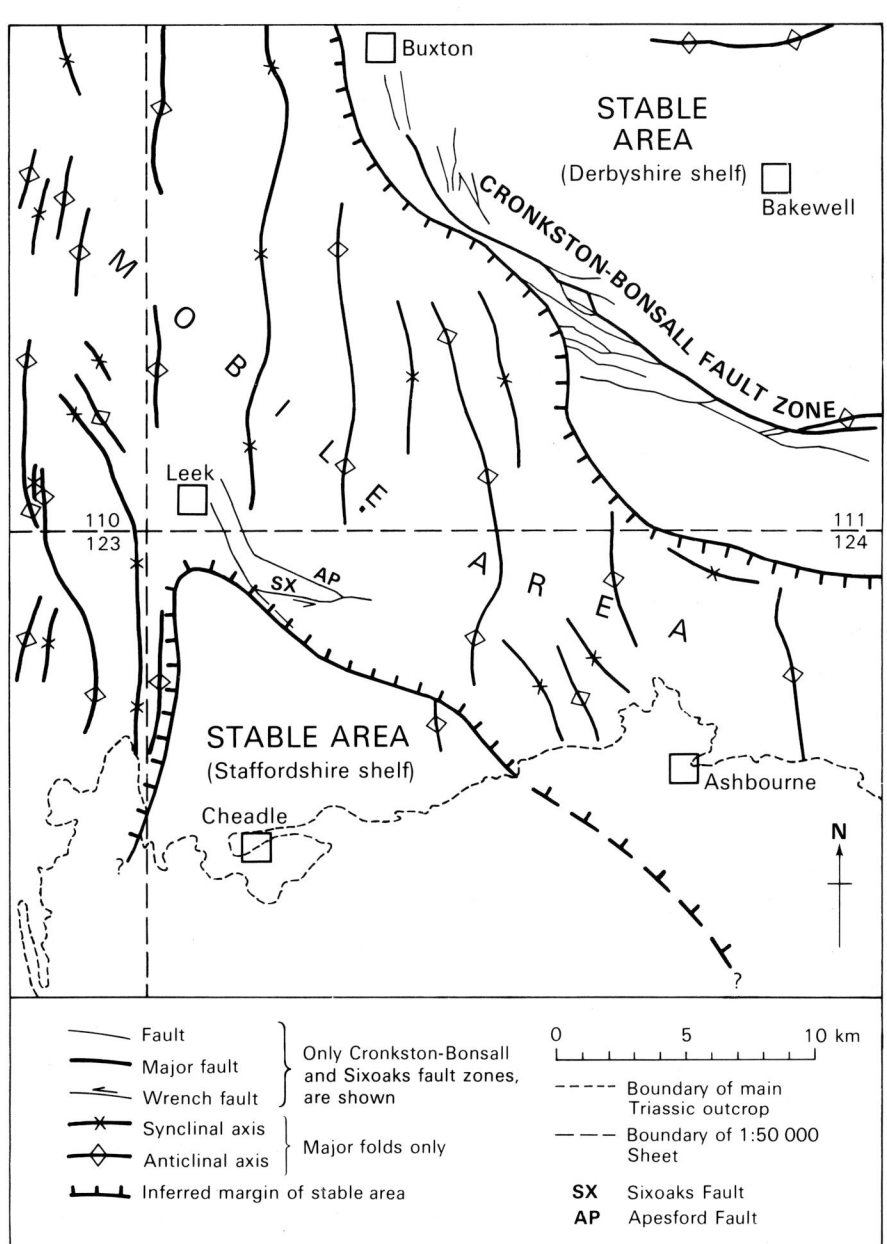

Figure 28 Main structural elements of the district and adjacent areas to the north and west

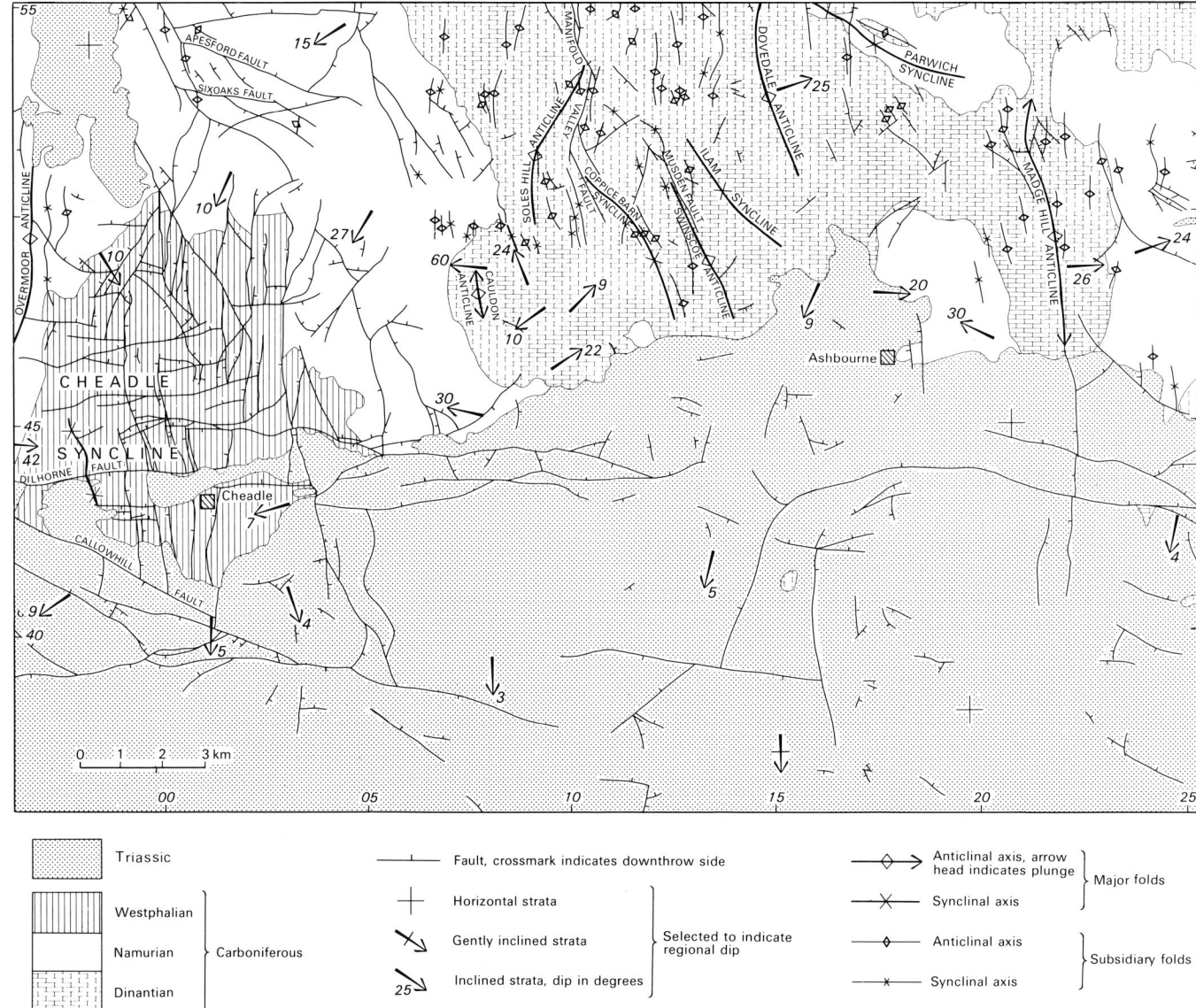

Figure 29 Structural features of the Ashbourne district

29), the rocks tend to be strongly folded, with major and minor fold axes trending between north and north-west. To the north-east of it lies the stable area corresponding with the Derbyshire shelf (Aitkenhead and others, 1985, p.109) and a similar stable area, corresponding in part with the Staffordshire shelf, lies to the south-west. The folds in the stable areas are mainly broad gentle structures of ill defined trend and faults are the most prominent feature.

The pattern of *en-échelon* folding in the mobile zone between two relatively stable areas suggests sinistral wrench movement between these structural elements, whereby the Derbyshire shelf has moved towards the north-west relative to the Staffordshire shelf (see, for instance, Wilcox and others, 1973, fig. 11). Such movement did not reach the stage of producing major wrench faults near the margins of the stable areas, as happened, for example with the Craven faults near the southern margin of the Askrigg Block (Arthurton, 1984). However, there is evidence for minor

sinistral movement along the Sixoaks Fault near the margin of the Staffordshire shelf.

DETAILS

Derbyshire shelf

Only a part of the southern margin of this stable area lies within the district (Figure 28). Dips within the area are mostly 10° or less and of variable direction. Steeper dips, with a largely depositional component directed towards the immediate off-shelf area, prevail in the highly indented marginal apron-reef.

Staffordshire shelf

The Dinantian limestones around Caldon Low [080 488] show rolling dips rarely over 30°, with no well marked fold axes. The structure is dominated by a larger dome-like upfold, the *Cauldon Anticline*, which has a vague culmination [078 479] near Caldonlow School. The eastern limb is ill defined but the western comprises a belt of steeper dips (50° to vertical) along the limestone margin. Normal faults in the Caldon Low area are few. Two with E–W trend and dips of 50° have been revealed in quarry workings [078 485]. More common in this area are north to north-west trending vertical fissures up to about 0.5 m wide, across which little displacement is evident. They commonly contain veins of calcite and hematite, and neptunian dykes and stringers of pink or bright red siltstone and sandstone. The sediments are of Triassic types and seem to indicate a pre-Triassic age for the fissuring.

The *Cheadle Syncline* is the only other major fold in this stable area. It is broadly oval in shape, with the deepest part in the south-west. Dips are generally low, except in the west, where it abuts against the mobile zone, and in the north-east where it adjoins the Cauldon Anticline. In the southern part of the syncline a rectilinear system of

N–S and E–W normal faults cuts up the Westphalian into small blocks. Calculations based on the positions of faults recorded during the working of successive coal seams show fault planes dipping at angles from 52° to vertical. In the northern and north-eastern parts of the syncline the fault-trends are less regular and tend more towards north-east and north-west directions. Movement on most of the Cheadle Coalfield faults took place in pre-Triassic times, but some show post-Triassic throws. N–S and E–W faults between Cheadle and Dilhorne are demonstrably of pre-Triassic age; their positions are known from underground workings but they do not displace the base of the Triassic sandstones. However, the outcrop pattern of the Triassic rocks roughly follows the fault pattern, an effect which is attributed to the influence of fault-scarps in the Triassic landscape at the time of deposition. Post-Triassic faults are evident

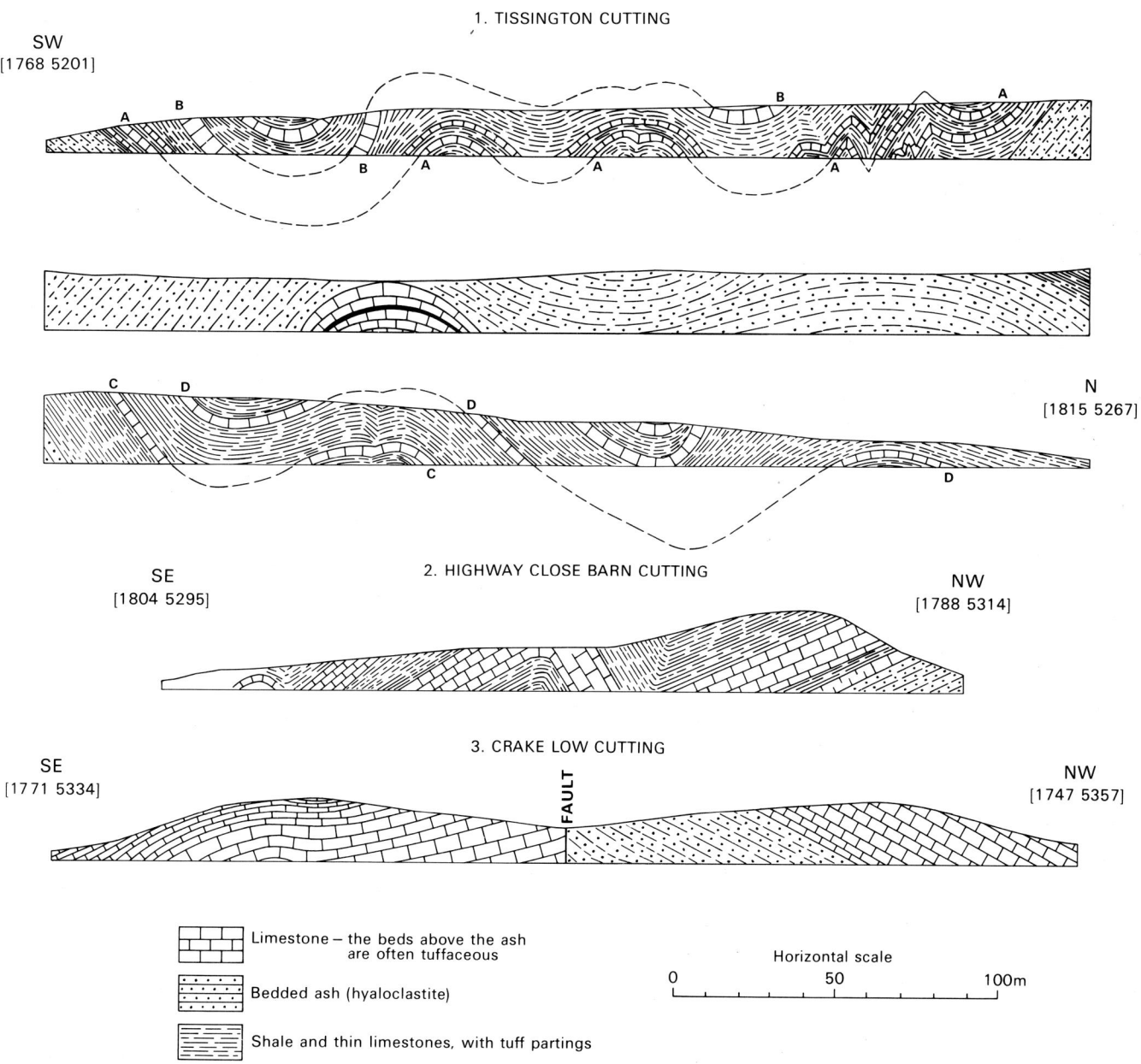

Figure 30 Diagrammatic sections showing folding in beds of the Widmerpool Formation and Tissington Volcanic Member formerly seen in cuttings of the Ashbourne to Buxton railway (now the Tissington Trail). From Arnold-Bemrose, 1899, plate 17. Reproduced by permission of the Geological Society

to the south and east of Cheadle. The *Callowhill Fault* is notable among these as marking the southern limit of coal extraction. Away from the Triassic outcrop it is usually impossible to prove which faults moved in post-Triassic times. However, an E–W fault exposed in a ravine [9807 4746] north-west of Broadoak shows purple-stained mudstone with sandstone bands near the base of the Kingsley Sandstone thrown against grey unaltered mudstone; if, as is generally supposed, the oxidation is an effect of Permo-Triassic weathering then the fault is a post-Triassic feature.

Mobile area

The main fold in the west is the *Overmoor Anticline*, which can be traced for 8 km from near Cheddleton to the Triassic boundary near Stansmore Hall [961 439]. Dips on the flanks of this fold range up to vertical, as can be seen in a prominent ridge of Rough Rock at Wetley Rocks [966 492] (Plate 7). A flanking structure immediately to the west, the *Shaffalong Syncline*, contains an outlier of Westphalian, but most of this lies outside the present district. In the Namurian outcrop to the east, groups of folds trending between north and north-west and with near-vertical axes are separated by areas of more gentle dip. A set of folds, with flanking dips commonly up to 55° but up to vertical in places, occupies the area between Sheephouse Farm [988 542] and Lower Lady Meadows [026 530]. Anastomosing fractures with trends between west and north-west cut through the folds. Fold axes on either side of the *Sixoaks Fault* do not match up, and it is likely that the movements here included an element of sinistral wrench-faulting. Another set of small steep folds affects the lowest Namurian mudstones east of Broomyshaw [067 497], while similar structures in the Dinantian area are well exposed [091 492] west of Huddale Farm.

In the Dinantian outcrop vertical and even overturned beds are present in the axial part of the *Soles Hill Anticline* [098 524]. The fold is least well defined where its axial trend changes from north-south to NNE–SSW as it crosses the valley of the River Hamps. This fold links up through the *Manifold Valley Fault* plexus with the Ecton Anticline in the district to the north. This fault is somewhat to the west of the position shown by Parkinson and Ludford (1964, p.173). The new line of the fault is indicated by several lines of evidence, including the presence of fault breccia on the valley side [1032 5413] near Beeston Tor, and the close proximity of a synclinal outlier of Widmerpool Formation to Milldale Limestones north-west of Throwley Hall [106 530].

The synclinorial form of the *Coppice Barn Syncline* is indicated by the sinuous boundaries between the Widmerpool Formation and the underlying Ecton Limestones and Milldale Limestones. The *Swinscoe Anticline* contains *en-échelon* subsidiary folds revealed on the map by anticlinal inliers of Milldale Limestones. A subsidiary anticline centred on the inlier of Milldale Limestones around Ilam Hall [131 506] is separated from the major fold by the *Musden Fault* which has a parallel NNW–SSE trend.

Similarly the *Ilam Syncline* contains subsidiary synclinal outliers of Widmerpool Formation between Ilam and Throwley Hall, also arranged *en-échelon*.

A broadly synclinal area lies between the Manifold valley and Dovedale. The subsidiary folds in this area are relatively gentle, with dips mostly less than 20° and there is a tendency for the anticlines to coincide with hills and the synclines with hollows. The general stratigraphic level is probably high in the Hopedale Limestones, just below the base of the more easily eroded mudstones of the Widmerpool Formation. The preservation of such a surface implies that the cover of Widmerpool Formation was removed in geologically recent times, perhaps during the ?mid-late Pliocene erosive phase of Walsh and others (1972, fig. 5.3).

The *Dovedale Anticline* has a mass of amalgamated Chadian knoll-reefs in its core, elongated subparallel to the fold axis. It is uncertain whether the presence of this mass of relatively rigid limestone has

determined the location of the anticlinal structure here or whether such reef masses are scattered beneath later cover over a wide area and are exposed in Dovedale because of the presence of a dissected anticlinal structure (see also p.19).

The *Madge Hill Anticline* is a broad north–south-trending anticlinorial structure with a core of Milldale Limestones including knoll-reefs. Both the major fold and some of the subsidiary folds form upstanding topographical features following the geologically recent removal of the soft Namurian mudstone cover in ?Pliocene times (see above).

The *Parwich Syncline* differs from all the other major folds in its WNW–ESE trend. Its probable extension eastwards to the area between Bradbourne and Brassington is interrupted by the Madge Hill Anticline, suggesting that it predates the other folds. This syncline may have been initiated by differential subsidence and compaction in the more argillaceous strata beyond the edge of the late Dinantian carbonate shelf that constitutes the stable area. This edge also trends in a general WNW–ESE direction though with several promontories and embayments that are probably original depositional features of the Asbian apron-reef.

The area lying to the south of the Parwich Syncline and between the Dovedale and Madge Hill anticlines contains no major structures though there are numerous subsidiary folds. Some of these were well displayed in the cuttings of the former Ashbourne–Buxton railway, now the Tissington Trail, but are largely grassed over except for an anticline [1688 5374] in the Hopedale Limestones, noted by Arnold-Bemrose (1903, p.338). Both this author (1899, plate 17) and Hind (1897) published diagrammatic sections that showed the style of folding as it affected the argillaceous beds of the Widmerpool Formation ('Yoredale Series') and the volcaniclastic rocks of the Tissington Volcanic Member ('bedded ash') (Figure 30).

POST-HERCYNIAN STRUCTURES

Structures affecting the broad outcrop of Triassic rocks that covers the southern half of the district are in marked contrast to those that dominate the Carboniferous beds to the north (Figure 29). Dips are generally to the south at 5°, or less, and rarely exceed 10°. This regional dip reflects the position of the area between the southerly plunging termination of the 'Pennine Axis' (George, 1963) and the Needwood Basin, a broad synclinal structure with a poorly defined east–west axis lying in the adjacent district to the south (Stevenson and Mitchell, 1955).

The faulting partly reflects the rectilinear pattern in the underlying Carboniferous but is less dense and dominated by generally east–west trending normal faults with down-downthrows up to 175 m. These produce a horst and graben effect well illustrated by the cross-section accompanying the published 1:50 000 geological map.

Structure contours drawn on the base of the Triassic (Figure 20) probably indicate the topography of the sub-Triassic erosion surface on which has been superimposed the post-Hercynian (mainly Alpine) southerly tilt. In some places, such as the area immediately north-east of Cheadle, it can be shown that this topography was controlled by fault scarps (p.119; Rogers and others, 1981, p.5).

The Triassic outlier extending northwards from [993 503] near Cheddleton (Figure 22) also occupies an erosional hollow in Carboniferous rocks and has, in addition, been affected by post-Hercynian movements (p.74; Aitkenhead and others, 1985, p.115).

NA,JIC

EARTHQUAKES

Several authors, notably Davison (1924) have compiled records which show that the Ashbourne district, in common with many other parts of the country, has been affected by earthquakes in historical times. A recent compilation by Neilson and others (1984) quotes some vivid descriptions, from contemporary local press reports, of the 'felt' effects of the tremors. Instrumentally determined epicentres of recent earthquakes are given by Turbitt (1984; 1985). Neilson and others draw isoseismal maps that indicate the location of the macroseismic epicentre, or location of greatest intensity, for each earthquake. In the present century, at least seven earthquakes have occurred with noticeable effects in the Ashbourne district; dates and macroseismic epicentres are given as follows: 24 March 1903 (Kniveton), 3 May 1903 (Mayfield), 3 July 1904 (a few km north of Ashbourne), 27 August 1906 (Matlock Bath), 14 January 1916 (Chebsey, north-west of Stafford), 11 February 1957 (Castle Donnington–Blackbrook) and 30 April 1984 (Loughborough/ Leicester area). The last event had an instrumentally determined epicentre at West Bridgford (Marrow, 1984). Intensities ranged mainly from 3 to 6 on the MSK scale (Burton and others, 1984), i.e. from the shock being felt by only a few people indoors (intensity 3) to the shock being felt by most people indoors and out (intensity 6). The strongest earthquake was that of 24 March 1903, with an exceptional maximum intensity of 7 at Hognaston; the village well and several springs were affected (Neilson and others, 1984). Other places in the district where effects of this earthquake were reported include Ashbourne, Bradbourne, Brassington, Denstone, Fenny Bentley and Wootton.

There is no good evidence to relate these earthquakes to movement along particular faults known at the surface and a deeper crustal origin seems more likely. NA

CHAPTER 11

Geophysical investigations

Some information on the deeper structure of the Ashbourne district can be derived from an examination of the regional geophysical data, in particular the aeromagnetic and Bouguer gravity anomaly maps (mainly Institute of Geological Sciences, 1980, and 1982b, respectively). The Bouguer gravity anomaly map (Figure 31), which is particularly significant in its relationship to the surface structure, is based on the regional survey coverage of observation points; more detailed surveys in places would considerably improve the interpretation of several of the anomalies. The aeromagnetic map in Figure 32 is based on data recorded at a height of 305 m (1000 feet) along east–west flight lines 1.6 km (1 mile) apart. Seismic reflection surveys have been carried out in the southern part of the district but the results are not generally available.

The quantitative interpretation of the gravity data is com-

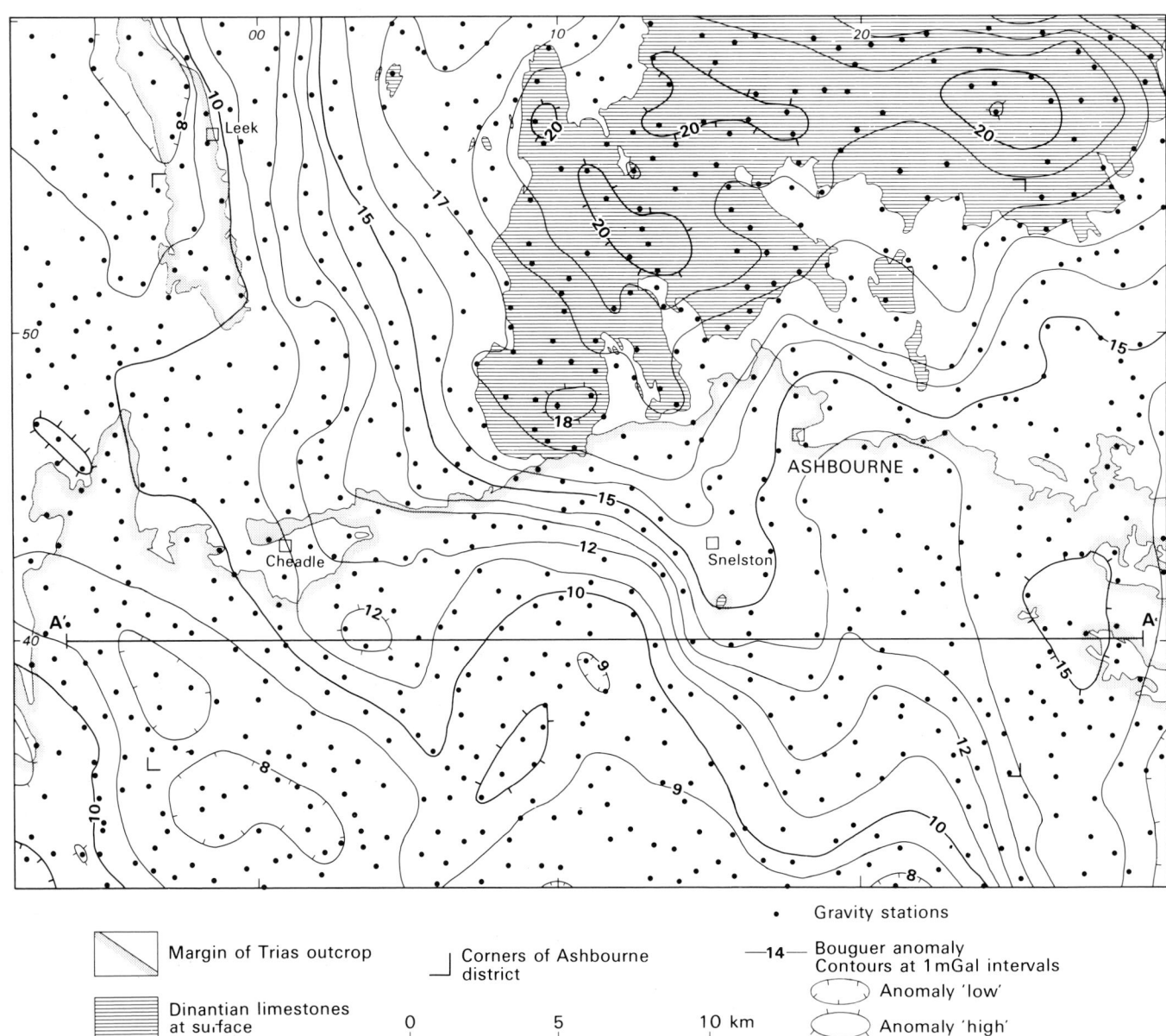

Figure 31 Bouguer gravity anomaly map of the Ashbourne district with contours at 1 mGal intervals. The Bouguer correction has been calculated using density values appropriate to the underlying geology. AA′ gives the location of the profile shown in Figure 33

Figure 32 Aeromagnetic map of the Ashbourne district with contours at 10 nT intervals. Based mainly on Institute of Geological Sciences (1980)

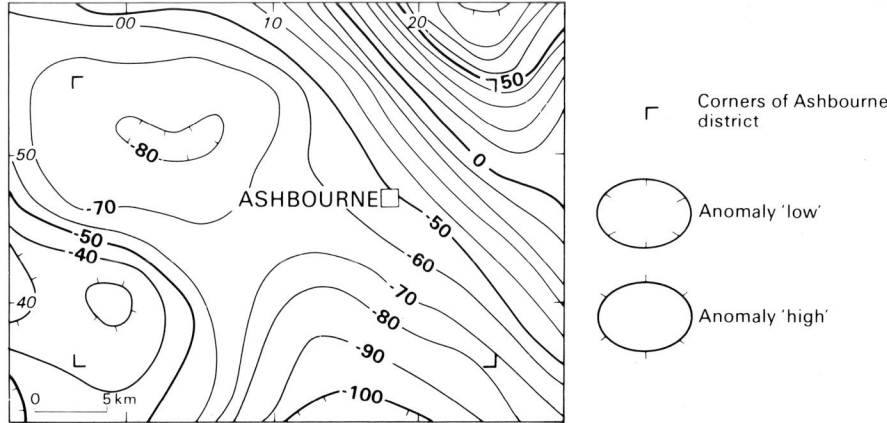

plicated by the number and variability of the density contrasts between the main rock units in the district. Triassic rocks have the lowest density (about 2.40 Mg/m³), while the Westphalian and Namurian have both been assumed to have a density of 2.50 Mg/m³. A similar value is applied to the dominantly mudstone Widmerpool Formation and, in the west, to the Mixon Limestone-Shales. The massive limestones of Dinantian age have densities of 2.70 Mg/m³ but a value of about 2.65 Mg/m³ is probably a more realistic average allowing for heterogeneities. The only pre-Carboniferous rocks known in the district are in the Caldon Low Borehole, where the ?Devonian Redhouse Sandstones have a density of 2.64 Mg/m³; however, Lower Palaeozoic rocks, with densities of perhaps 2.70 to 2.75 Mg/m³, could exist at depth. The uncertainties introduced by these density variations is increased by the lack of information, in many places, of the thickness of the rock units, especially for the Triassic rocks in the south of the district. In general, it would be expected that Bouguer gravity anomaly highs should occur over the Dinantian limestones and lows over the thickest Westphalian and Triassic sequences.

The various geophysical data have been examined to derive information on structures, ranging from the pre-Carboniferous basement to those affecting Triassic rocks in the south of the district; the main features recognised are shown in Figure 34.

PRE-CARBONIFEROUS BASEMENT

It has been suggested by Maroof (1976) that the Carboniferous rocks of the Derbyshire Dome are underlain at depth by high-density (2.80 Mg/m³) basement rocks, possibly Charnian in age. Rocks with densities as high as this have not been discovered in the few boreholes which have penetrated pre-Carboniferous rocks and it is clear that the deep basement is overlain by rocks of Devonian or older age at Woo Dale (Cope, 1973) and Devonian or early Carboniferous in the Caldon Low Borehole (p.5). In the model based on gravity interpretation for the southern part of the Ashbourne district (Figure 33) an extension southwards of the latter rocks is suggested.

The deeper structure along the Bouguer anomaly high extending from near Charnwood Forest to Ballidon on the edge of the Derbyshire Dome and including the Derby high

(Figure 33) has been studied using seismic refraction methods (Whitcombe and Maguire, 1981). The results indicate the presence of a refracting horizon with a velocity of 5.64 km/s which can be traced from the surface in Charnwood Forest northwards to depths of up to 2.1 km. The nature of this high-velocity basement is somewhat uncertain; Whitcombe and Maguire suggest that it is Charnian, on the basis of the studies carried out over Charnwood Forest (Whitcombe and Maguire, 1980) but a refractor with a similar velocity recorded on the LISPB seismic line farther to the north (Bamford and others, 1978) was interpreted as Lower Palaeozoic basement.

Bullerwell (*in* Stevenson and Mitchell, 1955) reports the results of seismic refraction surveys west of Burton upon Trent, just south of the Ashbourne district, in which a 5.9 km/s refractor was interpreted as 'Carboniferous Limestone'. However, on the basis of the velocities it is possible that this is the same basement as that recognised between Charnwood and Ballidon by Whitcombe and Maguire (1981); these authors assigned a lower velocity (5.0 km/s) to the 'Carboniferous Limestone' on the southern edge of the Derbyshire Dome. This 5.9 km/s basement lies at depths of between 1.2 and 2.0 km in an area of relatively low Bouguer gravity anomaly values between Rugeley and Burton upon Trent (Stevenson and Mitchell, 1955, fig. 19). As these depths are comparable with those reported by Whitcombe and Maguire the seismic results do not support the idea put forward by these authors that the areas of Bouguer anomaly highs are necessarily underlain by shallower high-velocity basement.

The most striking features of the aeromagnetic map of the district (Figure 32) are the long wavelength anomalies which suggest the presence of magnetic material only at considerable depth. Much of the central part of the area appears to be underlain by a thick north-west-trending zone of non-magnetic rocks, possibly Devonian and/or Lower Palaeozoic sediments. In the Burton upon Trent district there is some evidence that the thickest part of this sequence corresponds with a rise in the 5.9 km/s refracting horizon. Aeromagnetic data from surrounding areas suggest that the Ashbourne district coincides with a junction between two basement blocks, one characterised by a NW–SE Charnoid trend, the second extending down into central and south Wales and the Marches, with a NE–SW trend. There appears to be some overlapping of these trends and in Figure 32 it is the NW- or

Figure 33 Bouguer gravity anomaly profile AA′ (see Figure 31 for location), and a possible geological interpretation. The values approximating to the linear regional field were obtained by adding the gravity effect of the model shown (density contrast in Mg/m^3) to the observed profile

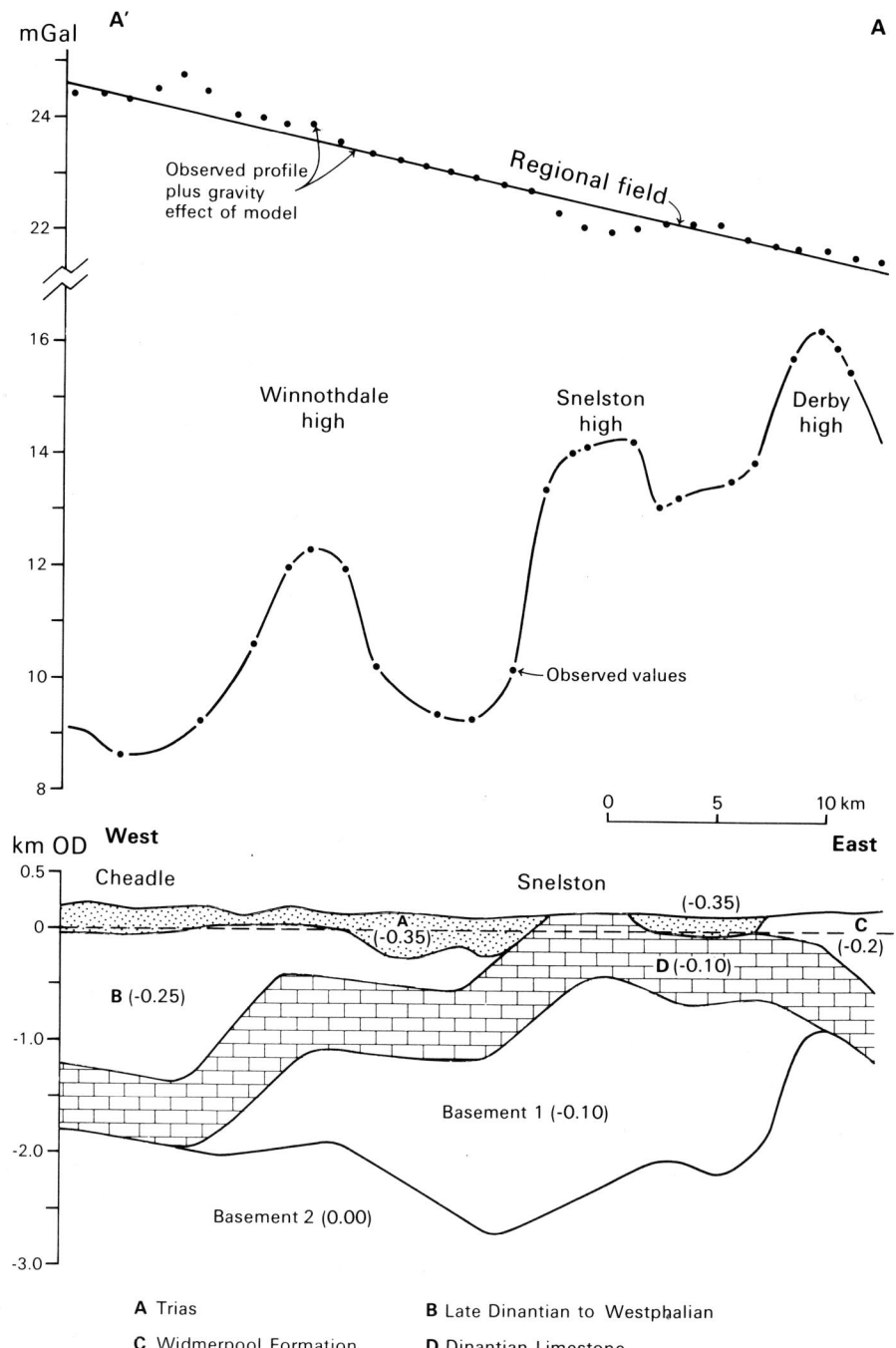

A Trias **B** Late Dinantian to Westphalian
C Widmerpool Formation **D** Dinantian Limestone

NNW-trend that dominates. The gradient zone crossing the north-east part of the district is particularly prominent (corresponding to the 'Derby Fault line' of Wills, 1978; F_1 in Figure 34) and forms part of an extensive zone crossing the Midlands (Cornwell *in* Aitkenhead and others, 1985). In the south-west corner of the district an anomaly of about 50 nT amplitude [04 00] indicates part of a block of magnetic material at a depth of about 3 km in an area covered by Triassic rocks. The block is probably fault-bounded Precambrian basement (cf. Wills, 1978) and extends westwards to underlie the Potteries Coalfield where a pronounced magnetic anomaly coincides with the position of the Red Rock Fault. The north-east margin of the block coincides

approximately with a step-like gravity feature (Figure 31) and near-surface faults downthrowing to the south-west. The south-east margin of the magnetic block is also thought to be defined by a fault (Figure 34) which could extend to the north-east to form a step in the deep magnetic basement and possibly even farther to intersect the extensive north-eastern magnetic basement.

Smith and others (1985) have postulated the existence of a growth fault affecting early Dinantian rocks and forming the north-eastern margin of a tilt block just to the south-west of the Caldon Low Borehole. This could correspond to the geophysical lineament F_2 (Figure 34) which forms an extension of a well defined gradient zone passing through the

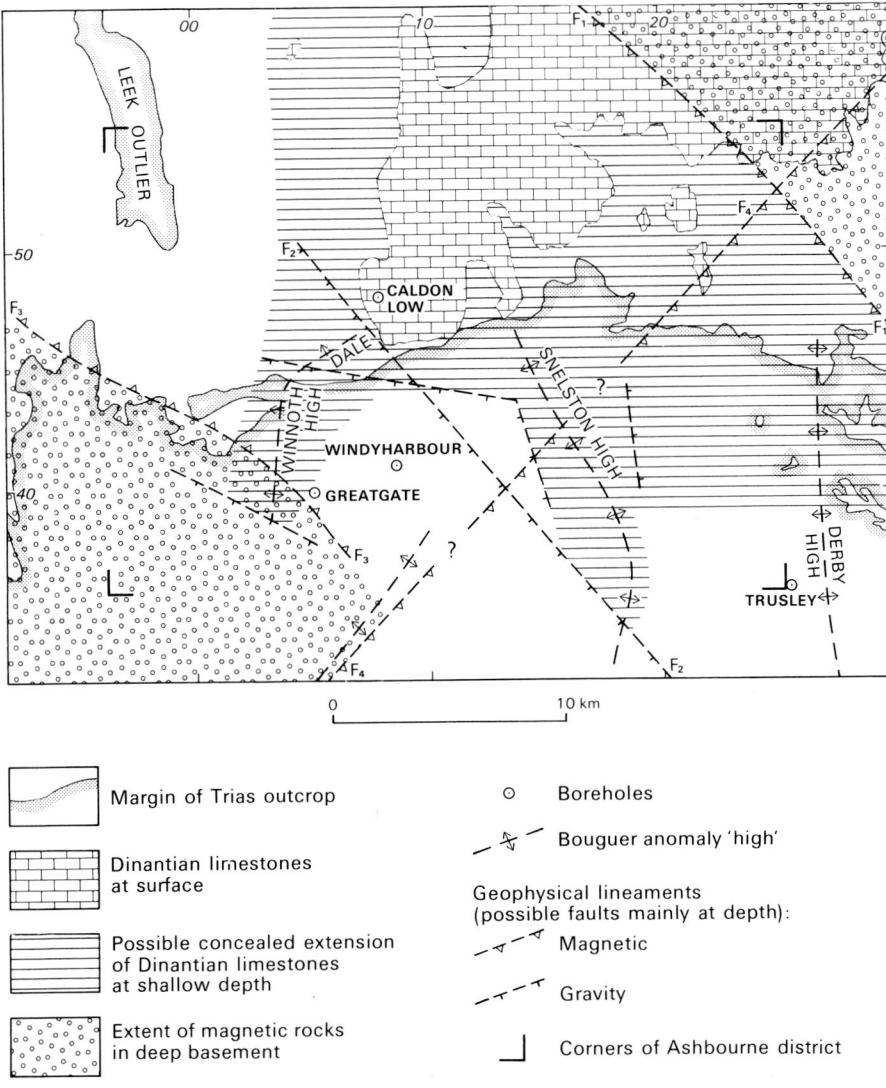

Figure 34   Compilation of geophysical and relevant geological features in the Ashbourne district

Leicestershire Coalfield and the southern margin of the Snelston high.

CARBONIFEROUS ROCKS

The exposed carbonate rocks of the Derbyshire Dome correspond in Figure 31 with a series of Bouguer gravity anomaly highs reaching about +20 mGal. There is a general decrease of values where the Widmerpool Formation and the Mixon Limestone-Shales appear, a reflection of the lower densities expected for these mainly argillaceous rocks, but the gravity data in areas of mixed limestones and mudstones can be misleading unless corrections for the gravity effect of near-surface geological variations are made. Detailed gravity traverses have been used (Cornwell, *in* Frost and Smart, 1979) to determine the form of the limestone surface where it is concealed by younger mudstones. These traverses confirm

that there is a significant density contrast between the two lithologies and this is also suggested by the appearance in Figure 31 of local Bouguer gravity anomaly highs over the limestone outcrops.

In the northern part of the area (Figure 31) the westward decrease of Bouguer gravity anomaly values to the west of the Derbyshire Dome is due mainly to the rapid thickening of Namurian rocks, with an additional contribution attributable to a change in the nature of the deeper basement rocks (Cornwell *in* Aitkenhead and others, 1985, figs. 42 and 45). This gradient is deflected slightly near the point where the Carboniferous rocks disappear beneath Triassic cover. It is suggested that slightly higher Bouguer anomaly values in the area south-west of Caldon Low are due to the presence of a concealed ridge of Dinantian limestones (Winnothdale high, Figure 34). In the same area, Namurian sediments are known to thin towards the western margin of the Dinantian outcrop.

TRIASSIC OUTCROP

The Bouguer gravity anomaly map shows no significant decrease of values at the margin of the main Triassic outcrop, which indicates that a rapid thickening of these rocks along a large fault line is unlikely, except perhaps between grid lines 05E and 12E (Figure 34). Within the area covered by Triassic rocks, however, several well defined anomalies occur, notably the elongated Bouguer anomaly highs extending southwards from the main high over the Derbyshire Dome. These anomalies will be referred to as the Derby, Snelston and Winnothdale highs (Figure 33). There is evidence from the surface geology that the first two of these coincide with topographic highs in the pre-Triassic floor, which bring Dinantian rocks to the surface as inliers (Figure 31). The Derby high extends across inliers of the Widmerpool Formation, mainly in the Derby district (Frost and Smart, 1979) around [29 39] and [29 42]. Northwards, within the main outcrop of the Widmerpool Formation, the Derby high appears to divide into two separate highs, one approximately coincident with the Madge Hill Anticline (Figure 29), the other with the Wirksworth Anticline (Sheet 125). The interpretation of the Snelston high as a ridge of shallow Dinantian limestones is supported by the occurrence near Snelston of an isolated inlier of these rocks (p.26).

Larger scale features on profile AA' (Figure 33), such as the thickening of the Westphalian rocks into the Cheadle Syncline and, to the east, the thickening of the Widmerpool Formation, produce Bouguer anomaly lows at the ends of the profile. To compensate for these and to produce the linear field shown (Figure 31) the model includes a basin of lower density pre-Carboniferous rocks ('basement 1')

perhaps comparable with the Redhouse Sandstones proved in the Caldon Low Borehole. The lower basement ('basement 2') is assumed to be Lower Palaeozoic rocks with density of 2.75 Mg/m^3. The model shown in Figure 33 is one of numerous alternative interpretations, which include those involving the high-density (2.80 Mg/m^3) basement favoured by Maroof (1976).

South of the Ashbourne district, Bullerwell (*in* Stevenson and Mitchell, 1955) has examined the Bouguer gravity anomalies associated with the deepest part of the Triassic basin (the Needwood Basin). The geophysical interpretation here has had to be made with little borehole control on the thicknesses of Triassic rocks and the Bouguer anomaly low is itself not well defined. A density contrast of 0.26 Mg/m^3 between the Triassic rocks and the underlying basement derived for the main part of the basin (Bullerwell *in* Stevenson and Mitchell, 1955) implies that the basement is more likely to consist of Dinantian limestones or older, more compacted sediments. The accuracy of this result is probably reduced by the uncertainties involved in its derivation.

The regional gravity station coverage is insufficiently detailed to reveal the response of the faults in the Triassic along the southern margin of the Cheadle Coalfield. North of the main Triassic outcrop, the isolated basin at Leek coincides with a small contour closure around [97 58]. The regional gravity data here are not inconsistent with other evidence (p.74) that the Triassic rocks, which probably have a density contrast of about -0.1 Mg/m^3 with the underlying Namurian, extend down to about sea level but more detailed gravity surveys would probably provide information on local thickness variations.   JDC

CHAPTER 12

Mineralisation

The Ashbourne district lies at the south end of the South Pennine Orefield, the general characteristics of which have been summarised by Ineson and Ford (1982) and Mostaghel (1985). Deposits of hydrothermal minerals, mainly in the form of veins and associated replacement bodies, are present in Dinantian limestones and dolomites and, more locally, in the overlying Triassic rocks, but the mineralisation is more patchy here than in the districts to the north. The south end of the main Derbyshire orefield enters the district in the north-east, around Brassington, and there are local concentrations of deposits in the Weaver Hills and near Stanshope, but the remainder of the Dinantian limestone outcrop contains only scattered occurrences (Figure 35). Mineralisation in the Triassic rocks, and along the Carboniferous–Triassic

unconformity, was discussed in its wider context by King and Ford (1968, pp.123–132).

The origin of the deposits has been much debated, but the mineralising fluids are now thought to have migrated laterally and upwards from the Carboniferous sedimentary basins that lie to the east, with some smaller contributions from the west and south (*summary in* Ineson and Ford, 1982). The minerals were apparently introduced over a long period, from late Carboniferous to Jurassic (Ineson and Mitchell, 1973), and may in part have been distributed by Triassic groundwaters (King and Ford, 1968, pp.123–132; Ford, 1969). Diagenesis of Triassic red beds is proposed by Holmes and others (1983) as an alternative source of the copper ores and baryte deposits in the Triassic sandstones.

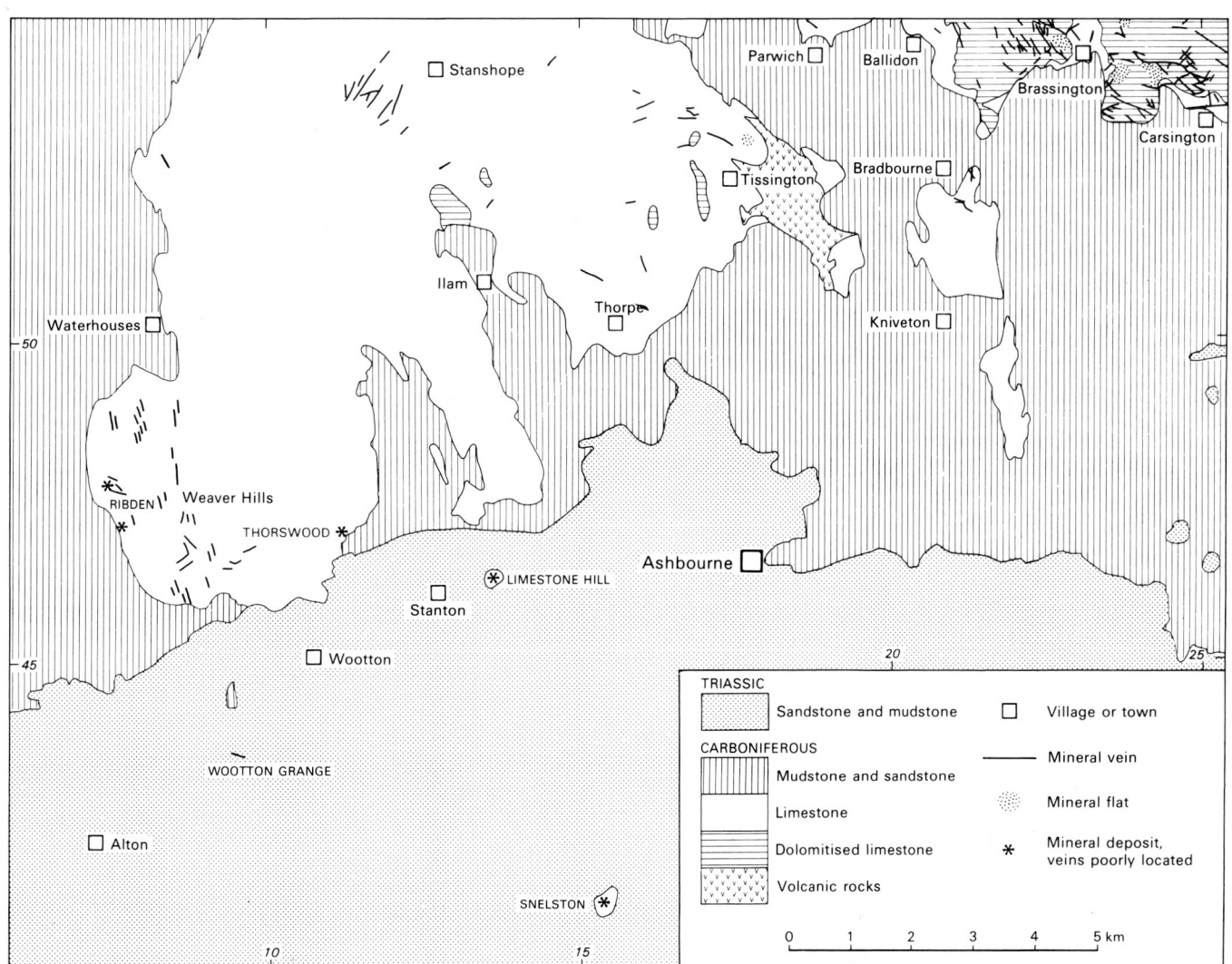

Figure 35   Mineral deposits of the Ashbourne district

The gangue minerals calcite, baryte and fluorite are accompanied by lesser quantities of the metalliferous minerals, which include sulphides of lead, zinc, copper and iron, oxidation products of the sulphides, and hematite. Workings for the metals are of great antiquity, but recent activity has concentrated on the gangue minerals. The deposits are classified as veins, pipes and flats, on the basis of their shape. The larger veins are also known as rakes, the smaller as scrins. They occupy near-vertical fissures that were probably initiated as wrench faults (Firman, 1977). Pipes are linear deposits, lying generally parallel to the stratification of the country rocks, and may contain a mixture of replacement and cavity-fill deposits. Flats conform roughly to the bedding of the country rocks but are irregular rather than linear in plan. They also contain both replacement and cavity-fill deposits. A more comprehensive discussion of the origin of these differently-shaped deposits is given by Aitkenhead and others (1985, p.118).

Maps showing the amount of lead, zinc and fluorine present as contaminants in the limestone country rocks, as distinct from the veins, are given by Harrison and Adlam (1985, figs. 16–18).   JIC

DETAILS

Brassington

The dolomitised Bee Low Limestones east and west of Brassington are extensively mineralised. Most of the veins occupy fissures trending roughly north-west, with a few of westerly and north-easterly trend. This area of deposits lies at the southern limit of the main mineralised area of Derbyshire, and the general description of the district to the north (Aitkenhead and others, 1985, pp.117–118) applies to it. The area is shown by Mueller (1954) to lie within a zone where, among the gangue minerals, calcite and baryte predominate over fluorite; the same conclusion can be drawn from the data of Wedd and Drabble (1908, plate 20), Firman and Bagshaw (1974) and Mostaghel (1983, fig. 2). Data recorded during the present survey indicate that baryte is more common than calcite, and confirm that fluorite is rare. Mostaghel (1984) records calcite, baryte and galena at three sample localities, with sphalerite in addition at one of them. Baryte was the mineral last worked in any quantity (Ford and Rieuwerts, 1983, p.130). A feature of the Brassington area is the presence of minerals in the Pocket Deposits (p.90), which occupy solution hollows in the dolomite and limestone. The lead ore in these cases is normally cerussite (Ford and Rieuwerts, 1983, p.132), associated with baryte.

North of Parwich, baryte occurs on the tips of a north-westerly vein [1883 5484] and east of Ballidon traces of fluorite are present on tips with baryte, calcite and galena [2082 5477]. To the west of Black Plantation a vein [2113 5471] some 0.7–1.5 m wide shows abundant baryte on tips. Farther east, the ground on the western side of Brassington is intensely mineralised. A plexus of closely-spaced discontinuous veins up to 2 m in width trends predominantly north-west and there is a probable flat [228 546]; tips yield relatively abundant baryte and lesser amounts of calcite. To the south-west of Brassington a confused section [2167 5383] in the wall of a Pocket Deposit shows a vein, about 1 m wide, with galena altering to cerussite in a clay matrix.

Between Brassington and Carsington lies the intensely mineralised area of Carsington Pastures. Here the veins trend mainly north-west, though some of westerly and north-easterly trends also occur. The names of many of the veins and mines are given by Ford and Rieuwerts (1983, pp.130–134). The most important vein is

Great Rake, seen at one point [2404 5356] as an openwork 8 m wide; tips from Great Rake Mine [2395 5358] show much baryte, the workings here having been largely for this mineral (Carruthers and Strahan, 1923, p.80). Yokecliffe Rake cuts apron-reef limestones [248 535] at the eastern margin of the district; few details are recorded, but in the adjoining district the vein occupies an east–west fault, with downthrow to the south (Frost and Smart, 1979, p.105). The form of Flaxpiece Rake [246 539] is uncertain; it trends north-east for a distance of 350 m and may be a pipe (Green and others, 1887, p.152). Several irregular areas of surface workings in this area are probably flats. The most extensive [243 541] is over 400 m across. Another, situated a little to the west, was worked from Nickalum Mine [2366 5397], which has been described as exploiting a 'pipe' (Green and others, 1887, p.152). Mostaghel (1984) recorded sphalerite here. A third probable flat lies farther north [238 548]. The Pocket Deposit at Wester Lane (p.90) [239 539] contained lumps of cerussite scattered through the sand and clay (Green and others, 1887, pp.152, 164).   IPS, JIC

Bradbourne and Kniveton

Standlow Lane Quarry [2122 5087], which is located in a partially dolomitised knoll-reef in the Milldale Limestones north-east of Kniveton, intersected old workings in a north-west-trending vein that appears not to extend far beyond the limits of the quarry. Subsidiary veins and old workings were penetrated to a depth of 20.32 m in a borehole (SK 25 SW/19) in the quarry floor. Vein minerals included calcite, fluorite and galena (Cox and Harrison, 1980, p.132).

Minor vein workings in the Hopedale Limestones are present to the north [213 525] and south [212 520] of Havenhill Dale, the former perhaps associated with Standhill Mine [adit at 2138 5238], which is shown as a lead working on the old Ordnance Survey map. Spoil tips contain calcite and baryte.   NA

Tissington and Thorpe

North-west of Tissington, there is surface evidence of scattered vein workings for lead, as at Nancy Mine [1690 5345] and Rusheycliff Mine [1774 5299], names shown on an old edition of the six-inch Ordnance Survey map. The veins are mainly aligned in a general east–west direction and cut the Hopedale Limestones; no subsurface information is available. One line of shafts [1667 5131 to 1676 5067] just west of Wash Brook is interpreted as a sough, though the reasons for its construction are not clear.

An oval-shaped area of workings [177 531] associated with Rusheycliff Mine, north-east of Tissington, indicates a probable flat. The Hopedale Limestones hereabouts are probably disposed in a broad anticline; interbedded tuffaceous beds may have acted as localised cap rocks and thus controlled the mineralisation.

South-west of Tissington, there are a few veins near Thorpe. The largest cuts reef-limestone at Thorpe Cloud, where there is an open working [1522 5100] 1 to 2 m wide.   NA, IPS

Stanshope and Ilam

A group of veins in the Hopedale Limestones [117 538] WSW of Stanshope was worked for lead, mainly in the 18th and 19th centuries, from the Bincliff Highfields and Oversets mines (Porter and Robey, 1974). Although output was evidently low, the veins represent the most intense area of mineralisation outside the main mining field. The veins trend generally north-east, range up to 600 m in length and are marked by numerous shafts. There was also access to the mines by adits, of which ten are known, located in the steep sides of the Manifold valley. Calcite, baryte and galena have been noted on tips around the shafts, together with traces of fluorite at one locality. The Hopedale Limestones exposed in places at the adits are mainly grey, partially dolomitised, medium to coarse, bioclastic, and thickly bedded. Mine explorations reported by Pedrick and Chapman (1974), and Critchley and Wilson (1985), suggest that the orebodies died out downwards in the dark limestones of the Milldale Limestones, which are exposed near river level.

The location of this group of veins here may be attributed to the opening up of north-easterly joints by localised tension during right-lateral tectonic movement along the Manifold Valley Fault plexus. Such movement is indicated by the deviation of fold axial trends from north–south to NE–SW in the vicinity of the plexus, which lies a short distance to the west (Figure 29). At the time of mineralisation the base of the predominantly argillaceous Widmerpool Formation probably lay just above the present topographical surface in this area and provided a suitable cap rock and also, perhaps, in its thicker development at depth to the south, a source for the mineralising fluids. Some little-known workings to the south-east around Ilam Tops [1354 5277, 1355 5212], again in partially dolomitised Hopedale Limestones and marked by a few old shafts and minor vein workings, are probably in similar orebodies. Mine spoil here contains calcite and baryte together with galena and traces of malachite. NA

Weaver Hills

Veins of calcite, locally containing ores of lead, copper, zinc and iron, are present in the Dinantian limestones of the Weaver Hills. Traces of copper mineralisation have also been found in the sandstones beneath the limestone (see below). None of the deposits is worked, but mines at Ribden, Thorswood and Stanton produced substantial amounts of lead, copper and zinc ores during the 17th, 18th and 19th centuries (Robey and Porter, 1971; Porter and Robey, 1972). The mineralising fluids may have come from Carboniferous rocks at depth to the south or west; the deposits of lead, copper and zinc lie along the southern flanks of the complex upfold of the Weaver Hills. The presence of copper suggests an affinity rather with the Ecton and Mixon areas (Aitkenhead and others, 1985, p.123), than with the main Derbyshire orefield.

The mines at Ribden worked several veins with a general westerly or north-westerly trend and steep northward dip (Porter and Robey, 1972, fig. 2; Robey and Porter, 1971, fig. 2). Among the surface traces that remain, Swallow Shaft [0764 4712], Ingleby's Shaft [0749 4774] and what is probably Ingleby's Vein can be identified from a map in Porter and Robey's account (1972, fig. 1). Ores of lead and copper were both produced. Minerals recorded include galena, copper carbonates and sulphides, hematite, quartz and calcite (Ford in Porter and Robey, 1972). Material collected on the tips during the present survey includes calcite, quartz and oxidised ores of copper, zinc and lead. Tips on a north-easterly vein [0861 4648] on Wredon contain calcite, iron oxides and malachite.

The limestones to north, east and south of the Ribden veins are extensively worked at Caldon Low [077 486], Cauldon [086 488], Wardlow [083 475], Wredon [087 468] and Kevin [089 460] quarries, but no veins containing lead or copper ores have been recorded. However, veins of calcite up to 0.5 m wide (rarely up to 2 m), generally containing hematite, are common. Most have a northerly to north-westerly trend and occupy near-vertical fissures with broad horizontal flutings that suggest a wrench-fault origin. The most easily accessible example is exposed on the west side [0748 4870] of Hemmings Low. Neptunian dykes of pink calcareous siltstone and red sandstone are present in many of the veins, suggesting a connection with the Permo-Triassic land surface (p.75; Table 3). The hematite was thought by Barnes and Holroyd (1897) to have come from the same source. The Caldon Low Borehole (SK 04 NE/36) proved veinlets of chalcopyrite in the Redhouse Sandstones (p.5) lying between 52.06 and 95.13 m below the base of the Dinantian limestones. Analyses for Cu, Pb and Zn, by P. Joseph of

the BGS Analytical Chemistry Unit, of sandstone samples taken every 0.5 m indicated that mineralisation is confined to veinlets and, is not generally disseminated through the host rock.

Veins in the limestone near Thorswood House contained ores of lead, copper and zinc. They were exploited in the 18th century and the workings were reopened in the 19th, as shown by surviving documents (Robey and Porter, 1971; Porter and Robey, 1972). Remains of several shafts can be seen in and near Thorswood Plantation [112 470], but the site of Gilbert's Shaft, shown in Robey and Porter's sections, cannot be identified. The location and trend of the veins is not evident from surface workings. Ford (in Porter and Robey, 1972, p.26) records traces of smithsonite (calamine) on tips; baryte veinlets in loose blocks of dolomitised limestone were recorded during the present survey. Three shafts were also noted at Softlow Wood [108 464], a short distance to the south-west of Thorswood House. JIC

Snelston

The small outlier [154 412] of Milldale Limestones near Snelston (p.26) was the location of a copper and lead mine. Some details of the workings, the minerals present and the value and tonnage of the output at certain times are given by Dewey and Eastwood (1925, pp.27–28). The mine was said to have been worked 'along numerous irregular levels approached by two shafts, and from an adit driven into the hill from the face of the quarry' (Birchwoodpark Quarry). The precise location of these workings is uncertain, but they were probably situated to the north or north-west of the quarry, where there is an old mine tip [1542 4142] with pieces of sandstone impregnated with malachite. An unpublished report by A. Russell (1918) quoted in Dewey's notebook (BGS archives) described the adit level passing through some 30 feet (9.14 m) of limestone before entering 'red marls and shales intercalated with sandstones'. The latter probably belong to the Denstone Formation. The Carboniferous-Triassic junction is described as 'appearing as a well defined wall ... which in places is slickensided and which at first dips at a steep angle but in depth apparently flattens out somewhat rapidly'. This junction is taken to be a steep unconformity at the base of the Triassic rocks, along which later movement has taken place.

Dewey and Eastwood state that the ores consisted of calcareous sandstone cemented with malachite; malachite coating nodules of chalcopyrite; galena and cerussite. The last two minerals were found both in the sandstone and in clay-lined fissures in the limestone. During the present survey calcite, baryte and fluorite veining was noted at several places in the limestone faces of the quarry, the most intensive mineralisation being a 1.58 m-wide vein complex trending ESE on the south-east face [1543 4115]; all three minerals were present.

Other occurrences

East of Ford there are surface indications [072 540] of a vein working in strongly folded Mixon Limestone-Shales. A spoil tip near a probable collapsed adit [0685 5390] contains a little calcite, galena and sphalerite.

Immediately north of Back o th Brook, a line of old shafts [0807 5222 to 0818 5209] is probably the mine 'between Waterfall and Grindon' referred to by Green and others (1887, p.158) as having produced copper. There are traces of galena on one of the spoil tips. East of Stanton, irregular disseminations of galena, up to 2 cm in diameter, are present in vughy dolomitised limestone exposed on the slopes of Limestone Hill [136 463]. Loose blocks of baryte can also be seen. This outcrop consists of a knoll-reef in the Milldale Limestones surrounded by sandstones of the Triassic Hawksmoor Formation. The deposits were worked in the 19th century (Porter and Robey, 1972, pp.15, 21) and a shaft [1369 4628] is still visible.

Ford (*in* Porter and Robey, 1972, p.25) considers the deposit to be a replacement along the Carboniferous–Triassic unconformity, like that at Snelston.

Higher in the Triassic sequence, an east–west fault cutting sandstones near Wootton Lodge contains a vein in which Hull (1869, p.94) noted traces of galena and copper ores. Trial adits known as Wootton Grange Mine [0953 4355] are still visible, with debris of baryte and some galena. In Rodsley No. 1 Borehole (SK 14 SE/3) veins of calcite and baryte were recorded in Triassic sandstone at 87 m depth.

Disseminated baryte is common as a cement in sandstones of the Hollington Formation (p.80) and baryte veins have been noted at several places. Charsley (1979, p.240) suggests that the presence of impermeable beds in the overlying Mercia Mudstone Group controlled the flow of mineralising fluids and the location of deposits in this formation. There is a good exposure [1074 4520] of sandstone with pink rosettes of disseminated baryte beneath a roadside building at Wootton. At Stanton Quarry [123 466], baryte is present as veins up to 4 cm across, as well as disseminations.   NA, JIC

CHAPTER 13

Mineral products

LIMESTONE

Limestone has been the main mineral product of the district since coal from the Cheadle Coalfield became largely worked out (see below). A detailed account of the limestone resources has been given by Bridge and Kneebone (1983) and the results incorporated in a guide to the limestone and dolomite resources of the Peak District as a whole by Harrison and Adlam (1985). At present there are five working quarries, all situated near the south-western boundary of the Dinantian limestone outcrop and outside the Peak District National Park. Three of these produce stone from the Milldale Limestones: Cauldon Quarry [086 488] (Blue Circle Industries); Caldon Low Quarry [077 486] (Tarmac Roadstone); and Wardlow Quarry [083 475] (Redland Aggregates). The other two, Wredon Quarry [087 468] (United Gravel) and Kevin Quarry [089 460] (Tilcon) are in the Kevin Limestones.

Bridge and Kneebone (1983) classify the Kevin Limestones as very high purity (98.5% CaCO₃) and the Milldale Limestones as high purity (97.0–98.5% CaCO₃). Despite this, the quarried stone, after crushing and grading, is used mainly as aggregate by the construction industry.

There are many small quarries, scattered over the limestone outcrop, which were mainly worked for stone for nearby walls and buildings. Some of the stone was also burnt in adjacent kilns to produce lime for agriculture. It is said that the kiln at Brownend Quarry, Waterhouses, was one of the last in the district to be used for this purpose, finally ceasing production during the late 1940s.   NA

SANDSTONE

Many of the sandstones in the Carboniferous sequence have been used as local sources of building stone, for example the Rough Rock around Wetley Rocks [966 495] and at Noonsun Common [015 497], the Chatsworth Grit at Cotton [064 459], and the Cheddleton Sandstones near Cheddleton Station [981 519].

The Triassic formations of the Sherwood Sandstone Group are more important, however. The cemented character and attractive colours of the sandstones, particularly those in the Hollington Formation (still referred to in the trade as 'Keuper Sandstone'), has made them suitable locally as building stones, and the number of disused quarries in the area testifies to their usefulness in the past. At present there are still four working quarries, three near Hollington: Hollington Red Quarry [055 398] (Staffordshire Stone Ltd), Tearne Quarry (also known as Oldham's quarry) [055 390] and Fielding's Quarry [055 402] (J Oldham & Co); and a small quarry at Wootton Hall [114 445] (J Oldham & Co). In the past stone was also quarried around Alton, Stanton and Mayfield. Buildings constructed

from the sandstone include Croxden Abbey (c.1120 AD), Wootton Lodge (c.1615), Alton Towers (c. 1817) and some was also used in the construction of the new Coventry Cathedral.   NA, TJC

COAL

Coal is present in the Upper Carboniferous rocks of the Cheadle and Shaffalong synclines, and has been worked over a long period (Molyneux, in Plant, 1881; Barrow, 1903). The lowest seams, which lie above the Roaches and Chatsworth grits, are thin and have been worked only locally at outcrop in the ground between Ipstones and Oakamoor. The lowest Westphalian coals, the Two Foot, Ribbon, Crabtree and Split, are also thin; the most persistent, the Crabtree, is pyritous and of little value. All were sporadically worked at outcrop in the valleys of the Churnet and its tributaries between Consall, Froghall, Ipstones and Oakamoor, and at Shaffalong. Considerable reserves of all these seams must remain at depth in the Cheadle Coalfield but none would be worth working under present conditions.

The higher seams, between the Woodhead Coal and the top of the preserved sequence, provided the bulk of the coal extracted in the Cheadle Coalfield, both by deep mining and opencast methods, and most of the accessible reserves of economically attractive coal have already been removed. The extent of known workings in each of the seams is described in Chapter 5; the Woodhead and Dilhorne coals were the most widely worked.

Exploitation of the Woodhead Coal by a small drift mine continues at Above Park Mine [977 464] and there may be other places where small mines would be successful in patches of coal remaining between abandoned workings and close to the outcrops. Further opencast operations in such areas may also be possible.

There are no reserves suitable for large-scale underground working left north of the Callowhill Fault; but to the south, around Draycott in the Moors, is an unexplored region where reserves large enough to justify deep mining may exist, concealed by Triassic rocks. The cross-section on the published 1:50 000 map shows the conjectural extent of the Woodhead and Dilhorne coals in this direction; the deeper of the two would be expected to lie at about 600 m below the surface. An earlier attempt to exploit this area was abandoned when shafts sunk into the Triassic sandstones encountered excessive volumes of water.

IRONSTONE

Hematite is common in the calcite veins that cut the Dinantian limestones of the Weaver Hills and Caldon Low (p.129), but there are no records of its having been worked. The amount visible in exposed veins is small. A parallel has been drawn between the origin of this occurrence and that of the much larger replacement deposits of Cumbria and elsewhere (Barnes and Holroyd, 1897).

The only bedded ironstone of note is the Froghall Ironstone (p.60), a bed of calcareous hematite and black-band ironstone near the base of Westphalian; the bed lies at the same horizon as the Two Foot Coal around Froghall and Ipstones and reaches 0.66 m in thickness (Figure 19). It was first worked as a source of iron at depths up to 137 m, but later only at outcrop and for making red paint (Barrow, 1903; Chester, 1979). Working ceased in 1923.　　　JIC

SILICA SAND

Silica sand of a quality suitable for making glass containers is at present produced by crushing and processing sandstone from the Rough Rock, at Moneystone Quarry [046 461] (British Industrial Sand Ltd) near Cheadle.

A silica sand used for the manufacture of low-temperature refractories is obtained from Pocket Deposits near Brassington (p.88) by Hoben Quarries Ltd and by Spencer Bros Ltd.

Further details of the economic aspects of these deposits are given by Highley (1975).

FLUORSPAR

The main area of fluorite mineralisation lies to the north-east of the present district and though minor quantities of the mineral have been noted at various places in the limestone outcrop, there is no record of fluorspar having been produced.

BARYTES

Barytes has been produced in the past, mainly in association with galena, from mines in the Brassington area including Great Rake Mine, Bees Nest Mine, Nickalum Mine, White Rake and Condway Mine (Ford and Rieuwerts, 1983). The first two of these mines were producing barytes in 1919 and the last was worked in the 1940s. Caulk, the amorphous form of the mineral, predominated in some of the workings. More recent production has been from some of the old mine tips in the area.

Triassic sandstones, mainly the Hollington Formation, show extensive cementation by baryte and may therefore constitute a resource of the mineral if a sufficient concentration is present. A few veins of baryte also occur in these sandstones.

LEAD

Lead ore was produced in the past from many small mines in the Brassington area (Ford and Rieuwerts, 1983; Slack, 1985) and from scattered mines elsewhere (pp.128–130), the most important of which were probably the Bincliff Mines west of Stanshope and the Ribden Mines.

COPPER

Copper ores were formerly mined at Ribden and near Thorswood House from 'before the 1680s to 1862 when the mines were abandoned' (Robey and Porter, 1971), and near Snelston (p.129; Dewey and Eastwood, 1925) up to the early part of the present century. Sulphides of copper and lead have also been worked in a vein near Wootton Grange (Hull, 1869, p.94).

SAND AND GRAVEL

The poorly cemented conglomerates and pebbly sandstones of the Sherwood Sandstone Group (formerly known as the 'Bunter Pebble Beds') provide an important source of aggregate used by the construction industry. Detailed assessments of the conglomerate resources in the Hawksmoor Formation south and east of Cheadle have been made by Rogers and others (1981) and Piper (1982). The main conglomeratic units are the Freehay Member and the Lodgedale Member (p.80). There are extensive workings in the former, two of which are now in production: Huntley Wood Quarry [995 415] (ARC) and Muddale Quarry north-east of Winnothdale [036 414] (Tarmac). Piper (1982) estimated that 'perhaps as much as half' of the potentially workable mineral had been extracted from the workings at Huntley Wood and Rogers and others (1981, table 4) estimated that about a quarter of the potential resources had been extracted from the area south-east of Cheadle. These authors stress that their estimates take no account of such factors as height of water table, public amenity, and high agricultural and land values, which might prevent the exploitation of the resources.

There are many other minor disused quarries and pits in the Hawksmoor Formation and in the undivided Sherwood Sandstone Group outcrop east of Ashbourne (p.84).

Sand and gravel deposits of glacial origin, and in the form of river terraces and other alluvial deposits, are shown on the published geological maps; they are largely unproved by drilling and little exploited. A compilation of the available information covering an area that includes most of the deposits in the present district has been given by Crofts and James (1984). The most extensive deposits probably underlie the present floodplain and terraces of the River Dove between Ashbourne and Crakemarsh near the district boundary [094 365].　　　NA

CHAPTER 14

Hydrogeology and water supply

The district lies within Hydrometric Area 28, and the water resources are administered by the Severn-Trent Water Authority. The principal drainage comprises the River Dove and its tributaries, the Blithe, the Tean and the Churnet. The south-east corner of the district is drained by the Shirley and Brailsford brooks.

The mean annual rainfall varies from about 980 mm over the high ground in the north, to about 750 mm over the low ground in the south-east. Annual evaporation is about 480 mm. Run-off is rapid from the northern highlands, which causes the flow of the River Dove to be rather flashy, although the groundwater component taken over the year amounts to between 50 and 60 per cent of the total flow (Downing and others, 1970; Monkhouse and Richards, 1984).

Previous work on groundwater in this district was published by Stephens (1929) and Downing and others (1970). The chemistry of groundwater in the Derbyshire Dome was studied by Edmunds (1971), and an analysis of potential borehole yields in the Mercia Mudstone Group was made by Monkhouse (1984).

The major aquifer within the district is the Sherwood Sandstone Group, while minor aquifers comprise the sandstone and grit horizons in the Namurian and Westphalian and the limestone beds of the Dinantian. Although minor abstractions for agricultural purposes are drawn from almost all the formations in the area, together with some small industrial yields near Ashbourne, public water supplies are pumped only from the Sherwood Sandstone Group (personal communication, Severn-Trent Water Authority).

The shales and sandstones of the Dinantian yield little or no groundwater, this being present in usable quantities only in the limestones. The limestone itself has a very low porosity and permeability, and groundwater flow is dominantly through fissures. Numerous springs issue from the limestone beds and support a number of local demands. There are few records of wells and boreholes in the Dinantian within the district, and yields are generally low. A borehole of 150 mm diameter penetrating 30 m thickness of saturated rock would be expected to have a mean yield of only 30 cubic metres per day (m^3/d) for a drawdown of 10 m. The groundwater is usually of good quality with total hardness in the range 250 to 350 mg/l (as $CaCO_3$), in general being mostly carbonate hardness. Where water infiltrates into heavily fissured limestones, the contact time with the rock is small due to rapid groundwater flow, and the total hardness may fall below 100 mg/l. The chloride ion concentration is not known to exceed 20 mg/l (as Cl). Fluoride is commonly present, and concentrations may approach 0.5 mg/l (as F). Thermomineral groundwaters have not been encountered within the Dinantian in this district (Edmunds, 1971).

Groundwater in the Namurian is obtained predominantly from the sandstones and grits. Flow may be intergranular or through fissures, the latter being usually the more impor-

tant. Failure to intersect fissures generally results in little or no useful yield. Sandstones that are soft and decalcified at outcrop tend to be hard and compact at depth and hence less permeable. For boreholes of 150 mm diameter constructed to depths of 40 m or less, the mean yield would be of the order of 230 m^3/d for a drawdown of 10 m; there would be about 10 per cent probability of a yield of less than 40 m^3/d.

The quality of groundwater in the Namurian strata is variable. Total hardness varies from less than 50 to more than 200 mg/l. Carbonate hardness is generally greater than non-carbonate hardness. The chloride ion concentration rarely exceeds 30 mg/l. The main problem is generally with a high concentration of iron, which often exceeds 1.0 mg/l and may approach 4.0 mg/l.

The outcrop of the Coal Measures is confined to a small area in the west of the district, and although sandstones are present, these strata appear to have little significance for water supply. Old coal workings may yield poor quality water, but there are no records of exploitation.

The Sherwood Sandstone Group forms the major aquifer in the district. Although some restrictions to groundwater movement are caused by the mudstone and siltstone bands present within the sandstones, hydraulic continuity does appear to exist throughout the group. Boreholes penetrating the sandstones beneath a cover of Mercia Mudstones may give an artesian flow.

Hydrogeologically, the group may be divided into three areas. The first, to the east of the River Dove, is characterised by low yields due to the poor development of fissures in the sandstones. Public water supplies are pumped from wells at Rodsley (SK 14 SE/8), Yeldersley (SK 24 SW/7), Sturston (SK 14 NE/18) and Cubley (SK 13 NE/2), but with an average yield of only 1000 m^3/d per site. In the second area, to the west of the River Dove, fissuring is better developed and cementation within the sandstones less complete. Yields averaging 6000 m^3/d are taken at each of six stations. Crumpwood (SK 04 SE/11), Cheadle (SK 04 SW/42), Greatgate (SK 03 NE/17), Draycott (SJ 94 SE/18), Teanford (SK 04 SW/1b) and Cresswell (SJ 93 NE/1). The third area lies in the north-west corner of the district. Fissuring is here well developed, and wells at Wall Grange (SJ 95 SE/63) pump over 10 000 m^3/d into supply.

Where the sandstones crop out, the total hardness is usually in the range of 100 to 300 mg/l. The chloride ion concentration is generally less than 40 mg/l, and the sulphate concentration less than 50 mg/l. Beneath increasing Mercia Mudstone cover, the total hardness tends to rise and may exceed 500 mg/l. The concentrations of chloride and sulphate also tend to increase. East of the River Dove, iron, manganese and fluoride also occur in above normal concentrations.

Little water is obtained from the mudstones within the Mercia Mudstone Group, but useful local supplies can often be taken from the sandstone beds ('skerries'). Groundwater flow is dominantly through fissures. Yields are generally better from the lower part of the sequence (Denstone Formation). The mean yield of a borehole of 150 mm diameter penetrating 30 m of saturated rock is of the order of 100 m³/d for 10 m of drawdown, but there is about 20 per cent probability of the yield being less than 50 m³/d. Boreholes failing to intersect skerries may yield little or no water. The natural recharge to the sandstone beds at depth is limited, and borehole yields tend to decrease with time as the storage is depleted.

Groundwater from the Mercia Mudstone Group is often hard, with a total hardness exceeding 400 mg/l. The concentrations of sulphate may locally exceed 100 mg/l, but the chloride ion concentration rarely exceeds 40 mg/l.

The extent of superficial deposits in the district is limited. The most extensive deposit, boulder clay, is generally impermeable, and is hydrogeologically important only in restricting the natural recharge to any underlying aquifer. Deposits of sand and gravel are too small to have any significance for water supply, while the alluvium is usually too thin and too impermeable to permit any useful development.   RAM

REFERENCES

AHR, W. M. 1973. The carbonate ramp: an alternative to the shelf model. *Trans. Gulf Coast Assoc. of Geol. Socs.,* Vol. 23, 221–225.

AITKENHEAD, N. 1977. The Institute of Geological Sciences Borehole at Duffield, Derbyshire. *Bull. Geol. Surv. G.B.,* No. 59, 1–38.

— and CHISHOLM, J. I. 1982. A standard nomenclature for the Dinantian formations of the Peak District of Derbyshire and Staffordshire. *Rep. Inst. Geol. Sci.,* No. 82/8.

— — and STEVENSON, I. P. 1985. Geology of the country around Buxton, Leek and Bakewell. *Mem. Br. Geol. Surv.,* Sheet 111.

— RILEY, N. J., BALL, T. K., NICHOLSON, R. A., PEACHY, D., BLOODWORTH, A. J., ROUSE, J. E., MILLER, M. F. and THRIFT, L. 1984. Carsington dam; geological, geomorphological and geochemical aspects of the site. [unpublished final report] (Keyworth: British Geological Survey.)

ALEXANDER, G. B. 1940. Report of field meetings for 1939: Buxton. *Proc. Yorkshire Geol. Soc.,* Vol. 24, 172–173.

ALKINS, W. E. 1921. Fauna of the Brachiopod Beds at Cauldon, Staffs. *Geol. Mag.,* Vol. 53, 367–369.

— 1923. Stones and shells of the Staffordshire moorlands. *Trans. North Staffordshire Field Club,* Vol. 57, 30–47.

ALLEN, J. R. L. 1974. Sedimentology of the Old Red Sandstone (Siluro-Devonian) in the Clee Hills area, Shropshire, England. *Sediment. Geol.,* Vol. 12, 73–167.

ANDERTON, R., BRIDGES, P. H., LEEDER, M. R. and SELLWOOD, B. W. 1979. *A dynamic stratigraphy of the British Isles.* (London: Allen and Unwin.)

ANON. 1899. Summary of progress of the Geological Survey of the United Kingdom for 1898, 159–164. *Mem. Geol. Surv. UK.*

— 1919. Fossils from the Keuper of Alton, Great Gate and Hollington. *Trans. North Staffordshire Field Club,* Vol. 53, 102–103.

— 1957. *Summ. Prog. Geol. Surv. G,B. for 1956,* 36.

ARNOLD-BEMROSE, H. H. 1894. Microscopic structure of Carboniferous dolerites and tuffs of Derbyshire. *Q. J. Geol. Soc. London,* Vol. 50, 603–644.

— 1899. Geology of the Ashbourne and Buxton Branch of the London and North-Western Railway: Ashbourne to Crake Low. *Q. J. Geol. Soc. London,* Vol. 55, Part 2, 224–238.

— 1903. Geology of the Ashbourne and Buxton Branch of the London and North-Western Railway: Crake Low to Parsley Hay. *Q. J. Geol. Soc. London,* Vol. 59, 337–347.

— 1904. Quartzite dykes in mountain limestone near Snelston (Derbyshire). *Q. J. Geol. Soc. London,* Vol. 60, Part 3, 364–371.

— 1907. The toadstones of Derbyshire: their field relations and petrography. *Q. J. Geol. Soc. London,* Vol. 63, Part 3, 241–281.

ARTHURTON, R. S. 1980. Rhythmic sedimentary sequences in the Triassic Keuper Marl (Mercia Mudstone Group) of Cheshire, northwest England. *Geol. J.,* Vol. 15, Part 1, 43–50.

— 1984. The Ribblesdale fold belt, N.W. England—a Dinantian–early Namurian dextral shear zone. *In* Variscan tectonics of the North Atlantic Region. *Spec. Publ. Geol. Soc.*

London, No. 14, HUTTON, D. W. H. and SANDERSON, D. J. (editors). (Oxford: Blackwell.)

ASHTON, C. A. 1974. Palaeontology, stratigraphy and sedimentology of Kinderscoutian and lower Marsdenian (Namurian) of North Staffordshire and adjacent areas. Unpublished PhD thesis, University of Keele.

BAMFORD, D., NUNN, K., PRODEHL, C. and JACOB, B. 1978. LISPB-IV Crustal structure of Northern Britain. *Geophys. J. R. Astron. Soc.,* Vol. 54, 43–60.

BARKE, F. 1894. Notes on sections in the drift in N. Staffordshire and S.W. Derbyshire. *Annu. Rep. & Trans. North Staffordshire Field Club,* Vol. 28.

— 1906. Report of the Geology Section. *Annu. Rep. & Trans. North Staffordshire Field Club,* Vol. 40, 85–86.

— 1907. Report of the Geology Section. *Annu. Rep. & Trans. North Staffordshire Field Club,* Vol. 41, 92..

— HIND, W. and SCOTT, A. 1920. Quartzose conglomerate at Cauldon Low, Staffordshire. *Geol. Mag.,* Vol. 57, 76–82.

BARNES, J. and HOLROYD, W. F. 1897. On the occurrence of haematite in veins and pockets of the Mountain Limestone at Cauldon Low. *Annu. Rep. & Trans. North Staffordshire Field Club,* Vol. 31, 137–139.

BARROW, G. 1900. 149 in *Summ. Prog. Geol. Surv. G.B. for 1899.* (London: HMSO.)

— 1903. The geology of the Cheadle Coalfield. *Mem. Geol. Surv. G.B.*

BEASLEY, H. C. 1892. The Trias of Cheadle and Alton, Staffordshire. *J. Liverpool Geol. Soc.,* Vol. 12, 37–41.

—1907. Report on footprints from the Trias. Part IV. *Rep. Br. Assoc. Adv. Sci.* (for 1906), 299–301.

— 1914. Some fossils from the Keuper Sandstone of Alton, Staffordshire. *Proc. Liverpool Geol. Soc.,* Vol. 12, 35–39.

BINNEY, E. W. 1855. On the origin of Ironstones, and more particularly the newly discovered Red Stone at Ipstones, near Cheadle, Staffordshire: with some account of the Ironstones of South Lancashire. *Mem. Manchester Lit. & Philos. Soc.,* Vol. 12, 31–45.

BOLTON, T. 1978. The palaeontology, sedimentology and stratigraphy of the upper Arnsbergian, Chokierian and Alportian of the North Staffordshire Basin. Unpublished PhD thesis, University of Keele.

BOSWELL, P. G. H. 1918. *A memoir of the British resources of refractory sands.* (London: Taylor and Frances.)

BOULTER, M. C. 1971. A palynological study of two of the Neogene plant beds in Derbyshire. *Bull. Br. Mus. (Nat. Hist.) Geol.,* Vol. 19, 359–410.

— and CHALONER, W. G. 1970. Neogene fossil plants from Derbyshire (England). *Rev. Palaeobot. Palynol.,* Vol. 10, 61–78.

— FORD, T. D., IJTABA, M. and WALSH, P. T. 1971. Brassington Formation, a newly recognised Tertiary formation in the southern Pennines. *Nature, London,* Vol. 231, 134–136.

BOUMA, A. H. 1962. Sedimentology of some flysch deposits; a graphic approach to facies interpretation. (Amsterdam and New York: Elsevier.)

BRAMWELL, D. 1964. The excavations at Elderbush Cave, Wetton, Staffordshire. *North Staffordshire J. Field Stud.*, Vol. 4, 46–60.

— and SHOTTON, F. W. 1982. Rodent remains from the caddis-bearing tufa of Elder Bush Cave. *Quaternary Newsl.*, No. 38, 7–13.

BRIDGE, D. McC. and KNEEBONE, D. S. 1983. The limestone and dolomite resources of the country north and west of Ashbourne, Derbyshire. Description of 1:25 000 SK 15 and parts of SK 04, 05, and 14. *Miner. Assess. Rep. Inst. Geol. Sci.*, No. 129.

BRIDGES, P. H. and CHAPMAN, A. J. 1988. The anatomy of a deep water mud-mound complex on the SW margin of the Dinantian platform in Derbyshire. *Sedimentology*, Vol. 35, No. 1, 139–162.

BROCKBANK, W. 1864. On the discovery of the bones of the mammoth in a fissure of Carboniferous limestone at Waterhouses near Leek. *Proc. Manchester Lit. & Philos. Soc.*, Series 3, Vol. 4, 46–50.

BROWN, E. 1865. Exploration of Thor's Cave. *Trans. Midland Sci. Assoc.*, Vol. 1, 1–6, 19–20, 34–38.

— 1867. The Weaver clays. *Geol. Mag.*, Vol. 4, 381–382.

BRYAN, R. B. 1970. Parent materials and texture of Peak District soils. *Z. Geomorphol.*, Vol. 14, 262–274.

BUREK, C. 1977. The Pleistocene ice age and after. 87–128 in *Limestones and caves of the Peak District*. FORD, T. D. (editor). (Norwich: Geo. Abstracts Ltd.)

BURTON, P. W., MUSSON, R. M. W. and NEILSON, G. 1984. Studies of historical British earthquakes. Global Seismology Unit Report No.237. (Edinburgh: British Geological Survey.)

CARRUTHERS, R. G. and STRAHAN, A. 1923. Special reports on the mineral resources of Great Britain. Vol. 26. Lead and zinc ores of Durham, Yorkshire and Derbyshire. *Mem. Geol. Surv. G.B.*

CAZALET, P. C. D. 1969. Correlation of Cheshire Plain and Derbyshire Dome glacial deposits. *Mercian Geol.*, Vol. 3, No. 1, 71–84.

CHAPMAN, A. J. 1984. The sedimentology and diagenesis of a Waulsortian-style carbonate mud-mound complex in the early Dinantian of the English Midlands. Eur. Dinantian Environments 1st Meeting 1984. Abstract, (Dept. Earth Sciences, Open University.)

CHARSLEY, T. J. 1979. Excursion to the Ashbourne area. *Mercian Geol.*, Vol. 7, No. 3, 239–241.

— 1982. A standard nomenclature for the Triassic formations of the Ashbourne district. *Rep. Inst. Geol. Sci.*, No. 81/14.

CHESTER, H. A. 1979. *The Iron Valley.* (Stafford: H. A. Chester and Ariel Printers.)

CHISHOLM, J. I. 1977. Growth faulting and sandstone deposition in the Namurian of the Stanton Syncline, Derbyshire. *Proc. Yorkshire Geol. Soc.*, Vol. 41, Pt. 3, 305–323.

— and BUTCHER, N. J. D. 1981. A borehole proving dolomite beneath the Dinantian Limestones near Matlock, Derbyshire. *Mercian Geol.*, Vol. 8, No. 3, 225–228.

CLAYTON, G. and SEVASTOPULO, G. D. 1981. Discussion on the recognition and division of the Tournaisian Series in Britain. *J. Geol. Soc. London*, Vol. 138, Pt. 1, 104–105.

CLAYTON, K. M. 1953a. The glacial chronology of part of the middle Trent basin. *Proc. Geol. Assoc.*, Vol. 64, 198–207.

— 1953b. The denudation chronology of part of the middle Trent basin. *Trans. Inst. Br. Geographers*, No. 19, 25–36.

COPE, F. W. 1946. The correlation of the Coal Measures of the Cheadle Coalfield, North Staffordshire. *Trans. Inst. Min. Eng.*, Vol. 105, 75–91 and 98–102.

— 1973. Woo Dale Borehole near Buxton, Derbyshire. *Nature, London*, Vol. 243, 29–30.

— 1979. The age of the volcanic rocks in the Woo Dale Borehole, Derbyshire. *Geol. Mag.*, Vol. 116, No. 4, 319–320.

COX, F. C. and HARRISON, D. J. 1980. The limestone and dolomite resources of the country around Wirksworth, Derbyshire: Description of parts of sheets SK 25 and 35. *Miner. Assess. Rep. Inst. Geol. Sci.*, No. 47.

COXON, R. E. 1986. Failure of Carsington Embankment. *Department of the Environment Report to the Secretary of State for the Environment.* (London: Her Majesty's Stationery Office.)

CRITCHLEY, M. F. and WILSON, P. J. 1985. A survey of the shafts of Bincliff, Oversetts and Highfields mines, Wetton, Staffs. *Bull. Peak Dist. Mines Hist. Soc.*, Vol. 6, No. 2, 73–81.

CROFTS, R. G. and JAMES, J. W. C. 1984. A desk study of the sand and gravel resources of the Dove-Derwent drainage and adjacent parts of the Trent valley. (Keyworth: British Geological Survey.)

CUMMINS, W. A. 1965. Sedimentary structures from the Keuper Sandstone at Alton, Staffs. *Mercian Geol.*, Vol. 1, No. 2, 153–160.

DAVISON, C. 1924. *A history of British earthquakes.* (Cambridge: Cambridge University Press.)

DEELEY, R. M. 1886. The Pleistocene succession in the Trent Basin. *Q. J. Geol. Soc. London*, Vol. 52, No. 168, 437–480.

— 1914. Ice-flows in the Trent basin. *Geol. Mag.*, Decade 6, Vol. 1, 69–73.

DEWEY, H. and EASTWOOD, T. 1925. Special reports on the mineral resources of Great Britain, Vol. 30. Copper ores of the Midlands, Wales, the Lake District and the Isle of Man. *Mem. Geol. Surv. G.B.*

DOWNING, R. A., LAND, D. H., ALLENDER, R., LOVELOCK, P. E. R. and BRIDGE, L. R. 1970. The hydrogeology of the Trent River Basin. *Hydrogeol. Rep. Inst. Geol. Sci.* No. 5.

DUNHAM, K. C. 1952. Age-relations of the epigenetic mineral deposits of Britain. *Trans. Geol. Soc. Glasgow*, Vol. 21, Pt. 3, 395–429.

— 1973. A recent deep borehole near Eyam, Derbyshire. *Nature Phys. Sci., London*, Vol. 241, 84–85.

EDEN, R. A. 1954. The Coal Measures of the *Anthraconaia lenisulcata* Zone in the East Midlands Coalfield. *Bull. Geol. Surv. G.B.*, No. 5, 81–106.

EDMUNDS, W. M. 1971. Hydrogeochemistry of groundwaters in the Derbyshire Dome with special reference to trace constituents. *Rep. Inst. Geol. Sci.,* No. 71/7.

ELLIOTT, R. E. 1961. The stratigraphy of the Keuper Series in southern Nottinghamshire. *Proc. Yorkshire Geol. Soc.*, Vol. 33, Pt. 2, 197–234.

EVANS, W. B., WILSON, A. A., TAYLOR, B. J. and PRICE, D. 1968. Geology of the country around Macclesfield, Congleton, Crewe and Middlewich. *Mem. Geol. Surv. G.B.*, Sheet 110.

FAREY, J. 1811. *A general view of the agriculture and minerals of Derbyshire*, Vol. 1. (London.)

FEARNSIDES, W. G. 1932. The geology of the eastern part of the Peak District. *Proc. Geol. Assoc.*, Vol. 43, 152–191.

FIELDER, G. and WILSON, L. (editors). 1975. *Volcanoes of the Earth, Moon and Mars.* (London: Elek Science.)

FIRMAN, R. J. 1977. Derbyshire wrenches and ores—a study of the rakes' progress by secondary faulting. *Mercian Geol.*, Vol. 6, No. 2, 81–96.

— and BAGSHAW, C. 1974. A re-appraisal of the controls of non-metallic gangue mineral distribution in Derbyshire. *Mercian Geol.*, Vol. 5, No. 2, 145–161.

FITCH, F. J., MILLER, J. A. and THOMPSON, D. B. 1966. The palaeogeographic significance of isotopic age determination on detrital micas from the Triassic of the Stockport–Macclesfield District, Cheshire. *Palaeogeog. Palaeoclimatol. Palaeoecol.*, Vol. 2, 281–313.

FORD, T. D. 1963. The dolomite tors of Derbyshire. *East Midland Geogr.*, Vol. 3, 148–154.

— 1969. The stratiform ore deposits of Derbyshire. *In* Sedimentary ores ancient and modern (revised). JAMES, C. H., (editor). *Proc. 15th Inter-Univ. Geol. Congr., 1967, Leicester, England.*

— 1972. Field meeting in the Peak District: Report of the Director. *Proc. Geol. Assoc.*, Vol. 83, Pt. 2, 231–236.

— (editor.). 1977. *Limestones and caves of the Peak District.* (Norwich: Geo Abstracts Ltd.)

— and BUREK, C. 1976. Anomalous limestone gorges in Derbyshire. *Mercian Geol.*, Vol. 6, 59–75.

— and KING, R. J. 1969. The origin of the silica sand deposits in the Derbyshire limestone. *Mercian Geol.*, Vol. 3, No, 1, 51–69.

— and RIEUWERTS, J. H. 1983. *Lead mining in the Peak District.* (3rd edition). (Bakewell: Peak Park Planning Board.)

FORSTER, S. C. and WARRINGTON, G. 1985. Geochronology of the Carboniferous, Permian and Triassic. 99–113. In *The chronology of the geological record.* SNELLING, N. J. (editor). *Mem. Geol. Soc. London, No. 10.* (Oxford: Blackwell.)

FROST, D. V. and SMART, J. G. O. 1979. Geology of the country north of Derby. *Mem. Geol. Surv. G.B.*, Sheet 125.

GAWTHORPE, R. L. 1987. Tectono-sedimentary evolution of the Bowland Basin, northern England, during the Dinantian. *J. Geol. Soc. London*, Vol. 144, Pt. 1, 58–71.

GEMMELL, A. M. D. and GEORGE, P. K. 1972. The glaciation of the west Midlands: a review of recent research. *North Staffordshire J. Field Stud.*, Vol. 12, 1–20.

GEORGE, T. N. 1963. Tectonics and palaeogeography in northern England. *Sci. Prog.*, Vol. 51, 32–59.

GLENNIE, K. W. 1970. Desert sedimentary Environments. *Dev. Sedimentol.*, No. 14. (Amsterdam: Elsevier.)

— and EVANS, G. 1976. A reconnaissance of the recent sediments of the Ranns of Kutch, India. *Sedimentology*, Vol. 23, 625.

GREEN, A. H. 1867. Distribution of white sands and clays subjacent to the boulder-clay. *Geol. Mag.*, Vol. 4, 335–336.

— FOSTER, C. LE NEVE and DAKYNS, J. R. 1869. The geology of the Carboniferous Limestone, Yoredale Rocks and Millstone Grit of North Derbyshire. *Mem. Geol. Surv. England and Wales.*

— — — 1887. The geology of the Carboniferous Limestone, Yoredale Rocks and Millstone Grit of North Derbyshire. 2nd edition with additions by A. H. GREEN and A. STRAHAN. *Mem. Geol. Surv. England and Wales.*

HAINS, B. A. and HORTON, A. 1969. *British regional geology: central England* (3rd edition). (London: HMSO for Institute of Geological Sciences.)

HARRISON, D. J. and ADLAM, K. A. McL. 1985. The limestone and dolomite resources of the Peak District of Derbyshire and Staffordshire. Description of parts of 1:50 000 geological Sheets 99, 111, 112, 124 and 125. *Miner. Assess. Rep. Br. Geol. Surv.*, No. 144.

HECKEL, P. H. 1974. Carbonate buildups in the geologic record: a review. Pp.90–154 in *Reefs in time and space.* LAPORTE, L. F. (editor). Spec. Publ. No. 18. (Tulsa: Society of Economic Paleontologists and Mineralogists.)

HESTER, S. W. 1932. The Millstone Grit succession in north Staffordshire. *Summ. Prog. Geol. Surv. G.B.* (for 1931), Pt. 2, 34–48.

HIGHLEY, D. E. 1975. Silica. *Miner. Dossier, Miner. Resour. Consult. Comm.* No. 18. (London: Her Majesty's Stationery Office.)

HILLS, E. S. 1972. *Elements of structural geology (*2nd edition). (London: Chapman and Hall Ltd.)

HIND, W. 1897. Description of the section in Carboniferous Limestone Shales at Tissington, on the new Buxton and Ashbourne Railway. *Trans. North Staffordshire Field Club*, Vol. 32, 114–116.

HOLLINGWORTH, S. E., TAYLOR, J. H. and KELLAWAY, G. A. 1944. Large-scale superficial structures in the Northampton Ironstone Field. *Q. J. Geol. Soc. London*, Vol. 100, 1–44.

HOLLIS, J. M. 1975. Soils in Staffordshire. *Rec. Soil Surv.*, No. 29, Sheet SK 05 (Onecote).

HOLMES, I., CHAMBERS, A. D., IXER, R. A., TURNER, P. and VAUGHAN, D. J. 1983. Diagenetic processes and the mineralisation in the Triassic of central England. *Mineral. Deposita*, Vol. 18, No. 2B (Supplement), 365–377.

HOUSE, M. R., RICHARDSON, J. B., CHALONER, W. G., ALLEN, J. R. L., HOLLAND, C. H. and WESTOLL, T. S. 1977. A correlation of the Devonian rocks in the British Isles. *Spec. Rep. Geol. Soc. London*, No. 8.

HOWE, J. A. 1897. Notes on the pockets of sand and clay in the limestone of Derbyshire and Staffordshire. *Trans. North Staffordshire Field Club*, Vol. 31, 143–149.

HOWE, J. A. (editor). 1920. Special reports on the mineral resources of Great Britain, Vol. 6, Refractory materials. Resources and geology (2nd edition). *Mem. Geol. Surv. G.B.*

HUDSON, R. G. S. and COTTON, G. 1945. The Lower Carboniferous in a boring at Alport, Derbyshire. *Proc. Yorkshire Geol. Soc.*, Vol. 25, Pt. 4, 254–330.

HULL, E. 1869. The Triassic and Permian rocks of the Midland counties of England. *Mem. Geol. Surv. G.B.*

— and GREEN, A. H. 1866. Geology of the country around Stockport, Macclesfield, Congleton and Leek. *Mem. Geol. Surv. G.B.*

HUNTINGTON, E. 1905. The basin of Eastern Persia and Sistan. 219–317. *In* Exploration in Turkestan. PUMPELLY and others. *Carnegie Inst. Publ.* No. 26.

INESON, P. R. and FORD, T. D. 1982. The South Pennine orefield: its genetic theories and eastward extension. *Mercian Geol.*, Vol. 8, No. 4, 285–303.

— and MITCHELL, J. G. 1973. Isotopic age determinations on clay minerals from lavas and tuffs of the Derbyshire orefield. *Geol. Mag.*, Vol. 109, No. 6, 501–512.

INSTITUTE OF GEOLOGICAL SCIENCES. 1968. *Annual report for 1967.* (London: Her Majesty's Stationery Office.)

— 1978. IGS boreholes 1977. *Rep. Inst. Geol. Sci.*, No. 78/21.

— 1980. 1:250 000 Series, Aeromagnetic anomaly map (Provisional Edition), East Midlands sheet, 52°N–02°W. (London: Institute of Geological Sciences.)

— 1981. IGS boreholes 1979. *Rep. Inst. Geol. Sci.*, No. 80/11.

— 1982a. IGS boreholes 1980. *Rep. Inst. Geol. Sci.*, No. 81/11.

— 1982b. 1:250 000 Series, Bouguer Gravity anomaly map (Provisional Edition), East Midlands sheet, 52°N–02°W. (London: Institute of Geological Sciences.)

JACKSON, J. W. 1919. On the occurrence of *Productus humerosus* (= *sublaevis*) in Dovedale, and its value as a zone-fossil. *Geol. Mag.*, Vol. 56, 507–509.

— 1941. *Spirifer bollandensis* Muir-Wood at Thorpe Cloud, with notes on the sequence in Dove Dale, Derbyshire. *J. Manchester Geol. Assoc.*, Vol. 1, Pt. 4, 233–237.

— and ALKINS, W. E. 1919. On the discovery of a quartzose conglomerate at Caldon Low, Staffs. *Geol. Mag.*, Vol. 56, 59–64.

— and CHARLESWORTH, J. K. 1920. The quartzose conglomerate at Caldon Low, Staffordshire. *Geol. Mag.*, Vol. 57, 487–492.

JOHNSON, G. A. L. 1981. Geographical evolution from Laurasia to Pangaea. *Proc. Yorkshire Geol. Soc.*, Vol. 43, Pt. 3, 221–252.

— and TARLING, D. H. 1985. Continental convergence and closing seas during the Carboniferous. *C. R. 10e Congr. Int. Stratigr. Geol. Carbonif., Madrid 1983*, Vol. 4, 163–168.

JOHNSON, R. H. 1965. The origin of the Churnet and Rudyard valleys. *North Staffordshire J. Field Stud.*, Vol. 5, 95–105.

JONES, C. M. 1980. Deltaic sedimentation in the Roaches Grit and associated sediments (Namurian R$_{2b}$) in the south-west Pennines. *Proc. Yorkshire Geol. Soc.*, Vol. 43, Pt. 1, 39–67.

JONES, P. F. 1979. The origin and significance of dry valleys in south-east Derbyshire. *Mercian Geol.*, Vol. 7, 1–18.

— and STANLEY, M. F. 1974. Ipswichian mammalian fauna from the Beeston Terrace at Boulton Moor, near Derby. *Geol. Mag.*, Vol. 111, 515–520.

— and WEAVER, J. D. 1975. Superficial valley folds of late Pleistocene age in the Breadsall area of south Derbyshire. *Mercian Geol.*, Vol. 5, 279–290.

— and CHARSLEY, T. J. 1985. A re-appraisal of the denudation chronology of south Derbyshire, England. *Proc. Geol. Assoc.*, Vol. 96, Pt. 1, 73–86.

JOWETT, A. and CHARLESWORTH, J. K. 1929. The glacial geology of the Derbyshire dome and the western slopes of the southern Pennines. *Q. J. Geol. Soc. London*, Vol. 85, Pt. 3, 307–334.

KELLAWAY, G. A. 1972. Development of non-diastrophic Pleistocene structures in relation to climate and physical relief in Britain. *Rep. 24th Int. Geol. Cong., Canada*, Sect. 12, 136–146.

KENT, P. E. 1957. Triassic relics and the 1000-foot surface in the southern Pennines. *East Midland Geographer*, Vol. 1, No. 8, 3–10.

KEREY, I. E. 1978. Sedimentology of the Chatsworth Grit sandstone in the Goyt-Chapel en le Frith area. Unpublished MSc thesis, University of Keele.

KING, C. A. M. 1960. The Churnet Valley. *East Midland Geogr.*, Vol. 14, 33–40.

— 1966. Geomorphology. 41–59 in *Nottingham and its region*. EDWARDS, K. C. (editor). (Nottingham: British Association.)

KING, R. J. and FORD, T. D. 1968. Mineralisation. 112–137 in *The geology of the East Midlands*. SYLVESTER-BRADLEY, P. C. and FORD, T. D. (editors). (Leicester: Leicester University Press.)

KOKELAAR, B. P. 1983. The mechanism of Surtseyan volcanism. *J. Geol. Soc. London*, Vol. 140, Pt. 6, 939–944.

LAMPLUGH, G. W. 1899. 160 in *Summ. Prog. Geol. Surv. G.B. for 1898*. (London: Her Majesty's Stationery Office.)

LEEDER, M. R. 1982. Upper Palaeozoic basins of the British Isles—Caledonian inheritance versus Hercynian plate margin processes. *J. Geol. Soc. London*, Vol. 139, Pt. 4, 479–491.

LEES, A. 1964. The structure and origin of the Waulsortian (Lower Carboniferous) 'reefs' of west-central Eire. *Philos. Trans. R. Soc.*, B.247, 483–531.

— HALLET, V. and HIBO, D. 1985. Facies variation in Waulsortian buildups, Part 1; A model from Belgium. *Geol. J.*, Vol. 20, No. 2, 133–158.

— MILLER, J. 1985. Facies variation in Waulsortian buildups, Part 2; Mid-Dinantian buildups from Europe and North America. *Geol. J.*, Vol. 20, No. 2, 159–180.

LINTON, D. L. 1951. Midland drainage; some considerations bearing on its origin. *Adv. Sci.*, Vol. 7, 449–456.

— 1956. Geomorphology. 24–43 in *Sheffield and its region*. LINTON, D. L. (editor.) (Sheffield: British Association.)

LIPPOLT, H. J. and HESS, J. C. 1985. ^{40}Ar/^{39}Ar dating of sanidines from Upper Carboniferous tonsteins. *C. R. 10e Congr. Int. Stratigr. Geol. Carbonif., Madrid 1983*, Vol. 4, 175–181.

LISTER, J. H. and STOBBS, J. T. 1917. Erratics in coal seams, with special reference to new discoveries in North Staffordshire. *Trans. North Staffordshire Field Club*, Vol. 51, 33–47.

— — 1918. Additional erratics from the Woodhead Coal of Cheadle, North Staffordshire. *Trans. North Staffordshire Field Club*, Vol. 52, 93–95.

LUDFORD, A. 1940. The Weaver Hills, North Staffordshire. *Proc. Geol. Assoc.*, Vol. 51, 217–219.

— 1951. Stratigraphy of the Carboniferous rocks of the Weaver Hills district, North Staffordshire. *Q. J. Geol. Soc. London*, Vol. 106, Pt. 2, 211–230.

— 1970. The stratigraphy and palaeontology of the Lower Carboniferous rocks of north-east Staffordshire and adjacent parts of Derbyshire. Unpublished PhD thesis. Chelsea College of Science and Technology.

McARTHUR, J. L. 1977. Quaternary erosion in the Upper Derwent basin and its bearing on the age of surface features in the southern Pennines. *Trans. Inst. Br. Geogr. New Series*, Vol. 2, 490–497.

McKENZIE, D. 1978. Some remarks on the development of sedimentary basins. *Earth & Planet. Sci. Lett.*, Vol. 40, 25–32.

MAGRAW, D. 1957. New boreholes into the Lower Coal Measures below the Arley Mine of Lancashire and adjacent areas. *Bull. Geol. Surv. G.B.*, No. 13, 14–38.

MAROOF, S. I. 1976. The structure of the concealed pre-Carboniferous basement of the Derbyshire Dome from gravity data. *Proc. Yorkshire Geol. Soc.*, Vol. 41, Pt. 1, 59–69.

MARROW, P. C. 1984. The magnitude 3.1 earthquake in the East Midlands on 30 May 1984. Global Seismology Report No. 240. (Edinburgh: British Geological Survey.)

MAW, G. 1867. On the distribution beyond the Tertiary districts of white clays and sands subjacent to the boulder-clay drifts, Part 1. *Geol. Mag.*, Vol. 4, 241–251.

MAYHEW, R. W. 1966. A sedimentological investigation of the Marsdenian grits and associated measures in north-east Derbyshire. Unpublished PhD thesis, University of Sheffield.

MILLER, J. and GRAYSON, R. F. 1982. The regional context of Waulsortian facies in northern England. 17–33 in *Symposium on the paleoenvironmental setting and distribution of the Waulsortian Facies.* BOLTON, K., LANE, R. H. and LE MONE, D. V. (editors). (El Paso: El Paso Geological Society and the University of Texas.)

MITCHELL, G. F., PENNY, L. F., SHOTTON, F. W. and WEST, R. G. 1973. A correlation of the Quaternary deposits in the British Isles. *Spec. Rep. Geol. Soc. London*, No. 4.

MITCHELL, G. H. 1954. The Whittington Heath Borehole. *Bull. Geol. Surv. G.B.*, No. 5, 1–60.

— and STUBBLEFIELD, C. J. 1941. The Carboniferous Limestone of Breedon Cloud, Leicestershire, and the associated inliers. *Geol. Mag.*, Vol. 78, 201–219.

MOLYNEUX, W. 1864. Report of the Committee on the Distribution of the organic remains of the North Staffordshire Coal-field. *Rep. Br. Assoc. Adv. Sci.*, 1864 (Bath), 342–344.

MONCKTON, H. W. and HERRIES, R. S. (editors). 1910. *Geology in the field*, Vol. 2. (London: Geologists' Association.)

MONKHOUSE, R. A. 1984. Groundwater yields from boreholes in the Midlands. *Water services*, Vol. 88, No. 1065, 465–467.

— and RICHARDS, H. J. 1984. Groundwater resources of the United Kingdom. Publication of the Commission of the European Communities (Hannover: Th. Schaefer.)

MORGAN, A. V. 1973. The Pleistocene geology of the area north and west of Wolverhampton, Staffordshire, England. *Philos. Trans. R. Soc. London*, (Ser. B), No. 265, 233–297.

— DUTHIE, H. C., MORGAN, A., FRITZ, P. and REARDON, E. J. 1977. The Stafford Project—a multidisciplinary analysis of a late-glacial sequence in the west English Midlands. *Abstr. 10th Inqua. Congress.*

MORGAN, N. 1980. Palaeoecology and sedimentology of Waulsortian reefs, lower Carboniferous. Unpublished PhD thesis, University of Oxford.

MORRIS, P. G. 1967a. The Namurian succession in the area around the Combes Brook, near Leek, north Staffordshire. *Mercian Geol.*, Vol. 2, 15–29.

— 1967b. The Namurian (E_1–E_2) strata between Waterhouses and Cauldon near Leek, North Staffordshire. *Proc. Geol. Assoc.*, Vol. 78, Pt. 2, 335–345.

— 1969. Dinantian and Namurian stratigraphy, east and south-east of Leek, North Staffordshire. *Proc. Geol. Assoc.*, Vol. 80, Pt. 2, 145–175.

— 1970. Carboniferous conodonts in the south-western Pennines. *Geol. Mag.*, Vol. 106, No. 5, 497–499.

MOSTAGHEL, M. A. 1983. Evolution of the South Pennine Orefield: I, Regional distribution of the major non-metallic minerals. *Bull. Peak Dist. Mines Hist. Soc.*, Vol. 8, No. 6, 369–372.

— 1984. Evolution of the South Pennine Orefield; II, Mineral associations. *Bull. Peak Dist. Mines Hist. Soc.*, Vol. 9, No. 2, 101–107.

— 1985. Classification of the South Pennine Orefield. *Mercian Geol.*, Vol. 10, No. 1, 27–38.

MUELLER, G. 1954. The distribution of coloured varieties of fluorites within the thermal zones of Derbyshire mineral deposits. *19th Sess. Int. Geol. Congr., Algiers 1952*, Sect. 13, Fasc. 15, 523–539.

NEILSON, G., MUSSON, R. M. W. and BURTON, P. W. 1984. Macroseismic reports on historical British earthquakes V: Midlands. Global Seismology Unit Report No. 228 (Edinburgh: British Geological Survey.)

PARKINSON, D. 1950. The stratigraphy of the Dovedale area, Derbyshire and Staffordshire. *Q. J. Geol. Soc. London*, Vol. 105, Pt. 2, 265–294.

— and LUDFORD, A. 1964. The Carboniferous Limestone of the Blore-with-Swinscoe district, north-east Staffordshire, with revisions to the stratigraphy of neighbouring areas. *Geol. J.*, Vol. 4, Pt. 1, 167–176.

PARSONS, L. M. 1922. Dolomitization in the Carboniferous Limestone of the Midlands. *Geol. Mag.*, Vol. 59, 51–63 and 104–117.

PATON, R. L. 1974. Capitosaurid labyrinthodonts from the Trias of England. *Palaeontology*, Vol. 17, 253–289.

PEDRICK, P. D. and CHAPMAN, G. J. 1974. A preliminary survey of the Bincliff lead mines, Wetton, Staffs. *Bull. Peak Dist. Mines Hist. Soc.*, Vol. 5, Pt. 5, 258–270.

PIGOTT, C. D. 1962. Soil formation and development on the Carboniferous Limestone of Derbyshire. 1. Parent materials. *J. Ecol.*, Vol. 50, 145–156.

PIPER, D. P. 1982. The conglomerate resources of the Sherwood Sandstone Group of the country east of Stoke-on-Trent, Staffordshire: Description of 1:25 000 resource sheet SJ 94. *Miner. Assess. Rep. Inst. Geol. Sci.*, No. 91.

PITTY, A. F. 1968. The scale and significance of solutional loss from the limestone tract of the southern Pennines. *Proc. Geol. Assoc.*, Vol. 79, 153–178.

PLANT, R. 1881. *History of Cheadle in Staffordshire.* (Leek and London.)

POCOCK, T. I. 1929. The Trent Valley in the Glacial Period. *Z. Gletscherkd*, Vol. 17, 302–318.

PORTER, L. and ROBEY, J. A. 1972. The metalliferous mines of the Weaver Hills, Staffordshire: Part II—the Ribden Mines. *Bull. Peak Dist. Mines Hist. Soc.*, Vol. 5, Pt. 1, 14–30.

— — 1974. A history of the Bincliff lead mines, Wetton. *Bull. Peak Dist. Mines Hist. Soc.*, Vol. 5, Pt. 5, 271–278.

POSNANSKY, M. 1960. The Pleistocene succession in the Middle Trent Basin. *Proc. Geol. Assoc.*, Vol. 71, 285–311.

PRENTICE, J. E. 1951. The Carboniferous Limestone of the Manifold valley region, North Staffordshire. *Q. J. Geol. Soc. London*, Vol. 106, Pt. 2, 171–210.

— 1952. Note on previous paper (Prentice, 1951). *Q. J. Geol. Soc. London*, Vol. 107, Pt. 3, 335.

RAMSBOTTOM, W. H. C. 1969. The Namurian of Britain. *C.R. 6e Congr. Int. Stratigr. Géol. Carbonif., Sheffield 1967*, Vol. 1, 219–232.

— 1977. Major cycles of transgression and regression (mesothems) in the Namurian. *Proc. Yorkshire Geol. Soc.*, Vol. 41, Pt. 3, 261–291.

— CALVER, M. A., EAGAR, R. M. C., HODSON, F., HOLLIDAY, D.W., STUBBLEFIELD, C. J. and WILSON, R. B. 1978. A correlation of the Silesian rocks in the British Isles. *Spec. Rep. Geol. Soc. London*, No. 10.

— and MITCHELL, M. 1980. The recognition and division of the Tournaisian Series in Britain. *J. Geol. Soc. London*, Vol. 137, Pt. 1, 61–63.

RICE, R. J. 1968. The Quaternary Era. 332–353 in *The geology of the East Midlands*. SYLVESTER-BRADLEY, P. C. and FORD, T. D. (editors). (Leicester: Leicester University Press.)

RITTMANN, A. 1962. *Volcanoes and their activity*. (New York: Wiley.)

ROBEY, J. A. and PORTER, L. 1971. The metalliferous mines of the Weaver Hills, Staffordshire. *Bull. Peak Dist. Mines Hist. Soc.*, Vol. 4, Pt. 6, 417–428.

ROGERS, P. J., PIPER, D. P. and CHARSLEY, T. J. 1981. The conglomerate resources of the Sherwood Sandstone Group of the country around Cheadle, Staffordshire. Description of part of 1:25 000 sheet SK 04. *Miner. Assess. Rep. Inst. Geol. Sci.,* No. 57.

SARJEANT, W. A. S. 1974. A history and bibliography of the study of fossil vertebrate footprints in the British Isles. *Palaeogeog., Palaeoclimatol., Palaeoecol.,* Vol. 16, 265–378.

— 1985. The Beasley collection of photographs and drawings of fossil footprints and bones, and of fossil and recent sedimentary structures. *The Geological Curator,* Vol. 4, Pt. 3, 133–163.

SCHOFIELD, K. and ADAMS, A. E. 1985. Stratigraphy and depositional environments of the Woo Dale Limestones Formation (Dinantian), Derbyshire. *Proc. Yorkshire Geol Soc.,* Vol. 45, Pt. 4, 225–233.

— — 1986. Burial dolomitization of the Woo Dale Limestones Formation (Lower Carboniferous), Derbyshire, England. *Sedimentology,* Vol. 33, 207–219.

SCOTT, A. 1927. A marine band in the Shaffalong Coalfield. *Trans. North Staffordshire Field Club,* Vol. 61, 87–88.

— 1927. The origin of the High Peak sand and clay deposits. *Trans. Ceram. Soc.,* Vol. 26, 255–260.

SHACKLETON, J. S. 1962. Cross-strata of the Rough Rock (Millstone Grit Series) in the Pennines. *Liverpool & Manchester Geol. J.,* Vol. 3, Pt. 1, 109–118.

SHOTTON, F. W. and WILCOCKSON, W. H. 1951. Superficial valley folds in an opencast working of the Barnsley coal. *Proc. Yorkshire Geol. Soc.,* Vol. 28, 102–111.

SLACK, R. 1985. Brassington mining 1792–1826. *Bull. Peak Dist. Mines Hist. Soc.,* Vol. 9, No. 3, 186–194.

SLEIGH, J. 1862. *A history of the ancient parish of Leek.* (London: J. Russell Smith; Leek: Robert Nall.)

SMITH, E. G., RHYS, G. H. and EDEN, R. A. 1967. Geology of the country around Chesterfield, Matlock and Mansfield. *Mem. Geol. Surv. G.B.,* Sheet 112.

SMITH, K., SMITH, N. J. P. and HOLLIDAY, D. W. 1985. The deep structure of Derbyshire. *Geol. J.,* Vol. 20, 215–225.

SMYTH, W. 1862. The Iron Ores of Great Britain. Part 4. Iron ores of the Shropshire Coalfield and of north Staffordshire. *Mem. Geol. Surv. G.B.*

STEPHENS, J. V. 1929. Wells and springs of Derbyshire. *Mem. Geol. Surv. G.B.*

STEVENSON, I. P. and MITCHELL, G. H. 1955. Geology of the country between Burton upon Trent, Rugeley and Uttoxeter. *Mem. Geol. Surv. G.B.,* Sheet 140.

— and GAUNT, G. D. 1971. Geology of the country around Chapel en le Frith. *Mem. Geol. Surv. G.B.,* Sheet 99.

STOBBS, J. T. 1905. The marine beds in the Coal Measures of North Staffordshire. *Q. J. Geol. Soc. London,* Vol. 61, 495–527.

— 1920. More erratics found in the coal-seams of the North Staffordshire and Leicestershire coalfields. *Trans. North Staffordshire Field Club,* Vol. 54, 100–101.

— 1922. Further erratics in and near coal-seams of North Staffordshire and India. *Trans. North Staffordshire Field Club,* Vol. 56, 97–99.

STRANK, A. R. E. 1985. The Dinantian biostratigraphy of a deep borehole near Eyam, Derbyshire. *Geol. J.,* Vol. 20, No. 3, 227–237.

— 1986. Foraminiferal biostratigraphy of the Woo Dale Borehole and the age of the Dinantian–Basement unconformity. *J. Micropalaeontol.,* Vol. 5, Pt. 1, 1–4.

STRAW, A. 1963. The Quaternary evolution of the lower and middle Trent. *East Midland Geographer,* Vol. 3, 171–189.

SWINNERTON, H. H. 1935. The denudation of the east Midlands. *Rep. Br. Assoc. Adv. Sci.,* Sect. C, 375.

SYLVESTER-BRADLEY, P. C. and FORD, T. D. (editors). 1968. *The geology of the East Midlands.* (Bath: Leicester University Press.)

TAYLOR, K. and RUSHTON, A. W. A. 1971. The pre-Westphalian geology of the Warwickshire Coalfield. *Bull. Geol. Surv. G.B.,* No. 35.

TAYLOR, P. W. 1917. Observations on the local distribution of glacial boulders. *Trans. North Staffordshire Field Club,* Vol. 51, 71–75.

TAZIEFF, H. 1974. *The making of the earth.* (Farnborough: D. C. Heath.)

THACH, T. K. 1964. Sedimentology of Lower Carboniferous (Viséan) limestones in north Staffordshire and south-west Derbyshire. Unpublished PhD thesis, University of Reading.

THOMAS, H. D. and FORD, T. D. 1963. A new tabulate coral from the Viséan of Derbyshire. *Proc. Yorkshire Geol. Soc.,* Vol. 34, Pt. 1, 45–50.

TREWIN, N. H. 1968. Potassium bentonites in the Namurian of Staffordshire and Derbyshire. *Proc. Yorkshire Geol. Soc.,* Vol. 37, Pt. 1, 73–91.

— and HOLDSWORTH, B. K. 1972. Further K-bentonites from the Namurian of Staffordshire. *Proc. Yorkshire Geol. Soc.,* Vol. 39, Pt. 1, 87–89.

— — 1973. Sedimentation in the lower Namurian rocks of the north Staffordshire basin. *Proc. Yorkshire Geol. Soc.,* Vol. 39, Pt. 3, 371–408.

TURBITT, T. (editor). 1984. Catalogue of British earthquakes recorded by the BGS seismograph network 1979, 1980, 1981. Global Seismology Unit Report No. 210. (Edinburgh: British Geological Survey.)

— 1985. Catalogue of British earthquakes recorded by the BGS seismograph network 1982, 1983, 1984. Global Seismology Unit Report No. 260. (Edinburgh: British Geological Survey.)

VARKER, W. J. and SEVASTOPULO, G. D. 1985. Dinantian conodonts. 167–189 in *A stratigraphical index of British conodonts.* AUSTIN, R. L. and HIGGINS, A. C. (editors). (Chichester: Ellis Horwood for British Micropalaeontological Society.)

VAUGHAN, A. 1905. The palaeontological sequence in the Carboniferous Limestone of the Bristol area. *Q. J. Geol. Soc. London,* Vol. 61, Pt. 2, 181–305.

WALKDEN, G. M. 1972. The mineralogy and origin of interbedded clay wayboards in the Carboniferous Limestone of the Derbyshire Dome. *Geol. J.,* Vol. 8, Pt. 1, 143–159.

WALSH, P. T., BOULTER, M. C., IJTABA, M. and URBANI, D. M. 1972. The preservation of the Neogene Brassington Formation of the southern Pennines and its bearing on the evolution of upland Britain. *J. Geol. Soc. London,* Vol. 128, Pt. 6, 519–559.

— COLLINS, P. I., IJTABA, M., NEWTON, J. P., SCOTT, N. H., and TURNER, P. R. 1980. Palaeocurrent directions and their bearing on the origin of the Brassington Formation (Miocene–Pliocene) of the southern Pennines, Derbyshire, England. *Mercian Geol.,* Vol. 8, No. 1, 47–62.

WARD, J. 1890. The geological features of the North Staffordshire Coal-fields. *Trans. North Staffordshire Inst. Min. Mech. Engrs.,* Vol. 10, Pt. 5, 189.

— 1900. On the occurrence of labyrinthodont remains in the Keuper Sandstone of Stanton. *Trans. North Staffordshire Field Club,* Vol. 34, 102–112.

— 1902. On a fragment of the tusk of a mammoth from Fenton, with notes on previous discoveries of mammalian remains in north Staffordshire. *Ann. Rep. and Trans. North Staffordshire Field Club*, Vol. 36, 90–93.

— 1906. Contributions to the geology and palaeontology of north Staffordshire. No. 6. Palaeontology of the Cheadle Coalfield. *Trans. North Staffordshire Field Club*, Vol. 40, 102–137.

— and STOBBS, J. T. 1906. A newly-discovered fish-bed in the Cheadle Coalfield; with notes on the distribution of fossil fishes in that district. *Trans. North Staffordshire Field Club*, Vol. 40, 87–101.

WARREN, P. T., PRICE, D., NUTT, M. J. C. and SMITH, E. G. 1984. Geology of the country around Rhyl and Denbigh. *Mem. Br. Geol. Surv.*, Sheets 95 and 107.

WARRINGTON, G. 1970. The stratigraphy and palaeontology of the 'Keuper' Series of the central Midlands of England. *Q. J. Geol. Soc. London*, Vol. 126, 183–223.

— AUDLEY-CHARLES, M. G., ELLIOTT, R. E., EVANS, W. B., IVIMEY-COOK, H. C., KENT, P. E., ROBINSON, P. L., SHOTTON, F. W. and TAYLOR, F. M. 1980. A correlation of the Triassic rocks in the British Isles. *Spec. Rep. Geol. Soc. London*, No. 13.

WARWICK, G. T. 1953. Essays in geomorphology and speleology. Essay A. The geomorphology of the Dove–Manifold region. Unpublished thesis, University of Birmingham.

— 1964. Dry valleys of the southern Pennines, England. *Erdkunde*, Vol. 18, 116–123.

WEDD, C. B. and DRABBLE, G. C. 1908. The fluorspar deposits of Derbyshire. *Trans. Inst. Min. Eng.*, Vol. 35, 501–535.

WELSH, A. and OWENS, B. 1983. Early Dinantian miospore assemblages from the Caldon Low Borehole, Staffordshire, England. *Pollen Spores*, Vol. 25, No. 2, 253–264.

WHITCOMBE, D. N. and MAGUIRE, P. K. H. 1980. An analysis of the velocity structure of the Precambrian rocks of Charnwood Forest. *Geophys. J. R. Astron. Soc.*, Vol. 63, 405–416.

— — 1981. Seismic refraction evidence for a basement ridge between the Derbyshire Dome and the W of Charnwood Forest. *J. Geol. Soc. London*, Vol. 138, Pt. 6, 653–659.

WILCOX, R. E., HARDING, T. P. and SEELY, D. R. 1973. Basic wrench tectonics. *Bull. Am. Assoc. Petrol. Geol.*, Vol. 57, No. 1, 74–96.

WILLS, L. J. 1937. The Pleistocene history of the west Midlands. *Rep. Br. Assoc. Adv. Sci.*, 71–94.

— 1970. The Triassic succession in the central Midlands in its regional setting. *Q. J. Geol. Soc. London*, Vol. 126, 225–283.

— 1978. A palaeogeological map of the Lower Palaeozoic floor. *Mem. Geol. Soc. London*, No. 8.

WILSON, G. H. 1937. Cave work in the Manifold Valley. *Caves & Caving*, Vol. 1, 61–69.

WILSON, P. 1979. Surface features of quartz sand grains from the Brassington Formation. *Mercian Geol.*, Vol. 7, 19–30.

WOLFENDEN, E. B. 1958. Paleoecology of the Carboniferous reef complex and shelf limestones in north-west Derbyshire, England. *Bull. Geol. Soc. Am.*, Vol. 69, 871–898.

YORKE, C. 1961. *The Pocket Deposits of Derbyshire: a general survey* (2nd edition). (Birkenhead: privately published.)

APPENDIX 1

Six-inch maps

Geological six-inch maps included wholly or in part in 1:50 000 Sheet 124 (Ashbourne) are listed below, together with the initials of the surveyors and dates of the survey; in the case of marginal sheets all surveyors are listed. The surveyors were: N. Aitkenhead, T. J. Charsley, J. I. Chisholm, W. B. Evans, G. H. Mitchell, D. P. Piper, I. P. Stevenson, P. J. Strange, A. J. Wadge and A. A. Wilson.

Copies of the fair drawn maps have been deposited in the BGS libraries at Keyworth and Edinburgh for public reference and may also be inspected in the London Information Office in the Geological Museum, South Kensington, London. Copies may be purchased directly from BGS either as black and white dyeline sheets or, where printed stocks are held, as published coloured sheets. The latter are indicated below with an asterisk.

	SJ 93 NE	Blithe Valley	IPS, TJC, AJW	1947, 1961, 1977
*	SJ 94 NE	Consall	AAW, JIC, DPP	1961–62, 1974–80
	SJ 94 SE	Dilhorne	WBE, TJC, JIC, DPP	1963, 1976–79
*	SJ 95 SE	Cheddleton	AAW, JIC	1960, 1973–78
	SK 03 NW	Checkley	TJC	1977
	SK 03 NE	Hollington	PJS	1974
*	SK 04 NW	Kingsley, Froghall and Ipstones	JIC, PJS	1974–79
	SK 04 NE	Cauldon and Weaver Hills	JIC	1975–77
	SK 04SW	Cheadle and Oakamoor	JIC, TJC, PJS	1974–79
	SK 04 SE	Alton	PJS, JIC	1973, 1975
	SK 05 SW	Combes valley and Ipstones Edge	JIC	1973–74
	SK 05 SE	Grindon, Waterhouses and Hamps valley	NA	1977
	SK 13 NW	Rocester	GHM, TJC	1947, 1974
	SK 13 NE	Great Cubley and Boylestone	GHM, TJC	1947, 1974
	SK 14 NW	Stanton and Blore with Swinscoe	NA, TJC	1976
	SK 14 NE	Ashbourne and Mayfield	TJC	1975
	SK 14 SW	Ellastone, Norbury and Roston	PJS	1973
	SK 14 SE	Clifton, Wyaston and Darley Moor	TJC	1973
	SK 15 SW	Throwley, Ilam and Dovedale	NA	1973
	SK 15 SE	Thorpe, Tissington and Parwich	IPS	1973–74
	SK 23 NW	Longford	GHM, TJC	1947, 1974–75
	SK 24 NW	Atlow and Hulland	TJC	1975–76
	SK 24 SW	Rodsley and Shirley	TJC	1973–78
	SK 25 SW	Kniveton, Bradbourne, Brassington and Carsington	IPS, NA	1974–75

APPENDIX 2

List of boreholes and measured sections

This list includes the permanent record number, location, total depth or thickness, and stratigraphical range of the selected boreholes and measured sections that are referred to in this memoir. Copies of these records may be obtained from the British Geological Survey, Keyworth, Nottingham NG12 5GG, at a fixed tariff. Other measured sections and non-confidential borehole data are given either on the six-inch geological maps listed on p.142 or are held on open file in the Survey's archives.

SJ 93 NE/1   Cresswell No. 1 [9736 3948]
Borehole, 356.62 m Sherwood Sandstone Group and Denstone Formation

SJ 93 NE/9   Stoke-Derby Motorway [9631 3837]
Borehole, (No. B18), 15.00 m Mercia Mudstone Group and drift

SJ 93 NE/12   Stoke-Derby Motorway [9641 3845]
Borehole, (No. B20), 11.00 m Mercia Mudstone Group and drift

SJ 93 NE/26   Stoke-Derby Motorway [9800 3761]
Borehole, (No. 42), 5.45 m Drift

SJ 93 NE/27   Stoke-Derby Motorway [9828 3755]
Borehole, (No. B22), 10.70 m Mercia Mudstone Group and drift

SJ 93 NE/28   Stoke-Derby Motorway [9834 3752]
Borehole, (No. 43), 6.20 m Mercia Mudstone Group and drift

SJ 93 NE/29   Stoke-Derby Motorway [9862 3749]
Borehole, (No. 44), 6.05 m Mercia Mudstone Group and drift

SJ 93 NE/30   Stoke-Derby Motorway [9884 3745]
Borehole, (No. 45), 8.00 m Mercia Mudstone Group

SJ 93 NE/31   Stoke-Derby Motorway [9913 3740]
Borehole, (No. 46), 10.00 m Mercia Mudstone Group and drift

SJ 93 NE/33   Stoke-Derby Motorway [9953 3740]
Borehole, (No. B24C), 14.60 m Mercia Mudstone Group and drift

SJ 93 NE/34   Stoke-Derby Motorway [9967 3741]
Borehole (No. B251), 8.20 m Mercia Mudstone Group and drift

SJ 94 NE/18   Out Wood, Consall [9764 4821 to 9806 4780]
Section, 163.95 m Namurian, *G. cumbriense* Band, to Westphalian A, Listeri Marine Band

SJ 94 NE/19   Consall Valley [around 9954 4804]
Sections, 38.16 m Westphalian A

SJ 94 NE/20   Consall Valley [9922 4786 to 9879 4759]
Sections, 144.95 m Westphalian A

SJ 94 NE/22   Hazlewall Colliery [9934 4615]
Shaft (downcast), 187.45 m Westphalian A

SJ 94 SE/1   Foxfield [9771 4316]
Borehole (No. 1), 135.64 m Westphalian A and B and Trias

SJ 94 SE/7   Foxfield Colliery [9764 4465]
Shaft, 229.29 m Westphalian A

SJ 94 SE/8   Foxfield [9988 4322]
Borehole (No. 8), 92.35 m Westphalian A and B and Trias

SJ 94 SE/16   Dilhorne [9848 4390]
Borehole (No. 1), 46.94 m Westphalian A

SJ 94 SE/17A   Delphhouse Colliery [985 426?]
Shaft, 85.13 m Westphalian B

SJ 94 SE/18 Draycott [9885 4122]
Shaft, 82.24 m Sherwood Sandstone Group

SJ 94 SE/20   New Haden Colliery [9925 4218]
Shaft (No. 8), 317.34 m Westphalian A and B

SJ 94 SE/21   Cheadle Park Colliery [9998 4409]
Shaft, 164.59 m Westphalian A

SJ 94 SE/22   Parkhall Colliery [9932 4442]
Shaft and borehole from shaft bottom, 351.35 m Westphalian A

SJ 94 SE/23   Old Brassworks, Cheadle [9959 4366]
Borehole, 149.66 m Westphalian A and B

SJ 95 NE/19   Great Longsdon Farm, Leek [9592 5595 to 9600 5606]
Section, 65.81 m Roaches Grit and Brockholes Sandstones

SJ 95 SE/2   Shaffalong [961 518 approx.]
Borehole, 284.7 m Namurian and Westphalian A

SJ 95 SE/26   Cheddleton Paper Mills [9771 5252]
Borehole (No. 1, 1923), 176.78 m Namurian, including *N. stellarum* Band, ?Triassic sandstone, and drift

SJ 95 SE/27   Cheddleton Paper Mills [9819 5214]
Borehole (No. 2, 1924), 67.97 m Namurian, including an *I. subglobosum* Band, and drift

SJ 95 SE/35   Cheddleton Paper Mills [9849 5089]
Borehole (No. 16, 1941), 122.53 m Namurian, including R_{1c} faunal bands, and drift

SJ 95 SE/58   Deep Hayes Reservoir, Cheddleton [9614 5332]
Borehole (No. 15), 25.58 m Rough Rock and drift

SJ 95 SE/62   Mosslee Mill, Basford Green [9971 5100]
Section, road cutting, 29.62 m Chatsworth Grit and Hawksmoor Formation

SJ 95 SE/63   Wall Grange [9754 5430]
Borehole, 100.00 m, ?Namurian, Hawksmoor Formation and drift

SJ 95 SE/64   Wall Grange [9754 5404]
Borehole, 100.00 m, ?Namurian, Hawksmoor Formation and drift

SK 03 NW/1   Fole Creamery [0453 3722]
Borehole, 21.95 m Mercia Mudstone Group and drift

SK 03 NW/2   Heath House, Tean [0304 3959]
Borehole, 69.65 m Hawksmoor Formation and drift

SK 03 NW/4   Fole Farm [0437 3677]
Borehole, 36.58 m Mercia Mudstone Group and drift

SK 03 NW/13   Stoke-Derby motorway [0215 3730]
Borehole (No. B27C), 14.10 m Mercia Mudstone Group and drift

SK 03 NE/1   Lawn Farm [0681 3685]
Borehole, 20.65 m Mercia Mudstone Group and drift

SK 03 NE/2   Creighton Park [0710 3687]
Borehole, 29.57 m Mercia Mudstone Group and drift

SK 03 NE/17   Greatgate No. 1 [0523 3994]
Borehole, 132.44 m ?Ipstones Edge Sandstones, Hawksmoor Formation including Freehay and Lodgedale Members

SK 04 NW/1   Key Wood [0391 4536]
Borehole, 204.83 m Namurian and Westphalian A

SK 04 NW/5   Ruelow Wood, Froghall [0205 4752]
Borehole (No. 3, 1963), 91.4 m Chatsworth Grit, Rough Rock, Subcrenatum Marine Band and drift

SK 04 NW/16   Foxt No. 9 [0372 4919]
Borehole, Chatsworth Grit

SK 04 NW/19   Crowtrees, Whiston [0498 4559]
Borehole (No. 8), 41.3 m Rough Rock and Subcrenatum Marine Band

SK 04 NW/21   Cloughhead, Froghall [0252 4909?]
Engine pit, 74.68 m Westphalian A

SK 04 NW/22   Booth's Wood, Ipstones [008 484 approx.]
Section, c.66 m Westphalian A

SK 04 NW/23   Ross Banks, Whiston Eaves [032 460?]
Shaft, 36.75 m Westphalian A

SK 04 NW/28   Near Glenwood House [0033 4887]
Section in ravine, 32.23 m Westphalian A

SK 04 NW/29   Consall New Lock [0042 4836]
Section by river, 39.74 m Namurian and Westphalian A

SK 04 NW/31   Foxt [026 477]
Shaft, 29.51 m Westphalian A
SK 04 NW/33   Gilmoor [023 480]
Mine section, 44.50 m Westphalian A
SK 04 NW/49   Shirley Hollow, Foxt [0379 4809 to 0439 4874]
Section, 32.06 m Roaches Grit, *R. superbilingue* and *D. sigma* bands
SK 04 NE/1   Ramshorn [0700 4558]
Borehole (1962), 87.27 m Ipstones Edge Sandstones, R_{2b} faunal bands and Chatsworth Grit
SK 04 NE/2B   Cauldon Low Pumping Station [0583 4800]
Borehole (No. 2, 1943), 76.2 m Ipstones Edge Sandstones and Roaches Grit
SK 04 NE/7   Wardlow [0871 4752]
Borehole, 54.0 m Pocket Deposits
SK 04 NE/10   Rue Hill [0888 4778]
Borehole, 61.01 m Milldale Limestones
SK 04 NE/20   Cauldon Low [0828 4983]
Borehole, 30.48 m Mixon Limestone-Shales and drift
SK 04 NE/31   Cauldon Shale Quarry [0812 4999 to 0834 5006]
Section, 104.30 m Namurian mudstones (E_1)
SK 04 NE/32   Ribden sand and clay pit [077 473]
Borehole, 30.48 m Pocket Deposits
SK 04 NE/33   Moorend Farm [0710 4862]
Borehole, 16.40 m Drift
SK 04 NE/34   Moorend Farm [0714 4863]
Borehole, 16.44 m Drift
SK 04 NE/35   Moorend Farm [0715 4880]
Borehole, 11.94 m Drift
SK 04 NE/36   Caldon Low [0804 4822]
Borehole, 535.37 m Redhouse Sandstones, Rue Hill Dolomites and Milldale Limestones
SK 04 NE/37   Kevin Quarry, Ramshorn [0837 4612 to 0877 4616]
Section, 131.1 m Kevin Limestones
SK 04 SW/1b   Teanford, Cheadle [0060 4066]
Borehole, 93.0 m Westphalian, Sherwood Sandstone Group and drift
SK 04 SW/11   Birches Colliery, Cheadle [008 424]
Shaft, 133.50 m Westphalian A
SK 04 SW/42   Cheadle Waterworks [0069 4350]
Well and Borehole, 73.46 m, Hawksmoor Formation including Freehay Member
SK 04 SE/4   Greatgate No. 3 [0535 4001]
Borehole, 153.92 m Hawksmoor Formation including Freehay and Lodgedale members, Hollington Formation and drift
SK 04 SE/11   Crumpwood No. 1 [0909 4271]
Borehole, 121.92 m Hawksmoor Formation and drift
SK 04 SE/15   Wootton No. 1 [0995 4394]
Borehole, 45.72 m Hawksmoor Formation and Hollington Formation
SK 04 SE/16   Windyharbour [0854 4100]
Borehole, 123.50 m Hollington Formation and Mercia Mudstone Group including Denstone Formation
SK 05 NE/10   Bullclough [0603 5502 to 0595 5500]
Section, 15.50 m, Mixon Limstone-Shales and Namurian mudstones (E_{1a})
SK 05 SW/6   Abovechurch, Ipstones [0130 5030]
Borehole, 91.97 m Chatsworth Grit and mudstones
SK 05 SW/8   Ipstones Edge [0258 5109]
Borehole (1980), 189.33 m Hurdlow and Cheddleton sandstones with interbedded mudstones
SK 05 SE/8   Winkhill [0589 5184]
Borehole (No. W1, 1969), 35.20 m Hurdlow Sandstones and interbedded mudstones
SK 05 SE/9   Winkhill [0601 5178]
Borehole (No. W2, 1969), 31.85 m Hurdlow Sandstones and interbedded mudstones

SK 05 SE/10   Winkhill [0612 5181]
Borehole (No. W3, 1969), 35.36 m Hurdlow Sandstones and interbedded mudstones
SK 05 SE/11   Winkhill [0619 5165]
Borehole (No. W4, 1969), 22.86 m Namurian mudstones, (E_{2b})
SK 05 SE/13   Winkhill [0635 5152]
Borehole (No. W6, 1969), 34.14 m Hurdlow Sandstones and interbedded mudstones
SK 05 SE/14   Winkhill [0627 5180]
Borehole (No. W7, 1969), 22.94 m Hurdlow Sandstones and interbedded mudstones
SK 05 SE/15   Winkhill [0607 5145]
Borehole (No. W8, 1969), 33.83 m Hurdlow Sandstones and interbedded mudstones
SK 05 SE/19   Grindon [0933 5410]
Borehole, 124.00 m Ecton Limestones
SK 05 SE/20   Waterfall [0826 5132]
Borehole, 100.00 m Hopedale Limestones and Mixon Limestone-Shales
SK 05 SE/21   Waterhouses [0861 5033]
Borehole, 51.93 m, Hopedale Limestones and made ground
SK 05 SE/22   River Hamps [0660 5370 to 0663 5370]
Section, 17.56 m Mixon Limestone-Shales and Namurian mudstones (E_{1a})
SK 05 SE/23   Back o' th'Brook [0771 5219]
Section, 1.20 m Mixon Limestones-Shales and Namurian mudstones (E_{1a})
SK 05 SE/24   River Hamps, School House [0831 5016 to 0821 5017]
Section, 50.63 m Namurian mudstones ($E_{1a} - E_{1b}$)
SK 05 SE/25   Pethills Gully, Winkhill [0594 5213 to 0587 5217]
Section, 16.20 m Hurdlow Sandstones
SK 05 SE/26   River Hamps near Ironpits [0662 5204]
Section, 9.22 m Namurian mudstones with *C. cowlingense* Band
SK 05 SE/27   River Hamps near Crowtrees [0737 5025]
Section, 2.00 m Namurian mudstones with *E. bisulcatum* Band
SK 05 SE/28   River Hamps near Winkhill [0687 5041]
Section, 24.96 m Namurian mudstones with *Ct. edalensis* Band
SK 05 SE/29   Brownend Quarry, Waterhouses [0910 5019 to 0897 5026]
Section, 95.11 m Milldale Limestones and Hopedale Limestones
SK 05 SE/30   Lee House Quarries, Waterhouses, [0868 5034 to 0851 5029]
Section, 75.03 m Hopedale Limestones
SK 05 SE/31   Field House Quarry, Waterhouses [0863 5084]
Section, 6.32 m Hopedale Limestones
SK 05 SE/32   Ladyside, Grindon [0955 5498 to 0943 5486]
Section, 110.82 m Milldale Limestones and Ecton Limestones
SK 05 SE/33   Calton [0971 5044]
Section, 12.39 m Hopedale Limestones
SK 05 SE/34   River Manifold, Weags Bridge [1015 5406 to 1000 5410]
Section, 76.0 m Milldale Limestones
SK 13 NW/2   Upwoods Farm [1162 3595]
Borehole, 59.13 m Mercia Mudstone Group and drift
SK 13 NE/2   Cubley Waterworks [1722 3808]
Borehole, 91.74 m Sherwood Sandstone Group, Mercia Mudstone Group including Denstone Formation, and drift
SK 13 NE/3   Cubley Trial Coal Boring [1526 3898]
Borehole, 102.57 m Sherwood Sandstone Group, Mercia Mudstone Group and drift
SK 14 NW/5   Caltonmoor House [1142 4880]
Borehole, 100.00 m Milldale Limestones and Ecton Limestones
SK 14 NW/6   Blore [1359 4944]
Borehole, 100.00 m Ecton Limestones
SK 14 NW/7   Stream near Coppice Barn [1280 4751 to 1274 4753]
Section, 33.50 m Widmerpool Formation

SK 14 NW/8   Quarry near Huddale Farm [0999 4892 to 1006 4897]
Section, 14.8 m Milldale Limestones
SK 14 NE/4   Yerley Farm [1519 4870]
Borehole, 45.70 m Widmerpool Formation and drift
SK 14 NE/7   Ashbourne Hospital [1739 4647]
Well, 35.05 m ?Carboniferous, Sherwood Sandstone Group and drift
SK 14 NE/18   Sturston [1998 4637]
Borehole, 39.19 m Carboniferous, Sherwood Sandstone Group and drift
SK 14 SE/3   Rodsley No. 1 [1973 4135]
Borehole, 87.78 m Sherwood Sandstone Group, Denstone Formation and drift
SK 14 SE/8   Rodsley [1964 4039]
Borehole, 98.40 m Sherwood Sandstone Group, Mercia Mudstone Group including Denstone Formation, and drift
SK 14 SE/9   Darley Moor [1680 4126]
Borehole, 115.76 m Sherwood Sandstone Group, Mercia Mudstone Group including Denstone Formation, and drift
SK 15 SW/7   Throwley Hall [1113 5244]
Borehole, 100.00 m Hopedale Limestones and Widmerpool Formation
SK 15 SW/8   Slade House [1062 5122]
Borehole, 100.00 m Milldale Limestones
SK 15 SW/9   Stanshope [1255 5374]
Borehole, 100.00 m Milldale Limestones and Hopedale Limestones
SK 15 SE/7   Tithe Barn, Parwich [1785 5458]
Borehole, 60.45 m Bee Low Limestones (apron reef) and Widmerpool Formation
SK 15 SE/8   Rusheycliff Barn, Tissington [1736 5318]
Borehole, 100.06 m Hopedale Limestones including Tissington Volcanic Member
SK 15 SE/9   Hollington Barn, Sharplow [1547 5258]
Borehole, 100.00 m Milldale Limestones
SK 15 SE/10   Pike House [1624 5122]
Borehole, 100.01 m Hopedale Limestones and Widmerpool Formation
SK 15 SE/12   Lees Farm [1818 5016]
Borehole, 251.49 m Widmerpool Formation including Tissington Volcanic Member, Namurian (E_1) mudstones and drift

SK 15 SE/14   Tissington [1901 5189]
Borehole (No. 2), 42.80 m Widmerpool Formation including Tissington Volcanic Member
SK 15 SE/16   Pike House Quarry [1621 5127]
Section, 20.25 m Hopedale Limestones
SK 15 SE/17   Standlow Farm, Newton Grange [1606 5386 to 1611 5384]
Section, 16.30 m Hopedale Limestones
SK 15 SE/18   Railway cutting, Newton Grange [1687 5373 to 1676 5372]
Section, 31.50 m Hopedale Limestones
SK 15 SE/19   Quarry near Moor Barn [1508 5271]
Section, 6.15 m Milldale Limestones
SK 15 SE/20   Parwich [1860 5434]
Section, 20.3 m Bee Low Limestones including apron-reef, and Widmerpool Formation
SK 15 SE/21   Quarry, Moat Low [1570 5432]
Section, 7.18 m Hopedale Limestones
SK 23 NW/2   Butt House [2426 3717]
Borehole, 123.75 m ? Carboniferous, Sherwood Sandstone Group and Mercia Mudstone Group
SK 23 NE/2   Trusley [2548 3588]
Borehole, 154.59 m Widmerpool Formation and Mercia Mudstone Group
SK 24 NW/8   Carsington Reservoir Site [2470 4986]
Borehole (No. R11, 1972), 30.00 m Namurian (E_{2c}–H_{1a})
SK 24 NW/19   Hulland [2465 4619]
Section, 5.15 m Namurian (?E_{2a})
SK 24 SW/5   Yeldersley Hall [2087 4410]
Borehole, 36.83 m Carboniferous, Sherwood Sandstone Group including Denstone Formation, and drift
SK 24 SW/7   Yeldersley [2254 4420]
Borehole (No. 1), 67.06 m Sherwood Sandstone Group, Denstone Formation and drift
SK 24 SW/9   Shirley Common [2206 4361]
Borehole, 61.18 m Sherwood Sandstone Group, Mercia Mudstone Group including Denstone Formation, and drift
SK 24 SE/4   North Farm [2561 4332]
Borehole, 26.82 m ?Carboniferous, Sherwood Sandstone Group, Denstone Formation and drift

APPENDIX 3

List of petrographical samples

E numbers refer to the Sliced Rock Collection of the British Geological Survey. Each number is followed by locality details; in the case of records in the Survey's borehole archives, the localities are indicated by borehole reference numbers (*see* Appendix 2).

E 49339   Stream near Breck Farm [2061 4938]. Lava in Tissington Volcanic Member

E 49340   Stream near Breck Farm [2059 4938]. Lava in Tissington Volcanic Member

E 51329   Old quarry near Lightoaks House [0470 4461]. Woodhead Hill Rock

E 51331   [SJ 95 SE/58]; borehole No. 15, depth 5.90 m. Rough Rock

E 51332   [SJ 95 SE/58]; borehole No. 15, depth 25.40 m. Rough Rock

E 51333   River Churnet, Consall New Lock [0043 4837]. Rough Rock

E 51334   Old quarry, Wetley Rocks [9667 4978]. Rough Rock

E 51335   Moneystone Quarry [0488 4647]. Rough Rock

E 51337   Old quarry, Blakeley Lane [9698 4713]. Chatsworth Grit

E 51338   Shirley Hollow [0381 4818]. Roaches Grit

E 51339   Ditch near Cotton [0657 4686]. Roaches Grit

E 51344   Old quarry near Crumwithies [0283 5102]. Kniveden Sandstones

E 51345   Sharpcliffe Rocks [0176 5184]. Cheddleton Sandstones

E 51346   Sharpcliffe Rocks [0176 5184]. Cheddleton Sandstones

E 51347   Near Upper Cadlow Farm [0425 5028]. Ipstones Edge Sandstones

E 51348   Near Crumwithies [0360 5027]. Ipstones Edge Sandstones

E 51349   Old quarry near Crab Tree Farm [0059 5116]. Brockholes Sandstones

E 51350   Near Cheddleton Railway Station [9833 5235]. Cheddleton Sandstones

E 51351   Stream near Cheddleton Railway Station [9846 5239]. Cheddleton Sandstones

E 51352   Near Sharpcliffe Hall [0043 5205]. Kniveden Sandstones

E 51353   Stream near Knowlbank Farm [9758 4974]. Brockholes Sandstones

E 51354   Stream near Cotton [0612 4609]. Ipstones Edge Sandstones

E 51355   Stream near Heywood Grange [9635 4559]. Protoquartzitic sandstone

E 51356   Stream near Heywood Grange [9626 4555]. Protoquartzitic sandstone

E 51357   Cutting near Cottonplain [0631 4801]. Ipstones Edge Sandstones

E 51358   Cutting near Cottonplain [0631 4801]. Ipstones Edge Sandstones

E 51359   Cutting near Longshaw Farm [0146 5435]. ?Cheddleton Sandstones

E 51360   Old quarry near Longshaw Farm [0104 5453]. ?Cheddleton Sandstones

E 51361   Old quarry near Bottomlane Farm [0266 5224]. ?Hurdlow Sandstones

E 51363   Near Garstones Farm [0298 5435]. Hurdlow Sandstones

E 51364   Stream near Apesford [0222 5355]. Hurdlow Sandstones

E 51366   Old quarry near Garstones Farm [0383 5414]. Minn Sandstones

E 51367   Sinkhole near Cottonplain [0707 4797]. Sandstone band in mudstone: early Namurian

E 51368   Old quarry near Parkhall Farm [9965 4372]. Huntley Formation

E 51369   Cutting near Scarletlake [0036 4158]. Huntley Formation

E 51370   Wardlow Quarry [0836 4755]. Neptunean dyke of sandstone in limestone

E 51371   Old quarry near Upper Park Farm [0942 4558]. Hollington Formation

E 51475   Brockholes Wood [0115 5130]. Brockholes Sandstones

E 51623   Garston Rocks [0507 4756]. Chatsworth Grit

E 51624   Old quarry near Froghall [0204 4832]. Woodhead Hill Rock

E 51625   Old quarry by Deep Hayes Reservoir [9591 5315]. Woodhead Hill Rock

E 51626   Kingsley Banks [0160 4731]. Kingsley Sandstone

E 51627   Ravine near Glenwood House [0037 4890]. Sandstone below Crabtree Coal

E 52427   Ravine near Westwood Hall, Leek [9594 5600]. Brockholes Sandstones

APPENDIX 4

Geological Survey photographs

One hundred and twenty photographs illustrating the geology of the Ashbourne district are deposited for reference in the headquarters library of the British Geological Survey, Keyworth, Nottingham NG12 5GG, the library at the BGS, Murchison House, West Mains Road, Edinburgh EH9 3LA, and in the BGS Information Office at the Geological Museum, Exhibition Road, London SW7 2DE. The majority of these belong to the L Series and were taken between 1976 and 1980 during and following the resurvey. The photographs depict details of lithostratigraphic units, geological features and also include general views and scenery. A list of titles can be supplied on request. The photographs may be supplied as black and white or colour prints and 2 × 2 colour transparencies at a fixed tariff.

FOSSIL INDEX

Page numbers in italics refer to figures, tables and plates. No distinction is made here between a positively determined fossil genus or species and examples doubtfully referred to them (i.e. with the qualifications aff., cf. or ?)

Acaciapora bradbournensis Dighton, Thomas and Ford 31
Acanthoplecta mesoloba (Phillips) 10, 12, 20, 22, 28
Actinopteria regularis (R Etheridge) 47
A. sp. 49
algae 7, 10, *11*, 14, 16, 19, 20, *22, 23*, 24, 25, 26
Alitaria panderi (Muir-Wood and Cooper) 9, 12
Ammodiscus sp. 62
ammonoid fragments 33
Amplexizaphrentis sp. 21
Amplexus sp. 28
Anthracoceratites vanderbeckei (Ludwig) 70
A. sp. 60, 70
Anthracosia aquilina (J de C Sowerby) 70
A. beaniana King 72
A. lateralis (Brown) 70, 72
A. ovum Trueman and Weir 70, 71
A. phrygiana (Wright) 71, 72
A. regularis (Trueman) 70
A. subrecta Trueman and Weir 71
A. sp. 70
Anthracosphaerium affine (Davies and Trueman) 71
A. turgidum (Brown) 71
Antiquatonia insculpta (Muir-Wood) 29
archaediscids 12, 29
Archaediscus angulatus Sosnina 17
A. reditus Conil and Lys 12
A. stilus Grozdilova and Lebedeva 12
A. spp. 12, 26, 30
Arenicolites carbonarius (Binney) 64
Aulina sp. 14
Avonia davidsoni (Jarosz) 12
A. youngiana (Davidson) 12, 28
Axophyllum vaughani (Salée) 9, 14, 31

Baituganella sp. 20
Beyrichoceras vesiculiferum (de Koninck) 12, 34
B. sp. 34
Bilinguites bilinguis see *Reticuloceras bilingue*
B. eometabilinguis see *R. eometabilingue*
B. gracilis see *R. gracile*
B. superbilinguis see *R. superbilingue*
bivalves 25, 26, 31, 33, 34, 39, 49, 50, 51, 60
Biorbis duplex Strank *23*
Bollandia persephone (G & R Hahn) 10, *23*
Bollandoceras hodderense (Bisat) 10

B. micronotum (Phillips) 14
B. sp. 30
bones/birds/mammals/remains *113*, 114
  amphibians *113*
  bear *113*, 114
  bison *113*, 114
  bovids *113*
  deer *113*, 114
  elephant 114
  fox *113*, 114
  hippopotamus *113*, 114
  horse *113*
  hyaena *113*
  lemming *113*
  lion *113*
  mammoth 114
  pig *113*
  rhinoceros *113*, 114
  rodents *113*
  watervole *113*
  wolf *113*
brachiopods/debris 7, 9, 10, 12, 14, 15, 16, 18, 20, 21, *22, 23*, 24, 25, 26, 27, 28, 29, 30, 31, *32*, 33, 34
Brunsia spirillinoides Grozdilova and Glebovskaya 10
bryozoa 18, 24, 26
burrows 20, *22*, 24, 63

Cancelloceras cancellatum see *Gastrioceras cancellatum*
C. cumbriense see *G. cumbriense*
Caneyella multirugata (Jackson) 62
Caninia cornucopiae Michelin 28
Carbonicola bellula (Bolton) 63
C. bipennis (Brown) 64
C. crista-galli Wright 68
C. discus Eagar 61
C. os-lancis Wright 69
C. pseudorobusta Trueman 66
C. rhomboidalis Hind 68
C. torus Eagar 64
C. venusta Davies & Trueman 70
C. sp. 61
Carbonita bairdiodes (Jones and Kirkby) 70
C. evalinae (Jones) 70
C. humilis (Jones and Kirby) 68
C. inflata (Jones and Kirkby) 70
cauda galli markings 21
Cinctifera medusa (de Koninck) 9, 14
Clisiophyllum ingletonense Vaughan *22*, 23
C. multiseptatum Garwood 10
C. rigidum Lewis 12, *22*
Cloghergnathus cravenus Metcalfe *11*, 20
C. globenskyi Austin and Mitchell *23*
C. rhodesi Austin and Mitchell *11*, 20
conodonts 9, 10, *11*, 17, 18, 20, *22, 23*, 24, 25, 26, 29

corals/debris 7, 10, 12, 16, 17, 20, 21, *22*, 23, 25, 26, 27, 29, 30, 31, 33, 34
Cravenoceras cowlingense (Bisat) 47
C. gairense Currie 47
C. holmesi Bisat *38*
C. leion Bisat 12, *32*, 35, 45, 46
C. subplicatum Bisat 47, 49
C. sp. 45, 46
Cravenoceratoides edalensis Bisat 49
crinoid columnals 49
crinoids/debris 15, 16, 18, 19, 20, 21, *22*, 23, 24, 25, 26, 27, 28, 29, 30, 31, *32*, 33, 35
Curvirimula belgica (Hind) 63
C. sp. 63
Cyathaxonia rushiana Vaughan 23, 28
Cyclotosaurus leptognathus (Owen, 1842) Paton, 1974 82
C. stantonensis (Woodward, 1904) Zittel, 1911 82

Dainella sp. 10, 20, *22, 23*
Darjella monilis Malakhora *22*
Davidsonina carbonaria (McCoy) 10, 17
D. septosa (Phillips) 9, 14, 15, 31
D. sp. 26
Delepinea notata (Cope) 26
D. sp. 26
Dibunophyllum bipartitum (McCoy) 12, 30
D. bourtonense Garwood and Goodyear 9, 12, 14
Dimorphoceras 49
Diphyphyllum lateseptatum McCoy 12
?Donetzoceras ?sigma (Wright) 52
Dorlodotia pseudocermiculare (McCoy) 10
Draffania biloba Cummings 12
Dunbarella papyracea (J Sowerby) 62, 70
D. persimilis (Jackson) 33
D. yatesae Brandon 49
D. sp. 60, 61, 62

Eblanaia michoti (Conil and Lys) 10
E. sp. 10
Echinoconchus punctatus (J Sowerby) 12
Endospiroplectammina conili Lipina 10, *22*
Endothyra laxa (Conil and Lys) 10, *11*
endothyrid 28
Eomarginifera derbiensis (Muir-Wood) 9, 10, 12, 20, *22*, 29
Eoparastaffella restricta Postoialko and Garini *23*
E. simplex (Vdovenko) 10, *22, 23*
Eotextularia diversa (N Tchernysheva) 10, 12, *23*
Eumorphoceras bisulcatum Girty 47, 48, 49
E. bisulcatum grassingtonense Dunham and Stubblefield 47
E. involutum Horn 46
E. medusa Yates 46
E. pseudobilingue (Bisat) 46
E. rostratum Yates 47

E. tornquisti Wolterstoff 45, 46
E. sp. 12, 46, 49

Fascipericyclus fasciculatus (McCoy) 10, 17, 24, 25, 26
F. sp. 24
Fayettevillea darwenense (Moore) 48
F. holmesi see *Cravenoceras holmesi*
fenestellids 18, 19, 24, 26
fish beds 65
fish debris/fragments 5, 50, 51, *57*, 60, 61, 62, 63, 64, 65, 66, 69, 70, 71, 72
fish fauna 62, 66, 67, 68
fish scales 46
foraminifera 7, 10, *11*, 12, 17, 20, *22*, *23*, 26, 27, 29, 70, 98
fossil-matrix tables 9

Gastrioceras cancellatum Bisat *38*
G. circumnodosum Foord 62
G. cumbriense Bisat *38*, 54
G. listeri (J Sowerby) 62, 77
G. subcrenatum C Schmidt 60
gastropods 15, 16, 20
Geisina arcuata (Bean) 61, 69, 70
Gigantoproductus crassiventer (Prentice) 12, 30
Gigasbia gigas Strank 29
G. sp. 12, 17
Globoendothyra delmeri Conil and Lys 12
Gnathodus commutatus (Branson and Mehl) *23*
G. girtyi Hass 26
G. homopunctatus Ziegler 10, *22*
G. texanus pseudosemiglaber Thompson and Fellows *22*, *23*
G. texanus texanus Roundy 29
goniatites 10, 12, 14, 24, 25, 26, 30, 31, *32*, 33, 34, 35, 36, 38, 39, 40, 42, 45, 46, 47, 49, 50, 51, 52, 53, 60, 61
Goniatites concentricus Hodson and Moore 12, 34
G. crenistria Phillips 30, 33, 34
G. falcatus Roemer *32*
G. granosus Portlock 12, *32*, 34
G. moorei Weyer 12, 33, 34
G. struppus Hodson and Moore 12, 34
G. sp. *32*, 33, 34

Haplolasma subibicina (McCoy) 10, 12
Hettonia fallax Hudson and Anderson 10, 30
Hindeodella segaformis Bischoff 10, *22*
Holinella claycrossensis Bless and Calver 70
Homoceras beyrichianum (Haug) 50
H. smithii (Brown) 50
Homoceratoides prereticulatus Bisat 50
Howchinia sp. 30
Hudsonoceras proteus (Brown) 50

insects *113*
Isohomoceras subglobosum (Bisat) 49, 50
I. sp. 50

Kazakhoceras scaliger Horn 47
Koninckophyllum praecursor Howell 20, 26, 28

Koninckopora inflata (de Koninck) Lee 12, *23*, 26, 30
K. sp. 10, *11*, 12, *22*, *23*, 30
Koskinotextularia sp. 12

labyrinthodont skull 82
Lamdarina manifoldensis Brunton and Champion *22*
Latiendothyranopsis menneri (Bogush and Juferev) 10, *11*
L. menneri solida Conil and Lys *22*
Levitusia humerosa (J Sowerby) 10, *11*, 14, 17, 18, 20, 24
Lingula mytilloides J Sowerby 62, 70
Lingula 49, 50, *57*, 61, 63
Linoprotonia hemisphaerica (J Sowerby) 28, 29
Lithostrotion arachnoideum (McCoy) 12, 14
L. aranea (McCoy) 9, 12, 14, 27, 29
L. ischnon Hudson 26, 27, 30
L. martini Milne, Edwards and Haime 9, 12, 14, 28, 29
L. pauciradiale (McCoy) 9, 12, 14
L. portlocki (Bronn) 9, 14, 31
L. sociale (Phillips) 14
Lonsdaleia floriformis (Martin) 31

maple leaves *113*
Mediocris sp. 10
Megachonetes magna (Rotai) 10, 20
M. papilionaceus (Phillips) 14, 28
M. sp. *11*
Merocanites applanatus (Frech) 10
Mestognathus beckmanni Bischoff *22*, *23*, 24, 25, 29
Michelinia megastoma (Phillips) 20
M. tenuisepta (Phillips) *22*
microplankton 86
miospores 10, 16, 39, 46, 47, 84, 86, 87
Muensteroceras sp. 26
mussel bands 65
'mussel' fauna 60, 61, 62, 63, 64, 66, 67, 68, 69, 70, 71, 72

Naiadites flexuosus Dix and Trueman 69
N. quadratus (J de C Sowerby) 70
N. sp. 70
nautiloid 6, 25, 26, 34, 49
Neoglyphioceras subcircularis (Miller) *32*
N. sp. 12, *32*, 35
Nodosarchaediscus sp. 26, 27
Nomismoceras vittigerum (Phillips) 14
N. sp. 33
Nuculoceras nuculum Bisat 48, 49
N. stellarum (Bisat) 47, 48, 49
Nudarchaediscus sp. 12

Obliquipecten costatus Yates 49
Orbiculoidea sp. 33
organisms 55
  lime-screting 12
  marine 1, 40
  skeletal 19
orthocone 49
ostracods 15, 16, 20, 26, 63, 68, 69, 70, 71

Overtonia fimbriata (J de C Sowerby) 9, 12, 14

palaeoniscid 5
Palaeosmilia murchisoni Milne, Edwards and Haime 9, 10, 12, 14, 20, *22*, 27, 30, 31
Palaeospiraplectammina mellina (Malakhova) 10
palaeotextulariid 12
Paragnathodus commutatus (Branson and Mehl) 26
patrognathus andersoni Klapper *23*
peloids 20
Pericyclus minimus Hind 10, 24
P. sp. 26
Phillibolina worsawensis Osmólska 10, 24
Phillipsia gemmulifera (Phillips) 10, 24
plants/debris/fragments 5, 39, 42, 47, 48, 50, 51, 63, 67, 82, 86, 89, 90
Pleuropugnoides pleurodon (Phillips) 14
Plicatifera plicatilis (J Sowerby) 9, 12, 14
Pojarkovella nibelis (Durkina) 12
Polygnathus bischoffi Rhodes Austin and Druce *22*, *23*
P. inornatus Branson 10, *11*
P. mehli Thompson *23*
Posidonia becheri Brom 34
P. corrugata (R Etheridge jun) 12, 25, 45, 46, 47, 48, 49
P. corrugata elongata Yates 49
P. corrugata gigantea Yates 49
P. gibsoni Salter 62
P. membranacea (McCoy) 12, 45, 46
P. membranacea horizontalis Yates 12, 35
P. sp. 46
Posidoniella minor (Brown) 91
P. vetusta (J de C Sowerby) 49
Productina pectinoides (de Koninck) 20
Productus hispidus Muir-Wood 12
P. productus J Sowerby 12
P. striatosulcatus Paeckelmann 30
Pseudolituotubella multicamerata Vdovenko *22*, 29
P. sp. *23*
Pseudopolygnathus minutus Metcalfe *23*
P. triangulus pinnatus Voges *22*, *23*
Pseudospatulina sp. 12
Pugilis pugilis (Phillips) 12, 30
Pugnax spp. 10
Pugnoides triplex (McCoy) 14
Pustula pyxidiformis (de Koninck) 29

Reticuloceras bilingue (Salter) 38, 52
R. circumplicatile (Foord) 51
R. dubium Bisat and Hudson 51
R. eometabilingue Bisat and Ramsbottom 38
R. gracile Bisat *38*, 51
R. metabilingue Wright 52
R. nodosum Bisat and Hudson 51
R. reticulatum (Phillips) 51
R. superbilingue Bisat *38*
rootlet bed 13, 16, 62
  horizon 39
rootlets 20, 52, 63, 64, 69, 70
Rotiphyllum sp. 21

Scaliognathus anchoralis Branson and Mehl
10, 17
S. anchoralis europeus Lane and Ziegler   *22*
Schizophoria resupinata (Martin)   25
Septabrunsiina perfecta (Conil and Lys)   *23*
S. ramsbottomi Conil and Longerstaey *in*
Conil, Longerstaey and Ramsbottom
22
serpulids   15, 16
Sinuatella sinuata (de Koninck)   9, 14
Siphonophyllia cylindrica Scouler   10, 20,
21, 26
S. garwoodi Ramsbottom and Mitchell   10
S. sp.   20, 21, *22*, 23, 26
Solenopora garwoodi Hinde in Garwood   20
S. sp.   20
Spinoendothyra mitchelli Conil and
Longerstaey *in* Conil, Longerstaey and
Ramsbottom   10, *11*, 12, *23*

S. sp.   10
Spirifer bollandensis Muir-Wood   10
S. coplowensis Parkinson   10
Spirorbis   70, 71, 72
spores   *11*
Streblopteria sp.   47
Striatifera striata (Fischer de Waldheim)
12, 30, 31
Sudeticeras crenistriatus (Bisat)   12, *32*, 34
S. splendens Bisat   *32*, 35
S. stolbergi Patteisky   12, 35
S. sp.   12, *32*, 33, 35
Sychnoelasma konincki (Milne, Edwards and
Haime)   20

Teichichnus sp.   63
tourneyellid   28
trace fossils   64, 82, 84
trilobites   10, 12, *23*, 24, 25, 26, 27, 31

Uralodiscus spp.   12

Vallites striolatus (Phillips)   51

Weania feltrimensis G and R Hahn   10, *23*
Winterbergia hahnorum (Miller)   12, *23*
worm trails   84

'*Zaphrentis*' *konincki* (Milne, Edwards and
Haime   *11*
Zaphrentites delanouei Milne, Edwards and
Haime   28

Zoophycos   21

GENERAL INDEX

Page numbers in italics refer to figures, tables and plates.

Abovechurch Borehole 52, 54
Above Park Mine 131
Accrington Mudstones 62
Adderley 72
adits 52, 128, 129, 130
aeolian grains 86
  silt 109
aeromagnetic map 122, *123*
Alder's Farm 97
Alecs Seam 65, 66, 68, 69, 70
Alkmonton 101, 109
Allenton (Beeston) Terrace 103
alluvial deposits 103, 107, 132
  fans 5, 77, 107
  flats 106
  gravels 103
  plain 5
alluvium 2, 92, 103, 104, 105, 106, 107,
  108, 109, 112, 134
Alpine movements 116, 120
  orogeny 1
Alportian Stage *38*
  strata 49, 50
Alton 1, 77, 80, 83, 85, 110, 131
  Castle 81, *82*, 83
  Towers 131
Amaliae (Tonge's) Marine Band 62
Anglian age 104
  glaciation 2, 95, 115
andesitic tuff 96
anhydrite 15
Anisian Stage 82, 84, 86
Anticlines *118*
  Cauldon 20, 28, *118*, 119
  Dovedale 24, 25, *118*, 120
  Ecton 120
  Kingsley 64, 65
  Madge Hill 33, *118*, 120, 126
  Overmoor 49, *53*, 55, *118*, 120
  Soles Hill *118*, 120
  Swinscoe 21, *118*, 120
  Wirksworth 126
Apesford *37*, 41, 47
apron-reefs 7, 9, 13, 14, 28, 33, 34,
  116, 117, 118, 120, 128
aquifers 133
archaeology *113*
Arley Mine 62
Arnsbergian Stage *38*, 46, 47, 48, 49
Arundian Stage *10*, 12, 13, *17*, 19, 20,
  25, 26, 27, 28, 29, 116
Asbian Stage 7, 9, *10*, 12, 13, 14, *17*,
  24, 26, 27, 28, 29, 30, 31, 34, 73,
  116, 117, 120
ash 31, 33

Ashbourne Airfield 100, 108, 111
  Gravel 92, 96, 103–105, *(104)*, 115
  Green 49
  Hey 64
  Hospital *96*, *104* to Buxton railway
  119, 120
  Waterworks *79*, 100
Ashcombe Park *37*, 49, 50, 51
Ashenhurst Mill 50
Ashes Farm 97
Ashover Grit 36, 40, 42, 51, 52, 53
Askrigg Block 118
Atlow 31, 33, 49, 100, 112
  Mill 112

Backhill Wood 48
Back o'th' brook 12, 27, 35, 45, 129
Baley Hill 24
Ballfields *37*, 46, 47
Ballidon 13, 73, 106, 107, 123, 128
  Quarry 14
Banbury Marine Band 70
Bank Sprink 64
Bank Top 62
Banktop Farm 46
  Wood 64
Barnfields 66
baryte 80, 83, 84, 96, 110, 127, 128,
  129, 130
barytes 132
basalt 6, 7, 31, 33, 34, 73
Basford Green 74, 80
basin facies 7, 40
Basset Wood 12
Bassy Mine 59, 61
Bates, The 69
Beamhurst Bridge 107
Beelow Hill 52, 54
Bee Low Limestones 7, 9, 14, 33, 128
Bees Nest Member 89, 90, 91
  Mine 132
  Pit 89, 90, 109
Beeston Terrace 103, 105
  Tor 19, 21, 24, 30, 111, 116, 120
Belgian Stages 9
Belgium 9, 19, 26
Belmont Hall 62
Bentley Brook 97, 103, 112
  Hall 97, 98, 101, 111
bentonite 39, 47, 50, 51
Beresford Dale 13
Bincliff Mines 128, 132
biotite 44
bioturbation 21, 26
Birchall Wood 46
Birches Colliery *58*, 65, 66, 67, 68
Birchwoodpark Stone Quarries 26, 83,
  129
Blackbank Wood 54
Blackbrook 121

Black Plantation 128
Black Rocks 14, 73, 111
Blackstone Edge Sandstones 41
'Blackwall' 84, 95, 97
Blake Hall 70, 72
Blakeley Bank 102
Blakeley Lane 65, 102
  Farm 64
Blakelow (near Bottom House) 47
Blakelow (near Upper Leigh) 98, 109
Blake Low 81
Bleach Farm 52
Bletch Brook 112
Blithe, River 98, 103, 107, 133
  Valley 102, 103, 105, 106, 107
Blore with Swinscoe 16, 26, 27, 96
Booth Hall 67
Booth's Farm 66, 67
  Wood *57*
boreholes and wells
  Abovechurch 52, 54
  Ashbourne Waterworks *79*, 100
  Bradbourne 73
  Butt House *79*
  Caldon Low 5, *6*, 7, 10, *11*, 12, 13,
    15, 16, 18, 20, 73, 75, 116, 123, 124,
    126, 129
  Callow 5
  Carsington Reservoir site investigation
    49
  Cauldon Low Pumping Station 52
  Cheddleton Paper Mills No. 1 48
    No. 2 50, 107
    No. 16 50, 51
  Cresswell No. 1 76, *79*
  Crowtrees No. 8 60
  Crumpwood No. 1 77, 107
  Cubley *79*
  Darley Moor *79*, 85, 98, *99*, 100, 101
  Dilhorne No. 1 *58*
  Duffield 31, 47, 49
  Eyam 15, 116
  Foxfield No. 8 *58*
  Greatgate No. 1 77, *79*, 80
    No. 3 *79*
  Heath House 80
  Ipstone Edge *41*, 42, 49, 50, 51
  Key Wood *57*, 62, 63
  Lees Farm *6*, 30, 31, 33, 34, 46, 73
  Merrivale No. 2 5
  National Coal Board 55
  Old Brassworks *58*, 70, 71
  Pike House 30, 31
  Ramshorn 52
  Ridgeway 62
  Rodsley *79*, 84, 85, 86, *99*, 100, 101
    No. 1 *79*, 130
  Ruelow Wood 60
    No. 3 53
    Rusheycliff Barn 30, 73

Ryder Point   13
Shirley Common   *79*, 84, 85, 86, *99*, 100, 111
Tissington No. 1   34
   No. 2   34
   No. 3   34
Whittington Heath   5
Windyharbour   *79*, 80, 83, 84, 85, 86, 87
Woo Dale   12, 116, 123
Yeldersley   100
   No. 1   *79*
Yeldersley Hall   *79*
Bostern Grange   25, 31
Bottom House   47, 95, 96, 112
Bouguer gravity anomaly highs   123, 125, 126
   lows   126
   maps   *122*, 126
   profile   *124*
boulder beds   19
   clay   *see* till
Boulton Moor   100
   terrace   102
Boundary   65, 71, 72
Boylestone   109
Bradbourne   13, 16, 19, 26, 27, 28, 31, 112, 120, 121, 128
   Borehole   73
   Brook   100, 106, 107, 111, 112
   Inlier   16, 19, 26
Bradbourne valley   107
Bradley   76, 84, 98, 100
Bradley Dumble   46
Bradley in the Moors   85
Bradley Nook Farm   46, 109
Bradley Wood   76, 84
Bradnop   102
Brailsford   83, 84, 109
   Brook   100, 105, 106, 108, 109, 114, 133
   valley   108
Brassington   9, 13, 14, 33, 73, 88, 89, 90, 109, 111, 114, 117, 120, 121, 127, 128, 132
   Formation   2, 88, 89, 90, 91, 109
   'Brassington pit'   90
breccias   *6*, 13, 15, 24, 28, 29, 89, 90, 95, 114, 120
brecciation   16, 24, 34, 73, 86
Breedon Cloud   13
Brigantian Stage   7, *10*, 12, 13, *17*, 27, 28, 29, 30, 31, 40, 117
Broadgatehall Drumble   85, 87
Broadhay   65, 66
Broadoak   64, 120
   Wood   63, 64
Brockholes Sandstones   40, 42, 43, 51, 52
Brocton Colliery   65
Brookend Farm   105
Brookfarm Dumble   85
   Lower   110
Broofieldhead   98
Brookhouse Farm   12, 31, 33, 34
Brookhouses   71, 72
Broomyshaw   47, 120

Brough's Wood   64, 65, 66
Brownend Quarry   10, 12, *12*, *22*, 23, 28, 29, 114, 131
Brown's Brook   111
buildup   *see* knoll-reef
Bullclough   34, 54
Bull Gap Shales   31
'bullions'   39, 45, 46, 49, 50, 51, 63, 77
Bull Pit   72
Bunster Hill   24, 33, 109, 116
'Bunter Pebble Beds'   132
'Bunter' pebbles   74, 94, 95, 96, 97, 98, 100, 101, 102, 103, 108, 109
Burton upon Trent   123
   district   103
Butterley Marine Band   51
Butterton   34
Butt House Borehole   *79*
Buxton district   1, 7, 13, 36, 40, 41, 47, 73, 88, 117

calamine   129
calcite   18, 19, 24, 26, 31, 75, 76, 80, 81, 84, 87, *97*, *104*, 105, 111, 114, 119, 128, 129, 130, 131
Caldon Hill Limestone Quarry   91, 129
Caldon Low   12, 13, 16, 19, 20, 28, 41, 43, 46, 49, 75, 90, 91, 95, 96, 114, 116, 118, 119, 125, 131
   Borehole   5, *6*, 7, 10, *11*, 12, 13, 15, 16, 18, 20, 73, 75, 116, 123, 124, 126, 129
   Conglomerate   12, 14, 19, 21, 26, 27, 28, 29, 30, 73
   Quarry   20, 28, 91, 131
Caldonlow School   118
Caledonian orogeny   116
caliches   5
Callow Borehole   5
Callowhill   71
   Fault   55, 65, 66, 68, 69, 72, 120, 131
Calton   16, 20, 21, 24, 27, 30, 33
Caltonmoor   96
   House   10, 21, 27
cannelloid band   70
Cannel Mine   62
carbonate   5, *6*, 13, 33, 34, 39, 46, 47, 49, 73, 125, 129
   concretions   5
   deposition   1
   sediments   12, 13
Carboniferous   7 – 73
   Period   1
   Basement Beds   5
   intra-Carboniferous movements   116
   pre-Carboniferous   5 – 6, 19, 116, 123, 124, 126
   sedimentary basins   127
   Upper   1
'Carboniferous Limestone'   7 – 35, 123
Carlton Formation   84, 85
'Carlton-type' beds   85, 87
Carnian Stage   86
Carr Wood   52
Carsington   13, 45, 46, 47, 49, 52, 73, 95, 97, 128
   Pastures   14, 90, 128

Carsington Reservoir site   47, *48*, 49, 51, 108
   boreholes   49, 50, 110
   dam   108
Carsington Reservoir aqueduct boreholes   52
Cartwright's Drumble   67
Castern   33
Castle Donnington   121
Castleton   14
Cauldon   12, 14, 27, 28, 34, 35, 45, 47, 109
   Anticline   20, 28, 118, 119
   Cement Works   45, 46
   Quarry   20, 28, *29*, 129, 131
Cauldon Low Limestone   16, 20
   Pumping Station   52
cave deposits   2, *113*, 114
caves   1
cavities   24, 25
cavity-fills   19, 23, 25, 128
Cecily Bridge   66
Cementstone Series   16, 24
Central Pennine Basin   *38*, 39, 40, 43, 53
cerussite   128
Chadian Stage   *4*, *10*, 12, 13, *17*, 18, 19, 20, 21, 23, 24, 25, 26, 27, 28, 29, 33, 116, 120
   post-Chadian   12
chalcopyrite   129
Chalk   98, 115
channel deposits   84
Chapel en le Frith district   1
Charnian   123
Charnoid trend   123
Charnwood Forest   123
Chatsworth Grit   36, 40, 42, 44, 51, 52, 54, 55, 80, 110, 131
Cheadle Coalfield   36, 42, 53, 55, *56*, *57*, *58*, 59, 60, 61, 64, 119, 126, 131
Cheadle Park   55, 68, 69, 71, 72, 77
   Colliery   *58*, 65, 67, 68, 69
Cheadlemoor   65
Cheadle Seam   55, 65
   Syncline   119, 126, 131
Chebsey   121
Checkley   98, 105, 115
Cheddleton   1, *37*, 41, 47, 48, 51, 102, 106, 107, 111, 112, 120
   Heath   80, 102
   Hospital   77, 80
Cheddleton Paper Mills Borehole No. 1   48
   No. 2   50, 107
   No. 16   50, 51
Cheddleton Sandstones   40, 41, 42, 43, 49, 50, 51, 131
Cheddleton Station   131
Cherryeye Bridge   60, 62
Cheshire Basin   85, 86
   Lowlands   93, 102
   Wood   30, 112
Chesterfield district   42, 73
'china clay'   91
chlorite   34

Chokierian Stage
  strata   49, 50
Church Mayfield   107
Churnet Grange   *37*, 50
  River   1, 2, 50, 60, 64, 102, 108, 133
  Valley   60, 61, 62, 64, 77, 81, 83, 92,
    102, 105, 106, 107, 111, 112, 115,
    131
clay wayboards   14
Clee Hills   5
Clifton   83, 105, 109, 112
Cloughhead   *57*, 63
  Shaft   62, 63
  Wood   61
coal   13, 16, 20, 39, 51, 52, 54, 55, 96,
  101, 103, 131
Coal Measures   133
  Westphalian A   55
  Westphalian B   55
Coal Seams
  Alecs   *57*, *58*, 65, 66, 68, 69, 70
  Arley Mine   62
  Bassy Mine   59, 61
  Cannel Mine   62
  Cheadle   55, 65
  Cobble   65, 66, 67
  Crabtree   56, 59, 61, 62, 63, 131
  Dilhorne   55, 65, 66, 68, 69, 70, 72,
    131
  Little Dilhorne   65, 66, 70
  Four Foot   70, 71
  Foxfield   65, 66, 67, 68
  Getley   72
  Half Yard   71, 72
  Hooster   65
  Huntley   69, 71
  Inch Mine   62, 63
  Ingleby's Vein   129
  King Mine   62
  Litley   71, 72
  Mans   65, 66,67
  Ouster   65
  Parkhall Sweet   68, 69
  Pasture Mine   62, 63, 64
  Ribbon   61, 131
  Rider   65, 66
  Split   62, 63, 131
  Stinking   61
  Sweet   61, 62
  Two Foot   *59*, 60, 61, 131, 132
  Two Yard   55, 65, 70, 71, 72
  Upper Mountain Mine   62
  Woodhead   55, 62, 64, 65, 66, 131
  Yard   70, 72
Cobble Seam   65, 66, 67
collapse hollows   75
Collieries, Mines and Shafts
  Above Park Mine   131
  Bees Nest Mine   132
  Bincliff Mines   132
  Birches Colliery   *58*, 65, 66, 67, 68
  Brocton Colliery   65
  Cheadle Park Colliery   *58*, 65, 67, 68,
    69
  Cloughhead Shaft   62, 63
  Condway Mine   132
  Delphhouse Colliery   *58*, 71, 72

Foxfield Colliery   *58*, 65, 66, 67, 69, 70
Gilberts Shaft   129
Gilmoor Mine   *57*, 61
Golconda Mine   73
Great Rake Mine   128, 132
Hazelwall Colliery   *58*, 65, 67
Highfields Mine   128
Ingleby's Shaft   129
Kingsley No. 2 Mine   65
Kingsley Holt No. 2 Mine   65
Longhouse Colliery   67
Madgedale Colliery   72
Moorland Colliery   65
Nancy Mine   128
New Haden Colliery   65, 66, 67, 68,
  69, 70, 71, 72
New haden (Draycott) Colliery No. 8
  Shaft   *58*
Nickalum Mine   128, 132
Oversets Mine   128
Park Hall Colliery   *57*, 61, 63, 65, 67,
  68, 69, 70
Rakeway Colliery   65
Ribden Mines   132
Rimmon's Shaft   67
Rusheycliffe Mine   128
Shawe Colliery   65, 67
Standhill Mine   128
Swallow Shaft   129
Wootton Grange Mine   130, 132
Coltstone   52
Colwick Formation   84
Combes Brook   *37*, 47, 102
  Valley   *37*, 40, 41, 46, 47, 48, 49, 50,
    51, 52
Combes, The   *37*, 42, 46, 51, 112
Combridge   105
Condway Mine   132
conglomerates   1, 5, 6, 12, 14, 16, 19,
  20, 21, 23, 26, 27, 28, 29, 30, 31, 33,
  34, 43, 44, 50, 73, 75, 76, 77, 80, 81,
  83, 84, 85, 97, 98, 100, 101, 105,
  108, 110, 116, 132
Consall   43, 49, 54, *57*, 59, 60, 61, 62,
  102, 131
  New Lock   *57*, 60
  Valley   *57*, 61, 62, 63
  Wood   52, 92, 107
copper   127, 128, 129, 130, 132
Coppice Barn   33
  Syncline   120
Cotgrave Skerry   85
Cotton   52, 131
  College   52
  Dell   52
Courceyan Stage   9, *10*, 12, 13, 15, 16,
  17, 18, 20, 23
Coventry Cathedral   131
Crabtree Seam   56, 59, 61, 62, 63, 131
Crake Low   27, 31
  railway cutting   *119*
Crakemarsh   103, 105, 106, 132
Crassiventer Beds   26
Craven Basin   40
  faults   118
Cravenoceras cowlingense Band   46, 47, 49
C. leion Band   35, 36, 45, 46

C. malhamense Band   45, 46
Cravenoceratoides edalensis Band   47, 49
Ct. nitidus Band   49
Ct. nititoides Band   46, 47, 48, 49
Creighton Park   101
Cresswell   84, 101, 103, 106, 107, 109,
  133
  Borehole No. 1   76, *79*
Cresswellford   65, 67
Cretaceous   1, 98, 115
  Upper   98
cristagalli belt   65
Croft Mill   106
Croppertop   87
  Farm   87
cross-bedding   41, 42, 50, 52, 54, 60, 64,
  75, 77, 80, *82*, 83, 84, 98, 100, 102,
  104, 105
Cross Close   98, 101
cross lamination   20, *22*, 25, 30, 86, 87,
  97
Crowgutter   52
'crowstone'   39
Crowtrees Borehole No. 8   60
Croxden   105
Croxton Abbey   86, 131
Crumpwood   77, 106, 107, 133
  Borehole No. 1   77, 107
  Weir   105
Crumwithies   51
crustal stretching   12
Crwbin   109
cryoturbation   105, 110
Cubley   101, 133
  Borehole   *79*
Cubleycommon Farm   110
cyclic deposition   39

Dairy House   67, 68
  Farm   64, 66, 106
Dale Abbey Farm   21
Dale, The   18, 20
Dandillions   67, 68, 69
Darley Moor Airfield   101, 108, 111
  Borehole   *79*, 85, 98, *99*, 100, 101
  'Surface'   111, 115
Daubhill   62, 64
Davidsonina septosa Band   *15*
Deepdale   27
Delphhouse Colliery   *58*, 71, 72
deltas   1, 39, 40, 41, 42, 53
Denstone   80, 84, 86, 121
  Formation   75, *76*, *82*, 84, 85, 86, 87,
    90, 91, 110, 111, 129, 134
Denudation Chronology   114 – 115
Derby district   36, 42, 47, 51, 73, 84,
  86, 110, 111, 114, 115, 126
  'Fault line'   124
  high   123, 126
Derbyshire   1, 128
  Dome   7, 42, 110, 123, 125, 126, 133
  orefield   127, 129
  shelf   7, 13, 14, 26, 27, 28, 40, 116,
    117, 118
Derwent valley   96, 115

Devensian 2, 93, 95, 100, 101, 102, 103, 105, 106, 107, 108, 109, 110, 111, 112, 114, 115
  Irish Sea ice sheet 92, 93
Devonian 1, 5, 10, 12, 116, 123
Dilhorne 1, 41, 66, 67, 77, 101, 102, 103, 109, 110, 119
  Borehole No. 1 58
  Common 65, 69, 70, 71
  Fault 55, 65, 66, 68, 69, 70, 71, 72
  Seam 55, 65, 66, 68, 69, 70, 72, 131
  Little Dilhorne Seam 65, 66, 70
Dinantian 1, 5, 7–35 (8, 9, 10, 10, 32), 74, 75, 88, 109, 111, 112, 116, 117, 118, 120, 123, 124, 125, 126, 127, 129, 131, 133
  biostratigraphy 7–9
  classification 7
  depositional history 12–13
  dolomitisation 73
  formations 8, 9, 10
  palaeogeography 12–13
  stratigraphy 14–35
disconformity
  pre-late Asbian 116
  pre-Namurian 117
dolines 2, 14, 114
dololutites 73
dolomitisation 73, 88
dolomites 5, 6, 13, 14, 15, 16, 26, 29, 30, 31, 39, 73, 76, 80, 84, 85, 86, 88, 89, 90, 95, 111, 114, 127, 128, 129, 131
Donetzoceras sigma Band 51
Dovecliff 112
Dovedale 1, 4, 9, 16, 19, 24, 25, 26, 27, 30, 95, 109, 120
  Anticline 24, 25, 120
  Church 25
  Limestone 16
Dove Holes 19, 25
Dove, River 1, 2, 4, 24, 25, 33, 74, 77, 81, 83, 84, 86, 87, 100, 101, 102, 103, 104, 105, 115, 132, 133
  Valley 24, 33, 92, 101, 103, 105, 106, 107, 111, 112, 115
drainage 3
Draycott 84, 133
  Cross 55, 72
Draycott-in-the-Moors 109, 131
drift deposits 92, 94, 95, 96, 97, 98, 100, 101, 102
drift mines 65, 131
dry valleys 1, 76, 77, 90, 108,. 111, 115
Duffield Borehole 31, 47, 49
dyke 33
  neptunian 119, 129

Earl Sterndale 14
earth movements 13
earthquakes 121
Eaton Barn 101
Eavesford 60, 61
Eaves, The 66, 68
Ecton 129
  Anticline 120

Limestones 12, 13, 16, 19, 20, 21, 24, 26, 27, 31, 33, 116, 120
Edlaston 100
  House 105
Edwalton Formation 84, 85
Elder Bush Cave 113, 114
Ellastone 106
Ellis Hill 20, 27
Engine Pit 57
ephemeral lakes 1, 86
erosion 1, 2, 4, 13, 19, 26, 29, 54, 55, 74, 81, 83, 85, 93, 98, 103, 104, 110, 111, 112, 114, 117, 120
  surfaces 13, 29, 74, 98, 111, 114, 120, 129
erosive bases 26, 29, 81, 83, 85, 104
erratics 93, 94, 95, 96, 98, 100, 101, 102, 103, 106
Eumorphoceras bisulcatum Band 47, 49
E. pseudobilingue Band 45
E. rostratum Band 49
eustatic changes 1, 13, 40
  transgressions 1
evaporites 6, 13, 15, 73
Eyam Borehole 13, 15, 116

fans 1
Far Kingsley Banks 62, 63
Farley 87
Farlow Group 5
Farwall 30
faults 1, 12, 16, 19, 24, 30, 31, 48, 49, 50, 52, 55, 60, 62, 64, 65, 67, 68, 69, 71, 72, 74, 80, 81, 84, 85, 87, 92, 108, 110, 116, 119, 124, 126, 130
  growth 24, 116
  micro 24
  reverse 116
  superficial 92, 110
  synsedimentary 116
  wrench 118, 128, 129
    Apesford 117, 118
    Callowhill 55, 65, 66, 68, 69, 72, 118, 120, 131
    Craven 118
    Cronkston-Bonsall 117
    'Derby Fault Line' 124
    Dilhorne 55, 65, 66, 68, 69, 70, 71, 72, 118
    Manifold Valley 116, 120, 129
    Musden 120
    Red Rock 124
    Sixoaks 41, 47, 117, 118, 120
    Whiston 65
    Woodhead 64, 65
feldspar 16, 39, 40, 42, 43, 44, 45, 51, 55, 60, 75
feldspathic sandstone 39, 40, 42, 43, 44, 51, 55, 60
Felthouse Wood 37, 51
Fenny Bentley 33, 103, 107, 121
ferric oxide 75, 76
Field House 30
Fielding's Quarry 83, 131
fills 93, 106, 108, 109, 112
fireclay 68
fish bed 65

'fish-eyes' 86
Fissure Cave 114
fissures 1, 20, 75, 83, 114, 119, 128, 129, 133
  deposits 114
flash floods 77
flats 128
Flaxpiece Rake 128
flood basin 86
floodplains 1, 84, 86, 103, 132
  deposits 77, 83
  Terrace 103
fluoride 133
fluorite 128, 129
fluorspar 132
fluvial conditions 1, 5, 40, 41, 42, 76, 77, 82, 84
  deposits 92, 94, 98, 101, 102, 103–108
  sequences 95, 100, 112
  terrace 92
fluviatile advance 13
  facies 50
folds/folding 1, 16, 21, 30, 33, 35, 47, 48, 55, 64, 65, 69, 74, 80, 108, 116, 118, 119, 120, 129
  en-échelon 117, 118, 120
  superficial 92, 110
Fole 105, 106, 111
  Creamery 106
  Farm 106
Ford 12, 35, 45, 46, 108, 112, 129
Forest Farm 21, 30, 31
'Forest Hollow Beds' 10, 12, 16, 21
Forsbrook 85, 103, 106
Four Ashes 93
Four Foot Seam 70, 71
Foxfield Borehole No. 8 58
  Colliery 58, 65, 66, 67, 69, 70
  Seam 65, 66, 67, 68
  Wood 69
Foxt 52, 57, 110
  Wood 63
Freehay 80
  Member 80, 81, 132
  Quarry 80
Froghall 60, 61, 102, 112, 131, 132
  Ironstone 57, 59, 60, 61, 132

Gag Lane Limestone 27
galena 128, 129, 130, 132
garnet 44, 75
Garstones 47
Garston Rocks 52
Gastrioceras cancellatum Band 52, 53, 54
G. cumbriense 53, 54
G. subcrenatum Marine Band 36
Geophysical investigations 122–126, (125)
Getley Seam 72
Gibralter 64
Gibridding Wood 62, 64, 65
Gilbert's Shaft 129
Gilmoor Mine 57, 61
Gimmershill 52
glacial deposits 2, 92–103, (93), 106, 109, 111, 114, 115
  sequences 95

Glenwood *57*
  House 61, 62
Godleybarn 69
Godleybrook 70
Gog 52, 110
Golconda Mine 73
Goldenhill Farm 52
Gondwanaland 1
goniatite bands
  Cravenoceras cowlingense 46, 47, 49
  C. leion 35, 36, 45, 46
  C. malhamense 45, 46
  Cravenoceratoides edalensis 47, 49
  Ct. nitidus 49
  Ct. nititoides 46, 47, 48, 49
  Donetzoceras sigma 51
  Eumorphoceras bisulcatum 47, 49
  E. pseudobilingue 45
  E. rostratum 49
  Gastrioceras cancellatum 52, 53, 54
  G. cumbriense 53, 54
  Hodsonites magistrorum 50, 51
  Hudsonoceras proteus 42, 49, 50
  Isohomoceras subglobosum 50
  Nuculoceras nuculum 47, 48, 49
  N. stellarum 47, 48, 49
  Reticuloceras bilingue 51, 52
  R. circumplicatile 51
  R. coreticulatum 51
  R. eometabilingue 52
  R. eoreticulatum 50
  R. gracile 51, 52
  R. metabilingue 51, 52
  R. paucicrenulatum 51
  R. reticulatum 50, 51
  R. superbilingue 51
  R. todmordenense 51
grabens 12, 120
gravels 95, 96, *97*, 98, 100, 101, 102,
  103, *104*, 105, 106, 109
Great Cubley 101
Greatgate 77, 80, 83, 111, 133
  Borehole No. 1 77, *79*, 80
  No. 3 *79*
  Quarry 82
Great Longsdon Farm 51
Great Rake Mine 128, 132
  Vein 128
Green Clay Pit 89, 90
Greenhead 67
Griffe Grange Bed 13
Grindon 12, 16, 26, 27, 35, 95, 129
  Church 35
groove and flute casts 83
gypsum 84

Haden House Farm 71
Hag Wood 64
Hales Hall 64
Halfway House 104, 105
Half Yard Seam 71, 72
Hall Dale 24, 26, 30, 111
Hammersley Hayes 67
Hamps, River 1, 2, 12, 35, 45, 47, 107,
  108, 120
  Valley 16, 18, 21, 24, 29, 30, 96, 106,
  107, 109, 112, 115

Hanging Bridge 105
Harboro' Farm 89
  Rocks 89
Harewood Hall 68
  Kennels 68
  Park 67, 68
Harlequin Formation 84, 85
Harlow Farm 109, 112
Harston Rock 52, 110
Hastarian Stage 9
Hatchley 68
Hathern 13
Havenhill Dale 112, 128
  Brook 31
Hawksmoor 76, 77, 82, 111
  Formation 77, 80, *81*, *82*, 83, 112,
  129, 132
  Nature Reserve 76, 77, 80
  Wood 64, 74, 77
Haywood Farm 104, 105
Hazelcross 64, 65
Hazelton Clump 27
Hazelwall Colliery *58*, 65, 67
  Farm 67, 68
head 2, 92, *94*, 96, 104, 106, 108, 109,
  110, 111, 112, 115
Headlow Fields Farm 110
Heath House Borehole 80
hematite 60, 75, 119, 128, 129, 131, 132
Hemmings Low 20, 129
Henmore Brook 100, 103, 105, 107,
  109, 111, 112
  Valley 92, 105, 107
Hercynian age 75
  earth movements 55
  orogeny 1, 74, 116
  structures 117–120
  post-Hercynian structures 120–121
Herdsman's Close Farm 110
Hermitage 60
Heywood Grange 49
Highshutt Quarry 80
Highway Close Barn railway cutting *119*
Hill House 62
Hilton Terrace 103
Hodsonites magistrorum Band 50, 51
Hoften's Cross 14, 28, 35, 46, 117
Hognaston 110, 112, 121
Holbrook Marine Band 60, 61
Holkerian Stage *10*, 12, 13, *17*, 19, 21,
  24, 26, 27, 29, 30, 116
Hollington (Staffs) 77, 80, 81, 82, 83,
  85, 87, 98, 101, 131
  (Derbys) 87
  End Beds 31
  Formation 75, 77, 80, 81, *82*, 90, 91,
  110, 130, 131, 132
  Red Quarry 131
Hollins 64, 66
  Wood 63
Hollywood 101
Homoceras beyrichianum zone 42
H. undulatum Band 42, 50
Honley Marine Band 60, 61
Hooster Seam 65
Hopedale 30, 111
  Limestones 7, 12, 13, 14, 16, 19, 20,

21, 23, 24, 26, 27–31, (*29*), *32*, 33,
  34, 35, 73, 112, 120, 128, 129
Hopestone Rock 110
Hopwas breccia 77
Horse Bridge 102
horst and graben effect 120
Hoxnian age 104
Huddale 20, 91, 109
  Farm 20, 91, 120
Hudsonoceras proteus Band 42, 49, 50
Hulland 1, 31, 45, 46, 47, 49, 52, 83,
  100, 109
'*Humerosus*-beds' 28
Huntley 76, 77, 102
  Formation 75, 76, 77, 80
  Seam 69, 71
  Wood 72, 76, 77, 80, 102, 103
  Wood Quarry 80, 102, 132
Hurdlow Sandstones 40, 41, 43, 46, 47,
  48, 49, 50
  Mudstones-with-Sandstones 40
Hurst Farm 28
hyaloclastite *6*, 30, 31, 33, 34
Hydrogeology 133–134
hydrothermal minerals 127

ice sheets 2
  limits 92, *93*, 95, 102, 111
  movements *93*, *94*, 96, 98, 100, 102
Ilam 7, 16, 33, 107, 116, 128
  Hall 21, 24, 28, 30, 109, 120
  Rock *4*, 24
  Syncline 120
  Tops 24, 30, 129
illite 5
imbrication 5
Inch Mine 62, 63
Ingleby's Shaft 129
  Vein 129
Intake Plantation 80
intermontane basins 1, 12
intertidal conditions 13
intraclasts 12, 16, 20, 27, 30, 34, 42
Ipstones 39, 42, 43, 50, 51, 52, 54, 60,
  61, 62, 63, 108, 110, 131, 132
  Park 52, 54
  Park Farm 52
Ipstones Edge 1, 41, 42, 49, 50, 96
  Borehole *41*, 42, 49, 50, 51
  Sandstones 40, 41, 43, 49, 50, 51, 52,
  112
Ipswichian 2, 100, 102, 103, 105, 114
iron 80, 128, 129, 132, 133
Irongate House 100
Ironpits 46, 47
ironstone/bands 39, 45, 46, 47, 48, 49,
  51, 55, 60, 61, 63, 64, 66, 68, 69, 70,
  72, 96, 100, 105, 106, 131, 132
  see also Froghall Ironstone
Isaac Walton Hotel 33
Isohomoceras subglobosum Band 50
Ivorian Stage 9
Jackfield Plantation 48
Jackson Wood 65
joints 129
Jurassic 1, 98, 127

kaolinite 75
karstic weathering processes 1
  solution 24, 111
  pillars *4*
Kenslow Member 89, 90, 91
'Keuper' 74
  'Building Stone' 82
  'Marl' 84
  'Sandstone' 82, 83, 131
  'Lower K. Sandstone' 84
Kevin Limestones 7, 9, 13, 14, *15*, 16,
    19, 20, 28, 29, 46, 90, 131
  Quarry 14, *15*, 49, 91, 117, 129, 131
Key Wood 61, 62
  Borehole *57*, 62, 63
Kinderscoutian Stage *38*, 50, 51
  marine bands 50
King Mine 62
Kingsley 60, 64, 66
  Anticline 65
  No. 2 Mine 65
Kingsleybanks 65
Kingsley Holt 112
  No. 2 Mine 65
Kingsley Moor 64, 65, 67
Kingsley Sandstone 55, 56, 62, 63, 64,
    65, 120
Kirkham Member 89, 90, 91
'Kirkham's pits' 90
Kniveden Sandstones 40, 41, 42, 43,
    50, 51
Kniveton 12, 13, 16, 19, 26, 31, *32*, 33,
    34, 73, 97, 109, 116, 121, 128
Knob Farm, The 110
Knob, The 100
Knockerdown 46, 49, 95, 96, 97
knoll-reef 1, *4*, 7, 10, 13, 14, 16, *18*,
    19, 20, 24, *25*, 26, 27, 28, 30, 31, 33,
    73, 74, 116, 120, 128, 129

Ladyside Wood 12, 21, *23*, 24, 27
lagoon 13
Lake District erratics 95, 96
Lake Sistan 86
Lancashire 60, 61, 62, 63, 64
landslips 2, 92, *94*, 100, 102, 107, 109,
    111, 112
lapilli 31, 33, 34
Laurasia 1
lava 28, 30, 31, 33, 34
Lawn Farm 60, 61
leaching 56, 75, 80
lead 128, 129, 132
  mines 90
  -zinc 1
Leafields 67, 68
Lee Brook 47
Lee House quarries 12, 29
Leek 42, 51, 52, 111, 126
  Golf Course 80
  outlier 74, 76, 77, 78
Leekbrook 45, 46, 102
Lees Farm Borehole *6*, 30, 31, 33, 34,
    46, 73
Leicester 121
Leicestershire Coalfield 125
Leighbank Farm 98

Lightwood 66
  Farm 64
lignite 90, 91
Lilleshall 13
limestone formations 7 – 35
  see Bee Low Limestones
    Ecton Limestones
    Hopedale Limestones
    Kevin Limestones
    Milldale Limestones
    Mixon Limestone Shales
    Monsal Dale Limestones
    Rue Hill Dolomites
    Woo Dale Limestones
Limestone Hill 20, 74, 114, 129
'Limestone Shale' 7
Lin Dale 24
Lingula bands 39, 49, 60, 61, 62, 63
  facies 42
Listeri Marine Band 62, 63
Litley Seam 71, 72
Little Dilhorne Seam 65, 66, 70
Little Harewood Farm 68
Littlepark 112
Llanvirn mudstones 116
Lockwood 64
  Hollow 64
Lodgedale Farm 80
  Member 80, 132
loessic beds 86
Longcroft Farm 66
Longford 105, 109
  Hall 105
Longhouse Colliery 67
Longsdon Farm 42
Longshaw Brook 52
Loughborough 121
Lover's Leap 25
Lower Above Park 68
Lower Delphhouse Wood 72
Lower Kinderscout Grit 51
Lower Lady Meadows 120
Lower Ladypark Wood 61
Lower Thurvaston 98
Lowtop 52
Lum Edge Sandstones 41, 42, 50

Macclesfield district 40, 41, 75
Madgedale Colliery 72
Madge Hill 112
Madge Hill 112
  Anticline 33, 120, 126
magma 31
Magog 52, 110
Majorsbarn 68, 70, 71
malachite 129
Malham 109
Mammerton 105
Mam Tor Sandstones 51
manganese 133
Manifold Limestone-with-Shales 16, 24
Manifold, River 1, 2, 24, 30, 33, 112,
    115
  Valley 2, 13, 16, 18, 19, 21, 24, 26,
    27, 30, 31, 33, 107, 109, 111, 112,
    114, 115, 116, 120, 128
  Valley Fault 116, 120, 129

Manor House 116
Mans Seam 65, 66, 67
Manystones Quarry 73
Mapleton 33, 77, 106, 111
marine bands 36, 40
  Amaliae (Tonge's) 62
  Banbury 70
  Butterley 51
  Gastrioceras subcrenatum 36
  Holbrook 60, 61
  Honley 60, 61
  Kinderscoutian 50
  Listeri 62, 63
  Meadow Farm 62, 63
  Seven Feet Banbury 70
  Springwood 60, 61
  Subcrenatum 53, 55, 59, 60
  Vanderbeckei 55, 65, 70, 71
marine inundation 12
  transgression 1, 13
Marsdenian Stage *38*
  strata 51, 52
Marston Montgomery 98, 101
Martin's Low 46
Massey's Wood 61
massif facies 7, 19
Massive Series 16, 24
Matlock Bath 121
Mayfield 96, 105, 106, 121, 131
  Quarry 83
Meadow Farm 67
  Marine Band 62, 63
meltwaters 2, 93, 100, 101, 102, 103,
    111, 112, 114, 115
Mercaston 84
Mercia Mustone Group 1, 74, 76, *79*,
    84 – 87, 98, 108, 109, 110, 111, 112,
    130, 133, 134
Merrivale Borehole No. 2 5
Mesothems *38*, 40
Mesozoic 1, 88, 110
metavolcanic rocks 76
mica 16, 43, 44, 75, 84, 85
Mickleton Rock 83
Middle Cliff 48, 50
Middle Mayfield 107
'Midland Barrier' 13
Midlands 5, 92, 110, 111
  Basin 85
Milk Hill Gate 91
Milldale 19, 24, 25
Milldale Limestones *4*, 7, *8*, 10, 12, 13,
    14, 15, 16, *17*, *18*, 19, 20, 21, 24, 25,
    26, 27, 28, *29*, 30, 31, 33, 46, 73, 90,
    116, 120, 128, 129, 131
  facies variation 16
  lithology 16
Mill Fields 84, 97
'Millstone Grit' 36, 40
  Series 36
mineral deposits *127*, 130
  see also flats, pipes and veins
mineralisation 127 – 130
mineralising fluids 127, 129, 130

Mineral products 131–132
see also barytes, coal, copper, fluorspar, ironstone, lead, limestone, sand and gravel, sandstone and silica sand
mineral sulphide 5, 128
minerals
  clay 5, *6*, 128
  gangue 128
  metalliferous 128
Mines—see Collieries, Mines and Shafts
Minn Sandstones 40, 43, 45, 46, 47, 48, 49
Mudstones-with-Sandstones 40, 45
  Beds 40
Miocene 1, 89, 90, 114, 115
Mixon 129
  Limestone-Shales 12, 27, 31, 34, 35, 45, 123, 125, 129
Moat Low 31
Mobberley 67, 68, 69, 70, 106
  Quarry 80, *81*
modal analyses (of sandstones) 44
Modiolaris Zone 65, 71
Moira breccia 77
Moneystone Quarry 43, 54, 132
Monsal Dale Limestones 14
Moor Barn 26
Moorend Farm 96
Moorland Colliery 65
  Cottages 65
  opencast site 65
Moorside 46, 47, 50
  Farm 66
Moor Top 46
moraine deposit 95, 96, 97, 105
Morridge 1, 40, 46, 47, 95, 102
  Side 45, 47
Moseymoor Wood 63
Moss Banks Quarry 83
Moss Fields Farm 60
Mosslee Hall 60
'Mountain Limestone' 7
mudcracks 84, 86
Muddale Quarry 80, 132
Mugginton 84
Musden Fault 120
  Grange 21, 24
  Low 24, 27
  Wood 24

Nabs Dale 24, 25, 109, 111
Namurian 1, 2, 12, 13, 14, 33, 34, 35, *36*–54, (*44*), 55, 56, 73, 81, 89, 90, 91, 102, 107, 108, 110, 112, 114, 115, 116, 117, 120, 123, 125, 126, 133
  biostratigraphy 39
  classification *36–39*
  composite sections *37*
  depositional history 40
  faunal bands *37, 38*
  formations *39*
  lithology 39–40
  nomenclature of sandstones 40–43
  petrography of sandstones 43–45
  stages and zones *38*
  stratigraphy 45–54
Nancy Mine 128

Narrowdale Hill 14
National Coal Board boreholes 55
Nature Reserve (Brownend Quarry) *21*
Needwood Basin 74, 120, 126
neptunian dykes 75
Nestlé Factory 77
Nether Sturston 100, 109
Newclosefield 71
New Haden Colliery 65, 66, 67, 68, 69, 70, 71, 72
New Haden (Draycott) Colliery No. 8 Shaft *58*
New House 26, 51, 98
  Farm 52
Newhouse Wood 60
New Inn 31
'New Red Marl' 84
Newton Grange 31
Nickalum Mine 128, 132
Nobut Hall 98
Noonsun Common 54, 131
Norbury 84, 100, 101
North Plantation 76
North Staffordshire Basin 36, 40, 41, 42
North Wales 5
Nothill Brook 105
Nottinghamshire 84, 85
Nuculoceras nuculum Band 47, 48, 49
N. stellarum Band 47, 48, 49
N V Miospore Zone 16

Oakamoor 52, 54, 60, 62, 74, 77, 83, 92, 96, 107, 111, 112, 131
Oaklea 68
Ochre Pit 90
  Wood 64
Oddo Hall 52
off-shelf 7, 13, 14, 34, 117
off-shelf province 7, 9, 10, 13, 15, 117, 118
  stratigraphy 14, 15
oil 33
Okeover Hall 77
  Park 105
Old Brassworks Borehole *58*, 70, 71
Oldengine Farm 70
Oldfield's Farm 95
Old Grammar School (Ashbourne) *104*, 105
Oldham's Quarry 83, 131
Old Laurence Rock 62
Old Red Sandstone 1, 5, 116
  Upper 5
Oldridge 52
Oligocene 1
Onecote 109
  Sandstones Member 34
opaque oxides 43, 75
opencast mining 55, 62, 65, 66, 67, 68, 69, 70, 71, 72, 131
opencast sites, pits and quarries
  Ballidon Quarry 14
  Bees' Nest Pit 89, 90, 109
  Birchwoodpark Stone Quarries 26, 83, 129
  'Brassington pit' 90

Brownend Quarry 10, 12, *21, 22*, 23, 28, 29, 114, 131
Bull Pit 72
'Caldon Hill Limestone Quarry' 91,
Caldon Low Quarry 20, 28, 91, 129, 131
Cauldon Quarry 20, 28, *29*, 129, 131
Engine Pit *57*
Fielding's Quarry 83, 131
Freehay Quarry 80
Greatgate Quarry 82
Green Clay Pit 90
Highshutt Quarry 80
Hollington Red Quarry 131
Huntley Wood Quarry 80, 102, 132
Kevin Quarry 14, *15*, 49, 91, 117, 129, 131
'Kirkham's pits' 90
Lee House quarries 12, 29
Manystones Quarry 73
Mayfield Quarry 83
Mobberley Quarry 80, *81*
Moneystone Quarry 43, 54, 132
Moorland opencast site 65
Moss Banks Quarry 83
Muddale Quarry 80, 132
Ochre pits 90
Oldham's Quarry 83, 131
Pike House Quarry 30, 34
Ribden Pit 90, 129
Sallymoor Pit 91, 96
'Spencer's pits' 90
Standlow Lane Quarry 128
Stanton Quarry 82, 83, 130
Surprise Pit 72
Tearne Quarry 131
Townhead Quarry 82, 83
Wardlow Quarry 14, 20, 29, 73, 91, 129, 131
Winkhill Quarry 47
Wonder Pit 72
Wredon Quarry 129, 131
Orchards, The 103, 105
Ordley Brook 74, 77, 112
Osleston 87, 98, 101
  Cottage 101
Osmaston 83, 100, 101
  Park 111
Ouster Seam 65
outwash deposits 92, 97, 98, 103, 106, 107
Out Wood *57*, 60, 61, 62, 63
Overfole 106
Overmoor Anticline 49, *53*, 55, 120
Oversets Mine 128
ovum belt 71

Padwick 41, 48
palaeocurrents *41*, 42, 50, 52, 54, *59*, 60, 64, *76, 77, 78*
palaeokarstic surface 20
Palaeolithic age 114
palaeoslopes 13, 19, 26, 33
Palaeozoic 116
  Lower 98, 101, 106, 123, 126
palagonite 31
palynomorphs 82, 86

Pangaea 1
Paper House 105
Paradise Cottage 98
parallel lamination *22*, 25, 27, 30, 48, 50, 51, 52, 64
Park Farm 96
Park Farm, Ipstones 61
Parkford 69
Parkhall Colliery *57*, 61, 63, 65, 67, 68, 69, 70
 Farm 68, 69, 71, 102
 Sweet Seam 68, 69
Park House Farm 63
Parva Formation 84
Parwich 9, 13, 14, 28, 33, 34, 45, 46, 73, 97, 106, 107, 117, 128
 Syncline 120
Pasture Mine 62, 63, 64
Paynsley Hall 107
P C Miospore Zone 16
Peak District 1, *7,8*, 13, 94, 131
'Peak District Upland Surface' 114
Peakstone Rock 110
Pearcroft Wood 68
peat 92, 106, 107, 108, 109, 112, 114
peat swamp 1
Pebble Beds 77
pedogenic crusts 14
Pendleian Stage *38*, 43, 45, 46, 47
peneplain 2
Pennines 1, 36, 40, 53, 55, 89, 114, 116
'Pennine Axis' 120
Pennine glaciation 95
periglacial deposits 92, 103, 108–111
permafrost 2
Permian age 73, 77, 114, 120, 129
Pethills 47
photic zone 19
phrygiana belt 71
physical features *3*
Pickering Tor *4*, 24, 111
Pike House Borehole 30, 31
 Quarry 30, 34
Pike Low 27
pillow lava *6*
pipes 128
pits—*see* opencast sites, pits and quarries
 also Collieries, Mines and Shafts
Plains Skerry 85
Plantation House 67
Pleistocene age 84, 88, 89, 92, 111, 114, 115
Pliocene 2, 88, 89, 90, 114, 115, 120
Pocket Deposits 2, 73, 75, *88*–91, 96, 114, 115, 128, 132
Polygnathus communis carina Conodont Biozone 9
Pool Close 97
Post-glacial deposition 2
 erosion 2
Potteries Coalfield 55, *56*, 61, 62, 70, 124
protoquartzite 39, 43, 47, 49, 50, 51, 52, 55, 56
pseudomorphs after halite 84, 86, 87
Punches Dumble 49

pyrite 34, 39, 53, 61

quarries *see* opencast sites, pits and quarries
quartzite *6*, 28, 56, 65, 75, 77, 84, 89, 94, 95, 96, *97*, 98, 100, 101, 102, 104, 105, 106
Quaternary Period 2, 86, 92–115
Quixhill Bridge 105

Radcliffe Formation 84, 86
'Radcliffe-type' beds 85, 87
Radfields 60, 61
Rainroach Rock 77, 83
Rainster Rocks 73, 111
Rake Edge 61
Rake Way 62, 64, 65
 Colliery 65
ramp 1, 13, 19, 26, 28
Ramshorn 41, 46, 50, 81, 96
 Borehole 52
Ravensdale Park 84
Ravens Tor 19, *25*, 109, 111
Recent age 2, 92, 106
red beds 127
Redhouse Sandstones 5, *6*, 7, 10, 12, 13, 116, 123, 126, 129
red jasper 28
Red Rock Fault 124
red staining 60, 74, 86
reef brachiopod assemblages 9, 10, 12
regularis belt 65
Reticuloceras bilingue Band 51, 52
R. circumplicatile Band 51
R. coreticulatum Band 51
R. eometabilingue Band 52
R. eoreticulatum Band 50
R. gracile Band 51, 52
R. metabilingue Band 51, 52
R. paucicrenulatum Band 51
R. reticulatum Band 50, 51
R. superbilingue Band 51
R. todmordenense Band 51
Reynard's Cave 25
Rhaetic 84
rhizoliths 14
'rib and furrow' structures 64
Ribbon Seam 61, 131
Ribden 14, 46, 90, 91
 Mines 132
 Pit 90, 129
Rider Seam 65, 66
Ridgeway Borehole 62
Rimmon's Shaft 67
ripple lamination 30, 41, 42, 47, 48, 50, 51, 52, 64, 84, 84, 85, 86, 87
river terrace deposits 92, 100, 102–108, 115, 132
Roaches Grit 36, 40, 42, 44, 51, 52, 131
 Syncline 36
Roaches, The 102
Rocester 86, 87, 101, 102, 105, 106, 107
 Bridge 107

Rodsley 111, 133
 Borehole *79*, 84, 85, 86, *99*, 100, 101
 Borehole No. 1 *79*, 130
Romano-British age 114
Roost Hill 46
Ross Banks 61
 Bridge 62, 65, 66
Rough Rock 40, 42, 45, 52, *53*, 54, 55, 60, 120, 131, 132
Round Hill, The 64
Rowfield 97
Rue Hill 20, 109
 Dolomites 5, *6*, 7, 10, 13, 15, 16, 18, 19, 73
Ruelow Wood Borehole 60
 No. 3 53
Rugeley 123
Rusheycliff Barn Borehole 30, 73
Rusheycliff Mine 128
Rushley 33
rutile 43, 55
Ryder Point Borehole 13

Sallymoor 75, 90, 91
 Pit 91, 96
salt deposits 1
sand and gravel 1, 84, 89, 92, 98, 100, 101, 102, 103, 105, 106, 107, 108, 109, 132, 134
 glacial 92, 94, 95, 96, 97, 98, 108, 109, 132
Sandhills Farm 101
Sandhurst Farm 90
sandstone 131
 nomenclature 40–43
 petrography 43–45
 see also Denstone Formation
 Onecote Sandstones Member
 Sherwood Sandstone Group
 Widmerpool Formation
Sandybrook Farm 107
 Hall 97
Saverley Green 103
Scarlet lake 65
School House 45
 Farm 20
Scow Brook 50
 Valley 110
screes 1, 92, 108, 109
 fossil 77
sea level changes 12
seatearth 53, 55, 60, 61, 62, 63, 64, 65, 66, 67, 68, 69, 70
sedimentary basins 116, 127
sedimentation 13, 19, 40, 116
Sedsall Rough 87
seismic evidence 116
 reflection 116
 refraction 123
 surveys 122
Seven Feet Banbury Marine Band 70
Shaffalong 55, 59, 131
 Syncline 53, 59, 60, 62, 63, 120, 131
Shafts—see Collieries, Mines and Shafts
Shale Grit 51
Sharpcliffe Conglomerate 42
 Rocks 42, 50

Shawe Colliery   65, 67
   Hall   65, 66
Shaw's Farm   31
shear planes in head   108
Sheephouse Farm   41, 80, 120
shelf   7, 9, 13, 14, 34
   provinces   7, 9, 14, 40, 88
   stratigraphy   14, 15
Sherwood Sandstone Group   1, 74,
   75–84 (76, 79), 92, 94, 98, 131, 132,
   133
Shiningford   49
Shirley   52, 83, 85, 100, 114
   Brook   105, 106, 107, 112, 133
Shirley Common   100
   Borehole   79, 84, 85, 86, 99, 100, 111
Shirley Hollow   52
   Sandstones   42
Shirley Mill   105
   Valley   105, 108
Shropshire Basin   86
silica sand   132
   see also Pocket Deposits
Siliceous bands   23
   pebbles   13, 28, 29, 116
silty loam   109–110
Silverdale Wood   67
sink holes   14, 46, 95, 96, 109
   see also dolines
Site of Special Scientific Interest   21
Sixoaks Fault   41, 47, 118, 120
'skerries'   84, 85, 86, 87, 133, 134
Slack Lane   84
Slade House   24, 27
slope   1, 13
   deposits   108, 109
slumping   19, 24, 26, 29, 34, 112
smithsonite   129
Snelston   7, 16, 26, 83, 85, 87, 126, 129,
   130, 132
   Common   84, 101
   high   125, 126
   Inlier   26, 126
   Rectory   106
Softlow Wood   20, 77, 129
soil development   56
   fossil   5
sole marks   41, 46, 83
Solenopora Beds   16
Soles Hill   16, 24, 109
   Anticline   120
solifluction   92, 93, 98, 103, 106, 107,
   108, 111, 114
South Pennine Orefield   1, 127
   see also Derbyshire orefield
spar   18, 75
'Spencer's pits'   90
sphaerosiderite   63
sphalerite   128
Split Seam   62, 63, 131
springs   133
Springwood Marine Band   60, 61
Stafford   93, 121
Staffordshire   1
   Lowlands   93, 102
   Nature Conservation Trust   21

Shelf   7, 9, 13, 14, 15, 26, 27, 28, 116,
   117, 118
Standhill Mine   128
Standlow Lane   26
   Quarry   128
Stanley Sandstones   41, 42
Stanshope   26, 28, 30, 127, 128, 132
Stansmore Hall   54, 120
Stanton   16, 20, 74, 77, 92, 96, 109,
   114, 129, 131
   Dale   20
   Quarry   82, 83, 130
Star Wood   52
Steeplehouse Farm   33
Stinking Seam   61
Stockport–Macclesfield area   75
Stoke on Trent   42
Stone Hole   66
stromatactis   19, 25
Structure   116–121, (117)
Sturston   133
Sturstonmill Bridge   107
Subcrenatum Marine Band   53, 55, 59,
   60
subtidal conditions   13, 15
sulphate   134
sulphides   129, 132
superficial structures   110
supratidal conditions   13, 15, 18
surfaces   74, 114
   see erosion surfaces
Surprise Pit   72
Surtsey   13, 31
Sutton Brook   108
   Valley   103, 105, 106
Sutton Valley   108
Swainsley Farm   116
Swallow-hole deposit   114
Swallow Shaft   129
Sweet Seam   61, 62
Swineholes Wood   50
Swinholm   107
Swinscoe   16, 20, 21, 26, 27, 33, 96
   Anticline   21, 120
Synclines
   Cheadle   118, 119, 126, 131
   Coppice Barn   118, 120
   Ilam   118, 120
   Parwich   118, 120

taxa   10, 30
Tean   105
   River   98, 133
   Valley   103, 105, 106, 107, 108
Teanford   133
Tean Leys   87
Tearne Quarry   131
tephra   6, 31
Tertiary   88, 89, 90, 111, 114, 115, 116
Third Grit   36
Thorpe   16, 27, 107, 111, 128
Thorpe Cloud   10, 24, 33, 116, 128
Thorpe Pasture   26
Thors Cave   16, 19, 21, 23, 24, 114, 116
Thorswood   31, 45, 129
   House   20, 21, 46, 129, 132
   Plantation   129

Threapwood   81
   Farm   83
Throwley Hall   30, 33, 120
till   1, 2, 92, 94, 95, 96, 97, 98, 99, 100,
   101, 102, 103, 104, 109, 110, 111,
   114, 115, 134
tilt-blocks   12, 13, 19, 116, 124
Tissington   27, 30, 31, 32, 33, 73, 97,
   109, 128
   Borehole No. 1   34
   No. 2   34
   No. 3   34
   Trail   31, 119, 120
   Volcanic Member   6, 13, 30, 31, 32,
      33, 34, 119, 120
Tissington Spires   24, 109
'toadstones'   7
Toothill Rock   83
Tors   73, 110–111
Totmonslow   84
tourmaline   43, 45, 55
Tournaisian Series   9, 16, 17
Town Field Farm   47
Townhead Quarry   82, 83
Trent Formation   84
   River   102, 103, 105, 111
   Valley   103
Triassic   74–87
   classification   74
   post-Triassic faulting   55
   pre-Triassic surface   74
   sedimentation   1
   structure contours on base   75
tuff   30, 31
turbidite deposition   13, 26, 33
   facies   31, 33, 41, 48
   origin   19, 39
turbidites   40, 41, 42, 45, 46, 47, 48, 49,
   50, 51
Turkestan   86
Two Foot Seam   59, 60, 61, 131, 132
Two Yard Seam   55, 65, 70, 71, 72

unconformity at base of Hopedale
   Limestones   12, 13, 28
   at base of Triassic   36, 55, 71, 72, 74,
      75, 107, 127, 129, 130
   see also disconformity
Upper Cotton   52
Upper Delphhouse Wood   72
Upper Ladypark Wood   63
Upper Leigh   87, 105, 106, 108, 109
Upper Mayfield   77
Upper Mountain Mine   62
Upper Tean   85, 86, 87
Upper Town   46
Upwoods Farm   87, 101

Vanderbeckei Marine Band   55, 65, 70,
   71
veins   127–130
Vernon's Oak Farm   101
Victoria Cottages   67
Viséan   19, 35, 45, 116
volcanic dust   39
   episode   34
   member   31, 33

origin   14, 16, 43
pebbles   97
rocks   7, 28, 31, 44, 73, 94, 103, 104,
   105, 116
volcanoes   1, 13, 31
vughs   16, 30, 33, 73, 84, 87, 129

wadi-infills   1, 77
Wales – Brabant Island   1, 7, 40, 41, 42
   see also 'Midland Barrier'   13
Walk Farm   13, 20
Walk, The   14
Wall Grange   133
wall rocks   89
Wardlow   13
   Quarry   14, 20, 29, 73, 91, 129, 131
Wash Brook   128
Waste Farm   81
   Wood   67
Waterfall   12, 26, 27, 34, 129
   Low   27
Waterhouses   10, 12, 13, 16, 21, 27, 29,
   30, 45, 46, 47, 91, 96, 106, 108, 112,
   114, 117, 131
   Limestones   26, 27
Waterstones Formation   84, 85
Waulsortian buildup   10, 18, 19
   'reef'   19, 26
Weags Bridge   24
weathering   1, 47, 56, 100, 102, 108,
   110, 111, 112, 120
Weaver Beds   16
   Farm   110
   Hills   9, 14, 16, 28, 73, 76, 77, 81, 84,
      88, 90, 95, 96, 97, 100, 109, 110,
      116, 127, 129, 131
   Villas   14
wells   133

West Bridgford   121
Wester Lane   90, 128
Westphalian   55 – 72
   sandstone petrography   55 – 59
   stratigraphy   59 – 72
Wetley Rocks   53, 54, 60, 101, 102, 120,
   131
Wetton   114
Whiston   43, 54, 96
   Fault   65
Whitehurst   64, 65
White Rake   132
Whittington Heath Borehole   5
Whympney Wood   66, 67, 68, 69
Widmerpool Formation   31 – 34
   'Yoredale Series'   120
   Gulf   13, 31, 40, 46, 73
Wigber Low   31
Windy Harbour   40, 50
Windyharbour Borehole   79, 80, 83, 84,
   85, 86, 87
Winkhill   40, 47, 96, 107, 108, 112
   Quarry   47
Winnothdale   80, 110, 132
   high   125, 126
Wirksworth Anticline   126
Wolfscote Dale   28
   Hill   7
Wolstonian glaciation   2, 102, 103, 104,
   105, 111, 112, 114, 115
   ice sheet   97, 100, 103
Wolverhampton   93
Wonder Pit   72
Woo Dale
   Borehole   12, 19, 116, 123
   Limestones   13, 14, 73
Woodeaves   27, 30
   Farm   34

Woodhay   83
Woodhead   65
   Fault   64, 65
   Hall   65, 66
   Sandstone   64
   Seam   55, 62, 64, 65, 66, 131
Woodhead Hill Rock   55, 59, 60, 61, 64
Woodside Farm   112
Wootton   80, 81, 82, 121, 130
   Hall   131
   Lodge   130, 131
   Park   50
Wootton Grange Mine   130, 132
Wredon   14, 129
   Quarry   129, 131
Wyaston   111
   Brook   109
Wyaston Common Farm   111
Wye Valley   96

Yard Seam   70, 72
Yeadonian Stage   38
   strata   53
Yeaveley   92, 98, 101, 109, 111
   'Yeaveley Surface'   111
Yeldersley   100, 133
   Borehole   100
   No. 1   79
Yeldersley Hall   85
   Borehole   79
Yeldersley Hollies   114
Yokecliffe Rake   128
'Yoredale Rocks'   7

Zechstein Sea   73
zinc   1, 128, 129
zircon   43, 45, 55, 75